SOCIAL WORK PRACTICE WITH CULTURALLY DIVERSE PEOPLE

SOCIAL WORK PRACTICE WITH CULTURALLY DIVERSE PEOPLE

Surjit S. Dhooper • Sharon E. Moore

Sage Publications, Inc.
International Educational and Professional Publisher
Thousand Oaks ▪ London ▪ New Delhi

For information:

Sage Publications, Inc.
2455 Teller Road
Thousand Oaks, California 91320
E-mail: order@sagepub.com

Sage Publications Ltd.
6 Bonhill Street
London EC2A 4PU
United Kingdom

Sage Publications India Pvt. Ltd.
M-32 Market
Greater Kailash I
New Delhi 110 048 India

Printed in the United States of America

Library of Congress Cataloging-in-Publication Data

Dhooper, Surjit Singh.
   Social work practice with culturally diverse people/by Surjit S. Dhooper and Sharon E. Moore.
      p.   cm.
   Includes bibliographical references and index.
   ISBN 0-7619-1296-7 (cloth: alk. paper)
   ISBN 0-7619-1297-5 (pbk.: alk paper)
      1. Social work with minorities–United States.   2. Minorities–United States.
I. Moore, Sharon E. II. Title.
HV3176.D49 2000
305.8´00973–dc21   00-009185

01 02 03 04 05 10 9 8 7 6 5 4 3 2 1

Acquiring Editor:	Nancy Hale
Editorial Assistant:	Heather Gottlieb
Production Editor:	Denise Santoyo
Production Assistant:	Candice Crosetti
Designer/Typesetter:	Siva Math Setters, Chennai, India

Contents

Preface

Our social scene is rapidly changing. It is projected that by the middle of the 21st century, the non-Hispanic white share of the country's population will fall to 53%, down from 76% in 1990. Thus, almost half of the population will then be made up of today's minorities. Because of the demographic and various other social changes, human service organizations and practitioners will be increasingly dealing with people who are more diverse, better informed, politically more active, and aware of their rights. This will demand significant changes in the nature, quality, and structure of human service organizations and changes in the knowledge, sensitivity, and skills of service providers. There is thus a need for ongoing efforts to develop new approaches to preparing culturally competent social workers and other human service providers. Fortunately, we have much to build on. Social work philosophy and values have always emphasized the unique along with the universal aspects of the lives of people. The unique dimensions of people's realities are influenced by their culture, history, and experiences. Social workers have all along acknowledged the need for understanding and accommodating the cultural dictates of the individuals, groups, and communities that they worked with. However, at the same time, social forces of the larger society—its ambivalence and ambiguities—have conditioned and constrained the willingness, ability, and efforts of social workers to provide culturally competent services to those different from mainstream Americans. Efforts to create cultural diversity-related social work knowledge, principles, and models of practice are a recent phenomenon, and those efforts of the profession are praiseworthy. Nevertheless, there are gaps in our response to the needs and problems of many of our fellow Americans. This book will contribute to addressing those gaps.

The following assumptions underlie the approach proposed in this book.

1. Human needs and problems are the result of the deficiencies of individuals as well as the faults of the world in which they live. Those needs and problems cannot be adequately dealt with through client-focused casework approaches alone. Therefore, your definition of social work with culturally diverse people should be inclusive of work with individuals, groups, and communities and at all levels—individual worker's activity; organizational programs and policies; and larger societal laws, rules, and regulations.

2. For effective work with disadvantaged populations, you need an understanding of the various client systems—individual, group, organization, community, social institution, and society at large—and basic skills in intervening at all different levels.

3. Self-awareness on your part is an absolute necessity. Self-awareness involves (a) learning about your own personal culture, that is, beliefs, values, perceptions, assumptions, and explanations of reality; (b) recognizing your own ethnicity and ethnocentricity; and (c) using this learning and recognition to treat others as culturally equal to you. This idea is beautifully expressed by Shimon (1976) in the poem "I Know Something About You":

Wouldn't this old world be better
If the folks we meet would say—
"I know something good about you!"
And treat us just that way?

Wouldn't life be lots more happy
If we praised the good we see?
For there's such a lot of goodness
In the worst of you and me!

Wouldn't it be nice to practice
That fine way of thinking, too?
You know something good about me,
I know something good about you?

4. History is a significant teacher. Our past influences the present, and the future is never completely divorced from the present. We cannot undo our past, and we should not disown our history. Those who do not learn from their history are likely to repeat the mistakes of the past.

5. The problem-solving process that you master as a part of your social work education is universally applicable to all entities and settings.

6. The ecological-systems theoretical framework is rich enough to capture the gestalt of the problem, the person-system, the situation, and their interaction and to generate ideas for assessments and interventions at all levels from individual to group, organization, community, and society.

Thus, our approach emphasizes that you (a) understand the *history* of the group to which the client belongs; its *culture and ethnicity*; major *intragroup variations* based on degree of acculturation, national or tribal origin, socioeconomic status, gender, and sexual orientation; and *environmental forces* affecting its well-being; (b) place the client system's problem in the larger context beyond the microsituation; (c) plan for a multipronged intervention; and (d) give equal importance to empowering the client and solving the problem. We have discussed the "what" and "how" of these in relation to five groups contributing most to the country's cultural diversity. These are Latino Americans, African Americans, Asian Americans, Native Americans, and biracial/mixed-race Americans.

The text is divided into seven chapters. Chapter 1 discusses the role of social work in the changing social world, reviews the cultural competence-related ideas and accomplishments of the profession, and introduces another approach to culturally competent social work. Chapter 2 discusses the essentials of the proposed approach, which are grouped into the following five clusters: (a) social worker's awareness of self—own culture, ethnicity, and identity; (b) an overall understanding of the commonalities among groups culturally different from the majority community; (c) general considerations for intervention with these groups; (d) general principles of culturally competent practice; and (e) stages of intervention with culturally diverse clients. Chapters 3 through 7 deal with each of the major disadvantaged groups of the U.S. population—African American, Latino Americans, Asian Americans, Native Americans, and biracial/mixed-race Americans. Each of these chapters (a) introduces the group; (b) provides a historical overview of its experiences; (c) discusses commonality of cultures and worldviews among its subgroups; (d) identifies intragroup differences; (e) highlights the major needs and problems of the group; (f) suggests general considerations for intervention with the group; and (g) discusses intervention at the micro-, mezzo-, and macrolevels.

Acknowledgments

In working on this book, we have benefited from the ideas, insights, and understanding as well as the assistance, encouragement, and inspiration of many. For Surjit Dhooper, these include his wife Harpal and children Amrit, Devinder, Manjot, and Nimrat. He also thanks Dr. Zafar Hasan and Dr. Kay Hoffman, the former and the current dean of the University of Kentucky College of Social Work, respectively, and Mrs. Egly Narevic, a student from Israel in the college's doctoral program. For Sharon Moore, these include members of her family—her father John W. Moore II; her beloved deceased mother, LaVerne; her brothers John III, David, and Lloyd; her sister Cynthia; sister-in-law Darlene; her nephews, Justin and John IV, and niece Brittany. She also thanks Dr. Candice Henry of Seton Hill College; Drs. Charlotte Dunmore and Anne Jones, professors emeritus of the University of Pittsburgh School of Social Work; and members of her extended and church family. With deep appreciation for their help, we are most sincerely grateful to all of these.

Cultural Diversity
and Social Work Practice

CHANGING SOCIAL SCENE AND SOCIAL WORK

America's social scene is changing significantly. The country is moving rapidly from a predominantly white society of European origin to a multiracial and multicultural one. Many major cities already have nonwhite majorities, and this trend is rippling out from urban centers to suburban and rural areas (Coile, 1990).

Increasing Diversity of the U.S. Population

Unprecedented demographic changes are projected for the 21st century. From 80 million in 1900, the population of the United States will have grown to 300 million by the year 2010. By the middle of the century, it is projected to be at 392 million. Not only will there be many more people calling this country home, but also the differences among them will be much more marked, visible, and complex. The non-Hispanic white share of the population will continue to fall steadily, from 76% in 1990 to 72% in 2000, 60% in 2030, and 53% in 2050. By the middle of the century, the black population will have doubled its 1990 size to 62 million. At an annual rate exceeding 4%, Asians and Pacific Islanders will be the fastest-growing racial-ethnic group (Day, 1993). It is forecast that by the middle of the 21st century, there will be 41 million Asian Americans, making up more than 10% of the population. The Hispanic-origin population will add more people to the country every year than will any other race or origin group (Day, 1993; Ulincy et al., 1995; U.S. Bureau of the Census, 1992a, 1992c). This population increase will be the result of both natural growth and immigration. Looking at the proportion of immigrants to the total number of Hispanics, compared with 15% in the 1960s (1960-1969) and 28% in the 1970s (1970-1979), more than half (50.7%) of the Hispanic foreign-born in the 1980s arrived in the United States between 1980 and 1990. In 1990, the more than 7.8 million foreign-born Hispanics represented 43% of all foreign-born persons in the country (U.S. Department of Commerce, 1993b). These projections, while giving an idea of the changing color of the U.S. population, do not speak to the increasing complexity of that population. The next section provides a glimpse of that complexity, which is reflected in the cultural diversity[1] within those groups.

The Hispanic immigrants are coming from North America (Mexico); Central America (Guatemala, Honduras, El Salvador, Belize, Nicaragua, Costa Rica, and Panama); the Caribbean (Cuba, Puerto Rico, and the Dominican Republic); South America (Venezuela, Colombia, Ecuador, Peru, Bolivia, Chile, Paraguay, Argentina, Uruguay, Brazil, French Guiana, Suriname, and Guyana); and Europe (Spain). The Asian and Pacific Islander Americans are people who claim descent from 28 different countries of Asia and 25 islands in the Pacific. Although those of Chinese, Filipino, Japanese, Indian, and Korean ancestry constitute the vast majority of Asian Americans, those of Bangladeshi, Burmese, Cambodian, Hmong, Indonesian, Laotian, Malaysian, Pakistani, Sri Lankan, Thai, and Vietnamese origin are also in the United States in significant numbers. People of Hawaiian, Samoan, and Guamanian descent form the majority of the Pacific Islanders. Others in substantial numbers are the people of Tongan, Tahitian, Fijian, Northern Mariana Island, and Palauan descent (U.S. Bureau of the Census, 1992a). African Americans are not only the descendants of those who have been a part of the American social scene for hundreds of years but also those whose forebears have lived on the various Caribbean islands and in many countries of Central and South America and those who have immigrated from different countries of Africa.

Also, the population of those who do not easily fit into the current racial categories is rising. Interracial marriages between whites and nonwhites and between people from different nonwhite groups are adding people who do not belong to a single racial or ethnic category. Such marriages have increased since 1960, when the estimate was 157,000, to the current census figure of 1.3 million in 1994;[2] since the early 1970s, the number of multiracial babies born has increased by 260%, compared with the 15% growth rate for monoracial babies (Alonso & Waters, as cited in Root, 1996).

Likely Future

The changes in the population will come more rapidly than the needed changes in society's institutions will. It is very likely that in the future the complexion of the country will have changed the most, its cultural norms some, and its power structure the least. The people of color, despite their increasing numbers, will continue to be disproportionately disadvantaged. As Turner (1995) put it, "Some minority leaders have felt that minority population growth would result in improved conditions for people of color, presumably by increasing the potential of minorities to advance their cause through use of the ballot. To date, the evidence does not support this line of reasoning" (p. 9). A general distrust of political systems by communities of color persists. A review of race relations in this country points to the validity of this forecast. Formal legal protections and informal norms have diminished but not eliminated discriminatory practices. According to Snipp (1997), antimiscegenation laws have been unconstitutional for a quarter of a century, Jim Crow is gradually becoming a thing of the past, Indian reservations have become homelands instead of concentration camps, and attacks on Asian immigration today are not likely to stir up the hysteria about "yellow peril" that the country experienced in the past. However, even as de jure discrimination is illegal and unabashed bigotry is publicly scorned, de facto discrimination is being practiced covertly.

Overt or covert, prejudice, hatred, and discrimination against minorities are still an ugly reality of American life today. Groups such as neo-Nazis, the Ku Klux Klan, and other white supremacists are attracting recruits to spread hatred and violence; gay men and lesbian women are suffering from "gay bashing" and verbal harassment; and women of all ages, races, and sexual orientations are experiencing sexual attacks (Kropf & Isaac, 1992). This intolerance of diversity is not going to disappear in the future. According to Wohl (1995), it is also difficult to forecast a brighter future because,

> The last decade has also witnessed the erosion of civil rights won over twenty years of street protest, organized social struggle, and legal challenge in the courts. The federal government has packed the Supreme Court with judges ready to reverse whatever gains were made by minority groups in employment and education and by women in the control of their reproductive lives.
>
> Civil rights are under siege not only in the courts, but in the workplace, in employment and in education. The Willie Horton distortion was used in the political arena for racist advantage. The "quota" distortion was used to reverse legal precedents in employment and education.
>
> This climate has darkened every aspect of public life. Multiculturalism is being pilloried in the media and in discussion about educational goals and direction as a play against national unity. Under attack are initiatives to discover through interchange across multiple diversities, the strengths of personal and group identity and the human treasure to be mined out of the richness of our cultural and historical differences. (p. 81)

All kinds of myths about affirmative action are being propagated. Plous (1996) has listed and debunked the most common myths, that: (a) the only way to create a color-blind society is to adopt color-blind policies; (b) affirmative action has not succeeded in increasing female and minority representation; (c) affirmative action may have been necessary 30 years ago, but the playing field is fairly level today; (d) the public doesn't support affirmative action anymore; (e) a large percentage of white workers will lose out if affirmative action is continued; (f) if Jewish people and Asian Americans can rapidly advance economically, African Americans should be able to do the same; (g) you can't cure discrimination with discrimination; (h) affirmative action tends to undermine the self-esteem of women and racial minorities; (i) affirmative action is nothing more than an attempt at social engineering by liberal Democrats; and (j) support for affirmative action means support for preferential selection procedures that favor unqualified candidates over qualified candidates.

Notwithstanding the advances made by minorities and women, judging affirmative action by the standards (based on the U.S. Commission on Civil Rights definition) of (a) whether the consequences of past discrimination have been eliminated, and (b) whether measures are in place to prevent future discrimination, its effectiveness is questionable.

> Overall, the one word that can be used to describe the effects of affirmative action across the three areas (education, employment, and business) is: fragile. While it is clear that gains have been made for women and minorities because of antidiscriminatory efforts, the longevity of this growth appears to be quite sensitive to legislative, political, and economic shifts in the country. (Murrell & Jones, 1996, p. 83)

Recent legislation and other developments at the federal, state, and local levels testify to the truth of the previous statement. For example, the Personal Responsibility and Work Opportunity Reconciliation Act of 1996 (Pub. L. 104-193) denies eligibility for supplemental security income and food stamps to most legal immigrants and gives states the option to deny them eligibility for Medicaid, TANF (Temporary Assistance to Needy Families), and state and local programs. Californians voted in favor of Proposition 187, which denies education to children of undocumented persons and requires that schools, hospitals, and police departments report suspected undocumented persons.

It seems that the doctrine of separate and unequal as a function of racial and ethnic discrimination will continue as the dominating philosophy of social status in America (Turner, 1995). "The separation of whites and minorities is so complete as to result in their possessing often contrary and conflicting views of the world" (Davis, 1995, p. 51). Large numbers in the disadvantaged groups will continue to feel alien and apathetic about access to political and economic power. Most of them will continue to share in common the characteristic of visibility, although a few who are invisible are not less disadvantaged:

> A person of color is quite visibly a different color. A woman is identifiable as female. A person with a physical handicap is noted as differently abled. However, gay men and lesbian women are not necessarily visible: despite widespread stereotypes, the vast majority of gay men and lesbian women can, if they choose, "pass" as heterosexual. This results in a double disadvantage because if they cannot be seen, neither can their oppression. (Haynes & Holmes, 1994, p. 147)

Social Work and the Changing Society

In the future, there will be many more culturally diverse people who are disadvantaged. Being disadvantaged means living in a world distinct and distant from that of mainstream America. Most service providers and their organizations do not have adequate knowledge of the disadvantaged and their world. However, the sheer numbers and potential political power of the latter will compel the former to strive to address their needs. Moreover, with increasing cultural diversity, it will become more likely that service providers and recipients will be of different backgrounds. Thus, there will be an ever-increasing need for practitioners to be equipped with cultural knowledge and cross-cultural skills:

> Consequences of cultural ignorance are ethnocentric, critical and condescending attitudes, and the inability to effectively provide needed services to clients, who are misunderstood and alienated. Without cultural competencies, social workers are likely to be part of the problem, rather than providing solutions to the difficulties which their clients face. (Winkelman, 1999, p. 17)

Competent practitioners can be effective only to the extent that their organizational environments allow for effective performance. Therefore, social service organizations will also need to be structurally and functionally responsive to the needs and realities of their clientele.

PREPARING FOR THE FUTURE

Preparing for the future does not require starting from scratch. We need to discover and build on our assets.

Discovering the Assets of Social Work

The philosophy and history of social work have significant strengths to draw from.

Richness of Social Work Philosophy

Social work philosophy is marked by a set of basic value orientations, norms, and ethical principles held in common by social workers. The most recent version of the National Association of Social Workers (NASW) Code of Ethics begins with the statement, "The primary mission of the social work profession is to enhance human well-being and help meet the basic human needs of all people, with particular attention to the needs and empowerment of people who are vulnerable, oppressed, and living in poverty" (NASW, 1996). Most social workers would agree to the profession's allowing for all kinds of differences, but not differences regarding ideology, as this ideology is essential for social work's character and role in the society. There is a traditional commitment to serve the poor and the needy.

The mission of social work is operationalized as humane and effective social services to individuals, families, groups, communities, and society in order to improve people's social functioning and quality of life. The optimal social functioning of the individual and good of the collective society demand a simultaneous focus on the individual, the environment, and the transactions between the two.

Social work's values[3] distinguish it from other helping professions. Those values represent the noblest ideas for conceptualizing, understanding, and working with people and for improving their societal conditions. The NASW has identified service, social justice, dignity and worth of the person, importance of human relationships, integrity, and competence as the core values of the social work profession. Over the years, social work values have led to the formulation of many practice principles: respect for the inherent worth and dignity of the individual, respect for the client's autonomy and self-direction, individualization of the client as a unique person, acceptance, empathy, genuineness, maintenance of a nonjudgmental attitude, respect for the confidentiality of the client's communication, impartiality, rationality, and self-awareness (Siporin, 1975). Some of these principles have been accepted as enforceable, and others as aspirational standards of practice (NASW, 1996).

A critical look at the fundamental social work values and practice principles shows that we have all the ingredients of effective social work with culturally diverse people. Powerful concepts such as *equality, justice, equity, human diversity*, and *tolerance*; individual's *uniqueness, inherent worth and dignity*, and *self-determination*; and *caring, competence*, and *professionalism* are the main elements of the social work philosophy and belief system. These ideas and our commitment to valuing diversity can serve as foundations for building an edifice of methodologies for culturally competent practice. Thus, the relationship between social work philosophy and cultural diversity is obvious.

Historically, social work philosophy has guided the translation of its values into practice principles and approaches for working with people. In the earlier days of the profession, most of the people that social workers served were culturally different from the social workers. However, the definition of cultural diversity was much narrower then: "the recognizably poor and chronically ill constituted a culturally diverse population in the midst of a larger, less tolerable society" (Kropf & Isaac, 1992, p. 4). That definition was later broadened to include white immigrants from countries of Southern and Eastern Europe. For a long time, the social work concern did not extend to those who were racially different, the people of color, whom the society at large considered as subhuman, enemies, or inferior. Our commitment to serve all people while respecting their differences has gradually grown in practice to match what it always was in principle.

Cultural Sensitivity/Competence-Related Intentions,
Ideas, and Accomplishments

Social work developed into a helping method in the second half of the 19th century and began aspiring to become a profession. At that time, an economic revolution was taking place, and the country's major characteristics—a small, prosperous, and homogeneous population (except for blacks and Indians) and a relatively simple economy—were becoming things of the past. Industries were growing, along with an explosive increase in population, massive and chaotic growth of cities, marked social stratification, a business cycle involving periods of depression and unemployment alternating with periods of growth, and a host of social problems (Popple, 1983, 1995). The increase in population was predominantly through immigration. Most of the new immigrants were from Southern and Eastern European countries, and they were different from the mainstream Americans in their cultures, customs, languages, and religion. The growing heterogeneity of the society was viewed by many as a threat. "With little new immigration to reinforce Old World cultures, ethnic minorities from Europe were met not only with relentless assimilation efforts but also with widespread discrimination" (Guzzetta, 1995, p. 2511). There was no societal incentive for appreciating and accommodating cultural differences in people. Individual effort and the traditional institutions of the family, the marketplace, and the church were no longer sufficient to handle social problems and ensure personal, familial, and community well-being. Social work organizations and approaches emerged to deal with the situation.

In order both to appreciate the distance covered and to realize the distance left to travel on the path to providing genuinely culturally competent social services, we will review our history of cultural sensitivity in terms of our intentions, significant ideas, and major accomplishments.

Intentions

Given the professional philosophy of social work, our intentions for acknowledging and accommodating diversity in our work were never suspect. However, the scope of our concern was limited. In a discussion of social work and diversity, Hoffman and Sallee (1994) observed that "[d]ifferences are not seen as barriers to be overcome, but as conditions that ought to be made known and celebrated. In a related sense, differences can be seen as a mark of the ordinary, a part of the human condition that does not set people apart, but, in a greater sense, binds us together" (p. 345). Despite their nobility, such conceptualizations of diversity led to a "treating everybody the same" or a "color-blind" approach, which pervaded the human service scene for a long time. In such an approach, "[t]here was no need to change programs, policies, and practices because they could be universally applied to everyone, regardless of race, creed, or color" (Sue, 1997, p. ix). This was also true of our acknowledging and addressing gender issues in social work practice, even though social work is largely a female profession. In their discussion of case-level social work assessment and intervention approaches, Norman and Wheeler (1996) have included the psychoanalytic model, behavioral models, the humanistic approach, cognitive models, Hollis and Wood's psychosocial approach, and Satir's conjoint family therapeutic model. Norman and Wheeler concluded that "[a]lmost without exception, the major approaches to psychological assessment and intervention developed to date neglect gender-based factors" (p. 206).

When minority groups began to challenge the monocultural views of the society, our intentions as social workers started becoming more real and our efforts more sincere. Our intentions regarding culturally competent social work practice are reflected in the pronouncements of the Council on Social Work Education (CSWE) and of the NASW. The first curriculum policy statement of the CSWE, issued in 1952, declared that all aspects of a person's growth—physical, mental, and emotional—should be considered in terms of how social, cultural, and spiritual influences affect his or her development (CSWE, 1952). The 1962 curriculum policy statement required that the social work curriculum enable the student to recognize, understand, and appraise "human behavior in the light of personal and cultural norms and values and varying conceptions of effective social functioning and well-being" (CSWE, 1962, pp. 4-5). Since the mid-1970s, all social work programs, at both the undergraduate and master's levels, are required to include content on ethnic and racial minorities and women. CSWE's curriculum policy statement calls for content on ethnic minorities and women and for attention to "patterns and consequences of discrimination and oppression" and to "the experiences, needs and responses of people that have been subject to institutionalized forms of oppression" (CSWE, 1983, sect. 7.4). The latest curriculum policy statement identifies nine specific curriculum areas for which all social work programs are responsible. Four of the nine areas are diversity, promotion of social and economic justice, populations at risk, and social work values and ethics (CSWE, 1994). In essence, the coverage of these content areas requires teaching students how to understand and work with culturally diverse people, most of whom are in at-risk populations, who are in need of economic and social justice and who serve as a challenge to the professional values and ethics. Similarly, the most recent version of the Social Workers' Code of Ethics, which became effective on January 1, 1997, spells out social workers' responsibility regarding cultural competence and diversity. Section 1.05 of the Ethical Standards section in the Code of Ethics states that:

(a) social workers should understand culture and its function in human behavior and society, [and] recognize the strengths that exist in all cultures;

(b) social workers should have a knowledge base of their clients' cultures and be able to demonstrate competence in the provision of services that are sensitive to clients' culture and to differences among people and cultural groups;

(c) social workers should obtain education about and seek to understand the nature of social diversity and oppression with respect to race, ethnicity, national origin, color, sex, sexual orientation, age, marital status, political belief, religion, and mental and physical disability. (NASW, 1996, p. 9)

Ideas

From the beginning of the history of social work, the organizations that arose in response to social problems, the people who provided social services, and the methods of service provision that were developed reflected ideas that have direct or indirect relevance for culturally competent practice. Over the years we have added to those ideas. We consider the following ideas especially important.

Bifocal Perspective. Social work organizations in the second half of the 19th century collectively had a bifocal thrust: They sought to change both the individual and the environment. Thus, they were concerned with social welfare as well as social reform. "The task of social welfare is to alleviate the distress of the poorest and the most disadvantaged groups. The task of social reform is to reduce the size of such groups or eliminate some of the disadvantages present in them" (Coll, 1984, p. 1504). This bifocal perspective, as an idea and an approach to human problems, has continued and has become the unique attribute of the social work profession. In the olden days, the charity organization societies (COS) and the settlement houses represented the two thrusts. The major technique of the COS was "friendly visiting," which consisted of "a wealthy volunteer befriending a needy family and through his or her example and guidance showing the family the way out of poverty" (Popple, 1983, p. 74). The underlying belief was that personal deficiencies and character flaws were responsible for people's poverty and problems. The COS also sought to make charity work scientific through ideas such as (a) a central referral system; (b) a systematic coordination of relief-giving agencies; (c) investigation and assessment of individual applications; and (d) intervention in the form of education, support, and community resources, aimed at helping the needy master their difficulties (Leiby, 1971). The settlement house workers, on the other hand, were guided by the idea of a "friendly neighbor" rather than a friendly visitor. They lived as neighbors of the poor in urban slums and impoverished neighborhoods and followed the principles of residence, research, and reform—a Three R's movement (Trattner, 1989). The approach to the settlement work was very broad:

> Characteristics of the settlement house movement include having a holistic rather than a specialization approach, advocating for social reform while giving services, bridging various groups and classes of people, identifying people as neighbors rather than as clients, transforming people from victims of outside forces to participants who are responsible for their own lives, exercising a large and flexible range of activities that are governed by a volunteer community board, and having an orientation to family and neighborhood strengths rather than to individual pathologies. (Smith, 1995, p. 2130)

The problems and situations of people different from mainstream Americans are complex, and that complexity largely results from their culture, values, worldview, life experiences, and self-concepts. Their problems would not respond well to narrow-scope approaches based on restricted views of their realities. A bifocal perspective is necessary.

Concept of Professionalism. Over the years, social work organizations and their methodologies changed: "By the turn of the century, COS representatives realized that the causes of poverty were social, economic, and psychological rather than the result of personal moral failure. If moral failure was not the cause of poverty, then friendly visiting was not the solution" (Popple, 1983, p. 75). The role of the volunteer friendly visitor gradually diminished, and that of the paid worker became prominent. By then Mary Richmond (1897), an outstanding social work practitioner associated with the COS organization and philosophy, was pushing for formal education for the "profession of applied philanthropy" (p. 186). Professions are groups whose characteristics include common knowledge and beliefs, skills and techniques, and values—all reflecting a commitment to service and acquired through formal, systematic, and rigorous training. The public comes to identify each such group "as being suited to fulfill the specific need and often gives it formal and legal recognition through *licensing* or other sanctions as the legitimate source for providing the relevant service" (Barker, 1999, p. 379).

Social Casework Based on "Social Diagnosis." An idea possibly borrowed from the practice of medicine, casework became the main approach to ameliorating social problems. Mary Richmond "formulated the first comprehensive statement of principles of direct social work practice" (Longres, 1995b, p. 2605). Casework was guided by the principle of individualization. It was Richmond who coined the term *social diagnosis*. Understanding the individual and his or her situation was considered essential for effective help. The social diagnosis by the worker had to be

> an attempt to arrive at as exact a definition as possible of the social situation and personality of a human being in some social need—in relation to other human beings upon whom he in any way depends or who depend on him, and in relation also to the social institutions of his community. (Richmond, 1917, p. 357)

Richmond's book *Social Diagnosis* became the bible of social workers:

> *Social Diagnosis* was a major intellectual creation of a profound and lucid mind, compounding wide reading with experience unremittingly testing and being tested. It was further reinforced by the discipline of teaching. Mary Richmond taught casework in the early years of what was then the New York School of Philanthropy and later the New York School of Social Work. (Klein, 1968, pp. 149-150)

For many decades, casework dominated the scene as the method of doing social work, and several models of casework were developed, including diagnostic casework, functional casework, problem-solving casework, sociobehavioral casework, and task-centered casework, as well as models based on psychoanalytic, Rogerian, gestalt, and existential theories. Most of these and other methods of intervention can be adapted to work with culturally diverse individuals.

Ecological-Systems Perspective. Despite the philosophical commitment of social workers to the person-in-environment framework, the medical model of study, diagnosis, and treatment guided social work practice for many decades. The narrowness of this model gradually became obvious. The search for other ideas led to the discovery of the utility of general systems theory and social ecology. General systems theory, which originated in the physical sciences, has been expanded to apply to living systems. The theory provides a useful model for understanding the relationships and dynamic processes of events affecting individuals, families, larger social groups, communities, cultures, and other larger systems. Similarly, ecological concepts were found to be helpful in practice not only with individuals, families, groups, and organizations, but also with communities and in political advocacy (Germain & Gitterman, 1995). Combining the two provided a perspective that "focuses on the total picture, with equal emphasis being placed on learning about the strengths and deficits of the environment and of the client" (Greif, 1986, p. 225). Despite criticisms[4] leveled at this perspective in the social work literature, we believe that the ecological-systems perspective can undergird the approach to effective work with culturally diverse clients.

Empowerment. This idea has become an important part of the social work ideology and approach. It refers to the process of gaining, developing, facilitating, and giving power. Simon (1994) has identified the following five components of the empowerment approach, which have existed in every phase of the history of social work: (a) construction of collaborative partnerships with clients; (b) the emphasis on their strengths; (c) focus on both individuals and their physical and social environment; (d) the recognition of clients' rights, responsibilities, and needs; and (e) the direction of professional energies toward helping disempowered individuals and groups.

> The process of empowerment addresses two objectives: the achievement of the more equitable distribution of resources and non-exploitative relationships between people and the enabling of people to achieve a creative sense of power through enhanced self-respect, confidence, knowledge and skills. (Rees, 1991, p. 66)

The importance of empowerment in culturally competent work is obvious.

Prevention. The focus of settlement house work was on preventing problems. Settlement workers turned to educating and organizing people of the neighborhood, not to coordinating their formal charities (Leiby, 1971).

> Settlement house staff worked on legislation attempting to combat slums and slum conditions. Pushing for municipal reforms, they worked to improve sanitation, sewage disposal, and clean water. They advocated for regulation and inspection of food to prevent disease and illness. They worked to create small neighborhood playgrounds, housing code improvement, reduction of congestion through city planning, and transformation of public schools and neighborhood social centers. (Brueggemann, 1996, p. 182)

They were more interested in changing social conditions than changing individuals. The typical settlement programs consisted of day care services for children, adult literacy classes, and recreation-social clubs (Trolander, 1975). The settlement house workers recorded their experiences and produced a stream of publications. The major techniques used in their work were what later came to be called social work group work and community organization. The group- and community-level interventions are essential for effective work with culturally diverse people.

General Accomplishments of Social Work

Besides the noble intentions and powerful ideas, there have also been impressive general accomplishments in the area of culturally competent social work practice.

Swimming Against the Current. During the early years of social work history, there was an atmosphere of extreme anti-immigration, with calls for rapid assimilation of immigrants into the American culture and with some social workers even helping new immigrants in the process of assimilation. There were many other social workers who focused on helping immigrants to master the challenges of adapting to the new country while maintaining their cultures and identities. Living among and interacting with the poor exposed settlement house workers to the conditions and cultures of these people. Jane Addams, the most prominent social worker associated with the settlement house movement, pressed for appreciation of differences. Settlement houses sponsored celebrations and exhibitions featuring crafts and customs of various cultures (Guzzetta, 1995). Social workers participated in political advocacy on behalf of the disadvantaged in the face of societal biases and prejudices, at times at great cost. For example, in the early 20th century, for their efforts to increase the government's role in maternal and child health, social workers were maligned as communists, subversives, endocrine perverts, and derailed menopausics (Siefert, 1983). Social workers participated in the civil rights movement of the 1950s and 1960s and in the welfare rights movement of the 1960s and 1970s.

Fighting for Broad Reform. As mentioned above, settlement house workers engaged in broader reform activities, aimed at improving the housing, neighborhoods, working conditions, family situations, diet, and health of the poor. They were in the forefront of the labor movement. They spearheaded the fight against child labor and were instrumental in the passage of progressive legislation, the establishment of the Children's Bureau, and the enactment of public welfare statutes. These societal changes benefited the poor and disadvantaged. The settlement workers also contributed to the cause of civil rights for blacks by assisting in the creation of such self-help organizations as the National Association for the Advancement of Colored People (Trattner, 1994; Trolander, 1975). At their best, settlements engaged "neighborhood residents in educational reform, environmental action, program development, intergroup relations, and broad arenas of social and economic development" (Weil & Gamble, 1995, p. 577).

Realizing the Inadequacy of the Melting Pot Theory. Social workers who saw the world of their clients from close quarters were gradually convinced that the reality of America was different from the image of the melting pot—the idea of Americans as a people who looked, thought, and acted alike. The melting pot idea ignored the enormous diversity of beliefs, values, traditions, and behaviors that persisted through successive generations among white Americans, and it had never applied to people of color. The latter truth is graphically depicted in Dudley Randall's (1971) poem "The Melting Pot":

> There is a magic melting pot
> where any girl or man
> can step in Czech or Greek or Scot,
> step out American.
>
> Johann and Jan and Jean and Juan,
> Giovanni and Ivan
> Step in and step out again
> all freshly christened John.
>
> Sam, watching, said, "why, I was here
> even before they came,"
> and stepped in too, but was tossed out
> before he passed the brim.
>
> And every time Sam tried that pot
> they threw him out again.
> "Keep out. This is our private pot.
> We don't want your black stain."
>
> At last, thrown out a thousand times,
> Sam said, "I don't give a damn.
> Shove your old pot. You can like it or not,
> but I'll be just what I am." (p. 141)

Moving Toward Professionalism of Social Work. The evolution of the COS into the family service agency, the significant increase in child welfare agencies, and the emergence of mental hygiene clinics in the 1920s provided the institutional demand for professional social workers (Leiby, 1984). The movement of professionalization of social work, among other things, led to the creation of educational institutions. In 1898, Mary Richmond organized a summer school of philanthropy, a 6-week course consisting of lectures, agency visits, and some field practice in the New York COS. This course became so popular that it was repeated in successive years and became known as the New York School of Philanthropy, the predecessor of the present-day Columbia University School of Social Work. The COS in other cities established similar programs. The Institute of Social Science was started at the University of Chicago in 1903 (Landon, 1986). The newly emerging schools of social work in the Northeast drew their support from COS and from many foundations and national associations. The University of Chicago School of Social Service Administration, on the other hand, had a different orientation, as its affinities were with the settlement house movement, with state and local public agencies, and later with the U.S. Children's Bureau. Thus social work education "responded to the various kinds of agencies and practice and reflected the confusion in the definition of the field and the competencies within it" (Leiby, 1971, p. 1469). Although professionalization of social work has involved efforts to become scientific by seeking, adapting, or creating practice theories, the public image and legitimacy of social work continue to come not from science but from altruism.[5]

Specific Accomplishments of Social Work

> Since the 1960s, social work has strongly supported cultural pluralism and diversity. Social work was one of the first and most consistent supporters of civil rights activity and built the commitment to oppose prejudice and discrimination into its organizational structure and code of ethics. (Guzzetta, 1995, p. 2515)

In response to the societal changes that acknowledged the demand for equal rights by the various disadvantaged groups, social work also turned to the task of making its methodology appropriate for effective work with those groups. Culturally sensitive and competent practice became a serious professional consideration, and over the years, social work education and practice have addressed a number of themes related to cultural diversity. These include

> race, ethnicity and power; therapy for ethnic minority families; approaches to minority youth intervention; race, gender, and class practice guidelines for individual, families, and groups; social work perspectives on the mental health of ethnic minority groups; and minority perspectives on human behavior in the social environment. (Lum, 1992, p. 4)

Over the past 25 years, some books dealing exclusively with cultural diversity issues and social work's response to those issues have appeared, as have related articles in social work journals. The frequency of these books and articles has gradually increased. *The Diverse Society* (Cafferty & Chestang, 1976) was the first publication by the NASW's press that dealt with questions related to cultural pluralism. CSWE published Norton's (1978) *The Dual Perspective* to bring diversity issues into the curriculum of social work programs. Until then, it was believed that the application of the basic social work principles, such as treating clients with respect and dignity and respecting their autonomy and self-determination, were sufficient for effective work with all. It was not realized that the "ethnicity and culture can influence what clients and social workers *perceive* to be respectful treatment" (DiNitto & McNeece, 1990, p. 299) and that in the absence of viable and significant options and choices, self-determination has no meaning. And, of course, all clients used to be judged by the standards and values of the majority culture.

The social work practice-related literature on cultural diversity can be categorized into: (1) more comprehensive generic models of practice that would accommodate the client's unique situations and needs; (2) information about distinctive conditions, cultures, situations, and needs of different "minority" groups; (3) practice principles in the form of "dos" and "don'ts" for work with culturally diverse clients; (4) specific models for culturally competent practice with culturally and ethnically diverse groups; (5) theoretical formulations for creating practice models or principles appropriate for intervention with diverse groups; and (6) approaches to teaching culturally competent practice.

1. Generic Practice Models Applied to Special Groups. The following are a few examples of such models. Devore and Schlesinger's (1981) *Ethnic-Sensitive Social Work Practice* was the first book that presented a model that adapts the traditional social work practice theory to ethnic issues. It emphasized the role of ethnicity and social class in the lives of people and how an understanding of these should inform social work assessment and intervention. Haynes and Singh (1992) presented an ethnic-sensitive practice model that integrates elements of ecological/social-systems theory and psychodynamic orientation. Ho (1987) proposed differential application of the existing family therapeutic social work models and approaches in working with different culturally diverse clients. For example, in his judgment, ecological family-centered (Hartman & Laird, 1983) and family task-centered (Reid, 1985) models are more suitable for second-generation middle-class Asian Americans, and behavior modification, family crisis intervention, and family mediation are more suitable for their more traditional counterparts.

2. Information on Distinct Cultures, Conditions, and Needs of Diverse Groups. There is an abundance of material on the distinguishing elements of the culture, values, and conditions of typical members of different ethnic and racial groups. Some of these are discussed in the group-specific chapters of this book.

3. Practice Principles for Work With Persons Outside the Mainstream. Some work has been done in formulating general principles of culturally competent practice. These principles include: (a) acknowledging diversity in terms of understanding how race, culture, and ethnicity contribute to the uniqueness of the individual, family, and community; (b) conducting cross-cultural self-assessment in terms of understanding how one's own culture shapes one's personal and professional beliefs and behaviors; (c) recognizing the dynamics of difference in terms of the client's and practitioner's interactions, behavioral expectations, degrees of self-disclosure, levels of rapport and trust, and the client's collective orientation (extended family and community); (d) acquiring cultural knowledge in terms of the client and his or her community; and (e) adapting social work skills to the needs and styles of the client's culture (Rounds, Weil, & Bishop, 1994). Gallegos (1984) has discussed the personal attributes, knowledge, and skills necessary for ethnically competent practice. Others have proposed specific "dos" and "don'ts" of such practice. For example, Davis (1995) has listed a number of "shoulds" for group workers.

4. Specific Models of Practice With Diverse Groups. We use the term *model* interchangeably with *framework.* Several models of culturally competent social work practice have appeared in the literature. These include a transcultural framework for assessment and therapy with Asian American, Native American, African American, and Latino American children and adolescents (Ho, 1992); a framework for therapy with culturally diverse families (Ho, 1987); a framework for integrating ethnic and gender identities of women of color in psychotherapy (Comas-Diaz & Greene, 1994); a sociocultural intervention model (De Hoyos, De Hoyos, & Anderson, 1986); and a framework for social work with people of color (Lum, 1996).

5. Theoretical Formulations for Culturally Competent Interventions. Efforts have been devoted to establishing and enhancing the relevance of the existing and emerging theories for culturally competent practice. For example, McMahon (1994) has suggested that Hoopes's seven-stage Intercultural Learning Process be used to gauge the movement in the process of professional self-awareness and growth. The stages delineated by Hoopes (1981) are ethnocentrism, awareness, understanding, acceptance-respect, appreciation-valuing, selective adoption, and multiculturalism. Ethnocentrism is one extreme, and it involves believing that one's culture is superior, is the right way, and should be imposed on others. Multiculturalism is the art of communicating and relating comfortably with people of any culture or with groups of people of any culture. Anderson (1992) has recommended that value orientation theory should inform multicultural family-centered practice approaches. Other relevant theoretical concepts include dual perspective (Norton, 1978); ethclass and ethnic reality (Devore & Schlesinger, 1981); intergroup interaction boundary (Green, 1982); sociocultural dissonance (Chau, 1989); and cultural dislocation (De Hoyos, De Hoyos, & Anderson, 1986).

6. Approaches to Teaching Culturally Competent Practice. Some attention has been given to devising effective approaches to teaching cultural sensitivity and competence. These involve the creation of measures for assessing attitudes related to cultural diversity and of models of cross-cultural training. Carrillo, Holzhalb, and Thyer (1993) have summarized the available instruments for measuring attitudes toward race, ethnicity, gender, sex stereo-typing, and so forth. Ho (1991) has presented an Ethnic-Sensitive Inventory of 24 practice skills covering an entire spectrum of client-worker interactions. He thinks that his inventory can be used by students, inexperienced workers, experienced educators, and field supervisors to enhance their skills. Teaching models and strategies include those by Pinderhughes (1979), Lister (1987), Ifill (1989), Chau (1990), Nakanishi and Rittner (1992), and Lum (1996). Carter and associates (1994) have proposed an approach to integrating content on women into the social work curriculum. Similarly, Norman and Wheeler (1996) have come up with a model of gender-sensitive social work practice that can readily be superimposed on existing models. Newman (1989) has discussed methods and resources for incorporating content on lesbian and gay issues into the social work curriculum.

Recognizing the Need for Another
Approach to Culturally Competent Social Work

Despite the noteworthy work mentioned above, there are gaps in our response to the needs and problems of culturally diverse Americans. Our values, practice wisdom, and policy statements have not fully guided our professional priorities, programs, activities, approaches, and techniques.

> The profession of social work has long prided itself on its recognition of the importance of ethnic, cultural, racial, and sexual differences and of the ability of social work practitioners to interact effectively with diverse groups. The actual performance of individual social workers who cross cultural or other boundaries, however, does not necessarily correlate with this benign view. (Zastrow, 1985, p. 245)

Similarly, judged by the CSWE curriculum and accreditation standards, social work education policies appear to reflect "a progressive development of humanitarian ideology (e.g., protection of the vulnerable, empowerment of the oppressed, and a redistribution of society's resources)" (Van Soest, 1995, p. 63). However, in the implementation of accreditation standards dealing with cultural diversity and women's issues, "few, if any of the educational programs could show clear-cut evidence of positive results" (Austin, 1986, p. 41), and the efforts to teach content on social justice and diversity "are uneven and at times unfocused. Only a handful of schools teach practice from a social justice framework" (Gutierrez & Nagda, 1996, p. 210). Thus, even after many years, the following conclusions about the state of social work education drawn by Dieppa (1984) still have significant validity:

1. There is little indication that social work curricula are providing the knowledge, skills, and intervention strategies for effective work with minority communities.

2. The social work profession has become more conservative, reflecting American society.

3. Doubts are raised about the validity of information provided on multicultural issues and the qualifications of faculty working in this area.

4. The social work profession has relied on material produced in the fields of psychology, sociology, anthropology, political science, economics, history, and education, and it has made only limited effort to develop its own body of knowledge.

5. There is a wide gap between the development of the relevant body of knowledge on cultural diversity and its integration into the social work curriculum.

6. Professional publications have paid limited attention to important and timely contributions of ethnic minority authors to social work knowledge.

7. More research is needed on social work practice with ethnic minorities.

The consequences of all these factors are the unevenness of competent practice with culturally diverse people and the continuation of the gap between what we profess and what we practice. Historically, although deeply concerned about the poor and having a commitment to serve the poor (which set social work apart from other helping professions), social work organizations have not been unaffected by the prevailing beliefs about the poor and the reasons for their poverty. Along with the strong cultural tradition of charity, there has existed the tradition of disapproval of the recipient of charity, who was judged, "*ipso facto*, as of low character, low endowment, shiftless and lazy, ready to exploit the good will of the charitable, and at times indeed a menace to the economic soundness and stability of the community" (Klein, 1968, p. 10). This is true not only of our distant past but also of recent times. Referring to the value of liberty, Klein (1968) wrote,

> In our day political liberty of the individual has been accepted as an undebatable condition of life, and for this country the Constitution is its exponent and guardian. We take this for

granted as the air we breathe, in happy unawareness of the thousands of years of history, East and West, of irresponsible domination, enslavement, whole sale slaughter, and cruelty, and we have been inexcusably remiss in making certain that Negroes and some other minority groups should be assured of that liberty and its accompanying benefits. (p. 6)

In the words of Turner (1971), "To the extent that members of minorities face conditions defined by ethnic status considerations, social services have rarely been significant resources in overcoming discrimination, barriers to opportunity, and in obtaining more equal rights" (p. 1068). Thus, despite its claim to serve as the conscience of the society, social work has at times not only failed to rise above the prevailing societal attitudes and ambivalence about the poor and the different, but also served as the instrument of conservatism:

Social work has, to some extent justifiably, been criticized as an instrument of conservative politics. Certainly, some aspects of the profession and the individuals involved in it suggest that more concern will always be given to controlling the ambitions of minorities than to reducing the domination of the majority. Those who provide social services are beholden to the majority because these services derive legitimacy and funding from them. Services exist to the extent that the more affluent and powerful are willing to mandate them and support them through taxes and philanthropic contributions. Furthermore, social workers have been tradi- tionally drawn from the ranks of the majority or from upwardly mobile groups that have used the majority as the reference point. It is thus more likely that social control will define the gen- eral parameters of service delivery. (Longres, 1982, p. 12)

Even when social workers are from minority communities, their behavior is influenced by several value systems. Mayadas and Elliot (1989) have identified four levels—social, ideo- logical, professional, and personal—that affect social work practice. As Mayadas and Elliot put it, "An individual may subscribe to the dominant norms of his/her culture, may subscribe to an ideology, and to a professional code, but it may also be that other combi- nations of values and priorities make up the individual's own code" (p. 1278). In addition, there is a strong tendency to use one's own cultural, social, and economic values as the norm (Zastrow, 1985).

Many social workers also share many of the misconceptions and prejudices of the larger society about those who are different, deprived, dependent, and deviant. Abramovitz (1991) has provided a glossary of terms found in the everyday personal and professional language of many social workers that convey stereotypical notions of women, poor people, and people of color. As she put it, "Although social workers know that conservative ideas have captured the social welfare policy agenda, few appreciate the extent to which their personal and professional language contains unspoken messages that may not be their own" (Abramovitz, 1991, p. 380). Nor do they know the unpleasant bases of many stereo- types. The following quote from Lum (1996) illustrates how sometimes strategies for sur- vival have given rise to racial stereotypes:

[T]he seemingly happy-go-lucky, obedient African American slave behaved in such a man- ner to avoid the wrath and whip of the owner. The quiet, smiling Asian American exhibited survival behavior to avoid being attacked and lynched by angry white mobs at the turn of the century. The sleepy Mexican American, sombrero over his face, epitomized the maxim "hear no evil, speak no evil, see no evil" in the midst of vigilante rule. The stoic Native American with an expressionless face, wrapped in a blanket, concealed feelings of defeat and frustration over reservation restrictions. These behaviors are masks that cover ethnic despair at social, economic and political oppression by a racist society. (p. 113)

We have earlier discussed the COS and settlement house approaches, the former focused on the individual and the latter on the community and environment; these two approaches are personified by Mary Richmond and by Jane Addams, respectively. These two sets of approaches, with their underlying ideas, assumptions, and philosophies, together had the potential for creating a profession of comprehensive scope. However, on our way to professionalism, we have looked to different places for direction, reacted to varied conditions, and experienced many a detour. In their book *Unfaithful Angels*, Specht and Courtney (1994) wrote,

> Social work seems to have taken shape in a way that neither Addams nor Richmond envisioned entirely. Richmond did not foresee a profession that would have anything like the current commitment social work has to psychotherapy, and Addams underestimated the political barriers to realization of the kind of community support system she tried to foster. Both of them started out with a vision of a profession that would help construct the city on the hill; but instead, at this century's end, we have a profession dedicated to building the church of individual repair. (p. 85)

This statement may not reflect the entire truth. There has always been tension between the social work profession and its social environment, because social work ideology, constituency, and membership differ in important respects from those of mainstream America. "Because of this tension, the profession searches for legitimacy and recognition from society, leaving it riven by two antithetical influences: anxiety about its status and commitment to preserve its ideological traditions" (Bisno & Cox, 1997, p. 373). The anxiety about the status tends to overshadow our ideological commitment and lets a number of factors—societal, organizational, and personal—dull our intentions, smother our abilities, and blunt our tools for serving those who are viewed with indifference or disdain by the society at large.

The quantity and quality of the professional literature produced that addresses multicultural themes leave room for more work. Lum (1996) did a content analysis of the 28 social work practice texts published between 1970 and 1995 as well as of all the articles published in the three most prestigious and widely read social work journals between 1970 and 1994. He found that the texts devoted only 4% of the chapters to multicultural themes, giving only 0.2% of pages to multicultural issues, 1% of pages to ethnicity, and 2% to culture. Similarly, of the 3,716 articles published, only 8% (296) dealt with multicultural themes both general and specific to the different groups of people of color. There was significant variance in the coverage among the three journals, with *Social Casework* publishing 10%, *Social Work* 8%, and *Social Service Review* only 4% of those articles. Similarly, Nichols-Casebolt, Krysik, and Hamilton (1994) conducted a review of eight selected social work journals for their coverage of women's issues between 1982 and 1991. They asserted that "inclusion of such content is not just a means for building the knowledge base; it also sends a message to educators, researchers, and practitioners about the importance placed on understanding women's experiences in society" (p. 349). They found that only 9.7% of the articles and book reviews published during the 1980s had women's content, which they considered to be quite a low figure. Discussing the quality of women's content in social work textbooks, Burden and Gottlieb (1987) observed that many of these texts provide merely perfunctory glances at women without offering a reexamination of the implication of gender for the rest of the material.

Social work response to the needs and situations of homosexuals is even less impressive. Both the NASW and CSWE have established committees to deal with gay and lesbian issues in social work practice and education. However, these organizations are not unaffected by the larger society's widely divergent views on the legitimacy of civil rights for homosexual men and women. The formal policies of these organizations discourage discrimination against and promote social justice for lesbians and gay men, but their impact has been inconsistent.[6] There is virtually nothing in the social work literature on either the unique situations, needs, and problems of biracial/mixed-race persons and families or effective approaches to working with them. It is believed that a large proportion of the 10 million Americans included in the "other" racial category on the 1990 U.S. Census are biracial individuals (Hall, 1992; Nash, 1992). The "other" is the fastest-growing racial category (Spickard, Fong, & Ewalt, 1995).

Reviewing the current state of ethnic-competent practice, Chau (1991) has identified the following three ideological premises underlying social work response to the needs of minorities:

1. The *cultural deficit perspective* prevailed in the 1950s and 1960s. From this perspective, all variations from the mainstream in cultural patterns were viewed as deficient or deviant. Social work emphasized the modification of the behavior and socialization of minority group members into the mainstream culture. "Shaped as it was by this ideology, social work subscribed to the function of social control in its practice with ethnic minorities" (Chau, 1991, p. 25).

2. The *minority perspective* gained importance during the civil rights movement and the Great Society program days. In this perspective, the attention shifted from individual deficiency to racism and structural deficiency. Organizational and social change became the focus of social work. "Its practice activities became more attuned to affirmative action, social reform, social action and advocacy, mirroring the perceived needs of minorities much more than the societal concern for social control" (Chau, 1991, p. 25).

3. An *ethnocultural perspective* is now being advocated, because although it addressed the issues of inequity and injustice, the minority perspective did not consider ethnic and cultural differences that affect the minority situations and needs, as well as approaches and services to meet those needs. "The overriding requirement of the ethnocultural perspective is a positive acceptance and a sensitivity to the cultural strengths, values, beliefs, and the unique conditions and visions of the ethnic groups served" (Chau, 1991, p. 26).

Nevertheless, there are significant gaps in our response to the needs of culturally different groups. The changes in the society demand continued commitment and efforts.

Presenting Another Approach to Culturally Competent Social Work

The approach to culturally competent social work presented here builds on our past successes while avoiding our failures, takes into account the broad societal trends in the nation's response to human suffering and social problems, and has a comprehensive definition of work with culturally diverse people. Our past successes include our abilities (a) to articulate our ideology, values, and intentions; (b) to participate in the civil and welfare rights movements of a generation ago; (c) to create some culturally sensitive models of practice; and (d) to embrace the concept of empowerment of clients who have tended to represent diverse disadvantaged groups. Our failures can be traced largely to an ineffective approach to bridging the gap between our ideology and practice. We have depended almost entirely on social casework as the method and the individual social worker as the instrument of action. Social casework focuses on helping individuals to adjust to and cope with their problems rather than addressing the conditions that generate those problems. As Mary and Morris (1994) put it,

> Social workers, since their work in the 19th Century settlement houses of the United States, have recognized the impact of the environment on human problems. Nevertheless, the history of this country's social work response to human need, even during the so-called Progressive Era, the New Deal, and the later War on Poverty, has been a repeated retreat to an individual deficit view of social problems, and to a casework/treatment mode of response. (p. 90)

In a more critical tone, Specht and Courtney (1994) have captured this historical tendency thus:

> There are occasional episodes—usually times of national crises—when social workers rediscover the group and the community. This occurred during the two world wars, the Great Depression, and the civil rights revolution. But when the crises subside, social workers return quickly to individualized therapy as the preferred means for dealing with social problems. When there are cuts in allocations for social problems, social agencies retreat unhappily to offering group treatment in place of psychotherapy. They perceive these communally organized substitutes for "the real thing" as inferior. (p. 28)

As reported by the Association for Community Organization and Social Administration, there are only 15 master of social welfare (MSW) programs in the entire country that offer a concentration in community practice and social administration (Pine & Mizrahi, as cited in Gutierrez, Alvarez, Nemon, & Lewis, 1996).

We believe that complex needs and problems of diverse populations cannot be met adequately through a casework approach. Our attention to social problems has to move from a concern with "precipitating" causes to "basic" causes (Boyer, 1989). Moreover, the impact of the efforts of individual social workers is minimal if the organizations and programs they represent are not culturally responsive to their diverse clientele. In order to be true to the social work creed, the structures, policies, procedures, and services of social work organizations must reflect the consciousness of the cultures of their clients. For meeting the challenge of the country's demographic shift and the need for greater equity, we have to develop multicultural human service organizations. This development requires (a) the representation and contributions of diverse groups in the organizational culture, mission, and outputs; and (b) concerted organizational effort to eliminate social injustices and oppression (Gutierrez & Nagda, 1996).

The present conservative climate—political and social—is likely to continue in the foreseeable future. It fosters intolerance of differences, despite the obviously increasing diversity of the country's population, and shrinkage of resources for human services, despite the persistence of major social problems. However, there is a bright and positive element in this otherwise drab and generally negative picture. There is a clear shift toward approaches that emphasize prevention of social problems and their early detection and treatment.

The definition of social work with culturally diverse people has to be inclusive of work with individuals, groups, and communities and at all levels—individual worker's activity; organizational programs and policies; and larger societal laws, rules, and regulations.

Assumptions of the Proposed Approach

The approach proposed in this book is based on the following assumptions:

1. You, the social work student, are learning the importance of self-awareness. In working with clients from groups different from your own, self-awareness also involves (a) learning about your own personal culture—beliefs, values, perceptions, assumptions, and explanatory frameworks about reality (Hogan-Garcia, 1999); and (b) recognizing your own ethnicity and ethnocentricity.

2. You are (a) gaining an understanding of the various client systems—individual, group, organization, community, social institution, and society at large—in terms of those systems' structural development and maturation, normative functioning, deviant function-ing or disorganization, and natural problem solving and change (Siporin, 1975); and (b) also acquiring basic skills in intervening at all different levels.

3. History is a significant teacher, because our past influences the present in numerous—obvious and not so obvious—ways and because the future is never completely divorced from the present. We cannot undo our past, and it is unwise to disown our history. Those who do not learn from their history are likely to repeat the mistakes of the past. The history of groups racially and culturally different from mainstream American society is not one that either those groups or the larger society can be proud of, but it has much to teach us all.

4. The problem-solving process that you master as a part of your social work educa-tion is universally applicable to all entities and settings.

5. The ecological-systems theoretical framework is rich enough to capture the gestalt of the problem, person system, situation, and interaction, and rich enough to generate ideas for comprehensive assessments and interventions at all levels, from individual, to group, to organization, to community, to society.

Thus, our approach to culturally competent practice suggests that you should: (a) under-stand the history of the group to which the client belongs; its culture and ethnicity, which subsume religious and spiritual beliefs; and major intragroup variations based on degree of acculturation, national or tribal origin, socioeconomic status, gender, sexual orientation, and environmental forces, all of which affect the group's well-being; (b) place the client system's problem in the larger context beyond the microsituation; (c) plan for multi-pronged interventions; and (d) give equal importance to empowering the client and solv-ing the problem. Exploring the history of a group's past and present experiences will provide you with a different perspective on the general societal view of history, and this exploration can be an enriching and mind-expanding activity. Learning about others' cul-ture and ethnicity will help you to become aware of your own culture and values and to appreciate other worldviews, perspectives on life, and ways of being human. Exploring other variables will help in individualizing clients and in uncovering powerful elements of their realities, which can be both generators of problems as well as contributors to solutions.

Attributes of the Proposed Approach

This approach has the following special attributes:

1. It is comprehensive in its scope in three different ways.

   a. The number of culturally diverse groups included is large. Besides African Americans, Latino Americans, Asian Americans, and Native Americans—the four major culturally diverse and disadvantaged groups—we have included the biracial/mixed-race group. We have also devoted special attention to the realities of gays and lesbians in these groups.

   b. Intragroup variations are considered in understanding and accommodating the uniqueness of client systems. These variations may reflect within the group: ethnic differences; class differences; differences due to the degree of acculturation; differences due to citizenship status and the reason for being in the United States for newcomers (e.g., immigrant vs. refugee); differences in the level of self-acceptance of one's identity (particularly for homosexuals); and the degree of comfort with racial status (i.e., biracial/multiracial status for biracial/mixed-race individuals and their families).

   c. The gender-specific issues within each of these five groups are addressed, thus acknowledging the differences in the attitudes, perspectives, needs, and problems of men and women.

2. The approach is process oriented, with special attention to the following:

   a. The process of problem solving with culturally diverse client systems is described.

   b. How culture influences the problem-solving process is brought out and discussed.

   c. Skills for identifying and mobilizing the client system's cultural assets for the success of intervention are discussed.

3. The approach is strength oriented in its philosophical and methodological thrust.

   a. At every stage of the problem-solving process—from problem definition, to intervention planning and implementation, to evaluation and termination—it is shown how strengths are identified and utilized to overcome deficits.

   b. Client empowerment-oriented techniques are suggested to help client systems to acquire new perspectives and skills.

4. The approach is built on a systematic theory and on practice principles.

   a. Ecological-systems theory, which combines the elements of human ecology and general systems theory, is used. It enables the conceptualization of the problem-person-situation gestalt of the case or issue that a social worker is dealing with. It provides a framework for understanding the situation in its totality and for combining and integrating other helping models to match that situation.

   b. Ethical principles are suggested that compel the worker to go beyond mere respect for the client's dignity and autonomy. These principles are derived from the social work values of justice, equality, and equity. Sohng (as quoted in Uehara et al., 1996) has aptly described the perspective that incorporates these principles:

      A social worker operating out of a multicultural perspective does not take for granted the surface manifestations of culture. She or he questions the [societal] power relations that have historically subordinated certain groups and rationalized their marginalized status as being the result of their "cultural" deficiencies. ... Multicultural social work entails not just the pleasure of diversity but the realities of exclusion that minority groups face. Its mission is to build bridges of understanding [that span] peoples stratified by race, class, gender, sexual orientation, language, and other social group memberships. (p. 614)

c. Other practice principles are drawn from professional work or from research on practice with disadvantaged individuals, families, groups, and communities of diverse cultures. Some of the principles are generic and apply to all such individuals, groups, and communities, whereas others are specific to particular groups. These principles help to address more adequately both the universal and unique dimensions of people's lives.

An Overview of the Text as an Introduction to the Proposed Approach

The text is divided into seven chapters. Chapter 2 is devoted to a discussion of the essentials of culturally competent social work practice with individuals and groups outside of mainstream America. These essentials are grouped into the following five clusters: (a) the social worker's awareness of self—his or her own culture, ethnicity, and identity; (b) an overall understanding of the commonalities among groups culturally different from the majority culture; (c) general considerations for intervention with these groups; (d) general principles of culturally competent practice; and (e) stages of intervention with culturally diverse clients. The stages of intervention correspond with the phases of the problem-solving process, that is, (a) engagement and problem identification, (b) assessment, (c) planning, (d) implementing the plan, and (e) evaluation and termination. Chapters 3 through 7 each deal with one of the major disadvantaged groups of the U.S. population—African Americans, Latino Americans, Asian Americans, Native Americans, and biracial/mixed-race Americans.

This organization is not based on a belief in the logic or stability of racial classification of the U.S. population but is more a reflection of the social reality.[7] We firmly believe that race as a biological concept has no meaning, as there are no biological differences between races. However, race as a socially constructed reality is tremendously powerful. In our judgment, race, ethnicity, and gender are major variables that determine people's place in society and their options and opportunities in life, as well as their attitudes, perspectives, and behaviors. The developmental literature also suggests that people's gender, racial, and ethnic identities are important constancies (see, e.g., Bernal & Knight, 1993). Each of these group-specific chapters (a) introduces the group; (b) provides a historical overview of its experiences; (c) discusses commonality of cultures and worldviews among its subgroups; (d) identifies intragroup differences; (e) highlights the major needs and problems of the group; (f) suggests general considerations for intervention with members of the group; and (g) discusses intervention at the micro-, mezzo-, and macrolevels.

It is expected that this text will enable you to:

- Acknowledge and understand the historical as well as current context of cultural diversity in the United States.

- Realize the increasing centrality of diversity for the country and for social work practice.

- Know yourself in relation to diversity and to know the diversity within (Baird, 1996).

- Own your ignorance and confront your own biases and prejudices.

- Respect your clients' worldviews.

- Understand several assessment and intervention approaches and learn how to use them judiciously and creatively.

- Acquire skills in intervening with varied client systems of different sizes.

NOTES

1. *Cultural diversity* refers to those human differences that account for the uniqueness of individual and group life. The term *culture* refers to beliefs; customs; traditions; habits; values; ideology; and religious, social, and political behavior of a group of people, and *diversity* is the condition of being different. Human differences cover a large range on many dimensions, such as "[r]ace, ethnicity, age, geography, religion, values, culture, orientation, physical and mental health, and many other distinguishing characteristics" (Barker, 1991, p. 105). Dixon and Taylor (as cited in Lum, 1996) make a distinction between primary and secondary characteristics of diversity. The primary characteristics are such generally visible traits of groups as race, gender, age, size, physical and mental abilities, and sexual orientation, about which group members have no choice. The secondary characteristics are often invisible and may change by individual choice. These include education, experience, occupation, socioeconomic position, marital status, political ideology, and religion. In the social work literature on diversity, the terms *ethnicity* and *minority* are often used to point to the differences of various groups from the mainstream culture. The term *ethnic* has traditionally been used to describe culturally different groups of European origin such as Italian, Irish, and Polish, whereas the term *minority* is reserved for people of color (DiNitto & McNeece, 1990). Another term that became popular in the 1980s is *multiculturalism*. The term refers to a sociointellectual movement that promotes diversity as a core principle and insists that all cultural groups be treated with respect and as equal (Fowers & Richardson, 1994). The boundaries of multiculturalism included women, people with disabilities, homosexuals, and other marginalized groups. Some advocates took up multiculturalism as a cause, stressing the empowerment of these groups in public life in opposition to Eurocentrism. "This stance sparked a debate in the academic community that pitted the 'pluralists,' who defend a common culture, against the 'particularists' or 'inclusionists,' who defend group interests and demand change to redress past exclusion" ("Publisher's Note," 1994, p. v). Because the term *ethnicity* indicated the acceptance of cultural diversity of groups of European origin, and the term *minority* signified the denial of the validity of the culture of other groups (McAdoo, 1987), we have decided against using these terms. Similarly, *multiculturalism* has generated a lot of futile debate, and the term "has picked up so much extraneous baggage that it is of questionable use as a construct" (Atherton & Bolland, 1997, p. 143). We have, therefore, preferred the term *cultural diversity*, which captures the cultural differences between the mainstream Americans and the historically disadvantaged groups as well as the differences among those groups.

2. In the 1990 census, nearly 10 million people (about 4% of the entire population) checked the "other" category. Of the 8 million write-ins under the "other" category, 253,000 identified themselves as "multi-racial," "inter-racial," "creol," "black-white," and "Asian-white" (Spencer, 1997). It is assumed that many more than these "other" were biracial or multiracial individuals. Wright (1994) estimated that in 1990 there were 1.5 million children living in families in which one parent is white and the other is black, Asian, or American Indian; furthermore, this figure did not include children of single or divorced parents. The U.S. Census Bureau (1992b) reported that although the number of monoracial black babies has grown by 27% and the number of monoracial white babies by 15%, the number of black-white biracial babies has grown by almost 500%. According to the 1990 census, there were 39% more Japanese-white births than monoracial Japanese American births that year. In Native American communities, there are 40% more racially mixed babies than there are

babies born to two parents who identify as American Indian. This trend was also present, although not as emphatically, for other Asian American and Pacific Islander American groups (Root, 1996, p. xv).

3. Siporin (1989) has compiled a comprehensive list of values that the social work profession considers of basic importance. It includes: (a) the inherent worth and dignity of the individual; (b) love, caring, tolerance, altruism, and the idea of service to people in need; (c) democratic fraternity, solidarity, and community along with individual uniqueness, human diversity, and religious and ideological pluralism; (d) self-determining liberty and autonomy, mutual aid, reciprocity, and interdependence; (e) rationality, competence, and professionalism; (f) personal and social responsibility; and (g) equality, justice, and equity.

4. The major criticisms are that this approach views humans as passive beings whose lives are determined by system processes and that it is value-neutral and mechanistic (Brueggemann, 1996; Simon, 1976; Winter, 1966).

5. According to Abbott (1995),

> Social work is unusual in having retained a public image based on a character trait. Most other professions have given up justifying themselves on the basis of character, which was the foundation of most professional authority in the nineteenth century. The military profession has turned "from warriors to managers," the doctors from trusted health advisors to technological sorcerers. Social work has claimed to be scientific, but the public, which has changed its opinion of soldiers and now, at last, of doctors, seems unwilling to believe it. The altruist image is reinforced by social work's public connection with populations despised and feared by the general populations—the poor, the criminal, the mentally ill. It is also reinforced by the field's pathetic salaries—on average, two-thirds of those of nurses with equivalent training—which the public imagines could attract only those whose true goal is to realize other values. Social work does, both in my experience and in the historical record, have more altruists in it than most other professions. And social work schools do not stamp out idealism in quite the same way as do medical schools. (p. 561)

6. With her focus on CSWE, Van Soest (1996) wrote: "The 1994 CSWE accreditation standards for BSW and MSW programs prohibit discrimination in any aspect of the program on the basis of race, color, creed, gender, age, ethnic or national origin, disability, political orientation, or sexual orientation (CSWE, 1994). However, gay men and lesbians are excluded from the CSWE nondiscrimination standards applied to the *host institutions* of social work programs. This distinction means that the institutions themselves, in hiring faculty, admitting students, and approving curricula, may discriminate against individuals on the basis of sexual orientation without jeopardizing their social work program's eligibility for CSWE accreditation" (pp. 57-58).

7. In 1980, the U.S. Census Bureau decided to list four racial categories: "white," "black or Negro," "Asian and Pacific Islander," and "American Indian," plus "other race" and "Spanish/-Hispanic origin." The Census Bureau was following the definition provided by the Office of Management and Budget Directive No. 15, issued in 1977 for use by federal agencies in implementing affirmative action programs as well as for enforcing the Voting Rights Act (Fuchs, 1997). It is true that this categorization of the American population does not recognize the state of flux that the country's race relations are in. For example, "[u]ntil recently, multiracial persons typically found themselves in the interstices of looming racial divisions. But as multiracial persons represent a growing part of American society, not only have they become less marginal, they are also presenting a challenge to beliefs about the stability of racial classifications" (Snipp, 1997, p. 669). However, the dropping of racial categories is not likely in the foreseeable future.

2

Essentials of Culturally Competent Social Work Practice

UNDERSTANDING ONE'S PERSONAL CULTURE AND APPRECIATING OTHERS' CULTURE

Everyone has a culture. However, we do not think of our attitudes, beliefs, and perspectives, as well as the "what" and "how" of our behavior, as the result of our culture. Our views and ways of life come to us as natural, as the only right views and ways.

> All of us grow up exposed to a variety of beliefs about other groups and interpretations of what is "good," or "right." This is part of what makes us a product of our culture. It is also what often makes us ethnocentric. We may conclude that things are "crazy," "odd," or "different" because they are not what we are used to. Thus, we tend to see life through a set of cultural sunglasses that colors all we experience, personally and professionally. (Kirst-Ashman & Hull, 1993, p. 403)

Self-awareness is essential for effective social work at every step in the intervention process, and it becomes even more important in working with individuals and groups different from ourselves. To be cross-culturally effective, one must have an awareness of one's own cultural characteristics and ethnicity. Ethnicity refers to the cultural heritage or aspects of culture that a group shares and that are learned from one generation to another (Hogan-Garcia, 1999). Without cultural self-awareness, one remains naive to the influence of culture on one's own behavior and incapable of sensitivity to the influences of others' culture upon their behavior. "By developing an awareness of one's own cultural influences, one can better appreciate the importance of others' culture for their own behavior, which will facilitate the acceptance and understanding of other cultures" (Winkelman, 1999, p. 47). Therefore, the first task in building skills for effective practice with culturally different clients is cultural self-awareness on your part. Carr-Ruffino (1996) has conceptualized building multicultural skills as a five-step process: (a) becoming aware of culture and its pervasive influence, (b) learning about one's own culture, (c) recognizing one's own ethnocentricity, (d) learning about other cultures, and (e) building interaction skills. We have subsumed the first three of these steps under cultural self-awareness. This section deals with approaches to developing cultural self-awareness. Cultural self-awareness should lead to culturally competent professional practice, but the movement from one to the other involves conscious and consistent work—affective, cognitive, and behavioral—in terms of appropriate attitudes, knowledge, and action.

Cultural self-awareness comes from recognizing and owning your cultural values:

> Values are among the most important cultural determinants of behavior, and frequently lie at the basis of unconscious motivations. Values are culturally determined emotionally charged priorities for decision making and social behavior which reflect the most important aspects of a culture's beliefs, goals and expectations. (Winkelman, 1999, pp. 51-52)

Recognizing your cultural values can be facilitated by asking questions and analyzing answers. There are several tools, such as self-awareness inventories and workbooks, for exploring one's cultural beliefs and values, including biases, fears, and prejudices (see, e.g., Brislin, Cushlin, Cherrie, & Yong, 1986; Hoopes & Ventura, 1979). We now suggest some ideas for this self-reflection.

Value Orientation

It may be interesting and less threatening to begin your cultural self-exploration by locating yourself and others on the variations of the basic value orientations that all cultures have. Kluckhohn (1961) has included: (a) human nature, (b) human-nature relationships, (c) time orientation, (e) activity orientation, and (f) human-human relationships as the dimensions of values orientations.

Human nature is variously viewed as (a) basically good, (b) basically evil, (c) neutral, or (d) both good and evil.

Human-to-nature orientation includes viewing humans as either (a) being at the mercy of nature and subjugated to its forces, (b) being in harmony with nature, or (c) having mastery over nature.

Time orientation is either (a) past: dwelling on the past, with traditions directing the current activities; (b) present: emphasizing the here and now with little regard for time and schedules; or (c) future: expecting the future to be better and improved, being obsessed about punctuality.

Activity orientation includes (a) being: emphasizing "what is" rather than developing the self into something else, (b) being-in-becoming: emphasizing the development of the self as an integrated whole, and (c) doing: emphasizing betterment and change judged by external accomplishments and standards.

Human relationships orientation is expressed in three dominant patterns: (a) individualistic: considering the individual as more important than the group, with individual's autonomy, freedom, rights, and progress seen as paramount; (b) lineal; and (c) collateral: emphasizing familial and group interest, rights, and well-being over individual freedoms and rights.

These dimensions outline a modified version of the values assessment exercise suggested by Winkelman (1999). The exercise can help you to discover your overall value orientation and can show how variations in these orientations create other views and ways of human life. Start by locating your cultural group on the continuum of values pertaining to each of the value orientations. Then repeat the exercise with focus on the self and ask such questions as: (a) Where am I on these value dimensions? (b) Am I different from my group? (c) How, if yes? (d) What does the difference mean for my personal and professional perspective on life and behavior?

Cultural Differences

Cultural and ethnic groups are different from others on various aspects of culture. Hogan-Garcia (1999) has listed the following as vital properties of cultures:

1. History: The immigration experience and the time period of a group's immigration.

2. Social group interaction patterns: Relations *within* the group and between *different* groups.

3. Social status factors: Attributed to education, occupation, and income.

4. Value orientations: Subjective ideals and standards by which members judge actions, their own and others'.

5. Communication forms and patterns: Verbal and nonverbal.

6. Family life processes: Gender roles, occupations, education, marriage customs, divorce practices (if applicable), and parental beliefs and practices.

7. Healing beliefs and practices: Attitudes, beliefs, and practices regarding health, the body, disease, pain, and death.

8. Religion: Spiritual beliefs and practices.

9. Arts and expressive forms: Including visual art, verbal art, and music.

10. Diet: The preferred foods eaten.

11. Recreation: Activities for enjoyment, leisure, and pastimes.

12. Clothes: The type, style, and extent of body covering.

Do the following: Answer questions pertaining to each of the above aspects of your culture and ask yourself: (a) How close or far am I from the mainstream or dominant culture? (b) What does being close or far mean in terms of meeting the basic human needs, leading a fulfilling life, and pursuing happiness? (c) What did I learn from this exercise? (d) How can I use that learning in my personal and professional life?

We suggest the following activity for discovering your attitude toward and developing sensitivity for those different from yourself. It is taken from Carr-Ruffino (1996). It is a four-step exercise that should be repeated for male and female members of culturally different groups.

Step 1. Associations

- Relax as deeply as you can. Close your eyes and take a few deep breaths.

- Focus on the phrase *black man*, and allow a picture to come up in your mind's eye.

- Notice the words and images that come to your mind as you "see" this person.

- Open your eyes and list 10 to 20 words in the order in which they occur to you.

- Review your list. Mark a plus sign beside the words that are positive, a minus beside the words that are negative, and a circle beside neutral words.

Step 2. Negative Associations

- Close your eyes and focus again on the image of the "black man." Formulate a negative opinion or judgment, perhaps one you typically hold about black men.

- Notice your *feelings* as you see the person in this negative way. What *thoughts* come up as you focus on the image?

- Write a few sentences about your feelings and thoughts.

Step 3. Positive Associations

- Formulate a positive opinion or judgment, perhaps one you typically hold about black men.

- Notice your *feelings* as you see the person in this positive way. What *thoughts* come up as you focus on this image?

- Write a few sentences about your feelings and thoughts.

Step 4. Insights

- Focus on the differences between your experiences when you had negative and positive judgments and opinions. What were the differences? What meaning does this have for you, your beliefs and feelings about people from this group, and about beliefs in general?

- Write your responses in a few sentences; include anything you like about your feelings, thoughts, and insights.

UNDERSTANDING OTHERS: COMMONALITIES AMONG GROUPS CULTURALLY DIFFERENT FROM MAINSTREAM AMERICANS

Understanding others is easier if we start by identifying commonalities among groups culturally different from mainstream Americans, commonalities that set them apart from those in the mainstream. We have described differences among and within these groups in the group-specific chapters (Chapters 3-7). Despite significant intergroup differences and intragroup variations, there are striking commonalities in the experiences and worldviews of these, such as the following.

Meaning of the Family. Family has a special meaning and place in the lives of these groups. Its meaning includes persons from outside the nuclear group. For example, most Asian Americans have retained the value placed on the family in Asian societies, where family, not the individual, is viewed as the basic unit. Family members are socialized to think of the family's needs, prestige, stability, and welfare as more important than the individual's aspirations, comfort, health, and well-being. The family's structure, roles of its members, and rules of relationships are prescribed and rigidly followed. Although the traditional Hispanic family structure—a bilateral extended family with a patriarchal emphasis and matricentric structure—has been replaced by several different structures, the traditions of the importance of the family and family obligations have persisted, and a significant value is placed on family cohesion and loyalty. The same is true for the African American and Native American family.

Extended Family Ties. In all these groups, great importance is placed on maintaining a wide network of kinship. The extended family has prevailed in the black community. The black family is "a multigenerational group of consanguineal and affinal kin, who form a kinship network extending into the African American community. It includes parents, full and half siblings, aunts and uncles from one or more marriages or unions, grandparents, cousins, family friends and other fictive kin" (Winkelman, 1999, p. 295). There are various forms of extended family among Asian Americans. For the Hmong, the extended family is the whole clan. Families belong to one of the 18 clans, all of which are represented among Hmong living in the United States. The extended family among Filipinos is a wider group in a different sense. Not only are the relatives of both parents incorporated into the extended family, but relatives acquired by marriage also play roles of importance equal to those related by blood ties.

> An additional source of members is the *"compadrazgo"* system, in which friends and allies can be recruited to serve as godparents to children. Thus incorporated into the family network, the godparent also assumes the responsibilities and obligations attendant to the role. (Ishisaka & Takagi, 1982, pp. 141-142)

The Native American family has been subjected to multiple destructive assaults. Native American children were either institutionalized, adopted by or placed in foster homes of European Americans, or housed in boarding schools, and large numbers of women of childbearing age were sterilized without their knowledge and permission. "Thus both reproductive and socialization roles of the Native American family were seriously compromised by the agencies of the U.S. government" (Winkelman, 1999, p. 252). Nevertheless, the extended family has remained the most important institution of Native Americans. Their kinship relations are based not upon blood alone but also on affinal relations, so that a wide variety of individuals belong to the family and kinship network. Because of the emphasis on kinship relations and the extended family system, children may have "multiple parents" (Winkler, 1999).

Place of Religion. Religion plays a significant role in the lives of the people belonging to these groups and their communities. It affects their attitudes and practices regarding food, medical care, mental health, recreation, schooling, and interpersonal relationships both within the family and in the external environment. Religious faith and religious institutions (represented by priests and indigenous healers) have a tremendous influence on their ability to deal with their problems. For example, church serves as an invaluable source of psychological, spiritual, and social support for African Americans and their families. However, the theology taught in the African American church emphasizes faith in God's ability to resolve problems, and many, particularly the elderly, are sometimes reluctant to depend on outside sources of assistance. The same is more or less true of other groups.

Experience as Americans. All of these groups share a history of being the victims of racism. The commonalities of their experiences as Americans include hostility from the white community, which has taken the form of prejudice, economic discrimination, political disenfranchisement, physical violence, immigration exclusion, social segregation, and denial of equality. Members of these groups continue to experience both social and institutional racism. Social racism involves negative attitudes of individuals and groups, which often result in such overt acts as name calling, social exclusion, and violence. Institutional racism is reflected in practices based on institutional policies and procedures that exclude or put persons from these groups at a disadvantage.

Poverty and Lower Economic Status. Poverty among these groups is another commonality. Large proportions of Native Americans, African Americans, Latino Americans, and Asian Americans (particularly Southeast Asian refugees) live below the poverty line. Contrary to the stereotypes, large numbers of these poor (a) are willing to work or are working; (b) believe in the American dream of success, wealth, and happiness; and (c) are eager to make the needed efforts to realize that dream but cannot lift themselves out of poverty.

Some in these groups have moved into the mainstream, succeeded in attaining middle-class status, reached positions of some power, and adopted the American middle-class culture and norms. However, even these often experience a lack of upward mobility. Their limited success at times generates unlimited jealousy and resentment in others, which find expression in various forms of discrimination, harassment, intimidation, vandalism, and violence.

Level of Acculturation. While pointing to intragroup differences, the level of acculturation of individuals and groups also speaks to the similarity of their experiences. This is true of the Native Americans, the original inhabitants of this land, as well as of the immigrants from Asia and South America, the most recent newcomers. Hodge (1981) reported that Native Americans respond to white society in different ways, based on their Indian identity. He separated them into three groups: bicultural, traditional, and marginal. Based on the level of acculturation, Ho (1987) has divided Asian American families into three types: recently arrived immigrant families, immigrant-American families, and immigrant-descent families. All these groups have concerns, needs, and priorities related to the level of their acculturation.

Culture-Related Disorders. There are culture-related disorders among many of these groups. Dana (1998) has included syndromes such as spirit intrusion, soul loss, root work, ghost sickness, and taboo breaking as culture-bound disorders among Native Americans. Also, many of their problems in living, such as marginal cultural orientation status, damaged sense of self, relationship problems, chronic alcohol or drug abuse, and lack of skills are directly related to their culture. Similarly, several culture-bound syndromes among Southeast Asian refugees have been reported in the literature. In many Asian cultures, physical and mental illness is attributed to natural and spiritual causes. Integration of body, mind, and spirit is viewed as essential for health. Lack of equilibrium in one is believed to result in disharmony for the entire being. Hence, medicine and religion are intertwined (Frye, 1995). Most Asian cultures discourage the owning and expression of emotional problems. Consequently, many Asian Americans tend to experience stress psychosomatically, so that many of their emotional and psychological problems are expressed as somatic complaints.

GENERAL CONSIDERATIONS FOR INTERVENTION

A Sense of Powerlessness. There is a sense of powerlessness among many members of racial and ethnic minority groups, which tends to feed their cultural belief in "fate." Therefore, your intervention with these individuals and their communities should use empowerment-oriented approaches. These approaches should be geared toward helping individuals to obtain appropriate tangible resources; to develop intangible assets such as a positive self-concept, hope and high morale, cognitive skills, interpersonal communication, and the American problem-solving skills; to acquire and maintain health and physical competence; and to use supportive social networks. Approaches should also be geared toward educating communities about how the country's civil, political, and legal systems work and how social institutions and service organizations can be made responsive to human needs.

Family—A Source of Both Strain and Strength. The family has traditionally been the hub of life and a bulwark against stress in these groups. However, a host of factors, including acculturation, is changing the family significantly. Devoid of resources of the larger kinship system, the family in its newer forms does not have the same vitality. At the same time, the family's roles, rules, and expectations put strain on individuals, who are torn between the conflicting pressures of the family and American culture. There is usually a discrepancy in acculturation between parents and children. The children's greater receptivity to the ideas of individualism and independence; their assertiveness; and their attitudes in relation to authority, sexuality, and freedom of individual choice become problematic (Dhooper, 1991). The individual is beset with feelings of alienation and conflict of identity, and the family is faced with marital and intergenerational conflict (Sue & Morishima, 1982). Nevertheless, most families deeply care for their members and are concerned about and willing to invest in the well-being of their members. Therefore, you should view the family as a resource and involve it in interventions with individuals. As structure is an element of the essence of many of these families, you will find models of family intervention that focus on the structure more effective in working with them.

Reluctance in Asking for Help. Most members of the racial and ethnic minority groups are reluctant to ask for help on their own. Many are used to fending for themselves, turning inward for strength, or seeking solace and support from their families. Others perceive human services as insensitive and unresponsive to their needs. For many others, particularly those who are new to this country and its culture, social work may be an alien concept (Dhooper, 1997a). Many, Asian Americans specifically, are also conditioned to control their feelings and have a low level of emotional expressiveness. They have difficulty in acknowledging and openly talking about their problems. These individuals should be reached out to in creative ways, ways that reduce their culture-based barriers. These may include using or going through the indigenous helping systems. In the group-specific chapters, we have provided examples of these systems. You can assume that the client is looking for a solution to the problem and an affirmation that he or she is not crazy, is embarrassed over having to seek help, and is confused or puzzled over how therapy can be helpful (Root, 1985).

Religious Faith and Institutions as Allies. Whereas religious faith can foster belief in fate, it is also a source of tremendous strength for facing life and its demands. In some cultures, priests, indigenous healers, fortune tellers, and the like have significant influence on people's ability to deal with their difficulties. View them as parts of the client's social support system. Their collaboration can improve the likelihood of the client's cooperation and the success of your intervention. Consider religious practices, such as special prayers for the client and the wearing of an amulet or talisman by the client, as psychological supplements to your counseling, educational, and resource mobilization activities.

Special Needs of Refugees. Although there are unique intergroup and intragroup differences among refugees, premigration stresses continue to predict depression and anxiety in many for years (Chung & Kagawa-Singer, 1993). In working with these refugees, make sure that your intervention approaches are informed by an extra sensitivity for their experiences. For example, a confrontational approach in which "identification and dissection of the psychological trauma is encouraged, and introspection is expected to be followed by verbalization" (Frye & D'Avanzo, 1994, p. 94) is antithetical to many, particularly Asian, cultures.

Different Perspectives on Problems and Their Solutions. Most in these groups do not believe in psychiatric dynamics and psychological explanations of behavioral difficulties. Instead, social, moral, and organic explanations are used. Similarly, they find loosely targeted and abstract long-term goals incomprehensible, unreachable, and impractical (Ho, 1987). Hence, remember that a structured, concrete, tangible, problem-focused, goal-directed, and result-oriented but realistic approach is needed for effective work with them. For example, the therapeutic approach that focuses on external stress (vs. internal conflict), emphasizes direct problem-solving techniques, and suggests active problem management (vs. internal resolution) is more effective with Asian Americans (Kim, 1985).

Standard diagnostic and treatment tools have questionable utility. It is often assumed that all people exhibit the same symptoms of problems, that Caucasian diagnostic and intervention methods are suitable for everyone, and that all people living in the United States wish to take on the culture of American society. Traditional diagnostic instruments such as the *Diagnostic and Statistical Manual of Mental Disorders* (*DSM-IV*; American Psychiatric Association, 1994) often overlook problems that are culture-specific. Similarly, mainstream approaches to intervention are not always applicable to people from racial and ethnic minority groups. Although some of these may yield positive results, others do not (Dana, 1998). However, many of those interventions can be adapted and used within the context of different settings and cultures (Hornby, 1992).

Trust building is extremely important. Before any intervention can take place on the micro-, mezzo-, or macrolevel, trust must be established between the client system and the helper. The preconditions of trust building with Native Americans that Dana (1998) has discussed are valid for other groups as well. You can develop and maintain trust to the extent that you: (a) are open to having new experiences; (b) take an active role in learning about other cultures through literature review, direct contact with those people, and participating in cultural immersion activities; (c) are open to challenging research and intervention methods based in European ideology; and (d) are able to communicate genuineness, sincerity, and warmth to the client. Fulfilling these conditions is hard, because to varying degrees, negative attitudes and beliefs about people in these groups abound in the larger society and are reflected even in everyday speech. Professionals including social workers are not unaffected by these negative images, and even social work terminology and jargon are not bias-free.

Therefore, you should recognize the need for conscious, constant, and sincere efforts on your part. The value of self-awareness cannot be overemphasized. Look for and acknowledge your own biases, prejudices, and concepts of what is normal and healthy; accept the validity of clients' perspectives on their lives and situations; and consider clients as culturally equal to yourself (Dhooper & Tran, 1987). Encourage clients to accept their unique values and traditions and to take pride in their culture and its positive aspects (e.g., the family's place in the individual's well-being; the importance of education, self-control, and religious faith). Explore with clients how these assets can be used for dealing with the problem.

GENERAL PRINCIPLES OF CULTURALLY COMPETENT PRACTICE

Five general principles undergird culturally competent practice: (a) acknowledging diversity in terms of understanding how race, culture, and ethnicity contribute to the uniqueness of the individual, family, and community; (b) conducting cross-cultural self-assessment in terms of understanding how one's own culture shapes one's personal and professional beliefs and behaviors; (c) recognizing the dynamics of difference in terms of the client's and the social worker's interactions, behavioral expectations, degrees of self-disclosure, levels of rapport and trust, and the client's collective orientation (extended family and community); (d) acquiring cultural knowledge about the client and his or her community; and (e) adapting social work skills to the needs and styles of the client's culture (Rounds, Weil, & Bishop, 1994). In Chapter 1, we have discussed approaches to using Principles a and b. Principle d is addressed in group-specific chapters. Principles c and e are used in the context of the worker-client relationship and are reflected in the discussion of the helping process.

STAGES OF INTERVENTION WITH CULTURALLY DIFFERENT CLIENTS

I. Engagement and Problem Identification Phase of Intervention

Whether the focus of social work intervention is on helping an individual client or organizing the whole community, engaging the client-system is extremely important for problem identification and subsequent activity and should be given considerable thought. According to Parsons (1995), three elements that must be present before the helping process can begin are: (a) a workable, warm relationship; (b) an atmosphere of acceptance and understanding; and (c) a show of confidence by the helper that the help seeker can develop or rediscover problem-solving skills. Whether a client—an individual or a group—comes to a human service agency for help or a social worker representing the agency reaches out to a potential client, and whether a client seeks help voluntarily or is forced to come, it is the worker's responsibility to engage that client and set the stage for effective work.

Engaging the Client

Engagement can be viewed as a two-stage process: (a) preparation, particularly for the first contact with the client or system; and (b) relationship building.

Preparing and Setting the Stage for Intervention. Preparations are important whether the client is coming to a human service agency voluntarily or involuntarily. The process takes on added significance when those coming in involuntarily feel that they are being forced to come against their wishes. Preparations require imagination and creativity when the worker is reaching out to potential clients and meeting them on their turf. Preparation is more than just arranging for a time and place that is convenient, comfortable, and conducive to good communication. The following suggestions can transform "preparation" from a mechanical to a creative activity.

1. Adhere to the principle of client self-determination, operationalizing it as giving the prospective client choices or maximizing that client's choices. Choices can be about the "when," "where," and "how" of the initial meeting. This will enhance the client's sense of control over the situation and project a positive image of the worker.

2. Start the initial meeting with greetings, and convey to the client that you not only are willing to assist but have positive regard for the client-system and that you believe in the client's ability to deal with the problem. You may follow the initial greetings with small talk or inquiries about social events (the news, etc.). This type of light conversation will help to put the client at ease. In the group-specific chapters, we have suggested culturally specific approaches to relationship building.

3. Anticipate that the client may be nervous, anxious, uneasy, or in other ways reacting to an "unknown" situation. Such feelings may result from unfamiliarity with the human service system, uncertainty about the nature of the helping process, apprehension about your ability to assist with the problem, or the fact that the client has not voluntarily chosen to participate in the process. Validate and address these feelings and try to reduce the element of the unknown.

4. Think of the questions that most people in the client's shoes are likely to have, and address those questions. This can be done by volunteering information about yourself, your agency, the agency's programs and policies, and how all of these come together in the service of clients.

5. In case of the client referred by a third party, an individual professional, or a human service agency, explain the "why" of the referral and "what" and "how much" about the client is already known to you. This will reduce the element of the unknown for the client and enhance his or her sense of control. Also identify and attend to the client's feelings about the referral.

6. In case of suspicion or the possibility that the help seeker is an undocumented alien, disassociate yourself from any immigration connection and thereby remove the client's fear of being reported to the immigration authorities.

7. Explain the "what" and "how" of the intervention and helping relationship. This can be done by asking if further information about you, the agency, or both is needed. Generally, areas requiring coverage or elaboration are:

   a. the worker's qualifications (degrees, certifications, experience);

   b. the nature of the agency and the services that can be expected;

   c. in the case of a referral, how the person came to be referred to the worker and the future role of the referring individual or agency;

   d. each party's roles and responsibilities;

   e. the limits of confidentiality;

   f. an initial agreement regarding goals;

g. the "what," "how," "when," and "where" of the problem-solving process;

h. "who" will be involved in the problem-solving process; and

i. issues regarding payment for services.

The issue of confidentiality is particularly important. Its discussion allows the client to decide what information he or she should share with the worker.

8. Encourage a discussion of the above areas. Such discussion will help to build mutual trust as the client begins to feel that you are qualified to provide the needed help, that you have been forthright regarding the nature and scope of what can and cannot be expected, and that you will act in his or her best interest.

9. Use empowerment-oriented approaches in relating to the client and discussing the client's problems. Empowerment involves helping client systems to gain or improve control over their lives through strengthening their internal resources and acquiring external resources so that they have the skills to change themselves and their environment and solve their problems.

10. Demonstrate respect for the dignity and worth of the client. This can be done by actively seeking and respecting the client's ideas, opinions, and suggestions; appreciating the client's life experiences and wisdom; recognizing the client's cultural and ethnic assets and supports; and involving the client in all phases of the helping process.

Building Relationship. Building a helping relationship with an individual client or a client system is the second and the harder part of the engagement process. The following characteristics of such a relationship are particularly meaningful for work with minority clients. Ideally, the relationship will be:

1. need-meeting for the client, in terms of solving the immediate problem as well as producing growth and improved functioning and coping with life;

2. motivating and energizing for the client;

3. socially integrative and inclusive, so that it becomes a source of social support;

4. transactional, so that there is an exchange of needed resources;

5. honest, genuine, and realistic; and

6. one of role complementarity, so that role performance behaviors of the worker and client are mutually completing (Siporin, 1975).

Building such a relationship with many persons from culturally diverse groups is difficult even for culturally sensitive social workers functioning in multicultural service delivery systems. This difficulty arises because of many barriers, which Lum (1996) has clustered under the following four headings:

1. Resistance: Most potential clients have varying degrees of resistance to the idea of seeking help from social service organizations and professionals. Some may not know what social work is and what social workers do, whereas others may have distorted views of the social work profession and its services. The experiences of others with social service organizations might not have been pleasant or positive. Others might have been

socialized not to disclose their personal problems to strangers. Undocumented aliens may also be afraid of being reported and consequently deported if they ask for help. Like most human beings, many may feel anxious and uncertain about the unknown, ashamed and guilty over their failure to solve their problems, and angry if they are coerced into using service. Some are reluctant to approach service agencies controlled and dominated by whites (Lum, 1996). They find it hard to cross the cultural boundary that separates social work practitioners, organizational structures, and operational procedures from the ethnic client, community, and history (Green, 1982).

2. Communication barriers: The standard communication skills that social workers learn as part of their professional education may not suffice for effective communication with many of these clients. The client's lack of mastery of the English language may not be the only barrier to communication. Verbal communication is marred when expression of feelings and explanation of situations are not adequately translated into English. Feelings are more often expressed through nonverbal communication, and nonverbal communication is almost always culturally conditioned. The worker and the client may also have different types of information to draw from, so that the worker cannot use examples relevant to the background of the client as an aid to communication. The worker may also not be familiar with what Brislin (1981) termed *conversational currency*, the range of topics considered appropriate subjects for conversation.

3. Personal and family background: Gathering information about clients' personal and family backgrounds is important for assessing clients and their needs, but most of these clients have been culturally or experientially conditioned not to share information about themselves and their families. Moreover, it is very likely that the personal and family backgrounds of many clients are different from those of the worker. Thus, there is not much commonality between the two to draw from and to encourage disclosure of information.

4. Ethnic-community identity: There is variance in the degree to which people relate to their ethnic community. However, most turn first to their own helping networks, and if they have to go beyond those networks, they prefer professional agencies, programs, and personnel that they can relate to. Commonality of language, culture, and experiences gives prospective clients the feeling and confidence that they will be understood and served appropriately. To the extent that human services lack personnel and resources that match the needs of those they seek to serve, clients' ethnic-community identity becomes a hurdle in the way of building a helping relationship.

You should acknowledge and deal with these barriers. Here are some helpful strategies:

1. Dealing with client resistance: Try to deal with clients' resistance at several—policy, program, procedural, and personnel—levels. Policies of many human service agencies often reflect the societal biases and distorted views of different groups of people and their needs. Many programs may not be tailored to the problems that they are supposed to eradicate or deal with. Agency procedures can similarly be a source of discouragement and frustration for clients unfamiliar with the ways of the larger society. Even well-meaning personnel are at times handicapped by their agency's policies, programs, and procedures, because their professionalism can only be expressed within the limits imposed by the agency. Human service agencies, a large proportion of whose current or potential clients are from these groups, should review the appropriateness of their policies, programs,

procedures, and personnel for effective and efficient services to such clients. Become instrumental in your agency's undertaking such a review.

Remember that clients look for something more than technical expertise in the helper. That something is made up of qualities reflected in the showing of respect, warmth, concern, genuine caring, empathy, and other appropriate efforts to create mutual trust. You will find that asking open-ended questions and listening attentively with feeling and understanding are helpful in creating that trust. Use a tone of acceptance that avoids confrontation (Ho, 1987). Your warmth, concern, and trustworthiness will break the client's resistance.

Observe appropriate formality in addressing the client by using his or her last name and *Mr., Mrs.*, or *Miss*, particularly in the beginning. Be prepared to share personal information about your work, family, and helping philosophy, and use this self-disclosure as a signal of openness, an invitation for the client to respond, and a chance to find a common point of interest. In this way, "[i]nstead of hiding behind professional policies and practices, the worker meets the client as a human being and initiates the relationship. Instead of focusing on the client's problem, the worker seeks to humanize the relationship by disclosing a topic common to both their backgrounds. Professional self-disclosure lays the groundwork for the reciprocal response of client self-disclosure" (Lum, 1996, p. 144). However, make sure that your self-disclosure has relevance to the client's problem.

If the whole family is being seen, respect the hierarchical role structure of the Asian, black, Hispanic, and Native American family by addressing and talking with family members according to their status. As you move beyond the "warm-up" period, you may use the idea of the *cultural story* as a nonthreatening way of finding out the relevant background information. This idea builds on humans' urge to tell their story.

> The cultural story refers to an ethnic or cultural group's origin, migration, and identity. Within the family, it is used to tell where one's ancestors came from, what kind of people they were and current members are, what issues are important to the family, what good and bad things have happened over time, and what lessons have been learned from those experiences. At the ethnic level, a cultural story tells the group's collective story of how to cope with life and how to respond to pain and trouble. It teaches people how to thrive in a multicultural society and what children should be taught so that they can sustain their ethnic and cultural story. (McGill, 1992, p. 340)

This story will also help you to determine the level of the client's acculturation.

2. Reducing the communication barriers: The suggestions made earlier will reduce the resistance of the client by conveying the message that you care, are sensitive to the client's culture and condition, and are willing to help. However, continuous efforts are needed to communicate effectively with the client. Pederson (1988) has presented a sixfold approach to decreasing communication barriers:

a. Decrease the language barrier by learning the language, finding someone who can speak the language, and asking for clarification if you are not sure what was said.

b. Decrease the nonverbal communication barrier by not assuming that you understand any nonverbal communication unless you are familiar with the culture, by not taking it personally if the nonverbal communication is insulting in your culture, and by developing an awareness of your own nonverbal communication that may be insulting in certain cultures.

c. Decrease the preconceptions and stereotypes barrier by making every effort to increase awareness of your own preconceptions and stereotypes of cultures being encountered; by reinter-
preting the behavior of people from another culture from their cultural perspective; and by
your willingness to test, adapt, and change your perceptions to fit your new experiences.

d. Decrease the evaluation barrier by maintaining objectivity, by recognizing that you cannot
change a person's culture overnight, and by not judging the other by your own cultural
values.

e. Decrease the stress barrier that is created by ambiguous and unfamiliar situations.

f. Decrease the organizational constraints barrier by identifying the authority/responsibility/
reporting relationships reflected in the formal organizational chart; by looking for patterns of
personal interaction that seem to deviate from the formal organizations; by recognizing that
an organization does not exist apart from people, checking and confirming the limits of formal and informal personal influence; and by clarifying your role, knowledge, and experience
with the other person to the extent that you maintain the integrity and loyalties demanded by
your position.

3. Recognizing the importance of personal and family background: The family has a
tremendously important place in the lives of most people from these groups. For many, the
family is also a much larger group than what goes by that name in mainstream American
society. Membership in the family generally means access to a source of strength and support as well as an obligation to help others in the group. Look at and explore the client's
personal and family background and his or her rights and responsibilities in the context of
that background. Doing so is likely to show a particular blend of the culturally universal and
individually unique elements. However, you need to remind yourself that information being
gathered has relevance to the problem in hand and the possible approaches to solve it.

4. Determining the relevance of the client's ethnic-community identity: All ethnic
communities have their unique history, triumphs, tragedies, problems, and strengths. The
lives of people are affected by their physical and psychological associations with these
communities. Try to relate to the client's ethnic identity. Doing so will assist not only in
building a helping relationship and in understanding the client in his or her situation, but
also in exploring the client's problem-relevant ethnic-community resources.

Identifying problems. As the engagement takes place; as the client feels freer to talk and
tell his or her story; and as the worker explores the client's personal and family background, ethnic-community identity, and level of acculturation, the identification of the
client's problem or problems becomes easier. Some problems become obvious, and others
come close to the surface and can be identified with some probing. The following are a few
suggestions for identifying problems:

1. Take advantage of the client's willingness to talk and your skill in exploring and
creating a rough psychosocial profile of the individual or family.

2. Build on the emerging relationship with the client, draw on the psychosocial profile
that you have created, obtain more information on the problems that have become obvious, and facilitate the disclosure of those that are not obvious but that are hinted at or
suspected.

3. Realize that most of these clients have probably come for help after having exhausted their own personal, familial, and ethnic-community resources. There may thus be a sense of desperation and urgency about the problem. However, many of them may view the problem as resulting from inadequacy in their role performance and as a personal failure. A nonpathological orientation should guide your response. You will find it helpful to universalize the problem as an encouragement to problem disclosure. Acknowledge the client's efforts to deal with the problem situation, and convey a positive view of those efforts.

4. Keep in mind that there is a connection between immigration status/acculturation level and the dominance of certain types of problems. In terms of family service needs, most Asian American and many Hispanic American families can be grouped into newly arrived immigrant, immigrant-American, and immigrant-descent families. Individuals and families in the first two groups are at greater risk for varied problems. Similarly, Native Americans can be divided into groups based on the level of their acculturation. Hodge (1981) reported that Native Americans respond to white society in different ways, based on their Indian identity. He separated them into three groups: bicultural, traditional, and marginal. You should explore the client's level of acculturation and its effect on the problems and their solutions.

5. Know that two of the major stressors faced by these clients are disempowerment and pollution. Pollution may be sociological or technological in nature. Social pollution involves such things as poverty and structural unemployment, whereas technological pollution encompasses environmental pollution that may extend to places of residence and work. Those subjected to pollution are forced to lead lives of economic, social, and environmental deprivation.

Many clients need help in defining their problems. The following are some helpful principles to consider:

a. The problems should be defined in terms of the specific social dysfunctioning, as manifested in particular behavior.

b. The problem definition should focus on an area of immediate concern and one that is open for constructive action.

c. The problem definition should indicate needs that have not been met and tasks that have not been accomplished, but the difficulties should be presented as resolvable (Siporin, 1975).

Without a comprehensive assessment, the picture of the client's problem and situation at this stage must be tentative.

II. Assessment Phase of Intervention

Assessment provides the basis for intervention. Its accuracy and comprehensiveness are essential for effective problem solving. Problems are experienced by people in a social context and cannot be thoroughly understood independent of the dynamics of the total situation. An assessment should therefore accomplish several tasks.

Tasks of Assessment

Major tasks of assessment include: (a) making a statement of the problem; (b) assessing the personality or character of the client (individual or system); (c) analyzing the situation; and (d) making an integrative evaluation of the case in terms of the problem, person or system, situation, and their interaction (Siporin, 1975). An assessment should enable you to arrive at a descriptive and prescriptive judgment about the problem situation so that you and the client can discuss and agree on what the problem is and what can be done about it.

Your understanding of the universal and the unique dimensions of people's lives and needs should go into the assessment. We are assuming that you have a good understanding of the universal elements of human existence—basic needs, developmental life stages, life transitions, and generally expected situational crises. Our focus, therefore, is on factors that account for the unique dimensions of the reality of the people from these groups.

In this section, we present principles of assessment and an approach to assessment.

Principles of Assessment

Because our focus is on groups that have historically been and continue to be disadvantaged, we believe that the assessment of people, problems, and situations should lead to and provide the basis for empowerment-oriented intervention. A positive attitude should pervade your assessment activity. The following principles should guide that activity.

1. Begin the assessment with a nonpathological orientation to problem identification. Such an orientation dictates that problems be defined as needs. Viewing problems as unmet needs and unsatisfied wants enhances clients' motivation to work on problem solving. This view provides a positive perspective and moves the focus from client pathology and blaming the victim toward a search for client's strengths, potential for change, and internal and external resources (Hepworth & Larsen, 1993; Reid, 1978). Moreover, the emphasis on the positive through this relabeling-reframing is consistent with the cultural value placed on respect and compassion for others among most of these groups. Besides the positive reframing, make helpful expectation another basic component of your problem orientation (Hepworth & Larsen, 1993). Convey a genuine belief in the client's ability to improve the problem situation. This will kindle or enhance hope in the client that the situation can change for the better.

2. Look for, acknowledge, and give credit for the client's assets, such as life experience, ideas, and wisdom. Let your assessment affirm the validity of the statement, "The client is best known as someone who knows something, who has learned lessons from experience, who has ideas, who has energies of all kinds, and who can do some things quite well" (Saleeby, 1992, p. 6).

3. Make your assessment highlight the present and potential positives in the situation, such as (a) the client's understanding, motivation, experience, and capability; (b) the family's concern, adaptability, resources, and social supports; and (c) the community's concern and resources.

4. Let your assessment uncover cultural strengths. Look for positive cultural strengths in the client's background. These strengths include commitment to the family, respect for

the elderly, a holistic view of life, religious faith, and an emphasis on a balance or equilibrium in life.

5. Make sure that your assessment yields a comprehensive understanding of the client situation. Look for and emphasize variables outside the client that may be responsible for creating or feeding the problem.

> Whereas traditional psychotherapy focuses on internal barriers within the person, the cultur- ally sensitive social worker starts with the assumption that many client problems are rooted in a racist society; that is, environmental and societal conditions are responsible for clients' unsatisfied wants. (Lum, 1996, p. 170)

6. Make the assessment process a motivating experience for the client. While assess- ing the client's failures, help him or her to differentiate between failure that he or she is responsible for and that which results from external factors. "When [clients] can recognize externally controlled failure, they reduce the amount of subjective stress, self-blame, and sense of worthlessness" (Lum, 1996, p. 197).

7. Make the assessment a worker-client joint activity. Allow the client to give direction to the assessment content and to feel ownership of the assessment process and product. Thus, your assessment should provide a mutually agreed-upon structure and direction for dealing with the problem (Cowger, 1994).

An Approach to Assessment

A review of psychosocial systems of the client—an individual, family, or community— will lead to a comprehensive assessment of that client. Review the systems covered in Table 2.1 in order to make an integrative evaluation of the person (or system), problem, situation, and their interaction.

When assessing a family system, add items that would elicit answers to such questions as the following:

1. Do family members live in the same household?

2. What is the hierarchy within the family?

3. Is status in the family related to gender or age?

4. Are the roles of family members clearly defined?

5. What environmental and familial factors impinge upon the members' role performance?

6. Who is the primary caregiver in the family?

7. What factors affect the general caregiving?

8. What are the parameters of acceptable child behavior?

9. What is the family's perception of health and healing?

10. Does the family rely solely on indigenous or culture-specific approaches?

11. Who is the primary provider of health and medical care?

12. What are the family's general feelings about seeking help—ashamed, angry, demand as a right, view as unnecessary? (Sodowsky, Kuo-Jackson, & Loya, 1997)

TABLE 2.1   Psychosocial Systems of the Client

1. Personal
   a. Age and gender
   b. Marital status
   c. Life-cycle stage
   d. Physical health and functioning
   e. Emotional health and functioning
   f. Cognitive functioning
   g. Sexual health and functioning
   h. Social roles performance
   i. Coping and problem solving
   j. Motivation and hopefulness
   k. Level of acculturation and English language proficiency

2. Familial
   a. Composition
   b. Roles
   c. Rules
   d. Pattern and quality of interactions
   e. Key decision makers and patterns of decision making
   f. Client's familial functioning
   g. Strengths and strains
   h. Family's social class
   i. Family's overall functioning

3. Social
   a. Immigration status, if applicable
   b. Acculturation
   c. Social network
   d. Quantity and quality of social supports

4. Educational
   a. Level of education
   b. School history
   c. School adjustment

5. Vocational
   a. Work history
   b. Present employment
   c. Future employment plans

6. Economic
   a. Source of income
   b. Other financial resources
   c. Adequacy of financial resources
   d. Money management

7. Religious
   a. Religion and its rituals
   b. Membership in the religious group
   c. Quality of religious ties
   d. Religious faith as a source of strength

8. Cultural
   a. Client's cultural identity
   b. Membership and involvement in a cultural or ethnic group
   c. Cultural factors related to psychosocial environment
   d. Cultural factors related to client's level of functioning
   e. Cultural meaning of the problem
   f. Cultural explanation of the problem
   g. Culturally dictated solutions to the problem

9. Physical Environment
   a. Neighborhood and community
   b. Housing and its adequacy
   c. Management of the physical environment
   d. Environmental barriers to client's functioning
10. Legal
   a. Immigration-related problems
   b. Other legal problems
   c. Issue of entitlements
   d. Other rights

You can identify and mobilize strengths by exploring the struggles that families and communities have experienced and how they have survived those struggles (Gutierrez et al., 1996).

When assessing a cultural or ethnic community, explore the following areas:

1. its population;

2. its proportion of the larger community in which it is situated;

3. any conflicts or tensions with the larger community and efforts to resolve the same;

4. time of arrival in the United States, the group's national origin, and main highlights of its history;

5. language spoken by the majority or significant groups;

6. its major problems and efforts to solve them;

7. its physical environment;

8. its resources—civic, economic, educational, health, recreational, religious, and social;

9. other strengths, such as areas of positive functioning, support networks, and collectivist worldview; and

10. its leaders—formal as well as informal—and how they use their power.

A review of the systems suggested above will reveal the client's needs and difficulties, suggest areas for further exploration, and lead to the "discovery" of problems. Exploring these systems should not be a mechanical exercise. Remember that gathering information for assessment and intervention can also be therapeutic for the client and helpful in building the worker-client relationship. The systems review will also hint at the presence of special needs and problems of particular subgroups, such as refugees. Explore those special needs and problems. The following ideas will help you in doing so.

Many problems are the result of a combination of socioeconomic stresses often compounded by poverty; racism; oppression; lack of access to educational, legal, health care, and social services; and the experience of acculturation (Romero, 1983). This is true of individuals and families as well as communities. Lum (1996) has suggested the following questions for grasping clients' resources for meeting their basic needs:

1. What are the family's practical needs pertaining to food and shelter, employment, finances, and other problems of living?

2. Does the client feel a sense of powerlessness due to lack of adequate resources?

3. What institutional barriers are obstructing socioeconomic survival and coping abilities?

4. What is the client's level of stress tolerance?

5. Does the client possess problem-solving skills that can be applied to the present situation?

6. Can the client differentiate between failures for which he or she is responsible and those caused by institutional barriers?

7. Have any somatic systems accompanied the personal or family problems?

8. Has the client seen a physician or ethnic healer in the past 3 to 6 months?

9. What natural family and community support systems are available to the client? (Lum, 1996, p. 200)

Look for the material generated by the systems review for answers to these questions. With his focus on psychosocial problems, Kim (as quoted in Lum, 1996) has recommended that a "minority assessment" should cover the following five areas:

1. Newcomer syndrome: Basic survival issues of food, housing, job or welfare, culture shock/ culture dislocation, language barrier, transportation, legal and immigration problems, and school for children.

2. Psychosomatic syndromes: Anxiety-depression, headache/backache/shoulder pain, hypertension or gastrointestinal disturbance, loneliness/isolation/alienation, and insomnia/weight loss/no energy.

3. Psychological and identity issues (for second and third generations): Ethnic-identity confusion, conflict, ambivalence, self-hatred/negative identification/rebellion, cultural value conflict, family role conflict/husband-wife role conflict, women's liberation/emancipation/sexuality/divorce.

4. Major mental illness (acute, chronic psychosis, affective disorder): Inadequate treatment in public or private facilities (few bilingual staff members), stigma of mental illness, family rejection, lack of social support.

5. Elderly problems: Isolation-despair, confusion, disorientation.

Try to identify and emphasize strengths throughout this process of gathering, reviewing, and exploring information. With this thrust in mind, there may be room for using some standard assessment tools, although it is hard to find standardized assessment tools that are not overwhelmingly concerned with individual inadequacies (Lum, 1996).

Wherever possible, supplement the systems review by the use of such tools as culturagrams (Congress, 1994), eco-maps and genograms (Hartman & Laird, 1983), FACES III (Olson, Portner, & Lavee, 1985), and social network mapping and social support instruments (Dhooper, 1990; Gottlieb, 1985). The culturagram can help the worker to clarify differences among individuals and families from similar racial and ethnic backgrounds. The topics included are: (a) reasons for immigration; (b) length of time in the community; (c) legal or undocumented status; (d) age at time of immigration; (e) language spoken at home and in the community; (f) contact with cultural institutions; (g) health beliefs; (h) holidays and special events; (i) impact of crisis events; and (j) values concerning family, education, and work.

The eco-map and genogram are paper-and-pencil simulations that can organize and objectify a tremendous amount of data about the family system in space and through time. They can lead to new insights, to altered perceptions, and thus to new ways of bringing change in complex human systems. (Hartman & Laird, 1983, p. 230)

The eco-map portrays the nature of family-environment exchanges and the flow of resources or deprivations. It organizes a lot of factual information and shows with a strong visual impact relationships among multiple variables in a situation. "As it is completed, then, family and worker should be able to identify conflicts to be mediated, bridges to be built, and resources to be sought and mobilized" (Hartman & Laird, 1983, p. 159). Similar to a family tree, the genogram is an intergenerational map of a family. It "can chart ethnic and religious background, major family events, occupations, losses, family migrations and dispersal, identifications, role assignments, and beginning information concerning triangles, coalitions, alignments, cutoffs, and communication patterns" (Hartman & Laird, 1983, p. 215).

FACES III is a 20-item instrument to assess family cohesion and adaptability. The scores on these two characteristics can be plotted on a circumplex model to identify the type of marital-family system. Families located near the center of the matrix are considered more functional and those at the periphery more dysfunctional. However, in families with different ethnic and cultural background, "if normative expectations of families support behavior extreme on one or both of these dimensions, families will function well as long as all family members are satisfied with these expectations" (Olson, 1986, p. 341). This instrument can also be used to measure family satisfaction. Family members can complete FACES III twice, once in terms of how they perceive their family and a second time in terms of how they would like it to be ideally. The discrepancy between the ideal and perceived versions indicates dissatisfaction. Approaches to social network analysis help clients to map out their social support system and to identify potential helpers who can provide specific types of support.

The basic review of the systems suggested in Table 2.1, further exploration of specific problem areas or experiences of special groups, and the use of appropriate assessment tools are likely to yield an integrative evaluation of the person, problem, situation, and their interactions as well as a descriptive and prescriptive statement of the problems that need intervention.

III. Planning Phase of Intervention

Once you have made a thorough assessment of the client system's problem, planning for action—or "goal setting," as it is also referred to—and contracting with the client become the next steps in the helping process. Planning is both a process and a product. It is a process of deciding how to move from problem identification to problem solution. It involves agreeing on the specific goals to be reached; discussing alternative approaches to goal attainment; and deciding on the particular approach to be used, strategies to be employed, tasks to be performed, and when and by whom. The agreed-upon plan for action is the product of that process.

Goals give direction to the efforts and energy to be expended on dealing with the problem situation. Without setting goals, there would be no order to the process, and our efforts would be purposeless. Goals can be both long-term and short-term. Although short-term and attainable goals should be the focus of intervention with racial and ethnic minority clients, a discussion of long-term goals is important. Long-term goals serve to give the client an expectation of accomplishment (Brille, 1998). They help the client look forward to further progress and goal attainment beyond the achievement of short-term goals.

Goals are often broken into more concrete objectives in order to increase the specificity of tasks involved in goal attainment and to improve the acceptance of responsibility for action. Objectives can also be conceptualized as immediate, intermediate, and long-term. They should be viewed also as a means for communication and relationship with others. Talking about objectives can become the basis for problem-related joint effort. This is particularly important in work at the group and community levels. The following section lists principles for setting attainable goals and objectives, which should guide the social work activity at this stage.

Principles of Attainable Goals and Objectives

1. Goals and objectives should result from the collaborative work of the social worker and client. Remember that the best-achieved goals result from a process that allows for maximal client involvement in deciding which goals are to be worked for and the manner in which this should occur. This can be harder with many clients, as they might have been culturally conditioned to defer to and obey those in authority. However, the best predictor for the outcome of intervention is the level of helping alliance between a helper and client (Dykeman, Nelson, & Appleton, 1996). When they are given maximum involvement in this phase of the process, clients are motivated to work harder toward achieving their goals. This also enhances their independence, which is essential for survival and success in the American society.

2. Goals should be based on a differential, individualized assessment of the client, problem, and situation and should be compatible with the clients' cultural and ethnic system. This requires on your part (a) an awareness of and sensitivity to the history, current situation, and concerns of the group that the client belongs to; (b) an appreciation for that group's cultural values and belief system; and (c) an exploration of the cultural identity (level of acculturation) of the individual client. This will ensure that the goals belong to the client.

3. Goals should be comprehensive, so as to yield maximum possible benefits from intervention in terms of meeting the needs; solving the problem; and leading to the growth, positive change, and enhanced problem-solving ability of the client. For organizations and communities as clients, the by-product will be improved organizational and community capacity, health, and resources.

4. Goals should be such that they require the best mix of intervention approaches, procedures, techniques, and other resources so that there is potential for optimal effectiveness and gains.

5. Goals should always be reasonable, realistic, and within the reach of the client. When goals are reasonable, the client is not set up for failure, which can negate the overall purpose of helping.

6. Goals should not be so fixed and set that they cannot be modified as needed. Allow for goal adaptation to changing needs, because people and life circumstances are dynamic and ever changing.

7. Goals should have other characteristics, such as being: (a) small, which makes them easier to achieve; (b) concrete, specific, and behavioral, which makes it easier to monitor progress; (c) focused on seeking the presence of something desirable rather the absence of something undesirable, as this improves outcome; (d) perceived by the client as involving "hard work,"

because the challenge of goals should make them worthwhile. This view of goals also protects the client's dignity, because if the client achieves the goal, the achievement is noteworthy, and if not, it means only that there is still more hard work to be done (Berg & Miller, 1992)

Practice the above principles in working with clients at this stage of the process.

Developing an Intervention Plan

An intervention plan specifies how the agreed-upon goals and objectives are to be reached. Depending on the particular dynamics of the client, problem, and situation and depending on the level of intervention—micro, mezzo, or macro—appropriate strategies, tasks, and procedures, as well as roles of the parties involved in intervention, will differ. However, the following guidelines are likely to be helpful.

1. Base the intervention plan on elements such as (a) the nature of the problem; (b) the client's experience of dealing with the same or a similar problem in the past; (c) the client's view of healing and the possible role of traditional healers; (d) the client's view of how the problem can best be solved; (e) the client's existing problem-related resources and skills; and (f) the availability of other resources—your agency's, client's social network's, and community.

2. Apply an ecological-systems approach to intervention planning. Such an approach will help make the intervention plan comprehensive and will combine strategies appropriate for addressing all aspects of the total situation.

3. Make sure that the intervention strategies (methods, techniques, roles, and tasks) are compatible with the client's life experiences, values, sense of appropriateness, and skills.

4. Make the intervention planning process an educational and growth-producing experience for the client while being cognizant of the client's concerns and capacities. This is especially important for those new to this country.

Contracting

After the desired goals and objectives have been agreed upon by both the social worker and client, a contract is established. A contract is a settlement reached between the two as to what each party is obligated to perform. It is a shared understanding of who does what, when, where, under what circumstances, and within what time frame. Contracts are helpful instruments, because they provide a framework for the helping process. A contract may be either written or oral. It is probably better to have a written contract to prevent misunderstandings between the parties involved. It can also allow the social worker to bring the client to the agreed-upon task if he or she tries to manipulate the worker. However, there may be clients who are afraid or uneasy about signing any document. In such cases, do not insist on a written contract.

We will end this section with a reiteration of the importance of your respect for clients and their culture, acceptance of those clients, and concern for their well-being from a holistic perspective. Without demonstrating these qualities, it will be very difficult to engage the client in setting goals and establishing a contract. Remember that the greatest impediments to building an alliance with a culturally different client are (a) ignorance on a worker's part of the differences between the majority culture and the customs, habits, language, and worldviews of people from minority groups; and (b) distrust of and contempt for the helper on the part of the client.

IV. Implementing the Agreed-Upon Plan Phase of Intervention

We have discussed the importance of a comprehensive assessment of the gestalt of client system, problem, situation, and their interaction, and we have also emphasized the need for the client and worker to act as partners and to jointly plan and agree on the "what," "how," "by whom," and "when" of the actions to be taken for dealing with the client need or problem. In implementing the agreed-upon plan, follow practice principles that are particularly helpful in intervening with people of color and their communities. These include the following principles.

1. Make the intervention multidimensional, systemic, and empowerment oriented. We have emphasized the importance of comprehensive assessment in the preceding section. The search for comprehensiveness will lead to multidimensional intervention. It will help not only to resolve the identified and agreed-upon problems but also to strengthen and accelerate progressive life forces, lessen restraining forces, and overcome obstacles, so that the client system arrives at a dynamic balance in an improved level of social functioning (Siporin, 1975).

2. Direct your intervention at modifying the client as well as the situation. Remind yourself that social work intervention is much more than *treatment*, as the term is generally understood. *Social work intervention* refers to "psychotherapy, advocacy, mediation, social planning, community organization, finding and developing resources, and many other activities" (Barker, 1999, p. 252).

3. Use a systems-oriented approach that obviates the dichotomy between "direct" and "indirect" forms of intervention. Such an approach will result in an attack on the problem from several points and increase the likelihood of success of the intervention.

4. See the client system as a source of resources, and focus on identifying, strengthening, and mobilizing that system's internal and external resources, both generic and situation-specific. An individual client's internal resources may include intelligence, imagination, creativity, sensitivity, motivation, optimism, hopefulness, courage, moral character, religious faith, physical health, strength and stamina, attractiveness, education, specific knowledge, and appropriate skills. A family's internal resources may include adaptability, cohesion, communication and expressiveness, hopefulness and optimism, lack of conflict, religious faith, shared decision making, and a positive coping style. The individual and family's external resources can include a secure job and steady income, property, prestige, helpful relatives, influential friends, other social and spiritual supports, and the right to benefits.

5. Assist clients to use their inner resources as a way of helping them to discover and actualize their creative powers and to realize their capacities and strengths for personality change and growth. These principles apply to work with families, other groups, organizations, and communities.

6. Use situational change interventions to make social situations more functional. These include mobilizing the client's own external resources or providing other external

material and social resources. Situational interventions include redefining the situation, reducing external stress, changing the situational behavior, changing the behavior setting, changing the climate of opinion, restructuring groups, rematching individual and group, strengthening the natural helping systems, and creating and implementing programs and projects (Siporin, 1975).

7. Use multiple approaches—individual, group, organizational, and community—and play different professional roles in order to match the type of client and the nature of the problem.

8. Tailor the approaches for empowerment-oriented practice to the needs and ethno-systems of culturally diverse individuals and groups. The mutual involvement of the client and worker in resolving the problem should aim at helping the:

   a. client perceive him or herself as a causal agent in achieving a solution to the problem;

   b. client perceive the worker as having knowledge and skills that he or she can use;

   c. client perceive the worker as a peer collaborator or partner in the problem-solving effort; and

   d. worker perceive the oppressive social institutions (schools, welfare departments, courts) as open to influence to reduce negative impact (Solomon, 1976).

Because a sense of powerlessness pervades the lives of many people of color and their communities, you should address that reality at every level of intervention.

Microlevel. At the microlevel, in working with individuals, families, and small groups, you should help clients:

   a. feel pride in their culture and its positive aspects;

   b. have or regain faith in civil, legal, political, and service systems while working to make those systems responsive to client needs;

   c. retain hope and maintain morale in the face of discouraging experiences and a belief in the forces of fate (a common cultural characteristic among many groups);

   d. learn skills—communication, life, problem-solving, assertiveness, self-advocacy, resource-accessing, and other social skills—that they may be deficient in; and

   e. meet their needs and resolve their problems in the context of their community, simultaneously acknowledging, strengthening, and mobilizing the community's resources and power.

Accomplishing the above tasks is easier when you make the following efforts:

1. You are aware of your own opinions and biases about culturally different people, and you are aware of your own personal identity and of your internalized racial and ethnic stereotypes. This helps to maintain objectivity by curbing prejudicial tendencies, distin-guishing dysfunctional from normative behavior, and empowering clients (Root, 1994).

2. You use a nonoppressive theoretical perspective in working with these clients. Helpful ideas can be drawn from feminist theory. This involves conscious and concerted effort to separate pathological from nonpathological behaviors in assessing clients (Deters, 1997).

3. You refine the following therapeutic skills:

a. Develop a working relationship with extra sensitivity to the racial factors that may influence that relationship.

b. Allow clients to ventilate feelings about identity, and validate the normality of their feelings.

c. Help them identify and refine their coping skills.

d. Provide support and help them build self-esteem.

For these skills, the use of such tools as the genogram, eco-map, and culturagram can be a helpful strategy.

4. You involve the families of clients and enhance their ability to meet the needs of their members. Some helpful suggestions include the following:

a. Give them ideas and encouragement to assert themselves in dealing with health, human, and other service systems.

b. Assist them to improve their informal social network by forming a support group.

Mezzolevel. Mezzolevel systems are neither micro nor macro. There is no consensus as to which systems fall into this category. Groups, neighborhoods, and small organizations can be included. At the mezzolevel, in working with ethnic communities and organizations, your intervention should be bifocal.

On the one hand, you should educate, involve, and mobilize the community for addressing its needs and problems. On the other hand, you should act as a catalyst in improving the commitment of service agencies to social justice through changes in their policies, procedures, personnel, and programs. This is done through the use of the appropriate organizational change approaches and tactics. Garvin and Seabury (1997) have provided an impressive list of organizational and community change strategies. Generally, community organization is harder for outsiders because of the difficulty of attaining the required degree of knowledge of, intensity of contact with, and depth of identification with the community. Rivera and Erlich (1998) have conceptualized a community organizer's contact intensity as a three-level phenomenon. They have called these primary, secondary, and tertiary contacts. The primary-level contact requires racial, cultural, and linguistic identity and full ethnic solidarity with the community. A Chinese American will not be able to have this level of contact with the Vietnamese American community. The secondary level does not require the same degree of personal identification with the community and its problems. The same language, although helpful, is not an absolute necessity. A Puerto Rican may be able to work effectively at this level in a Mexican American community. The tertiary level does not require cultural or racial similarity. The organizer works for the common interest and concerns of the community. Organizers at the secondary level work as liaisons with the outside community and as resources, and those at the tertiary level function as advocates and brokers for the community. Even at the secondary and tertiary levels, the generic community organization knowledge and skills should be supplemented with an awareness of the uniqueness of the community. Rivera and Erlich (1998) have identified several attributes of successful community organizers in communities of color. Such organizers are:

1. able to identify culturally, racially, and linguistically with the community;

2. familiar with the community's customs, traditions, values, and social networks;

3. knowledgeable about the community's major group language and subgroup slang;

4. able to work with the community's existing leaders and train emerging leaders;

5. able to do a political and economic analysis of the community;

6. able to structure the organizing strategies and activities within the community's historical framework;

7. skillful in conscientization and empowerment, that is, empowering people through the process of developing critical consciousness;

8. skillful in assessing community psychology, that is, knowing what will motivate the community and keep it allied and synergized;

9. knowledgeable about organizational behavior and decision making (so that the creation of dysfunctional arrangements can be avoided);

10. skillful in evaluative and participatory research;

11. skillful in program planning, development, and management; and

12. aware of themselves—their personal strengths and limitations.

Most social workers have quite a few of these attributes. You can strengthen the ones that you have and acquire those that you do not have in order to work effectively at the community level.

The other mezzolevel social work intervention focuses on improving the responsiveness of human service organizations to the needs and realities of vulnerable groups and communities. This should be done through the education and sensitization of agency personnel about the needs of those groups and through changes in the organizational policies and procedures.

Within your own agency, you will find the following measures, recommended by Hogan-Garcia (1999), helpful in creating an organizational atmosphere that allows or encourages cultural awareness and culturally competent services:

1. Provide cultural diversity training for all employees at all levels.

2. Incorporate diversity training into the orientation for new employees.

3. Review the organizational policies to ascertain that they support cultural diversity.

4. Provide ongoing follow-up forums on cultural issues.

5. Provide mentoring in identifying cultural issues and problem solving.

6. Appoint a staff manager responsible for cultural diversity issues.

7. Establish culturally diverse management teams.

8. Encourage culture-sensitive social events.

9. Recruit culturally diverse employees.

10. Establish a system that rewards behavior and makes use of and supports cultural diversity.

11. Establish performance evaluations based on actual documented achievement and results.

12. Monitor working procedures with employees who resist change.

Hogan-Garcia (1999) has also suggested a number of external organizational strategies. These are grouped into four sets:

1. Establish effective relationships with client communities. This can be accomplished by: (a) setting up a steering committee comprising agency staff, community leaders, practitioners, and educators to facilitate program development; (b) promoting community organizations such as mutual assistance associations; (c) seeking the help of indigenous community workers; (d) fostering friendly neighborhood sharing and support services; (e) soliciting community input and participation in organizational policy making; and (f) promoting highly visible presence of the agency at local restaurants, businesses, community events, and places of popular social interactions.

2. Review the ethics and social responsibility of the organization. This can be done by setting up an ethics committee made up of culturally diverse members. The committee should evaluate and promote the organization's social responsibility efforts, measure its impact on the community, and deliberate complex moral issues while taking into account the issues of cultural diversity.

3. Strive for client satisfaction in a culturally diverse way. Approaches to doing this include: (a) initiating policies that encourage agency personnel to be sensitive to clients' current and future needs, (b) starting programs in which personnel can truly partner with clients, (c) establishing a practice for regular debriefing and documenting information about clients, and (d) having criteria for gauging client satisfaction.

4. Work respectfully and responsively with culturally diverse clientele. This type of work will result from: (a) encouraging clients to participate actively in decisions about their care; (b) maintaining communication with the community through diverse strategies such as readily intelligible annual reports; educational material on physical, mental, and social health; press releases; and local advertisements; (c) selecting culturally homogeneous target audiences when planning informational campaigns and program messages; (d) charting a step-by-step service delivery system for culturally diverse clients; (e) setting up accessible community sites for concrete practical help; (f) creating organizational procedures for allowing or supplying appropriate mediators from the culturally diverse community; and (g) setting up process-evaluation procedures for monitoring and assessing the agency activities and services.

Macrolevel. At the macrolevel—dealing with complex organizations or large geographic populations—the agenda for the social worker as a community organizer should include:

1. coalition building, to enable disenfranchised communities and groups to present a united front to external political forces;

2. political and legislative reform, to resuscitate civil rights and address economic disparities;

3. addressing racism through communities of color coming together, discussing mutual concerns, and strategizing; and

4. nurturing the growth of true cultural pluralism (Rivera & Erlich, 1992).

Lum (1996) has suggested several client-worker joint intervention strategies that are drawn from a set of fundamental themes, such as: (a) oppression versus liberation,

(b) powerlessness versus empowerment, (c) exploitation versus parity, (d) acculturation versus maintenance of culture, and (e) stereotyping versus unique personhood. His assumption is that most persons of color encounter problem situations that reflect oppression, powerlessness, exploitation, acculturation, and stereotyping in their relationship with the dominant society. For each problem state there are corresponding intervention strategies involving liberation, empowerment, parity, maintenance of culture, and unique personhood. You can contribute to the elimination or alleviation of problems at the larger societal level. Combine your intimate understanding of the realities of your clients as individuals and your community organizational and advocacy skills for maximum impact.

V. Evaluation and Termination Phase of Intervention

A cumulative overall evaluation of the total intervention and its termination constitute the last stage of the helping activity. This stage marks the formal closure of the activity, whereas an informal evaluation or monitoring of the helping activity is an ongoing process. Monitoring occurs from the very beginning of the initial phase and continues through termination, and monitoring allows the worker and the client to assess the efficacy, practicality, and success of intervention.

Types of Evaluation

Evaluation can take two forms. It can be either formative or summative. *Formative evaluation* is what we have referred to as "monitoring." The focus of this evaluation is on the process rather than the product or outcome of activity. Formative evaluation is conducted at various times throughout the helping process to help the worker and client to determine the appropriateness of continuing the process or modifying the plan of action. Formative evaluation is done by the client and social worker during times set aside to discuss the progress made up to a certain point. It also helps the client to prepare for the eventual cessation of the helping relationship. With all that may be happening in the life of the individual, family, or community, some clients may forget that there will eventually be a time to bring closure to the helping process. For instance, a social worker may have been called upon to serve as an advocate for a piece of legislation on behalf of a group or community. This work, spread over a long period of time, may create the expectation that the worker will be available on an indefinite basis.

The second type of evaluation is summative. A *summative evaluation* is done toward the end of the intervention activity. It allows both the client and worker to determine if the agreed-upon goals were attained and if termination is appropriate. Its utility goes beyond the specific case situation. It can help sort out the methods, techniques, and skills that are or are likely to be effective and efficient in serving similar clients or dealing with the same or similar problems. It can also help to assess the effectiveness of the agency's policies, programs, services, and procedures. Both the formative and summative evaluations are as important in working with clients from racial and ethnic minority groups as they are with others.

Termination

Termination is more than a graceful end of the social work intervention and of the worker-client relationship that sustains it. There are multiple client-related tasks of termination. These include (a) examining the total problem-solving experience and the progress made;

(b) considering how this experience can be transferred to other problem situations in the future; (c) recognizing the skills developed and other gains made; (d) examining how those gains can be stabilized; and (e) attending to the affective dimensions of that experience, such as the feelings of insecurity and of impending loss of relationship with someone who is concerned, empathic, involved in the client's life, and significantly helpful.

Depending on the depth and length of involvement, for many clients as well as helpers, the thought of terminating the helping relationship can be threatening and may arouse feelings of ambivalence. Both may feel uncertain about the client's ability to function independently. Both may experience pain and a feeling of loss as the time for the interaction to end nears. These feelings are associated with bringing to closure a relationship into which both have invested a great deal of time (Shulman, 1999). Client transference of negative feelings and thoughts from the present to future helpers becomes a potential problem if these issues are not resolved.

Termination is appropriate in the following circumstances:

1. The agreed-upon goals have been achieved. The problem has been resolved, and the client's functioning has improved.

2. The client requests that the relationship should end. For several reasons, a client may wish to end the helping process. He or she may feel that enough progress has been made, or perhaps the issues being addressed are too painful to deal with at the moment.

3. It is deemed that the client can be better served by another agency or helper.

4. There is nothing further to be gained by maintaining the helping relationship. Sometimes there is a deadlock, or negative outcomes have occurred to which no resolution can be found. Sometimes involvement with the worker and the agency becomes a way of life, a source of major secondary gain for the client. In such situations, termination is called for.

Principles of Evaluation and Termination

As compared with the mainstream Americans being served by social workers from majority or minority communities, in cases of clients from minority groups, there are many elements of the unknown both for those clients and for workers unfamiliar with them. You should recognize this reality. You may find the following suggestions helpful:

1. Favor formative evaluation over summative evaluation. This will ensure that clients are satisfied with the nature, direction, and pace of success being made in dealing with their needs and problems. This will also reduce the likelihood of premature termination by clients. Premature termination or dropout by clients is a much-neglected area of human services. The client dropout may be a reflection of the lack of fit between a service agency's resources and the needs of its clients. Agency resources—broadly defined as its policies, protocols, procedures, programs, services, personnel, and their skills—may be inappropriate, inadequate, inaccessible, inefficient, and ineffective in addressing client needs. In the ongoing monitoring, you should evaluate all dimensions of the service being provided. This can lead to desirable changes in the agency's working and services.

2. Monitor the helping process continuously. During the evaluation stage, both the worker and client make an analysis of the successes or failures that have occurred and

determine the appropriateness of continuing, terminating, or making modifications to the plan.

3. Make positive feedback an integral part of the evaluation phase. Doing so allows for a discussion of the positive aspects of intervention. Devote attention and care to valuing what has transpired, considering the time, effort, and energy that both client and worker have put into trying to obtain desirable outcomes (Shulman, 1999).

4. Prepare clients for termination from the very beginning of the helping process. By doing so, you reduce the likelihood of fostering a dependent environment. Make it clear from the beginning that the helping relationship is not designed to be permanent and that its primary purpose is to restore or enhance clients' social functioning, thereby enabling them to operate independently at their maximum potential.

5. Never end the relationship with clients abruptly, for instance, as in the case when a helper transfers the client to another professional without giving any explanation. Terminating the relationship in an orderly fashion facilitates a smoother transition to ending the helping relationship and decreases the chances for any misunderstandings.

6. Make sure that the mutually agreed-upon goals deal with both the process and outcome of intervention and are stated clearly and in empirically measurable terms. This will make the evaluation easier and yield clearer findings.

7. Include clients in the decision to terminate and in the actual process. Both the client and you should have a clear understanding of why termination is taking place, and both should express their feelings about ending the helping relationship.

8. Stress to the client that the termination is not necessarily permanent or absolutely unchangeable. As people change and move through the life span, their life circumstances and situations also change. At any point in time, additional assistance may be needed to work on resolving old issues or new challenges that may arise.

9. Focus the termination experience on the specific helping objective of stabilizing and generalizing the client's learning.

Begin the process of termination when it is determined that termination is warranted and when both the client and you agree that no further services are needed. The process itself should be guided by the following suggestions, most of which are taken from Parsons (1995).

1. Review the presenting problem. Discuss with the client an overview of why the client initially came for help. This review serves as a baseline from which the amount and degree of progress made can be determined.

2. Assess the client's current situation. While discussing the progress made in dealing with the client's needs or problem, point out the abilities and skills that the client has developed during the helping process.

3. Review the strategies that were used by both the client and you that fostered goal attainment. This review can serve as an educational tool. Clients can be encouraged to generalize positive coping strategies to other situations, and you can increase your understanding of what strategies are best used with such clients under what circumstances.

4. Respond to any questions that the client may have. By doing so, you may avoid the development of false beliefs or misconceptions.

5. It is vital that clients gain the ability to transfer what they have learned from one situation to another. Encourage such transfer. Clients are better able to cope with new and related problems in the future if they are able to transfer coping strategies from one situation to another.

6. Explore the client's feelings in relation to termination of the helping relationship. Some clients may be unsure about their ability to function independently. Give the client an opportunity to express these feelings, and provide appropriate feedback.

7. Throughout the termination process, emphasize the "positives"—the needs met, the problem solved, the situation handled, the growth experienced, and the skills acquired, rather than the impending separation, loss of relationship, and the withdrawal of the help and resources.

8. Make sure that termination helps shape the client's growth pattern. This takes place through appropriate follow-up aimed at reinforcing the change that the client has experienced and encouraging the client to continue the progress made. This can be done through invitation for periodic progress reports, notes, or phone calls.

9. Assist clients in locating or rediscovering resources and supports within their informal social networks and community that can be utilized when necessary. These resources should include supportive elements in the client's ethnic world and its belief system.

> We believe this type of reunification with ethnic roots is significant dimension in termination. Ethnic identity, or a new sense of what it means to be African American, Asian American, Latino American, or Native American, is a powerful motivator for coping with the kind of living and problem situations that the client confronts. (Lum, 1996, pp. 283-284)

10. Finally, give a final adieu in a manner appropriate to both the client and you only if it has been mutually agreed that no further services are needed and that the client is free to seek assistance should future assistance be warranted.

We end this chapter with a reminder that effective social work with culturally diverse clients—individual, groups, organizations, or communities, at all levels of intervention— begins with you, the worker. You are the most important element in the complex picture of organized human services, and you can make your agency's mission, policies, programs, and services real for its clients. You may have little or no control over the conditions of clients' lives or even over the environment of your work. However, you should consciously, constantly, and deliberately cultivate and practice the essential personal competencies that Hogan-Garcia (1999) has identified and framed as mandates:

1. Be nonjudgmental—shut down the general tendency to see people different from yourself in an unfavorable light.

2. Be flexible—readjust quickly and effectively to changing situations.

3. Be resourceful—skillfully obtain the things required to deal with the situation.

4. Personalize observations—express your personal feelings, beliefs, ideas, and thoughts in a warmly personal way. Communicating with "I-messages," paraphrasing what the other person is saying, and listening actively will help in this.

5. Pay attention to your feelings—keep in touch with your inner reactions to the other person. This will put you in better charge of yourself.

6. Listen carefully—this will increase sensitivity to the whole message.

7. Observe attentively—this too will increase sensitivity to the message.

8. Assume complexity—recognize that in a culturally diverse environment, there are multiple perspectives and possible outcomes.

9. Tolerate the stress of uncertainty—avoid showing annoyance or irritation about the ambiguity of the culturally diverse situation.

10. Have patience—remain calm in challenging and trying situations.

11. Manage personal biases and stereotypes—move beyond your personal outlook and point of view, and treat the other person as an individual, not as typifying a group.

12. Keep a sense of humor—avoid taking things so seriously that you cannot laugh at yourself and with others.

13. Show respect—go out of the way to express your understanding, esteem, and honor for the other person.

14. Show empathy—experience the other person's attitudes, beliefs, feelings, and perspective as if these were your own.

These competencies will make your work with culturally different clients professionally fulfilling.

3

Understanding and Working With Latino Americans

LATINO AMERICANS: WHO ARE THEY?

Latino Americans are the second-largest group contributing to the cultural diversity of the United States. However, there is a lack of consensus on what this group should be called. The government agencies use the term *Hispanic*, whereas many within the group prefer the term *Latino*. Hayes-Bautista and Chapa (1987) introduced the term *Latinos*, restricting the name to persons living in the United States whose ancestries are from Latin American countries. Both terms enjoy wide use, depending on the region of the country (e.g., Latino in California and Hispanic in Texas; Suarez & Ramirez, 1999). We will use *Latino*, although *Hispanic* will appear from time to time as an equivalent term. The 1990 census recorded more than 22 million Hispanics (U.S. Bureau of the Census, 1993b), and the 1995 population projection put their number at 26.5 million, at a growth rate of over 30 per 1,000 between 1990 and 1995. It has been estimated that by the middle of the 21st century, one in three births will be Hispanic (Day, 1993). Their rising number is a result of both natural growth (related to their relative youth, fertility rates, and cultural practices) and immigration. Some of them were here when the United States became a nation. Others became a part of this country because of historical events. Still others are very new to this country. Those who have been here for generations claim that:

> They were here first, before the English, French, or Dutch. When U.S. arms seized California and the Southwest, more than three hundred years had passed since the hooves of Spanish horses had imprinted Florida's beaches, stirred the dust of Texas, and trod up the Rio Grande Valley past the Sangre de Cristo Mountains. And for all that time these had been the lands of Spain and of Mexico. (Weyr, 1988, p. 1)

The major historical events that have shaped the presence of other Latinos in the United States include

> the Louisiana Purchase, admission of Florida and Texas into the Union, the Treaty of Guadalupe Hidalgo which ended the Mexican-American War, the Spanish-American War, the Mexican Revolution, labor shortages during World War I and World War II, the Cuban

Revolution, and political instability in Central and South America in the recent past. (U.S. Department of Commerce, 1993b, p. 1)

Whereas race separates African Americans from mainstream Americans, it fails to function similarly when applied to Latinos. Unlike in the United States, where race is an "either-or" phenomenon,

> Among Latinos race is perceived in continuous terms. People of mixed ancestry are neither white nor nonwhite, but if their complexion is relatively white their European ancestry takes precedence over any other. Thus, most racially mixed people in Spanish-speaking nations think of themselves as white or some intermediary designation such as *mestizo* (European/indigenous) or mulatto, *trigueno*, or *moreno* (all variations of African/European ancestry). (Longres, 1995a, p. 1217)

In many countries of Latino Americans' origin, people speak languages other than Spanish, which may be a second language for many Latino immigrants. There are immigrants from highland Guatemala, highland Peru and Bolivia, and coastal Honduras where, respectively, Mayan, Quechua and Aymara, and Garifuna (a creole language) are spoken (Castex, 1994). However, a majority of Latinos speak or understand Spanish, and for most, one of their distinguishing marks is the Spanish language, which helps to preserve their cultural identity. Estimates of those speaking Spanish fluently, reporting Spanish as their first language, and speaking Spanish at home vary from 50% to 91% for different groups (Acosta-Belen, 1988; Bean & Tienda, 1987; Padilla & Ruiz, 1976; Rodriquez, 1989; U.S. Bureau of the Census, 1993b). Of all Latinos, about 78% spoke Spanish at home in 1990. Of these, about half also spoke English very well (U.S. Bureau of the Census, 1993b). Thus, most are learning English, but not as a replacement for Spanish. Unlike the experience of other immigrants, the use of Spanish has not disappeared among the second or third generations of Latinos reared in the United States (Nelson & Tienda, 1997). "For every Hispanic who transitions into English, another Hispanic already comfortable in English rediscovers his Hispanic heritage and takes up Spanish again. At the same time two other Hispanics appear in the country who speak only Spanish" (Weyr, 1988, p. 224). It is possible to live and die in Spanish in most major U.S. cities:

> A Hispanic doctor will snatch a baby into life and a Hispanic priest will baptize it. The child can go through school in Spanish. He can marry in Spanish, vote in Spanish, worship in Spanish, pay taxes in Spanish, receive unemployment insurance, Medicaid, Medicare, and Social Security in Spanish. A Hispanic undertaker will bury him in Spanish. (Weyr, 1988, p. 8)

There is appearing a common Latino identity, *latinismo*, an emergent Latino culture that blends several cultures:

> This includes the appearance of remarkable musical fusions, Mexican and Salvadoran restaurant combinations in San Francisco, Miami, and Washington, D.C., and the transformation of Cinco de Mayo from a holiday for Mexican Americans into a Dia de la Raza, a celebration of Latino culture. (Romero, 1997, p. xvi)

However, significant differences among Latino Americans persist. Their major groups are Mexican American,[1] Puerto Rican,[2] Cuban Americans,[3] Central and South Americans,[4] and Caribbeans.

A HISTORICAL OVERVIEW OF LATINO AMERICANS: COMMONALITY OF EXPERIENCES

There is a remarkable similarity in the experiences both of subgroups of Latinos who have been a part of the United States for a long time, and of those who are new to its shores. We have organized this section according to such themes as the desire for political independence, the search for personal security, the lure of wealth and prosperity, the needs of the U.S. economy, and the pervasive nature of racism and color prejudice in the country.

Desire for political independence of Latino populations and groups results instead in their becoming minority groups in the United States. Mexican Americans are those who themselves or whose ancestors either came from Mexico or lived in those parts of the United States that were once part of Mexico. Prior to the annexation of Texas by the United States in 1845 and the subsequent Mexican-American War, Texas, New Mexico, Arizona, and California were provinces of Mexico.

> In the years following Mexican independence from Spain in 1821, the northern areas of the new nation (America's Southwest) were centers of unrest. In brief wars and a series of conflicts that fell just short of being "official" wars, Mexican Americans were the "enemy." The first war was the War for Texas Independence in 1835; the second was the Mexican War of 1846. (Locke, 1998, p. 153)

The Treaty of Guadalupe Hidalgo, which formally ended the Mexican-American War in 1848, resulted in Mexico's ceding to the United States territory that now forms Arizona, California, Nevada, New Mexico, Utah, and part of Colorado and giving clear title to Texas (Meier & Rivera, 1972). Many Mexicans who had hoped to become independent of Mexico became a people conquered by the United States. The United States also acquired an additional 45,532 square miles of Mexican territory in the Gadsden Purchase in 1853 (McWilliams, 1990). The treaty gave Mexicans the right to remain in the United States or to withdraw to Mexico, the option of either Mexican or American citizenship, and guaranteed property rights (Lum, 1996). Most chose to stay, but they were treated as a conquered people occupying an inferior social position. They lost their land, either because the burden of proof of ownership fell on Mexican landholders or because of a series of land schemes, and were forced into agricultural labor and unskilled jobs. "The cultural and ideological confrontations between the resident Mexicans and Americans, and their competition for land, resulted in the creation of cultural stereotypes to legitimize the Anglo dominance in the area" (Cruz, 1997, p. 163). Their social treatment by the Anglo population in Texas became the pattern everywhere in the Southwest:

> Because more than 80 percent of early Anglo migrants to Texas came from the Deep South, racial attitudes toward black people were readily transferred to Mexicans. As a result of their distinctive culture, Mexican Americans were considered innately inferior and an obstacle to the establishment of a progressive economy and society. (Curiel, 1995, p. 1234)

Segregation included establishment of separate schools for Mexican American children. "This practice, continued until the 1970s, left a heritage of barely literate generations, underfunded school districts, and high dropout rates" (Locke, 1998, p. 152). Mexican Americans not only were denied equal educational opportunities, but also were discriminated against in jobs and housing. They could not vote because of such exclusionary practices as the rule that one could not vote unless one could read and write English.

> Thus, the Mexicans lost their property and their political power and became foreigners in their own land. Their position rapidly changed from that of settlers in a Mexican frontier society to that of an American ethnic group, marginal to both the Mexican and the Anglo American culture. (Curiel, 1995, p. 1233)

There are close to 3 million (2,728,000) Puerto Ricans living in the United States mainland, and they represent about 42% of all Puerto Ricans. Thus there are almost as many of them here as are living on the island of Puerto Rico (U.S. Bureau of the Census, 1993b). The presence of Puerto Ricans in this country can be traced to the days when Puerto Rico was a Spanish colony. Earlier Puerto Ricans here were merchants, students, and factory workers (Sanchez Korrol, 1993). In the last three decades of the 19th century, New York became a center for revolutionary exiles from Puerto Rico who were fighting for the independence of their homeland from Spanish colonial rule. The most famous of these freedom fighters were Ramon Emeterio Betances, Eugenio Maria de Hostos, and Bonocio Tio and his wife, the poet Lola Rodriguez de Tio. Francisco "Pachin" Marin and Sotero Figueroa published newspapers to propagate their political ideals and to maintain solidarity in the Puerto Rican community (Acosta-Belen, 1988). Instead of becoming an independent nation, Puerto Rico was forced to become a part of the United States in 1899.

As a Spanish colony, Puerto Rico was granted autonomy in 1897, but it became a battleground for foreign countries. It was attacked 26 time, with the United States being the last attacker (Locke, 1998). One of the final battles of the Spanish-American War was fought in Puerto Rico in 1898. Under the Treaty of Paris of 1899, Puerto Rico was given to the United States, and for the first two years it was ruled by the U.S. military. The Foraker Act of 1900 replaced the military rule with a civil government, but the governor was an American appointed by the president of the United States. The Jones Act of 1917 conferred U.S. citizenship on all Puerto Ricans (Campos, 1995) but without giving the island autonomy or self-government. The relationship between the island and the mainland stayed unchanged for the first half of the 20th century. The end of World War II prompted more significant changes:

> The difficulties of maintaining direct authority over the territory, at a time of mounting world sentiment for decolonizing the Third World and when island support for political independence was at a peak, forced the United States to redefine its relationship to the possession. In the compromise that was struck, the U.S. government turned over some autonomy to Puerto Rico, while still retaining domination over economic, legal, and military matters. An important outcome was the promotion, by U.S. and cooperating Puerto Rico authorities, of a massive migration, with New York as the primary destination. (Torres, 1995, p. 17)

On the island, people were allowed to elect their own governor in 1948, and two years later the U.S. Congress authorized Puerto Rico to draft its own constitution, under which people could elect not only their governor but also members of the two houses of legislature. In 1952 the Commonwealth of Puerto Rico came into existence (Campos, 1995). However, this commonwealth is neither an independent country nor a state of the United States. Over the years, that in-between status has become the island's identity crisis, which has become a chronic problem, with Puerto Ricans oscillating between desiring independence and desiring statehood for their land's future. Although Puerto Ricans, both on the mainland and on the island, are U.S. citizens, the relationship of Puerto Rico to this country has essentially been colonial. There have been efforts on the part of the U.S. government to conceal the island's colonial status.[5]

By the end of the 19th century, about 10,000 Cubans had settled in New York City, the Key West and Tampa areas of Florida, and New Orleans. They had turned the Tampa area into a major cigar manufacturing center. Their cultural and political activity manifested itself through the proliferation of several newspapers, such as *El Eco de Cuba, El Cubano, La Voz de America, La Independencia, El Republicano*, and *La Republica*. These became vehicles for propagating ideas of independence of Cuba from Spanish colonial rule, generating moral and financial support for separatist leaders back home, and giving the U.S. Cuban community a sense of unity and a commonality of purpose (Acosta-Belen, 1988; Poyo, 1984). Although the early Cubans established migratory patterns for others who came after them, there is little connection between the early immigrants and those who have come since the 1960s. Different circumstances propelled large numbers of Cubans out of Cuba. The United States used those circumstances to serve its international needs.

Whereas most Mexican Americans became an ethnic minority when the United States conquered and annexed parts of Mexico, and Puerto Ricans started coming to this country after Puerto Rico became a U.S. colony and U.S. citizenship was forced on them, a majority of Cuban Americans or their parents came as political refugees in waves beginning in 1959. The Treaty of Paris in 1898 ended the Spanish-American War and gave the United States the rights to occupy Cuba briefly, to acquire the military base at Guantanamo, and to intervene in Cuban affairs. The United States still has the military base, but its economic and political hold on the island ended in 1959, when Fidel Castro overthrew the government of Fulgencio Batista and created the first communist government in the Western hemisphere (Jimenez-Vazquez, 1995).

> The military defeat at the Bay of Pigs and the secret United States-Soviet agreements during the 1962 missile crisis marked a shift in the United States geopolitical strategies toward Cuba from military to ideological-symbolic concerns. The United States now wanted to transform Cuba into a negative showcase by imposing a trade embargo that would limit its trade with the Western Hemisphere. (Grosfoguel, 1997, p. 124)

Cuban refugees became an example of the superiority of capitalism over socialism. Their success was crucial for the United States to gain symbolic capital (Grosfoguel, 1997).

The first wave of refugees consisted of the political and economic allies of Batista, who hoped to return home after Castro's regime was overthrown, with their help, by the United States. That hope was gone after the failure of the Bay of Pigs invasion, in which

> Cuban refugees, recruited from an all-party coalition, financed and aided by the CIA, and trained in Florida and Guatemala, attempted in 1961 to invade Cuba at the Bay of Pigs, but President John F. Kennedy at the last moment denied air support to the invaders and the venture collapsed. (Gann & Duignan, 1986, p. 101)

Theirs became an involuntary stay in the United States, even though they had come here voluntarily. The desire for political independence, deepened by conditions in Cuba, has brought others here over the years. Castro had at first successfully posed as a nationalist leader with a commitment to social justice.

Castro progressively tightened the screws and imposed a system of control over Cuba's citizenry far beyond the restrictions imposed on the people by traditional Latin American oligarchies. There were no more elections of any kind. Professional organizations and trade unions became mere instruments of state control. The authorities enforced far-reaching restrictions on internal travel. The media turned into crude instruments of propaganda, exhorting the people to never-ending sacrifices for the fatherland. The government constructed a thoroughgoing system of block vigilance committees to encourage political denunciation. The secret police (*Seguidad del Estado*) set up a sophisticated system of repression modeled on those in Eastern Europe. Deviations from the official line were punished by a variety of sanctions, ranging from short confinement in jails and prison camps (*granjas*) to long sentences of forced labor and possible execution. (Gann & Duignan, 1986, p. 99)

The result was that thousands of people began to flee the island. This was the second wave of refugees. The third wave began in 1965 and went on until 1973. During this period, the United States provided "Freedom Flights" for family reunification. Thousand of family members of Cubans here, including parents of 23,000 unaccompanied children who were sent here through religious organizations, were airlifted to this country (Jimenez-Vazquez, 1995). The fourth wave of Cuban immigrants lasted from 1973 to 1978 and covered those sponsored by their Cuban relatives in the United States. The fifth wave covered the period from 1978 to 1980, and about 20,000 former political prisoners and their families came during this time (Szapocznik & Hernandez, 1990). The sixth wave started in 1981. The most significant group to come in this wave consisted of the 125,000 "Marielitos"— Cubans boatlifted from the Port of Mariel to Key West. These included some 4,000 "social undesirables"—people with criminal records; mental hospital patients; gays and lesbians; and Santeros, who are practitioners of a religion called Santeria (Clark, Lasaga, & Reque, 1981). Hence, over the years and through these waves, Cubans of most socioeconomic statuses and skill levels have come here.

The federal government under President Eisenhower, as well as local governments and voluntary organizations, provided financial and social services to Cuban refugees. Under President Kennedy, the Cuban Refugee Emergency Program was created. The government took full advantage of the refugees' exodus from Cuba to discredit and delegitimize Castro's communist regime, and the assistance provided was significant. As political refugees, Cubans received resettlement and cash assistance, availed themselves of special education programs (including retraining of professionals) and college tuition loans, and took advantage of relaxed citizenship requirements. Even with a socioeconomic status much higher than that of other Latinos, Cubans have realized that they are an ethnic minority subject to discrimination and subordination by the dominant society (Safa, 1988).

Political and economic instability in their native lands and their personal sense of insecurity bring many Latinos to the United States. The political and economic conditions in Mexico have also been pushing Mexicans across the border into the United States. The first major wave was precipitated by the Mexican Revolution of 1910. Over 1 million Mexican immigrants came to the United States (Meier, 1990), and the inflow continued until the Great Depression of the 1930s. The conditions in Mexico pushed them, and opportunities in the United States pulled them. Rich mineral deposits in Arizona and New Mexico, agricultural development, and expanding railroads attracted them, but most found themselves harvesting fruits, vegetables, and cotton and living in extremely poor and unsanitary conditions (Cruz, 1997).

Central and South Americans have come not only from a variety of lands but also from different socioeconomic classes. Although their reasons for coming are many, the concerns about political instability and personal safety and the desire for economic security and prosperity are prominent.

> In the 1970s, there were the radical democracies of Allende and Sandinistas in Chile and Nicaragua, insurrectional movements in Colombia and Peru and civil war in El Salvador and Guatemala. Dictatorships flourished in many countries in Latin America during 1970-1980s. (Bejar, 1998, p. 287)

The democracies restored in the last 20 years continue to be weak, dominated by economic monopolies, pressured by organizations of corruption, and threatened by militarism (Bejar, 1998).

The most prominent reason for many Central Americans to come here has been their countries' political instability and their personal insecurity. Until the 1950s, immigration from Central America was negligible. From the beginning of the 1960s, the loss of civil liberties and a pervasive sense of insecurity resulting from the civil strife in their lands forced thousands of Salvadorans, Panamanians, Guatemalans, Hondurans, and Nicaraguans to seek refuge in the United States, both legally and illegally. On the other hand, most of those from the South American countries, such as Argentina, Chile, and Uruguay, followed the pattern of Western European immigration during the post-World War II years.

> The Argentines and Chileans who came to the United Sates did not face hunger at home; their motives for emigrating were more complex. Some Argentineans departed because they were fearful of left-wing terrorists or right-wing repression or of their country's economic future, or because they were Jewish and worried about the long-term prospects of their community. (Gann & Duignan, 1986, p. 120)

Another large group is made up of Dominicans. Their immigration increased in the 1960s because of the political instability and economic stagnation in their land. The United States has a tremendous appeal for those yearning for political stability and those dreaming of economic prosperity, as it combines "liberty and stability with economic opportunity" (Gann & Duignan, 1986, p. 113).

U.S. economic and political policies vis-à-vis Latin American countries encourage many to migrate to this country. There is truth in the view that the presence and policies of the United States in many countries of Central and South America have contributed to their sociopolitical instability, and that therefore the United States cannot escape being a part of the solution to their problems. Portes (1982) considers the flow of undocumented workers into the United States a response to the economic hegemony exercised by this country over economically peripheral countries, which produces patterns of industrialization that increase pressure on the working classes and maintain high levels of unemployment in those countries. A careful analysis of the massive population movements in Central America has led Hamilton and Chinchilla (1997) to conclude that several factors are responsible, including

> an economic crisis, a consequence of the changes in the capitalist world economy and their specific forms in each Central American country, combined with political conflict

arising from the growing contradictions between capitalist modernization and the backward socioeconomic structures maintained by the repressive state apparatus. U.S. involvement in these conflicts has prolonged and intensified them without resolving the structural contradictions from which they emerged. Prolonging the conflicts has in turn aggravated the economic crisis, which cannot be expected to disappear once the conflicts ended. Thus one effect that can be anticipated is the continued dislocation, displacement, and migration of substantial sectors of the Central American populations. (p. 96)

In his discussion of the geopolitics of the Dominican and Haitian migration, Grosfoguel (1997) wrote that only after the 1961 United States-backed military coup against Trujillo did emigration to the United States increase. This emigration was politically induced and was viewed as a safety valve against social unrest and political instability. The people forced to out-migrate included not only political activists but also thousands from the middle sectors of the working classes, which were the social bases of the political opposition. Grosfoguel quotes John Barlow Martin, the U.S. ambassador in the Dominican Republic:

> The riots mounted. Cautiously, the Consejo [the Council of State] began to deport agitators under the Emergency Law. ... And we became involved—we had to issue U.S. visas for people that the Consejo deported to the United States. ... The Consejo forbade airlines and steamships to sell returning tickets. It had already asked us to impose departure control on people deported to the United State—that is, to keep them there. (quoted in Grosfoguel, 1997, p. 128)

Labor shortage and needs of the U.S. economy propel its government to attract and import Latino manpower. The labor shortage in the country during World War II led the United States to look toward Mexico for cheap labor. It entered into an agreement with Mexico to obtain seasonal laborers. Millions came and worked on the agricultural fields, in factories, and on railroads. The arrangement continued after the war and was formalized in 1958 as Public Law 58, known as the Bracero Program (Curiel, 1995). *Bracero* means manual worker. Although these workers were guaranteed minimum wage, the program was "legalized slavery, nothing but a way for big corporate farms to get a cheap labor supply from Mexico under government sponsorship. The braceros were hauled around like cattle in Mexico and treated like prisoners in the United States" (Amott & Matthaei, 1991, p. 79). The Bracero Program continued until 1964. Many bracero workers remained in the country and made it their permanent home.

Similarly, the inflow of thousands of Puerto Ricans was an important part of the solution to the U.S. problem of labor shortage during the postwar boom years. These Puerto Ricans filled secondary jobs in garment production, building maintenance, the hospital sector, and the tourist industry, and they occupied social positions on the margins of the society. After those boom years, the size of the Puerto Rican migration varied according to the job opportunities here and the economic conditions on the island. There was a back and forth movement. "Responding to a variety of forces—from economic incentives to family and personal triumphs and tragedies—migration from and to Puerto Rico by Puerto Ricans has been a complex and dynamic process that has not been systematically studied" (Campos, 1995, p. 1250).

The lure of U.S. wealth and the prospect of personal prosperity motivate many to migrate hither. Mexicans have continued to come legally as well as illegally in search of jobs and prosperity. Those who come by swimming the Rio Grande River are called "wetbacks," and smuggling undocumented Mexicans into the United States is a lucrative business. Thus, Mexican Americans

> represent a variety of historical experiences ranging from the descendants of the original set-
> tlers in the Southwest; through Mexicans who migrated to the United States, became natural-
> ized U.S. citizens, and produced subsequent generations of U.S.-born individuals of Mexican
> descent; to the transient Mexican populations with visas or work permits; to the undocu-
> mented workers. (Acosta-Belen, 1988, p. 92)

Undocumented and documented Mexicans who come here take the jobs that no one else wants and often experience the worst working conditions in agricultural and manufacturing industries.

Other factors also encourage many to come to the United States. Vargas (1992) referred to several Latin American and Caribbean countries as suffering from the "megalopolis syndrome." These countries have a few large cities where most of the industries; other sources of income; and centers of education, medicine, and leisure are concentrated. This syndrome results in the depopulation and poverty of towns and villages and changes in the conditions and lifestyles of the people who flock to cities. "But probably one of the most important results is that the population abandons its traditional culture, to adopt the urban pattern, which is usually a form of the so called Western cosmopolitan way of life" (Vargas, 1992, p. 8). This internal migration in a way prepares many of them for what they will likely experience in the United States and encourages them to come to this country.

Mexican immigrants from across the border have also been coming partly because of the nature of the United States-Mexico border. In the words of Weyr (1988),

> It is after all not much of a border, a line cartographers scratched in the sand of the cactus-
> strewn desert, or narrow river-bed that most of the year is a dried-up creek. Mexicans never
> accepted the borders drawn up by the 1848 treaty, and most historians concede it doesn't
> make geographic sense. Better river and mountain formations on which to structure political
> divisions are found north and south. Mexicans have always come and gone pretty much as
> they pleased, ignoring the signposts the Americans put up to mark national boundary lines.
> Marking the border was a vain effort. Visible U.S. power along the frontier was never strong
> enough to make a difference. The geography worked against Washington's design. (p. 6)

We have alluded to geopolitics determining the U.S. immigration policy and strategies and the subsequent inflow of people from Central American countries. In the words of Grosfoguel (1997),

> Puerto Rico was transformed into a positive symbolic showcase of the United States develop-
> ment model for the Third World; Cuba suffered a trade embargo as part of a strategy to trans-
> form it into a negative symbolic showcase of the Soviet model of development in the region;
> the Dominican Republic was militarily invaded by the United States for fear of another Cuba
> in the Western Hemisphere; and, Haiti's Duvalieran dictatorship received continued support
> from the United State as an anti-Communist state that guaranteed its security interests in the
> region. (p. 119)

Pervasive Intolerance of Diversity in the United States Culture. Despite the U.S. Constitution, which proclaims equality for all, the society at large is indifferent to the idea of equality. Those from minority groups are treated as unequal. We have briefly mentioned how the native Mexicans who became American were deprived of their property and political power; despised because of their language, religion, and culture; and exploited in the workplace and the marketplace. Those who came from across the border, familiar with exploitation at home, accepted the grievous economic conditions in the United States. This acceptance on their part became a reason to treat them differently:

> Being representatives of a culture that still was viewed as an enemy by the Americans in the Southwest, their acceptance of the social and economic conditions with which they were faced only revitalized and reinforced the old stereotypes of Mexicans as childish, dirty, dishonest, and irresponsible. (Cruz, 1997, p. 166)

Every situation was used as justification for ill-treating them.

The heightened patriotism of Americans during World War I awakened the negative feelings against Mexicans, and these feelings became a demand—"Greasers go home" (Acuna, 1981, p. 123)—during the Depression days. Massive deportation of Mexicans, many of them Americans by birth or naturalization, took place in order to reduce the pressure on the welfare system (Estrada, Garcia, Macias, & Maldonado, 1981).

World War II affected the Mexican Americans in significant ways. The participation of Mexican Americans in the war effort promoted their Americanization. The military service tended to distance young Mexican Americans from their traditional Mexican life:

> Their service in the war boosted an awareness of their patriotic contributions to winning the war effort and gave them new status and respect. In short, the Mexican American participation in the war had a marked impact on their identity as Americans rather than on their Mexican past. As participants in the war, they were to feel a part of the American mainstream, and this contributed to the distinction they increasingly made between themselves and Mexican immigrants. (Cruz, 1997, p. 168)

However, their experiences in the war did not bring them any closer to the larger community. A local newspaper report on the Fourth of July celebrations in two Texas towns in 1943, as quoted by Sanchez (1977), stated:

> Several hundred citizens of the United States of Mexican extraction were told over the loudspeaker that they should go home because the dance being held in a public square was for white people only. Among the persons ejected were many wearing United States soldier's uniforms. (p. 210)

Most Americans do not understand the history of Puerto Rico and its relationship with the United States and do not treat Puerto Ricans as fellow Americans. Puerto Ricans are culturally different from mainstream Americans and do not fit the societal black and white classification. For over 400 years, there has been such an extensive intermingling of African and European populations in Puerto Rico that it is not uncommon to find many shades of skin color within a family. As Rodriguez (1996) put it,

> For within the U.S. perspective, Puerto Ricans, racially speaking, belong to both [whites and blacks] groups; however, ethnically, they belong to neither. Thus placed, Puerto Ricans find themselves caught between the two polarities and at a dialectical distance from both. (p. 35)

In the words of Montserrat (1994),

> Puerto Ricans are the only racially integrated group in the United States, as we have come to know the meaning of the word integrated. As such, they suffer the peculiar problem of not being understood either by their black brothers or by their so-called white neighbors. (p. 318)

Most Puerto Ricans are born and brought up in the United States. Many have never visited Puerto Rico and may not speak the Spanish language. They have not experienced being a Puerto Rican in Puerto Rico (i.e., not being a "minority" and having freedom from institutionalized discrimination). Nevertheless, everything in their environment constantly reminds them that they are Puerto Ricans. They are seen as minority and as different, which is equated with being "less than" or inferior to others (Montserrat, 1994).

The achievements of Cubans in business and economics, politics, arts, and literature are impressive. However, their successes have not been without a price. The portrayal of spectacular rags-to-riches transformations of Cubans in the popular media has created a "success" myth that denies the existence of poverty among them. Not only is the Cuban American household income substantially lower than that of non-Latino households, but there are also high rates of poverty among recent Cuban immigrants, Afro-Cubans, and Cuban American children (de Haymes, 1997). Cuban businessmen met the bitter criticism that their relative success was owed to special favors of the U.S. government. Cuban intellectuals encountered discrimination in academia for their real or alleged political views. All Cubans faced social disapproval, because many Anglo Americans resented hearing or having to speak Spanish whenever they went shopping, and because they associated rising crime rates and soaring housing costs with the Cubans' presence (Gann & Duignan, 1986). On the other hand, Cubans internalized this myth of success and superiority, with the result that the unsuccessful ones among them masked their need for services (Jimenez-Vazquez, 1990). During the turbulent 1960s, Cuban refugees and immigrants could not understand, appreciate, and participate in the civil rights movement, because they were grateful for the hospitality of this country, busy finding jobs and getting established in the land of their refuge, and afraid that they might be sent back if they got involved in the social movement (Jimenez-Vazquez, 1990). This created resentment in other minority groups, which the "success" myth kept alive: "Many blacks became embittered at the extent of the Cubans' success, all the more so because most Cubans were white" (Gann & Duignan, 1986, p. 111).

Because Latinos come in all skin colors, their internalization of the pervasive racial norms of the larger society tends to adversely affect their interpersonal relationships. It creates barriers between those with lighter and those with darker skin complexions. In the larger society, those who are classified as African Americans experience racial discrimination with its detrimental effects on their self-esteem, social relationships, and real opportunities (Castex, 1994).

COMMON CHARACTERISTICS: COMMONALITY OF CULTURES AND WORLDVIEWS

Despite the historical and other differences, there is unity in diversity among the various Latino groups, represented by common cultural values shared by all Latinos to a greater or lesser extent. In the following section, we list their most common cultural characteristics.

Familismo. The meaning and place of family in the lives of most Latinos determine their attitude toward the family and the world beyond the family. For the individual, the family represents a solid refuge from a difficult world (Bernal, Martinez, Santisteban, Bernal, & Olmedo, 1983). It involves a group that extends beyond the nuclear family and that may include not only extended relatives but also members of other social networks, such as friends and neighbors (Kirst-Ashman & Hull, 1993).

> Family is often an extended system that encompasses not only those related by blood and marriage but also *compadres* (coparents) and *hijos de crianza* (informally adopted children). *Compadrazgo* is the institution of *compadres comadres* (godparents), a system of ritual kinship with binding mutual obligation for economic assistance and encouragement. (Locke, 1998, p. 176)

Godparenthood is an honor that involves commitment and extensive responsibility to the family and children (DiNitto & McNeece, 1990). Thus, members from outside the blood and legal relationships assume special roles and responsibilities within the family. Despite its size, the family is close-knit, with a lot of interdependence among its members. An individual's identity, security, and worth are determined by his or her relationship to other family members. Because of its importance to the individual, there is a deep sense of family obligation. During good times or crises, the family's name and welfare always come first (Ho, 1987). Upholding the family name and ensuring that one does not bring shame to the family name become powerful motives and methods for controlling the behavior of family members. Hence, the importance placed on preserving, respecting, and being loyal to the family is an integral part of the Hispanic culture. Individuals turn to family members during times of stress—emotional, social, or economic—and often consult them before seeking help from an outside source. Any attempt to conduct psychotherapy without the involvement of the client's family is the route to failure (Paniagua, 1994).

Sense of Hierarchy. The family structure and functioning, in terms of both leadership and roles, are guided by a hierarchy that is both gendered and generational. The father occupies the position of authority, makes major decisions, and expects to be obeyed by other members, including the mother. His role is to earn a living and to ensure the family's economic well-being, and that of the mother is to run the household and to balance the father's authoritative role. "Even if children see their father unsuccessfully cope with life and begin to drink, they remain loyal to him as the family authority and head of the household. He is recognized as the provider for the family" (Lum, 1996, p. 54). This emphasis on hierarchy, as reflected in children's obeying their parents, also applies among the children themselves. "Younger children are expected to obey older children who serve as role models" (Ho, 1987, p. 126). The gender-based hierarchy allows for more and earlier independence for sons than for daughters.

Personalismo. Latinos are people oriented and value personal relationships. They feel uncomfortable when treated as "things." This feeling can lead to the perceptions that there is a wide distance between the client and the helper, that the helper lacks "warmth," and that he or she avoids sharing personal information (Paniagua, 1994). Latinos value the inner qualities that constitute a person's uniqueness:

> Along with the concept of familism, a Hispanic defines his self-worth in terms of those inner qualities that give him self-respect and earn him the respect of others. He feels an inner dignity (*dignidad*); and expects others to show respect (*respeto*) for that "dignidad." (Ho, 1987, p. 125)

This phenomenon is known as personalism. It can affect a client's choice of a helper, the degree of cooperation, and forms of appreciation for the help received.

Machismo. Several qualities highly prized in men are collectively called *machismo*. These include altruism, bravery, courage, pride, responsibility, steadfastness (Mirande, 1988), and "a style of personal daring by which one faces challenge, danger, and threats with calmness and self-possession" (Ho, 1987, pp. 125-126), as well as physical strength, sexual attractiveness, masculinity, aggressiveness, and the ability to consume an excessive amount of alcohol without getting drunk (Comas-Diaz, 1988). Men see themselves as more masculine and protective of women and younger members of the family and community (Wodarski, 1992b). In general, *machismo* also denotes a sense of respect from others. For marginal men, *machismo* has been distorted to "symbolize masculine entitlement, sexual potency, and toughness, which include the right to drink, especially as a reward for earning a living in a milieu that offers only limited economic opportunities" (Lex, 1987, p. 297).

Marianismo. In contrast with *machismo*, the qualities valued in women are submissiveness, obedience, dependence, docility, timidity, gentleness, sentimentality, and virginity until marriage (Comas-Diaz, 1988; Martinez, 1988). These qualities are collectively called *marianismo*, which is based on the Catholic veneration of the Virgin Mary, who is considered both a virgin and a Madonna (Comas-Diaz & Duncan, 1985). Because of this image,

> The wife/mother is expected to be pure and spiritually better than men; but at the same time, like the Virgin, she will be long-suffering and will place the needs of her husband and children before her own wishes and needs. (Enos, 1997, p. 307)

These qualities do not make women entirely powerless. Falicov (1982) observed that although there is an outward compliance with the cultural ideal of male dominance and female submission, there is culturally acceptable "undercover power and family centrality of the self-sacrificing mother" (p. 139). Nevertheless, an insistence on retaining these qualities under the larger American cultural and social conditions can create problems, particularly for first-generation immigrants.

Respeto. We have mentioned a sense of hierarchy that pervades the Latino family. This hierarchy is maintained by *respeto*. In the context of *machismo* and *marianismo*, *respeto* is seen as an example of submission by the wife and children to the authority of the man in the family. Beyond the immediate family, this concept also guides interpersonal relationships. In their study of "Identity, Conflict, and Evolving Latino Communities," Rosaldo and Flores (1997) explain the concept of *respeto* by quoting the following words of a Chicana activist:

> About *respeto* my father gave me this advice: the first, first thing about *respeto* is to listen to the person. Second, don't tell them that they don't feel something just because you don't. Even if the temperature is 106 we can't tell you that you're not cold when you tell us that you are. Third, if you see something and they see something different, accept what they tell you. Fourth, ask a lot of questions to make sure you respect and understand. Fifth, you can be angry, but show *respeto*. Do not raise your voice, break things, or belittle the other person. Do not put yourself in a position where you have to apologize for yourself. Sixth, don't lie. (p. 69)

A person is expected to show respect to parents, elders, and others in authority. One who does not do so is called uneducated: "the implicit assumption in the Hispanic community is that his child did not receive education from his or her parents concerning the treatment of others (particularly persons in a position of authority) with *respeto*" (Paniagua, 1994, p. 41).

Spiritualism. Latinos emphasize spiritual values, which are an amalgam of American Indian cosmology and Christianity (Ramirez, 1985). Catholicism is the predominant religion among them, but their spirituality transcends the formal church. "Hispanics believe they can make direct contact with God and the supernatural without the assistance or intervention of clergy" (Ho, 1987, p. 126). Objects such as the crucifix, pictures and jewelry showing the suffering Christ, the Sacred Heart, and so on not only reflect their personal identification with their religion but also are symbolic reminders of the ever-abiding presence of God and His protection and care. In times of need, the religious rituals include "going to many Catholic churches and making promises; making novenas; lighting candles; and praying to a Patron Saint" (Wodarski, 1992b, p. 75). Latinos have special devotion to Jesus's mother, the Virgin Mary, who is seen as helpful because she is an understanding mother. In a discussion of religion and philosophy in Latin America, Hilton (1973) stated that there is scarcely a country in Latin America that does not have a special, national Virgin Mary. "In Latin America the Church promotes the cult of the Virgin, or rather of statues of the Virgin. Christ is practically forgotten" (Hilton, 1973, p. 141). Along with faith in God's will, many Hispanics turn to *curanderos* (faith healers—*el curandero* for men and *la curandera* for women) and the practice of *espiritismo* (exorcising evil spirits).

Fatalismo. Latinos tend to accept hardships of life as the will of God. "There is a pervading sense that much of what happens is beyond one's control" (Wodarski, 1992b, p. 74). They value the spirit and soul as more important than the body and physical possessions. Their thinking is more in terms of transcendent qualities such as justice, loyalty, and love than about mastering the world (Ho, 1987). "Fatalism could imply a sense of vulnerability and lack of control in the presence of adverse events, as well as the feeling that such events are 'waiting' to affect the life of the individual" (Paniagua, 1994, pp. 43-44). Fatalism may also be seen as an adaptive response to uncontrollable life situations (Neff & Hoppe, 1993), and it can soften "the sense of despair or personal failure that is the common by-product of the middle-class American values system" (Ho, 1987, p. 127).

Other Values. Latinos have a worldview and a set of attitudes that are different from those of the larger American society. In a discussion of Mexican Americans, Locke (1998) stated that material objects are considered necessities but not ends in themselves, that work is viewed as necessary for survival but not as a value in itself, and that life is to be lived and experienced completely in the present:

> It is much more valuable to experience things directly, through intellectual awareness and through emotional experiences, rather than indirectly, through past accomplishments and accumulation of wealth. The philosopher, poet, musician, and artist are more often revered in this culture than the businessperson or financier. (Locke, 1998, p. 163)

Whereas in the dominant American culture responsibility is often equated with punctuality, among the Latinos the concept of responsibility is based on different values. There is no compulsive time orientation. For example, attending to the immediate needs of the family or a friend is seen as more important than being punctual. Unlike the value placed on openness, frankness, and directness in the dominant culture, the concern and respect for the feelings of others dictate the manner of communication among Hispanics/Latinos. They use tact and diplomacy instead of frankness and directness. "The manner of expression is likely to be elaborate and indirect because the aim is to make the personal relationship at least appear harmonious, to show respect for the other's individuality" (Locke, 1998, p. 162). The characteristics of the Puerto Rican values and attitudes identified by Banks (1987) are true of other Latino groups as well. These include interdependence, group centrality, cooperation, dignity, respect of persons, and comfort with human contact.

We want to end this section with a cautionary statement. The common cultural values among Latino Americans identified here are not fixed and absolute but changing and evolving. Moreover, depending on the level of acculturation, there are different degrees of acceptance and observance of these values by individuals and groups. It will be impossible to find an individual who shows absolute conformity with traditional values (Queralt, 1984).

DIVERSITY WITHIN: SUBGROUP AND INTRAGROUP DIFFERENCES AMONG LATINO AMERICANS

The commonality of cultural values identified previously is the result of a very broad-brushed portrayal of those values. There are significant intergroup and intragroup differences. Moreover, although people are influenced by their culture, they are not controlled by it. They do not accept all of the culture's values with equal intensity; they tend to emphasize some and de-emphasize others (Kirst-Ashman & Hull, 1993). There are layers of differences, differences among subgroups and differences within subgroups. The following are a few examples of these differences.

Differences Based on Immigration-Related Factors. Not all Latinos are immigrants. Some Mexicans had become foreigners in their own land when the United States took over parts of Mexico, and others have been immigrating from Mexico. Puerto Ricans are technically not immigrants, but like immigrants, many of them struggle with the tasks of mastering the English language and adjusting to the mores and values of the larger society. Then there are immigrants from the various Central American, South American, and Caribbean countries. There are differences in the needs and problems of subgroups of immigrants and their families, such subgroups as: (a) newly arrived immigrant families, (b) immigrant-American families, and (c) immigrant-descent families (Casas & Keefe, 1980; Padilla, Carlos, & Keefe, 1976). The newcomers are the first-generation immigrants, and their children constitute the second generation. Loneliness, isolation, a sense of loss, hopelessness, and depression are seen in adult immigrants from both Mexico and Central America (Cervantes, Salgado de Snyder, & Padilla, 1989). Those who immigrate as refugees have needs different than those of other immigrants.

> "Becoming" a refugee, with its psychological, political, and economic ramifications, is a catastrophic life change. It is an upheaval of all that is known and familiar. It is a series of losses, which include country, home, family members, and friends. Previous support systems may be lost and earlier coping patterns may no longer be useful. (Fox, 1991, p. 55)

The age at immigration is also an important variable. Padilla, Alvarez, and Lindholm (1986) found that those who immigrated at an older age and second-generation individuals experienced the most stress, lower self-esteem, and high externality. Second-generation individuals are likely to experience more stress as a result of being caught between the cultural values of their parents and those of the larger society. The erosion of beliefs and practices begins with the second generation even when there are no intermarriages between Hispanics and non-Hispanics. The history of intermarriage is long, and the trend seems to continue (Ho, 1987).

Differences Based on Degree of Acculturation. Acculturation is a powerful factor responsible for differences among Latinos. On the one hand, there are subgroups with a long history of settlement and acculturation reflecting the trends in family and household structures characteristic of the larger U.S. population (Bean & Tienda, 1987; Vega, 1990) and other elements of the dominant culture. On the other hand are those experiencing a continual reinforcement of the traditional patterns of family organization and values prevailing in the country of origin. They "are not yet 'settled,' but continue expanding and changing in response to uninterrupted immigration and to close contact with events in the home countries" (Portes & Truelove, 1987, p. 361). Many move back and forth between the United States and their home countries, which keeps them exposed to their native culture:

> The ease with which Dominicans, Puerto Ricans, and Mexicans can return to their respective countries—the former two by relatively inexpensive plane flights from the East Coast; the latter, by plane, car, or bus—permits the cultural roots of their communities to be constantly affirmed. (Klor de Alva, 1988, p. 111)

Because of these forces, there is significant heterogeneity among Latinos. There are several classifications based on the degree of their acculturation. Hernandez and Carlquist-Hernandez (1997) classified Mexican Americans into: (a) the *traditional* Mexican American, who identifies strongly with family, community, ethnic group, and members of the extended family; (b) the *duotraditional* Mexican American, who is semiurban and ethnically heterogeneous and has moderate ties to his or her family; and (c) the *atraditional* Mexican American, who has assimilated into the community at large, has few familial ties, is urban, and speaks English as his or her primary language. Chavez and Roney (1990) have proposed the term *decultured* to describe the Mexican American who culturally belongs neither to the Mexican American culture nor to the larger culture and is on the margins of both. Matute-Bianchi (1986) identified five categories of ethnic identity within the Mexican American student population: (a) recent Mexican immigrant (Mexican-born, Spanish-speaking, *Mexicano* identity); (b) Mexican oriented (bilingual, strong ties to both Mexico and the United States); (c) Mexican American (born in the United States, assimilated, prefers English over Spanish); (d) Chicano (identifies as Mexican or *Mexicano*, alienated from mainstream-oriented activities); and (e) Cholo (marginal, disaffected, frequently associated with gangs).

Differences Based on National Origin. These differences persist and affect Latino Americans in different ways. Different national-origin groups have different racial backgrounds. They may be divided into three categories depending on the type of racial mixing most common to them:

> One set of countries—Panama and countries in the Caribbean Islands and northern South America—have large populations that are of mixed European and African ancestry. Another set—Mexico and countries of Central America and western South America—have large

populations that are of mixed European and indigenous (Indian) ancestry. A third set of countries—Argentina, Uruguay, and to a lesser extent, Chile—are composed almost entirely of people who are European in ancestry. (Longres, 1995a, p. 1217)

Race and color are the major bases for social stratification in the United States, and race distinctions not only shape the experience of different groups in the United States but also influence their socioeconomic positions (Suarez & Ramirez, 1999). Different groups are also affected by the histories of their countries of origin and by the relationships between those countries and the United States. These are among the reasons for Latinos' resistance to the idea of uniting into a single category of "Hispanic" to reflect a panethnic identity. Romero (1997) has articulated their objections thus: "One is the depoliticization of each group's distinct history with the U.S. (colonized, conquered, exploited, etc.); the other is the emphasis upon Hispanic (European) culture and ancestry, rather than African and indigenous cultures" (p. xv). Many Hispanics have no ancestors from the Iberian Peninsula (Castex, 1994).

The self-interest of various national-origin groups also brings out differences among them. For example, Montiel and Ortego y Gasca (1998) observed that

more than three-fifths of the Hispanics in the United States are Chicanos. Yet many are concerned that by subsuming themselves under the Hispanic rubric, they will lose their edge in numbers to Cuban Americans, who make up less than 5% of the U.S. Hispanic population but, like Jewish Americans, are influential beyond their numbers in the population. (p. 57)

The experiences of these groups in the United States also validate and strengthen their differences. With his focus on Dominicans in New York, Guarnizo (1997) stated:

Partly due to their subordinate social position in the city, partly because of their nostalgia for their homeland, partly because of their sheer numbers, their high concentration, and their physical appearance (which may lead to their being misidentified as either African Americans or Puerto Ricans), Dominican immigrants reaffirm and re-create their origins to a degree rarely seen among other Latin American groups. (p. 167)

The strength of the local community of a particular subgroup also makes a difference. Numbers create and maintain the ethnic consciousness, which serves both as a way of validating themselves and improving their collective self-esteem and as a defense against exploitation and discrimination (Acosta-Belen, 1988). Dominicans, Colombians, Panamanians, and others who have congregated residentially in large cities have a sufficient mass to maintain some degree of public subcultural identity (Klor de Alva, 1988). The result of all these differences is more discord than unity among the various subgroups of Latinos. Weyr (1988) has illustrated this by the following story, which he claims that Chicanos tell on themselves:

A man sits on the banks of the Rio Grande pulling crabs out of the river. His pail is already full. A passerby asks if he doesn't worry about the crabs climbing over the edge to freedom. "Naw," the man says tranquilly, "them's Mexican crabs"—meaning, of course, that they pull each other down. (p. 13)

Differences Based on Sociodemographic Factors. As a group, Hispanics are a young population. In 1992, their median age was 27 years, which is a decade younger than the median age of non-Hispanic whites. However, intragroup variation in age structure is quite wide. Whereas Mexican Americans were the youngest group, with a median age of 25 years, followed by Puerto Ricans, with a median age of 27 years, the median age of Cuban Americans was 44 years. This difference will have an effect on the prevalence of such chronic diseases as cancer, cardiovascular disease, and diabetes among subgroups (Suarez & Ramirez, 1999). Similarly, subgroup differences are quite significant in the levels of education attained, occupational positions held, and income categories occupied. A higher proportion of Cubans than Mexicans and Puerto Ricans are in managerial and professional jobs. For example, in Miami, almost one third of all businesses and 40% of industries are owned by Cubans, and 20% of the banks are controlled by them. Seventy-five percent of the workforce in construction is Cuban. "Unlike other minorities, Cubans rejected by the unions did not simply return to low-wage, unskilled work. Instead, Cuban immigrants began creating their own, nonunion firms and competing for housing contracts" (Nelson & Tienda, 1997, p. 26). Their other strongholds include textiles, food, cigars, and trade with Latin America. Cubans are doing equally well elsewhere in the country. Of their presence in New York, Weyr (1988) said:

> Cubans own the major Hispanic advertising agencies. Cuban lawyers work out of corporate suites, not storefront offices as do other Hispanic attorneys. Cubans run theaters, write plays, and own restaurants. They are cultural potentates. They get money from the New York Council on the Arts. (p. 149)

On the other hand, Puerto Ricans and Mexicans, along with Dominicans, are worse off. For example, even after half a century, most Puerto Ricans in the United States are not any closer to their American dream. During the 1970s and 1980s, the economic status of Puerto Ricans deteriorated both absolutely and relative to other minority groups. By 1990, Puerto Rican families were three times as likely as other families to fall below the official poverty line, and nearly four out of every ten of these families were impoverished (Campos, 1995; Tienda, 1989). Overall, more than 30% of Dominican, about 30% of Puerto Rican, 23% of Mexican, 21% of Central American, 11% of Cuban, and 10% of Spaniard individuals were below the poverty level in 1990 (U.S. Department of Commerce, 1993b).

Differences Based on Religious Affiliation and Beliefs. Although the majority of Latinos are Catholic, more and more are turning to churches of other Christian denominations. Even Catholics may be practicing a form of Catholicism quite different from the one dominant in the United States.[6] Many Puerto Ricans are also adherents of spiritism, and many Cubans are adherents of Santeria, while still regarding themselves as Catholics (Gann & Duignan, 1986). Moreover, not every Puerto Rican who came to the mainland was Catholic. With the U.S. invasion of the island had also come Pentecostalism, which gradually became the largest and fastest-growing religion in Puerto Rico because of the importance it places on religious experience, which reinforces the Puerto Rican desire for intimacy with the supernatural. "After migrating to New York, many Puerto Ricans found the Pentecostalism provided a means of escaping the cultural and social aimlessness they experienced in the transition from rural to city life" (Locke, 1998, p. 175).

Differences Based on Belief in Different Theories of Human Illness and Suffering and Approaches to Healing and Help. For many Latinos, the meaning of suffering and approaches to alleviating it reflect the persistence of beliefs in different theories of health, illness, and misfortune.

> There is general belief that the physical-physiological body constitutes an envelope for the spirit being cycled through reincarnations. A spiritual body (*perispiritu*) forms an invisible link between the corporeal and incorporeal bodies. External sources, including invasive spirits and discomfort from others' enmity, are often credited with causing distress and bizarre behaviors. (Dana, 1998, p. 177)

For health, mental health, and other problems of living, individuals and families in Hispanic communities turn for help to several sources in place of or along with the formal health and human services. These sources of help and solace include not only priests but also folk healers such as spiritists, Santeros, herbalists, santiguadors, and curanderos:

> These folk healers address particular needs experienced by individuals who are in distress and use unique culture-specific methods to diagnose and treat ailments. The santero and spiritist focus primarily on emotional and interpersonal problems, the herbalist and santiguador focus on physical ailments, and the curandero maintains a balance between the physical and mental spheres. (Wodarski, 1992b, p. 97)

Differences Based on Family Forms and Status. Despite the centrality of the family in the Hispanic culture, there are significant variations in the form and status of the Latino family. Families are affected by what is happening in the society at large, as well as by regional, historical, political, and socioeconomic factors, such as the level of urbanization, degree of intermarriage, and extent of employment of women outside the home. Like other American families, Latino families have shown a decrease in husband-wife families and an increase in female-headed families. However, there are marked intragroup differences.[7] In 1990, 60% of Mexican American and 57% of Central and South American households were married-couple families compared with 46% of Puerto Rican households (U.S. Bureau of the Census, 1990). Like Puerto Ricans, Mexicans are likely to be poor, but the percentage of female-headed households among Mexican Americans is lower than among Puerto Ricans. Although divorce and separation are a significant source of female-headed households, a number of others factors contribute to changes in the family structure and pattern of living. Married-couple families and female-headed families are not the only forms of the Latino family. For example, Fitzpatrick (1987) has identified four types of Puerto Rican families: (a) the extended family, with strong bonds and frequent interaction among a wide range of natural or ritual kin providing a source of strength and support; (b) the nuclear family, consisting of the mother, the father, and their children not living close to relatives and having weak bonds with the extended family; (c) the father, the mother, their children, and the children of another union or other unions of husband or wife; and (d) the mother-based family, with children of one or more fathers but with no permanent male in the home.

Differences Based on Gender. Whereas *sex* refers to the biological aspects of a person, involving characteristics that differentiate females and males by chromosomal, anatomical, reproductive, hormonal, and other physiological factors, *gender* involves social, cultural, and psychological aspects linked to males and females through a particular social context (Lindsey, 1990). Gender determines the differences between the roles, behaviors, opportunities, and life experiences of men and women. We have earlier discussed *machismo, marianismo, familismo,* and a sense of hierarchy as the common cultural characteristics of Latino Americans. Although these point to clearly defined and prescribed gender-based roles and responsibilities, the life conditions of both men and women make it hard for them to perform those roles and discharge those responsibilities. For example, the limited incomes of Latino men necessitate women's employment, which makes the traditional patriarchal subordination difficult to maintain. Many men have not developed the positive traits of *machismo*, such as bravery, courage, self-defense, responsibility, respect, altruism, pride, protection, steadfastness, individualism, and honor (Mirande, 1988). Others try to live up to this image of *machismo*. Many fail in an environment of poverty and racism. Nevertheless, gender-based differences persist. Although the employment of Hispanic women outside the home has begun to undermine the economic and cultural bases of male power in the family (Taylor, 1994), results are not always clear-cut. Fernandez-Kelly and Garcia (1997) studied the effect of employment on Cuban and Mexican garment workers in California and Florida. The marital profiles and household compositions of the two groups were similar, with intact marriages predominating in both. They found that,

> On the one hand, paid employment expands the potential for greater personal autonomy and financial independence. This should have a favorable impact upon women's capacity to negotiate an equitable position within the home and in the labor market. On the other hand, women's search for paid employment is frequently the consequence of severe economic need; it expresses vulnerability rather than strength within the home and in the marketplace. Under certain conditions, women's entry into the labor force also parallels the collapse of reciprocal exchanges between men and women. (Fernandez-Kelly & Garcia, 1997, p. 226)

Similar is the situation of most women from Central America. In a study of these women in Washington, where their labor force participation is very high (87%), Repack (1997) found that they experienced a greater degree of personal autonomy and control over domestic resources but not any greater freedom from household work. "Even when women worked full-time outside the home, these men still expected their partners to do most of the cooking, cleaning, and caring for children in the household" (Repack, 1997, p. 249). In their study of work-family role allocation in dual-earner Chicano families, Coltrane and Valdez (1997) also found that the simple fact of employment is not sufficient to bring about changes in the division of domestic labor. For many, the myth of the "Superwoman," who "works outside the home but also retains her traditional home-making and child-rearing roles and fulfills all of her roles with stunning aplomb" (Fassinger & Richie, 1997, p. 86), becomes a reality as they try to live up to it. This is, of course, at a price. Assuming multiple roles is stressful for them and taxing for their intra-familial relationships.

MAJOR NEEDS AND PROBLEMS
OF LATINO AMERICAN GROUPS

We are discussing needs and problems that are both common to most subgroups and experienced by the most vulnerable of all Latino Americans. Our focus is on needs rather than problems. We believe that in the absence of adequate and appropriate resources, unmet needs become or generate problems.

Needs Related to Poverty. In 1992, 26.2% of Hispanic families had incomes below the poverty level, compared with 10.3% of non-Hispanic families. The 1992 median income of non-Hispanic white households ($33,388) was 46.1% higher than that of Hispanic households ($22,848; U.S. Bureau of the Census, 1993a, 1993b). A look at poverty among the vulnerable populations also reveals high rates of prevalence. Twice as many (24%) elderly (over 65 years of age) Hispanics lived in poverty than elderly non-Hispanics did (12%). Similarly, about 27% of Hispanic females, compared with 13% of non-Hispanic females, were poor. Twelve percent of the children in the United States were Hispanic in 1992, but 21% of children living in poverty were Hispanic (U.S. Bureau of the Census, 1993a; U.S. Department of Commerce, 1993b).

Poverty breeds all kinds of problems. The poor are forced to live in unhealthy and often dangerous environments, eat nutritionally deficient food, and acquire detrimental lifestyles. For example, in comparison with Anglos, alcohol consumption among Hispanic men is heavier, with 43% reporting alcohol problems nationally (Lex, 1987). The inability to find employment and provide for their families creates personal crises for many men, in which feelings of inadequacy and guilt dominate. Tran and Dhooper (1997) sought to understand the relationship between poverty and psychological distress in elderly Cubans, Mexicans, and Puerto Ricans. They found that all these elderly people, irrespective of gender, marital status, educational background, and facility with the English language, are equally vulnerable to psychological distress.

Needs of the Elderly. As pointed out previously, the Latino elderly are vulnerable to psychological distress. Different types of stress have differential effects on their distress. The stress of poor health and disability is strongly associated with distress in both poor and nonpoor elderly. Similarly, social stress, operationalized as loneliness-isolation and dependence on others, has more potential for causing psychological distress than other types of stress in all elderly. There are some subgroup differences. Puerto Rican elderly, both poor and nonpoor, are more vulnerable to distress than other elderly populations are. In general, elderly Latino Americans are not sharing in the economic prosperity enjoyed by other elderly Americans. Many struggle to make ends meet. Serious health problems and physical impairments compromise an independent lifestyle. Families are a major source of their support, but long-term care inflicts enormous financial and emotional burdens on family caregivers (Andrews, 1989). There is a widely held belief that Hispanic families are willing and able to care for their elderly. However, willingness and ability do not necessarily go together. Hispanic familism seems to prevent the use of services that the elderly and their caregivers desperately need (Purdy & Arguello, 1992).

The senior author has been involved in exploring the human service needs of Hispanic elderly and their ability to use the needed services. One of the studies (Tran & Dhooper, 1996) found that the needs of these elderly for social services were influenced by their ethnicity (Cuban, Mexican, or Puerto Rican) as well as by their gender and education. More Mexican and Puerto Rican elderly needed services than Cuban elderly. From 9 to 20% of Cuban, 19 to 37% of Mexican, and 18 to 46% of Puerto Rican elderly men reported needs for specific social services. As compared to these groups of men, the three ethnic groups of the elderly Hispanic women showed a different pattern of needs. Similarly, elderly with different educational backgrounds had needs for different social services. In general, the Hispanic elderly are at risk of having their needs remain unmet.

Needs of Recent Immigrants. Like all immigrants, Latinos new to this country struggle with the problems of acculturation. The acculturation stress in an atmosphere of prejudice and discrimination tends to be taxing emotionally and physically. This is particularly so for women. Palacios and Franco (1986) have described the problems of Mexican

American women trying to reconcile the preservation of traditional values and customs with adoption of new values and behaviors from the dominant society. Smart and Smart (1995) have used the concepts of *role entrapment* and *status leveling* to describe the effect of acculturation stress on the physical health, decision making, and occupational functioning of Hispanic immigrants. Role entrapment results from stereotypes that stigmatize language ability, skin color, speech, and educational level in damaging ways. Status leveling reduces all newcomers to the lowest common denominator, regardless of individual differences.

The society deals with diversity in stereotypical ways, but stereotypes are damaging to their victims. The uniqueness of the particular entity—individual, group, or community—is ignored, generally to the disadvantage of that entity. There is also the danger of that individual, group, or community believing in the stereotype, with damaging consequences. We have mentioned earlier that unsuccessful Cubans have sometimes denied their need for services because they had internalized the myth of Cuban success and superiority. In an assessment of the stereotypes about persons of Mexican descent held by three generations of Mexican American and Anglo American adolescents, Buriel and Vasquez (1982) found that with each successive generation, the attitude of Mexicans became more negative and more closely approximated the Anglos' stereotypes of persons of Mexican descent.

The foreign-born Hispanics are the largest group in the country's foreign-born population, and most are newly arrived. For many, adjusting to the life in the United States is strenuous.

> Now when Latinos come to this country and have to face strangers outside of their world, they suffer incoherence: they really don't know what to do with them. To resort to the old relationships would be a disaster since these others do not share the same web of life. The Anglos do not respond to *respeto* except to see it as weakness and therefore to take advantage of us. How can traditional Latinos bargain with people who have fixed prices, laws, and boundaries for everything? In this context the web of life cannot be sustained. The children especially no longer feel secure and see their parents hesitant and silent in front of authority figures. (Abalos, 1986, p. 170)

The lack of proficiency in English becomes a handicap for many. Status leveling is the experience of most newcomers. Even Cubans, the most successful of Latinos, were not exempt from a widespread downward occupational mobility. A comparison of their occupational positions in Cuba with those they hold in the United States showed that the percentage of unskilled laborers in Miami had doubled. The proportion of professionals, managers, and technicians had dropped from 48% in Cuba to 13% in the United States (Casal & Hernandes, 1975).

Needs of Children of Recent Immigrants. The cultural contradictions and tensions experienced by most new immigrants are magnified for the children of those immigrants.

> Parents are unable to mediate as children attempt to find their niche in a new society, particularly when the parents are forced to work long hours away from home or are compelled to separate because of domestic problems. Alienation within the family increases with time as children become acculturated more quickly than their parents and lose respect for parental authority. ... In the process of becoming "Americanized," trying to be like their peers, or even trying to help the family with extra income, immigrant youths may be sorely tempted by the easy money and fast life of drug dealing. They may also join street gangs, which confer a sense of safety and belonging. (Repack, 1997, p. 251)

The skin color of individuals also determines how the society at large receives and treats them. Light-skinned Latinos face fewer obstacles than their dark-skinned compatriots. Also, the poor, dark-skinned Central Americans contrast with the white immigrants from inland Columbia, Argentina, and Uruguay, and with other Latin Americans. "In the extremely race-conscious environment of the United States, these different shades of humanity translate into different experiences of reality" (Klor de Alva, 1988, p. 114). Being different from the majority in the larger society affects these new Americans profoundly. There are also differences in their help-seeking behaviors, so that some will ask for assistance, whereas others will need to be reached out to.

Needs of Refugees. Refugees require special attention because of their special vulnerabilities. Potocky (1996), who studied refugees who had arrived here as children and were now adults, has described some of the problems experienced by them, and Gonsalves (1992) has delineated stages of acculturation that refugees go through. The U.S. government has not treated all Hispanic refugees alike. Unlike the Cubans, who were given blanket asylum, Haitians and Nicaraguans were required to prove on a case-by-case basis that they had been persecuted or had had a well-founded fear of being persecuted in their home countries. The vast majority of these cases are denied, and many of these refugees living in the United States are considered illegal aliens. As such, they are ineligible for any benefits as refugees (Potocky, 1996). With her focus on those from Central America, many of whom came here to escape political persecution in their countries, Repack (1997) said that migration for them becomes a catch-22 situation:

> Individuals move north in order to help maintain the family back home or to ensure their safety by relocating family members to the United States; but the separations and cultural distances they must traverse enhance the loneliness that causes some to look for new partners, peers, or gangs upon resettlement. Families are torn apart amid the contradictions and struggles surrounding them, and unexpected outcomes may be worse than the problem that inspired the migration in the first place. (p. 251)

Needs of the Undocumented Immigrants. We have earlier mentioned many undocumented Latinos from Mexico and various Central and South American countries. Some of them might have taken advantage of the laws offering protection and amnesties and regularized their immigrant status. The fear of being deported might have kept many others from owning their undocumented immigrant status. In the current anti-immigrant climate, the undocumented immigration status of these people becomes their most serious problem. They cannot find employment. "This creates an underclass of workers who can find subminimum wage employment only in the ethnic enclave, the domestic, and secondary labor sectors" (Cordova, 1998, p. 193). Although the American Civil Liberties Union and the United Nations High Commission on Refugees have declared their position that Salvadorans and Guatemalans in the United States are prima facie refugees and should not be deported, many government officials engage in immigrant bashing, blaming immigrants for the ills of society (Cordova, 1998).

Needs of Some Little-Known Special Groups. One group of Hispanic women with special needs is made up of what Comas-Diaz (1996) termed *LatiNegra*, who are perceived as black by both the American and Hispanic communities. They are doubly marginalized: racially excluded within their own group as well as in the larger population. In the words of Comas-Diaz (1996), "Due to her socially imposed low self-esteem and inferior social standing, the LatiNegra experiences powerlessness and learned helplessness" (p. 187).

Another little-known group is a subgroup of the male youth, unmarried teenage fathers who have special needs. Many male youth from families unable to inculcate the values of familism, who are often abused and witness to the battering of their mothers and sisters, model alcohol and drug use and a tough, violent street persona (Belitz & Valdez, 1994). Over and above the dilemmas of adolescence, they must deal with the demands of the relationship with the unwed mother as well as family, social, and economic pressures (Hendricks, 1988).

The third little-known group is homosexuals, because of the high degree of homophobia in the Latino community. There is a double standard of sexual permissiveness among Latinos. Whereas men participating in sexual activities with other males may not consider themselves or be viewed by others as homosexual, lesbians are frowned upon. B. Greene (1994) suggested that the declaration of homosexuality may be viewed as an act of treason against the Latino culture and family. Hence, the pressure to deny their homosexuality is so strong that many Latino gays and lesbians remain silent about their sexuality.

SOCIAL WORK PRACTICE: GENERAL CONSIDERATIONS FOR INTERVENTION WITH LATINO AMERICANS

In this section, we present some general ideas, insights, and suggestions that should guide social work intervention with Latino Americans.

Importance of the Spanish Language for Most Latinos. Romero (1997) has mentioned a 1995 court case in which a judge decided in favor of a father's right to prohibit the mother of his daughter from speaking Spanish to the child. He claimed that teaching the child Spanish would condemn her to a future of servitude as a maid. This reflects one of several beliefs that the larger society holds about people different from the majority community. However, the reality is always more complex than the simple "truths" about it. An example of this complexity is provided by a comparison of the socioeconomic status of Puerto Ricans with that of Cubans. Puerto Ricans have the highest levels of English language proficiency but the lowest levels of socioeconomic achievement. On the other hand, the least linguistically proficient Cuban immigrants have been more successful in the labor market (Nelson & Tienda, 1997). For many Latinos, Spanish is more than a mere medium of communication. It helps to preserve and strengthen their cultural identity and to create a sense of unity among them.

The Spanish language is thriving in many parts of the country despite discouragement of and opposition to bilingualism (Padilla et al., 1991). There is a constant inflow of newcomers, the mother tongue of most of whom is Spanish. In 1990, the total foreign-born population in the United States was close to 20 million. Of these, the largest group (42.5%) was made up of those from Latin American countries. The media, print as well as radio and television, are also helping to keep the Spanish language alive:

> Dominican and Puerto Rican newspapers are on sale in Manhattan the day of publication or a day or two later. Mexican newspapers arrive in Los Angeles as quickly. On television the Spanish International Network has wired the country, claiming more than three hundred outlets, from small cable operations to anchor stations in New York, Los Angeles, San Antonio, and Miami. (Weyr, 1988, p. 7)

Large proportions of Latinos (e.g., 95% of Mexicans, Cubans, or Salvadorans) speak Spanish at home. More than half of those who speak Spanish at home do not speak English "very well," and 43% of Mexican and nearly half of the Salvadoran foreign-born are "linguistically isolated" (U.S. Department of Commerce, 1993a). Hence, there are likely to be large numbers of people who may not be adequately served if the level of their proficiency in English is not considered.

We have also discussed the desire of many native-born Latinos to rediscover their Hispanicity by learning or mastering the Spanish language. Many bilingual-bicultural persons also have strong preferences regarding which language should be used in working with them. Moreover, people in crisis may have additional difficulties communicating in a second or third language (Castex, 1994). With a focus on the psychiatric examination of Hispanics, Marcos (1994) said that services in a second language can disguise or exacerbate psychopathology and influence any self-presentation by alterations in motor activity, speech, affect, and general attitude. Therefore, in dealing with Hispanic clients, you should find out which language the client communicates best in and respect his or her language-related preference.

Race-based discrimination affects racially diverse Latinos differently. Latinos are racially diverse, and therefore the race-based discrimination in this country affects them unequally. Individuals may be characterized as white or European American, Native American, African American, East Asian, South Asian, or some other racial type.

> Clients who may have become classified as African American only after their arrival in the United States may be experiencing serious racial discrimination for the first time. As a result, the practitioner must keep in mind the need to consult with the client regarding his or her racial status and to be sensitive to the possibility that he or she may have experienced a dramatic change in social status because of the U.S. system of racial ascription. Such a change can affect self-esteem, relations with others, and real opportunities. (Castex, 1994, p. 293)

You should avoid verbal and nonverbal behaviors that clients can view as reflective of prejudice and discrimination.

Poverty Affecting Large Proportions of Latino Population. We have discussed the poverty among Hispanic/Latino families, the elderly, and children. In a study of economic stress on high school students' views of work and the future, Jones, Agbayani-Siewert, and Friaz (1998) found that Latino students reported more mental health difficulties and felt less confident about finding a job after graduation. The economic and social conditions of poor inner-city communities are contributing to the growing population of angry youth engaged in behaviors destructive to themselves and society (Hughes, 1995). Even those—children, the elderly, and families—who are eligible for existing health and human services underutilize those services. You should acknowledge the existence of poverty and its impact on Latino victims and deal with it through approaches that involve investments in education, employment, family, and community. Examples of such approaches are appearing in the literature. Lord and Kennedy (1992) have described a model that transformed a micro-oriented casework agency into a progressive community center that advocates social and political empowerment at the grassroots level.

Prevalence of AIDS Among Latinos. AIDS is no longer the disease of homosexual males concentrated in a few large cities. It is shifting to minority communities, and large proportions of minority populations, both male and female, are represented among the HIV-positive and AIDS patients. The victims of AIDS and their caregivers are a growing part of the Hispanic/Latino communities. Puerto Ricans are the group most disproportionately affected by AIDS, followed by Dominicans. The most common means of contracting HIV and AIDS among Hispanic women is intravenous drug use. The needs of female AIDS caregivers, many of whom are infected themselves, have not been adequately studied and understood (Land & Hudson, 1997). The health care issues pertaining to Hispanics infected with HIV disease that were identified by Jimenez and Jimenez (1992) are still valid. These included the facts that many persons with AIDS do not have private insurance, that undocumented persons may not be eligible for Medicaid, and that many may have lost the social support from their extended familial network. You should take leadership in understanding the situations of and responding to the needs of AIDS victims and their caregivers. Innovative approaches are needed to reach them. These must involve all sectors of the Latino community and must reach out to those unwilling or unable to access conventional programs. Delgado and Santiago (1998) have described a "Projecto Cooperacion" that involved in its HIV/AIDS-related work botanical shops, which are indigenous culture-based institutions in Puerto Rican and Dominican communities.

Alcohol Abuse and Alcohol-Related Problems. There is a high prevalence of alcohol abuse and alcohol-related problems among Hispanic men and women. They continue to be at greater risk than whites for developing a number of alcohol-related problems (Caetano, 1998). Hispanic immigrants are particularly vulnerable. Grossman (1990) studied 102 Hispanic immigrants admitted to an alcoholism treatment program and found a significant association between several aspects of the immigrant-acculturation experience and an exacerbation of alcohol-related problems after immigration. Those with the highest levels of acculturation had the greatest increase in those problems. In a longitudinal study of lifetime, past year, and magnitude of use of cigarettes, alcohol, and illicit drugs among a large sample of Hispanic, African American, and non-Hispanic white adolescents, Warheit, Vega, Khourey, Gil, and Elfenbein (1996) also found that foreign-born Hispanics reported a positive relationship between the length of time in the country and substance abuse.

In dealing with the alcohol and drug abuse problem among Latino Americans, you should modify approaches to make them consistent with Latino cultural values. Aguilar, DiNitto, Franklin, and Lopez-Pilkinton (1991) have described how Mexican American families' cultural values have been incorporated into a psychoeducational approach to the problem of chemical dependency. Women alcohol and drug abusers are helped to view recovery as a gift to others in their family, to children by becoming a better mother and to the husband by becoming a better wife. Inclan and Hernandez (1992) have found the application of the concept of codependence to poor Hispanic patients to be counterproductive, because the changes expected of the patient and family for recovery are in conflict with their cultural value of familism. They have suggested strategies for more effective treatment of codependence in Hispanic families. Weave these ideas into your work with such clients.

Acculturation a Source of Both Problems and Their Solution. The variation in the levels of acculturation among Latinos is tremendous, with those who are completely acculturated on the one extreme and those who are almost strangers to American culture on the other. The process of acculturation is stressful for most people. Acculturative stress for Hispanics is lifelong, pervasive, and intense, involving loss of social support, self-esteem, and identity (Smart & Smart, 1995). The discrepancy in the degree of acculturation among family members creates conflict. This is particularly true in relationships between parents and children and between husbands and wives. Major issues are the "what" and "how" of dating for adolescent girls and the "how much" of autonomy and freedom for women (Bernal & Gutierrez, 1988; Comas-Diaz & Duncan, 1985). The differential commitment to the traditional values by the different family members results in partial observance or even total disregard of culturally approved behaviors. The dynamics of these actions and reactions wreak havoc with the mental health of individuals, quality of interpersonal relationships, and atmosphere of the family.

Acculturation tends to reduce the intensity of traditional beliefs, but it does not provide a guarantee against problems and stress. Burnam, Hough, Karno, Escobar, and Telles (1987) studied acculturation and lifetime prevalence of psychiatric disorders among Mexican Americans and found that those born in the United States had higher rates of alcohol and drug abuse, depression, phobias, and antisocial personality with increasing acculturation. We have mentioned other studies also showing a correlation between the length of stay in the country and alcohol and drug abuse. There may be a number of reasons for these correlations, including the second generation's greater awareness of discrimination by the dominant society. Nevertheless, it is helpful to explore the client's level of acculturation and to discuss how he or she and his or her family interpret this concept. Acculturated and bicultural clients may benefit from culture-general intervention; traditional clients often require culture-specific interventions; and marginal clients may respond to a combination of culture-general and culture-specific interventions (Dana, 1998).

SOCIAL WORK INTERVENTION AT THE MICRO-, MEZZO-, AND MACROLEVELS: PRINCIPLES AND APPROACHES

In Chapter 2, we discussed at some length all phases of intervention with clients and client systems from diverse cultures and communities, and we suggested appropriate practice principles and strategies. Those ideas and approaches are applicable to Latino American clients and communities as well. In this chapter, we focus on assessment and intervention at the micro-, mezzo-, and macrolevels. As seen in the preceding sections, there are simultaneously powerful commonalities and significant differences among members of the various Latino American subgroups. People as individuals, groups, and communities also experience problems in varied social situational contexts. Their response to problems is thus influenced by a number of variables reflecting the client or system's universal human needs, urges, and aspirations; cultural conditioning, perspectives, and values; unique needs, hopes, and worldviews; values, standards, and demands of the larger society; and a host of situational factors. This complexity highlights the significance of accurate and comprehensive assessment as the basis for effective intervention. You will find the following ideas and suggestions helpful for intervening with Latino Americans.

Assessment-Related Practice Principles and Approaches

1. Recognize that accurate assessment depends on your ability to engage and build a positive relationship with the client or client system. Whether the focus of social work intervention is on helping an individual client or organizing the whole community, engaging the client or system is extremely important for problem identification and subsequent activity. You will find the principles and approaches for engagement given in Chapter 2 to also be helpful with Latino clients.

2. View engagement as a two-stage process: (a) preparation, and (b) relationship building. Preparation is especially important for the first contact with the client-system. Operationalize the principle of client self-determination as giving or maximizing the prospective client's choices about the "when," "where," and "how" of the initial meeting. Reduce the element of the unknown for the client by anticipating questions that someone in the client's shoes is likely to have and by giving information about yourself, your agency, and its programs and policies, as well as what you already know about the client from the referral and other sources.

3. Recognize that building relationship with Hispanics/Latinos is difficult because of:

a. Resistance to the idea of seeking help in general and disclosing their personal problems to strangers, a sense of shame and guilt over their failure to solve their problems, anger if they are coerced into using service, and the fear of being deported (on the part of the undocumented).

b. Communication barriers due to a lack of mastery over the English language or to the difficulty in adequately translating into English their expressions of feelings and explanations of situations. Even bilingual Hispanic Americans may vary their emotional expressiveness when using English:

Hispanics generally offer more carefully weighted, rational, and intellectualized messages in English ... Hispanics may come across as relatively guarded and businesslike in English, and yet when switching to Spanish, they frequently become much more open, expansive, informal, jovial, friendly, jocose, explosive, negative, or positive. (Queralt, 1984, p. 119)

Moreover, feelings are more often expressed through nonverbal communication, and nonverbal communication is almost always culturally conditioned.

c. Differences in personal and family backgrounds of clients and the worker. Family has a special place in the lives of most Hispanics, and it may be structurally different from the mainstream family. Most Hispanics do not feel free to talk frankly about their families to strangers.

d. Variance in the ethnic-community identity of clients. Although the degree to which people relate to their ethnic community varies, most turn first to their own helping networks, and if they have to go beyond those, they prefer agencies, programs, and personnel they can relate to.

Thus, engaging the client system for effective social work intervention should involve acknowledging and dealing with these reasons.

4. Build relationship with the client through appropriate affect, words, and deeds that are oriented toward motivating and energizing clients and meeting their needs. Remember that Hispanics value *personalismo* and place much emphasis on inner qualities, an inner dignity within themselves and others. Hispanic clients look for these qualities in the helper. It is not hard for clients to recognize the worker's warmth, concern, and trustworthiness and size him or her up in terms of his or her sincerity of concern, degree of warmth and empathy, and level of trustworthiness. You can demonstrate these qualities by showing respect, warmth, concern, genuine caring, and empathy and by making other appropriate

efforts to create mutual trust. Asking open-ended questions, listening attentively with feeling and understanding, and using a tone of acceptance that avoids confrontation (Ho, 1987) will help in creating that trust and breaking the client's resistance.

5. Realize that Latinos are people and contact oriented more than other cultural groups are. They value highly the human dimension of organizations and the warmth of professionals, and they are comfortable with body touch. The Mexican American cultural values of pleasantness and dignity, agreeableness, avoidance of negativism, simple courtesies, and collectivism (Marin & Marin, 1991) are shared more or less by most Latinos. "All clients appreciate/respond to high frequencies of affiliative/affectional behaviors (*simpatico*) or respect (*respeto*); personal, informal, individualized attention (*personalismo*); chatting to create warm atmosphere (*platicando*)" (Dana, 1998, p. 189). Being *simpatico* requires that one always be personable and pleasant in interactions with others. "It emphasizes avoiding disagreements, confrontation, and any kind of dissension. It values the notion of seeking consensus rather than conflict in intergroup relationships" (Enos, 1997, p. 315). Respecting this belief and using other key dimensions of Hispanic culture such as dignity, integrity, honor, and pride will be conducive to establishing trust in the client-worker relationship.

6. Begin with *platica*, a friendly conversation. *Platica* stresses mutuality and reciprocity, taking the form of worker-initiated open, personal, and warm conversation about noncontroversial subjects (Valle, 1980). Use self-disclosure as a signal of openness, an invitation for the client to respond, and a chance to find a common point of interest with client.

> Instead of hiding behind professional policies and practices, the worker meets the client as a human being and initiates the relationship. Instead of focusing on the client's problem, the worker seeks to humanize the relationship by disclosing a topic common to both their backgrounds. Professional self-disclosure lays the groundwork for the reciprocal response of client self-disclosure. (Lum, 1996, p. 144)

Whenever possible, make your self-disclosure relevant to the client's problem.

7. Be willing to disclose personal information such as food preferences, music, and hobbies, as well as information about work, family, and helping philosophy. This will help to enhance the client's trust and confidence in you. As Torres (1998) put it, "regardless of which culturally sensitive intervention approach is used, the practitioner's authentic presentation of self will remain his or her most valuable therapeutic tool" (p. 24).

8. Observe appropriate formality in addressing the client by using his or her last name and the form Mr., Mrs., or Miss. If you can speak Spanish, address the client as Senor (Mr.), Senora (Mrs.), or Senorita (Miss).

> Among Hispanics, the term Senor is used with adult males regardless of marital status; the term Senora is generally used to address women who are married. A Senorita is a woman who is at least 15 years, not married, and considered a *virgin* (i.e., without a history of a sexual relationship with a man). (Paniagua, 1994, pp. 47-48)

Also remember to use the polite form of the pronoun *you* (*usted*) with adults (Ho, 1987).

9. If the whole family is being seen, respect the hierarchical role structure of the Hispanic American family by addressing and talking with the father first. In a family conflict involving children (considered by parents) as the center of the problem, interview the father alone for a few minutes during the first session.

> This approach is a recognition of the father's authority by the therapist. Because of the value that Hispanics attach to the father's authority, the brief meeting between the therapist and the father could be the signal to the family that the therapist is sensitive to cultural variables among Hispanics and that he or she is ready to respect and to support them during the course of therapy. (Paniagua, 1994, pp. 49-50)

10. As you move beyond the "warm-up" period, you may use the idea of the *cultural story* as a nonthreatening way of getting background information. It builds on the human urge to tell a story.

> The cultural story refers to an ethnic or cultural group's origin, migration, and identity. Within the family, it is used to tell where one's ancestors came from, what kind of people they were and current members are, what issues are important to the family, what good and bad things have happened over time, and what lessons have been learned from those experiences. At the ethnic level, a cultural story tells the group's collective story of how to cope with life and how to respond to pain and trouble. It teaches people how to thrive in a multicultural society and what children should be taught so that they can sustain their ethnic and cultural story. (McGill, 1992, p. 340)

This will also be a way of determining the level of the client's acculturation.

11. Make the assessment comprehensive and multidimensional in order to ensure that intervention is appropriate and effective. In Chapter 2, we suggested a systems-oriented approach to assessment. Given the nature of the problem, you will need to explore some systems of a client's world more than others. We have also provided ideas for assessing communities.

12. Let your assessment efforts be guided by some fundamental assumptions. These include the following ideas:

a. Culture and ethnicity affect people's attitudes, perspectives, and behaviors differently.

b. Culture and ethnicity do not pervade all dimensions of people's lives in uniform ways.

c. Culture and ethnicity may not have a direct bearing on the causation, persistence, and solution of people's problems. Culture and ethnicity are powerful forces in human life, but their role in the specific problem of a particular client should be determined rather than assumed.

13. Consciously guard against stereotypical views of people and their problems. Remind yourself that stereotypes of Latinos abound and that it is easy to blame the victims of social problems for their plight. Be aware of your biases and the need for not letting preconceived ideas color your assessment of the clients and their needs and problems.

14. Recognize the importance of personal and family background of clients. As was pointed out earlier, the family has a tremendously important place in the lives of most Latino Americans. For them, the family is a much larger group than what goes by that

name in mainstream American society. Membership in the family generally means access to a source of strength and support as well as an obligation to help others in the group. Exploring the rights and responsibilities of the individual in the context of the specific personal and family background is likely to show the particular blend of the culturally universal and individually unique elements. However, you should remind yourself that information being gathered has relevance to the problem in hand and to the possible approaches to solving it.

15. Explore the client's level of acculturation and discuss how the client and his or her family interpret this concept. There are several acculturation rating scales for different groups of Hispanics, such as the Acculturation Questionnaire (Smither & Rodriguez-Geigling, 1982), the Acculturation Rating Scale for Mexican Americans (Cuellar, Arnold, & Maldonado, 1995), the Brief Acculturation Scale for Hispanics (Norris, Ford, & Bova, 1996), the Cuban Behavioral Identity Questionnaire (Garcia & Lega, 1979), the Cultural Life Style Inventory (Mendoza, 1989), the Multicultural Acculturation Scale (Wong-Rieger & Quintana, 1987), and the Multicultural Experience Inventory (Ramirez, 1984). Paniagua (1994) has recommended the use of a brief acculturation scale. There are only three items, each of which has five response categories. These items include the person's generation in the United States, with a score from 1 to 5; the language preferred, with a score of 1 for *Mine only* and 5 for *English only*; and preference to engage in social activity, with a score of 1 for *Only within my racial group* and 5 for *Only with a different racial group*. Knowledge of a client's acculturation status will ensure a better fit between the client's problem and the intervention.

16. Determine the relevance of the client's ethnic-community identity. Depending on the individual and familial level of acculturation, some people need the comfort and security of their ethnic community and prefer to live in ethnic neighborhoods; others do not live in ethnic neighborhoods but maintain meaningful contacts with people in those neighborhoods; and still others live away from those neighborhoods and feel comfortable in using the mainstream services. All ethnic communities have their unique history, triumphs, tragedies, problems, and strengths. The lives of people are affected by their physical and psychological association with these communities. Relating to the client's ethnic identity will assist not only in building a helping relationship and understanding them in their situations but also in exploring problem-relevant ethnic-community resources.

17. Make the assessment process an active and positive experience for the client. In conducting yourself, engaging the client, asking questions, providing information, identifying problems, seeking clarification, giving opinions, suggesting solutions, and so forth, make sure that the client feels good about sharing the problem with you and has a better understanding of the problem situation, faith in your skills and resources, hope for resolving the problem, and greater confidence in realizing that hope.

Intervention-Related Practice Principles and Approaches

At the Microlevel. You will find the following principles and approaches helpful.

1. Observe the communication-related formalities (discussed in the preceding section) with Hispanic clients during the intervention phase as well. This will help sustain the positive and trusting relationship that you have established with them.

2. Accept the validity for the clients of their perspective on life's problems, and examine your views on people like your clients and their problems. This will help to remind you that there is not one standard way of being human and that your own cultural perspective on and approach to problems may not be the best.

3. Examine the assumptions of your intervention model, and judge its compatibility with Hispanic values. The traditional Anglo models of psychological counseling reflect assumptions inconsistent with Hispanic values, particularly the values of those who are bicultural and of low acculturation levels. "Among these is the view that it is appropriate and beneficial to discuss personally sensitive issues, and the belief that achieving an intellectual understanding of a problem is likely to reveal a course of action that can rectify it" (Torres, 1998, p. 21). You should, therefore, use caution in using such models.

4. Use cultural sensitivity and creativity when applying most mainstream microlevel approaches with Latino individuals, groups, and families. Fenster (1996) has examined the benefits of group therapy in treating African Americans and Hispanics, and Goodman, Getzel, and Ford (1996) have described an innovative group-work project targeting 16- to 20-year-old African American and Latino young men on probation and at high risk for rearrest. They creatively blended an interactionist mutual aid approach with the cognitive-behavioral approach that reflected the culture of the youth.

5. Realize that most Hispanic clients come for help after exhausting their own personal, larger familial, and ethnic-community resources to deal with the situation. There may be a sense of desperation and urgency about the problem. However, many may view the problem as an inadequacy of their role performance and a personal failure. Universalizing the problem will help in problem disclosure. It is important that you acknowledge the client's efforts to deal with the problem and convey a positive view of those efforts.

6. Be sensitive to the possibility that many problems are the result of external environmental stress and American racism expressed in prejudice and discrimination. "Part of problem identification is uncovering the dynamics of racism, prejudice, and discrimination that may be present in the problems of the multicultural client" (Lum, 1999, p. 39). Race is associated with prejudice and discrimination as well as economic insecurity. Nonwhites in the U.S. society are likely to experience stigma, prejudice, and discrimination, which in turn cause distress. Similarly, they are likely to experience poverty, unemployment, and a sense of insecurity and unsafety. Icard, Longres, and Spencer (1999) explored the place of race in a theory of distress. Their study, involving 918 children, found significant differences on self-reported worry among groups based on racial heritage. Hispanic children reported the highest level of worry. This remained so even when factors such as gender, age, socioeconomic status, and social support were controlled.

7. Use empowerment-oriented approaches that on the one hand emphasize a concrete here-and-now problem focus, and that on the other hand involve the client's natural support system, including the extended family, religious group, folk healers, and social clubs. Empowerment-oriented work calls for interventions at multiple levels—individual, family, group, and community. With her focus on women, Gutierrez (1990) suggested the following techniques for microlevel empowerment: (a) accept the client's definition of the problem, thereby giving the message that the client is capable of identifying and understanding the problem situation; (b) identify and build upon existing strengths, thereby

getting in touch with the client's current sources of functioning and power; (c) engage in a power analysis of the client's situation, thereby understanding the client's conditions of powerlessness and identifying potential sources of power; (d) teach specific skills, such as problem solving, parenting, job seeking, self-defense, assertiveness, and self advocacy; and (e) mobilize resources and advocate for clients with their active participation.

8. Keep in mind that the different family structures and patterns impose different responsibilities on men and women, generate different problems, and require different interventions. With his focus on Puerto Rican men, Torres (1998) observed,

> The symptomatic behavioral reactions of many Puerto Rican men to such personal crises tend to be aggressive rather than depressive, and aimed at protecting personal vulnerability. Drinking, gambling, fighting, and promiscuity are common reported manifestations of attempts to maintain *hombria* (manhood). (p. 20)

Alcoholism and domestic abuse are major social problems among Hispanic American men. These in turn lead to divorce and separations, which are a significant source of the larger percentage of female-headed households among Spanish-origin groups (Taylor, 1994).

9. Recognize the connection between immigration status/acculturation level and the dominance of certain types of problems. In terms of family service needs, Hispanic families are grouped into: (a) newly arrived immigrant families, (b) immigrant-American families, and (c) immigrant-descent families. Families in the first two groups are at greater risk for varied problems.

> Newly arrived immigrant families need information, referral, advocacy, and such concrete services as English language instruction. Due to cultural and language barriers, they seldom seek personal or family therapy. Immigrant-American families are characterized by cultural conflict between foreign-born parents and American-born children. They need help in resolving generational conflicts, communication problems, role clarification, and renegotiation. (Ho, 1987, p. 134)

10. Remember that *familismo* is one of the strongest core values of traditional Hispanic culture. Therefore, family-focused interventions are likely to be more effective than individual-focused interventions.

11. Remember that honor is an important aspect of *familismo* and that protecting and preserving the family's honor is the responsibility of all family members. This creates "a rigid boundary of privacy that guards conflict or suffering within the family from exposure to the outside world" (Inclan & Hernandez, 1992, p. 248). Be creative in using this concept as a means of motivating and energizing Latino clients.

12. Base intervention with Latino men on a thorough understanding of the positive as well as negative dimensions of *machismo* in its historical, sociopolitical, and cultural context. "Reframing the client's concerns about treatment, addressing his strong sense of obligation and responsibility for himself and his family, and appealing to his sense of honor may also be in keeping with his own gender-role expectations" (Torres, 1998, p. 23). You should make the treatment active, structured, time limited, and goal oriented.

13. Acquire good understanding of *espiritismo*. This is especially important in working with Puerto Ricans:

The espirita is a spiritualist, medium, or fortune-teller. She usually gives advice about such things as life, love, and fortune. However, much of her "trade" centers upon psychosomatic problems and illnesses. She can be a key person to consult in the attempt to understand the relationship between the physical and psychological difficulties that the client may be experiencing. (Enos, 1997, pp. 314-315)

14. Use culture-specific interventions "whenever presenting symptoms and idioms of distress signal the presence of culture-specific disorders consistent with traditional health/illness beliefs" (Dana, 1998, p. 198). These interventions often involve mixing the traditional and professional approaches. In a discussion of the treatment of Puerto Rican psychiatric patients in New York, Swerdlow (1992) said that in one program a majority of the patients were also being treated by spiritists, informal home remedies, and community-based religious approaches, such as prayer for Catholics and group ceremonies for Pentecostals.

15. Recognize that undocumented Hispanics have special needs and problems. The fear of being deported complicates their help-seeking behavior. It is wise to remember that "[a]ll noncitizens, even undocumented noncitizens, have rights, however. These include a child's right to schooling, the right to basic medical care, and the right to due process" (Castex, 1994, p. 294). Castex suggested that in order to serve these clients effectively, social workers should (a) become acquainted with the services available to people with various immigrant statuses; (b) emphasize the degree of confidentiality they can offer as well as legal advice about the agency, local, and federal policies; and (c) keep abreast of the current immigration regulations.

At the Mezzolevel. At the mezzolevel, the focus of social work can be on increasing the sensitivity and responsiveness of human service agencies to the needs of Latino Americans, thereby improving their effectiveness. The following principles and approaches will help you as an agency director, program planner, and quality assurance and service utilization manager.

1. Acknowledge that there is resistance on the part of Latino American clients to seeking and taking full advantage of human services. This is particularly important for those agencies for which a large proportion of current or potential clients are Hispanic/Latino.

2. Accept the possibility that the resistance to using services is the client's reaction to the agency's policies, programs, procedures, or personnel. Agency policies often reflect the societal biases and distorted views of different groups of people and their needs. Programs may not be tailored to the problems that they are supposed to deal with. Agency procedures can similarly be a source of discouragement and frustration for clients unfamiliar with the ways of the larger society. Even well-meaning personnel are handicapped by the agency policies, programs, and procedures, because their professionalism can only be expressed within the limits imposed by the agency.

3. Review the appropriateness of the agency policies, programs, procedures, and personnel for effective and efficient services to Latino clients. Seek ideas, opinions, and suggestions from Latino clients, Latino community representatives, or both about the "what" and "how" to improve agency services. This will make the review an effective approach to agency improvement.

4. Ensure that your agency employs Spanish-speaking workers, particularly if it serves a large number of Hispanic clients. Such workers can effectively relate to these clients. "Each language evokes a distinctive cognitive, affective, and behavioral pattern. Disturbed Latino patients manifest more psychopathology when they are interviewed in English than when they are interviewed in Spanish" (Lum, 1996, p. 148). In his study of Puerto Rican elderly, Delgado (1997a) used a community forum approach to data collection. In response to the question, "Why are elders not fully utilizing an extensive array of formal services even though their functional needs indicate that it would be appropriate to do so?" he stated that "[m]any elders had stories to share about miscommunication, lack of trust, and a total lack of understanding concerning cultural values when providers did not speak Spanish or know the culture" (p. 326).

5. Provide for the delivery of culturally competent services if, for whatever reason, the agency cannot employ Spanish-speaking workers. This can be done by allowing agency workers to: (a) learn and master culturally competent practice approaches through a continuing education program and through access to appropriate consultants, and (b) have available to them services of Spanish-speaking translators-interpreters who have been sensitized about the dimensions of psychosocial assessments and the importance of confidentiality.

6. Urge and help your agency to become "culturally sophisticated" (Grant & Gutierrez, 1996). Culturally sophisticated organizations integrate the needs and strengths of the ethnic communities they serve into their mission, staffing, programs, and activities.

7. Familiarize yourself with the philosophy and technology of Continuous Quality Assurance (CQA), which is also known as Total Quality Management. CQA demands that: (a) customers (clients) come first and that the organization should have a formal process to meet all customer needs and expectations, (b) there be organizational commitment to continuous improvement in quality of services, (c) there be an organizational culture that encourages participation by all users of the organization's services, and (d) there be continuous feedback from customers as well as service providers. The concept of customer is much broader in this philosophy and applies both internally and externally. External customers of an organization are clients, families, payers, volunteers, and the community, and all employees are its internal customers (Dhooper, 1997b).

8. Enrich your agency services with the resources of the local Hispanic/Latino community. This can be done by identifying, approaching, cooperating, and coordinating with formal sources of social support in the community. Delgado (1997b) studied the multifaceted role Latina-owned beauty parlors play in Latino communities and found owners of these parlors willing to involve themselves in leadership roles on social agency boards, advisory committees, and task forces. He concludes that "[b]eauty parlors and other small businesses can help distribute public education information (in Spanish), make referrals, perform crisis intervention, help interpret correspondence for non-English-speaking clients, and fulfill other important roles" (p. 450).

9. Take personal responsibility for establishing strong relationships with the Latino community your agency serves. As an administrator or a program director, visit the community periodically

to speak personally with community leaders and other community stakeholders so as to build and maintain *personalismo* (personal relations) and *confianza* (trust) and to demonstrate a "commitment from the top" in giving an ear and voice to the community in relation to program goals and objective. (Castro, Cota & Vega, 1999, p. 161)

10. Show your commitment to culturally competent and effective service. Castro and associates (1999) listed the qualities of the best administrators of health promotion programs for Latino populations. We are using these to recommend the following practice principles for social work agency administrators:

a. Have knowledge of the community and a vision of the agency's purpose and direction for serving that community.

b. Communicate that vision and purpose to the agency staff on a regular basis.

c. Build commitment and morale among the agency staff.

d. Give all the staff appropriate voice regarding agency policies and procedures.

e. Maintain a balance between scientific agendas and cultural competence agendas in the ongoing evolution of the agency programs.

f. Be proactive in anticipating problems and in searching for solutions.

g. Inspire staff and community confidence in their abilities to work for enhancing the welfare of the community.

h. Show strength and integrity in responding forcefully on behalf of the agency and its programs when accosted by political or social opposition.

11. Ensure that the evaluation of the agency's programs includes culturally relevant measures. These should assess both the processes of the program and the program impact in terms of its outcomes.

At the Macrolevel. Macrolevel interventions deal with social, political, economic, and environmental forces that affect the human condition. These are aimed at bringing about improvements in societal institutions through changes in laws, creation of resources, and modification of public opinion. The social, economic, political, and legal institutions must also allow poor Latino Americans to experience the American dream and to make their best contributions to the larger society. Social workers should help Latino groups and communities organize for systemic changes. The need for such intervention is obvious.[8] You will find the following suggestions helpful.

1. Acknowledge that the community can be a source of healing and growth, because it has traditionally been one. "Community is the context in which healthy selves develop. Without community, the social bonds and relationships that give purpose and meaning to life, and friendships that fulfill the need for affiliation and connectedness with others, are not formed" (Brueggemann, 1996, p. 126). Assume that: (a) the community has the capacity to deal with most individually experienced problems; (b) working with community groups is the preferred way of meeting social needs, because it increases the community's overall problem-solving ability while solving the individual's problems (Specht & Courtney, 1994); and (c) social work can enhance the community's problem-solving capacity.

2. Assess your readiness for community work. Brueggemann (1996) has suggested a threefold approach for this assessment: (a) sizing up the community by learning about and

analyzing it; (b) sizing up the problem by learning about, understanding, and defining it; and (c) sizing up yourself by examining your own concerns, ideological beliefs, and personal strengths.

3. Use appropriate strategies for setting the stage for community work. These may include the following strategies:

a. Collect information, both factual and subjective, about the community. Factual information about the community demographics, history, neighborhood associations, cultural groups, religious institutions, human services, and leadership is important. Such information can be obtained from formal official sources. Equally important is the subjective meaning humans attach to people and places, actions and experiences, and situations and problems. This information comes from face-to-face encounters with people. Use both types of information for an appreciation and assessment of the community.

b. Build trust in the community by using both generic and culture-specific approaches. Generic approaches include being visible in the community, hanging out at places where people congregate, and becoming close to key people (Brueggemann, 1996). Culture-specific approaches should be based on the major cultural values of the community. For example, *personalismo* expects that contact with the community members is personalized through face-to-face encounters and socializing, so that they can feel your caring personality.

c. Use planned group discussions for drawing out people's experiences, their ideas about the "what" and "why" of their problems, and their suggestions about "what" should be done about those problems and "how." Value people's participation in discussions, encourage them to speak their mind, and listen carefully. Use your knowledge of the history and context of the community for engaging them (Morales & Reyes, 1998).

d. For organizing meetings, ensure the appropriateness of the location and time, availability of transportation and child care, agenda for discussion, and your communication skills. This may involve going to where people are or tend to congregate. "Language must be appropriate to the group one is working with. This may mean addressing people as Don or Dona, avoiding or explaining professional language and technical terms, and utilizing idiomatic expressions" (Morales & Reyes, 1998, p. 87).

4. Modify the traditional approaches to community organizing in order to address (a) the racial, ethnic, and cultural aspects of the community; (b) the implication of this uniqueness in particular communities; and (c) the empowerment of the community through the process of development of a critical consciousness (Rivera & Erlich, 1995). Rothman (1995) has categorized community intervention approaches into (a) *locality/ community development*, (b) *social planning/policy*, and (c) *social action* models. Locality/ community development emphasizes building community competency and social integration. Social planning emphasizes technical competencies for problem solving, and social action aims at making fundamental changes, including redistribution of power and resources and gaining access to decision making for marginal groups.

The modification of approaches will require borrowing ideas and strategies from these three models. The resulting model is likely to be more community development oriented.

Pantoja and Perry (1998) have defined community development as work through which members of the community accept to work together for: (a) understanding the forces and processes that have made them and kept them in their state of poverty and dependency; (b) mobilizing and organizing their internal strengths represented by political awareness and a plan of action based on information, knowledge, skills, and financial resources; (c) eradicating from individuals and from group culture the mythology that makes them participate in their dependency and powerlessness; and (d) acting in restoring or developing new functions that a community performs for the well-being of its members. They have also described the processes of community development.

5. Acknowledge and address different beliefs among Latinos about their problems. In a discussion of community work with Puerto Ricans, Morales and Reyes (1998) stated, "Some may not view themselves as oppressed, marginalized, or discriminated against. Others may blame themselves for the social, economic, and political problems they face" (p. 76). Address these beliefs and show how private and personal troubles are related to public problems.

6. Look for ways of empowering the community. These are reflected in the following "dos."

a. Do resist the temptation to blame the victims (individuals and groups) for their problems.

b. Do connect personal troubles with public problems.

c. Do foster positive identities by looking for and highlighting pluses in people and situations.

d. Do counter internalized negative stereotypes that the larger society holds of Hispanics.

e. Validate the past struggles of community, and capitalize on those problem-related efforts (Morales & Reyes, 1998).

f. Avoid illusions about people's abilities or dysfunctions, and depend on objective assessment.

7. Use multiple approaches to community work, such as the following approaches:

a. Build coalitions with like-minded groups within the community and outside, because there is strength in numbers and because there are powerful individuals and systems in the community—employers, landlords, politicians, and others—who benefit from the status quo.

b. Neutralize opposition from those who may feel threatened by your presence.

c. Raise consciousness of the people regarding the reality of their situation and their understanding of how their problems are created and fostered by the larger economic and social forces. With their focus on organizing women of color, Gutierrez and Lewis (1998) emphasize the importance of consciousness raising thus:

> By examining the nature of their lives, women can begin to understand the commonality of their experience and its connection to community and social issues. Consciousness raising can be carried out in one of two formats: group discussion or praxis, the integration of action and reflection. (pp. 100-101)

d. Share with people information and knowledge about social problems and societal institutions, and give them skills and values that will be a source of empowerment.

8. Familiarize yourself with the various models of community empowerment, and create a model that best suits your community. Among the models of community empowerment are Paulo Freire's method and the Theology of Liberation model, which have been used in various Latin American countries as well as with Central American refugee communities in several U.S. cities. The emphasis here is on selection and training of low-income refugees who work as refugee rights promoters and advocates. "The promoters provide services to the refugee community, speak in public forums, and monitor and attempt to impact legislation affecting the Central American refugee community at the municipal, state, and national levels" (Cordova, 1998, p. 191). A study by Hardy-Fanta (1991) has challenged the view that Hispanic communities are apathetic and apolitical. Bonilla-Santiago (1989) has described successful legislative work of the Hispanic Women's Task Force in New Jersey.

NOTES

1. Mexican Americans make up 60% of all Latino Americans. They are a much younger group, with 25 years as their median age. This may reflect a higher percentage of immigrants (who tend to be younger) in their population and a higher rate of fertility (resulting in a larger number of children). Their educational level is the lowest, with only 46% graduating from high school. Although 81% of men and 52% of women are in the labor force, their earnings are the lowest of all the Latino groups. The median earnings of Mexican Americans are $13,622 for men and $10,098 for women. They are concentrated in the Southwestern states of California, Texas, Colorado, New Mexico, and Arizona (Ortiz, 1997).

2. Puerto Ricans remain the Latino group with the overall lowest socioeconomic indicators (Acosta-Belen, 1988). The 1990 census found the following. In educational attainment, a little over half (53%) of those 25 years old and over had completed high school, and less than 10% had received a bachelor's or a higher degree. Next to the Dominicans, Puerto Ricans had the largest proportion (37%) of female-headed households. The median family income of these households was $8,912, the lowest of all such Latino households. About 30% of Puerto Rican families were below the poverty level. The distribution of poverty among subgroups of their population was equally bad. Thirty-five percent of women, 22% of children, and about 30% of the elderly were poor (U.S. Department of Commerce, 1993b).

3. Cuban Americans are better off than most other Latino groups in terms of level of educational attainment; median family income; and rates of poverty among families, females, children, and elderly. In 1990, 57% of Cubans 25 and older had high school or higher education, and about 17% had at least a bachelor's degree. These figures are higher than those of Puerto Ricans, Dominicans, Mexicans, and Central Americans, but they are lower than those of South Americans and Spaniards. Similarly, Cubans' median family income of $32,417 is much higher than that of Mexicans, Puerto Ricans, and Dominicans, but lower than that of Spaniards. Despite their economic success, over 11% of Cuban families and 24% of their elderly were living below the poverty level in 1990 (U.S. Department of Commerce, 1993b).

4. The population of the Central and South American Hispanics has also been growing dramatically. Compared with a 19% growth rate in the 1970s, this population grew at 67% between 1980 and 1990. Seventy percent of all Central Americans and 51% of South Americans have come here during this period (U.S. Department of Commerce, 1993b). Although people from every country in Central and South America are represented in this group, the majority are Salvadorans, Guatemalans, Nicaraguans, and Hondurans from Central America and Colombians, Ecuadorians, Peruvians, and Argentineans from South America. In terms of their socioeconomic status, there are significant differences within and among the subgroups of these Latinos. Whereas 77% of Spaniards and 71% of South Americans 25 years old and older are high school graduates, only 46% of Central

Americans and 43% of Dominicans have completed high school. Similarly, 20% of Spaniards and South Americans have at least a bachelor's degree, whereas the corresponding figures for Central Americans and Dominicans are 9% and 8%, respectively. The differences in the family income of these groups are equally significant. The Spaniards' median family income of $36,680 is almost double that of Dominicans, which is $19,726. The rates of poverty among these groups also highlight this intergroup variance. Compared with less than 10% of Spaniard and 12% of South American families, 21% of Central American and over 33% of Dominican families were poor in 1990 (U.S. Department of Commerce, 1993b).

5. After World War II, U.S. foreign policy was aimed at increasing its military security as well as its ideological-symbolic geopolitical capital. One of the programs was the Point Four Program run by the State Department. The international training ground for that program was located in San Juan, Puerto Rico. Therefore, it was necessary to transform Puerto Rico into a symbolic showcase of the American capitalist model of development for the Third World. This was done through a combined approach that included: (a) concealing the island's colonial status by a subtle form of relationship called Commonwealth; (b) including Puerto Rico in the federal programs for health, education, and housing without requiring Puerto Ricans to pay federal taxes; (c) attracting U.S. labor-intensive industries by offering tax exemptions and a cheap wage-labor force; and (d) fostering migration of thousands of Puerto Ricans to the mainland by federal funds for massive recruitment and pressures on the Federal Aviation Administration to set low airfares for transportation between the island and the United States (Grosfoguel, 1997).

6. This may be partly the result of the lack of accommodation of the needs and aspirations of Hispanic/Latino Americans by the Catholic church dominated by the Irish. It is alleged that for more than 100 years until the 1970s, Hispanic Catholics were treated as serfs of the Irish Church.

> The Irish were harsh cultural enforcers, who showed little compassion for or understanding of New Spain's indigenous Catholicism, with its mix of Indian ritual and Aztec architecture, and the touch of voodoo bred in the Caribbean jungles. Nuns insisted on English in the parochial schools the Spanish-speaking children attended. The Church became a foreign scourge, and its legacy was bitter. Intellectuals were alienated, while simpler folk looked elsewhere for the emotional support they had once found in their religion. Pentecostals, Jehovah's Witnesses, Adventists, Mormons, and Baptists moved into the void. They held services in Spanish and encouraged a high emotional content which the Irish-run Church did not offer. (Weyr, 1988, pp. 9-10)

With his focus on the relationship between the Church and the Puerto Rican community in New York, Torres (1995) also concluded that the Catholic Church has fallen short of the community's expectation:

> With no Puerto Rican clergy and a severely limited economic foundation in Puerto Rican areas, the Catholic church in New York City has not been particularly aggressive in the promotion of policies and programs to enhance the community's political strength. (p. 71)

7. Because of other factors, Puerto Ricans, in comparison with Cubans, have lower education, labor force participation and employment, and income, but a higher degree of endogamy and residential segregation as well as a higher percentage of households headed by women (Gurak & Kritz, 1985).

8. In an insightful review of the history of Chicano organizations in the United States, Montiel and Ortego y Gasca (1998) concluded that "[t]he Chicanos of this generation are busy professionalizing their lives, fashioning them on the templates of the dominant culture, and they have apparently lost interest in Chicano politics, particularly the politics of protest" (p. 57), although the social circumstances of barrios and communities have not changed. Puerto Ricans and Latinos from Central American and Caribbean countries have the larger society's social problems multiplied manifold.

4

Understanding and Working
With African Americans

AFRICAN AMERICANS: WHO ARE THEY?

African Americans number approximately 33.5 million and constitute about 13% of the population of the United States (Walker & Wilson, 1997). They are largely urban dwellers. As of 1992, they resided in central cities 2.2 times more often than whites did, with the majority living in the southern part of the United States. On average, African Americans live 6 years less than whites and have an infant mortality rate 2.4 times higher than that of whites. However, during the past 20 years, there has been an improvement in their educational attainment. The proportion of African American youth who have completed high school increased from 27% in 1975 to 36% in 1993. Likewise, the number of those who had attended college rose from 9% to 22% during those years. The percentage of those who completed college between 1975 and 1993 increased even faster than that of whites. Despite these educational gains, however, the unemployment gap between African Americans and whites has grown. Whereas in 1975 African Americans were 1.8 times as likely as whites to be out of work, in 1993 they were 2.2 times as likely to be unemployed as whites. Similarly, although the number of African Americans working in white-collar occupations has increased, the disparity in wage earnings between African American and white workers continues (Daniels, 1998).

On the basis of their history and experiences, African Americans can be divided into three distinct groups: (a) those who were brought here against their will as slaves and have been a part of the American social scene for hundreds of years, (b) those who experienced slavery on various Caribbean Islands and have been coming to the United States on their own over several generations, and (c) those who have come on their own as immigrants from different countries of Africa. We will call these: (a) U.S. African Americans, (b) Caribbean African Americans, and (c) African immigrants. The three groups share similar physical features, trace their common roots to Africa, identify themselves culturally with the continent of Africa to varying degrees, experience the effects of white supremacy and racism, have minority status, and occupy lower socioeconomic levels within the larger society. The first two groups also have in common a history of slavery,[1] despite the difference in the locale of that experience.

A HISTORICAL OVERVIEW OF AFRICAN AMERICANS: COMMONALITY OF EXPERIENCES

Africa the Land of Their Ancestors. In order to justify the exploitation of Africa and Africans by Europe, European historians have depicted Africa as a deep, dark, savage continent so that "[n]ot only America, but also much of the rest of the world, regards Africa as the primal continent: the most backward, the least developed, by almost every modern measure" (Hacker, 1992, p. 33). This is far from the truth about that continent and its people. Africa is a land rich in natural resources such as gold, ivory, bronze, salt, and cotton. One of the world's longest rivers, the Nile, and the one that contains the world's largest volume of water, the Congo River, along with the world's largest desert, the Sahara, are located in Africa. Recent archeological and anthropological evidence lends credence to the theory of Africa as the continent upon which man originated. The literary, mathematical, and architectural contributions of Africans cannot be understated. The creation of the first calendar and the majority of the names of the Greek gods originated in Africa (Asante, 1995). Slaves were not the first Africans to come to America. Five hundred years earlier, Africans had traveled as free people to the Caribbean; to North, Central, and South America; and to lands of the East, such as China and India. The African influence on the Mexican culture, for example, is seen in the Mexican pyramids and in various carved sculptures and statues that carry African physical features. They came from a continent that is four times larger than the United States, is divided into more than 54 countries, and has a total land mass of almost 12 million square miles. They came from among 2,000 distinct ethnic groups and tribes, such as the Yorubas, Mandinkas, Igbos, Fantis, Krus, Tivs, Angolans, and Zulu, representing a broad array of religious beliefs and practices, values, and customs, and they spoke more than 100 dialects (Asante, 1995).

Transatlantic Slave Trade. The cruel system of chattel slavery was established by European countries, first by Portugal, then Spain, followed by Britain and others, for the sole purpose of economic gain. The transatlantic slave trade began in 1515. Forcefully removed from the African continent, primarily from the West, Gold, and Ivory Coasts, Africans were displaced to the Caribbean Islands and to the North and South American continents. Starting in the beginning of the 17th century, America began importing slaves from Africa. Slavery has existed for centuries in many countries and cultures. Under some circumstances individuals became slaves for the purpose of debt repayment or as spoils of war (Asante, 1995). The transatlantic slave trade was distinctly different from other forms of slavery, in terms of the brutality with which it was conducted; the treatment of slaves as personal property; and the numbers of people who were captured as slaves, possibly as high as 50 million. It was done strictly as a profit venture, and its existence was the longest ever recorded in history. Millions died as a result of disease, starvation, revolt activities, infanticide, and suicide during and after the 1- to 3-month-long passage across the Atlantic. One of the major consequences of the slave trade for Africa was the economic and political disruption due to the continent's loss of people, including those who produced goods and services and those who carried out political and governance functions.

Experience of Racism and Race-Related Issues. The history of African Americans is an account of their experience with racism. Racism is a universal system of white supremacy and domination under which the people of color of the world are subject (Cress-Welsing, 1991). *Racism* has been defined as white supremacy, because none of the world's other races has asserted itself to be the superior race and invested political or economic resources to perpetuate oppression of others based on race. Inherent in this philosophy is the belief that a person's successes or failures in life are genetically predetermined. Racism asserts that African Americans are genetically inferior to whites and justifies discriminatory practices against them, practices that deny them equal access to opportunities in socioeconomic and political spheres. Racism is thus a universal behavioral system of which the generating force is power and of which the manifest objectives are the cultural and social stigmatizing and stereotyping of a whole people (Bowser, 1991). Racism continues to be an integral variable in all spheres of life for African Americans (Singleton-Bowie, 1995). Individual and institutional racism remain very strong forces that govern the "norms and mores" of people's daily activity (Longers & Seltzer, 1994). These are manifested in virtually every aspect of the nation's political, economic, and social arenas and have far-reaching consequences.

To be an African American is to be or to be made cognizant of one's racial background at all times and everywhere, regardless of one's social class. "Since Europeans first embarked on explorations, they have been bemused by the 'savages' they encountered in new lands" (Hacker, 1992, p. 26). These backward people, as so described, were in most cases viewed as inferior by the Europeans. Europeans never envisioned that the Africans with whom they came in contact could ever match the achievements of whites. It was assumed that people of African heritage did not have the mental faculties to achieve in education and therefore could never rise to professional levels to become physicians, lawyers, dentists, and academicians. They could be entertainers: "When everything is added up, white America still prefers its black people to be athletes, musicians and comedians" (Hacker, 1992, p. 34). These assumptions were supported and continue to be espoused by social scientists (such as Jensen, Shockley, and Murray; see Hacker, 1992) who have questioned the intelligence of people of African ancestry and postulated theories of African genetic inferiority.

African Americans are often stereotyped and negatively portrayed in the print media. It is assumed that individual African Americans can speak for all members of the race. When history is discussed, they are told that the role played by African Americans was minimal to nil. If they choose to travel across country, it is in their best interest to carefully plan their route and rest stops according to the known or reported level of racial tolerance of the areas in question. They may not be warmly received in the neighborhood where they can afford to and wish to live (Hutchinson, 1996; McIntosh, 1998).

Discrimination against African Americans is evident in such areas as one-way busing, employment, and school and residential segregation. They are subjected to residential segregation irrespective of good financial means and a respectable character. Most residential areas are either majority black or majority white. Once the African American population for a particular area exceeds 8%, "white flight" begins, regardless of the economic and social position of the African Americans (Hacker, 1992). It appears that the presence of African American people produces images of crime, residential deterioration, and poor educational advancement in the minds of many white Americans. Discrimination is not restricted to the U.S. African Americans. Newcomers from the Caribbean Islands or from African countries are not exempt from racism. A commonality among all people of African descent is that they have been compelled to come here, either unwillingly—by the institution of slavery—or willingly—by the poor economic, political, or social conditions of their country. Many African immigrants came to America in hopes of bettering their life situations, with the expectation of going back to share their resources with the less fortunate. For sundry reasons, many were unable to do so. As residents of America, they have all, to a greater or lesser degree, experienced racism and its outgrowths, that is, discrimination and prejudice. Many work in occupations for which they are overqualified and may never partake of the American dream.

The Importance of the African American Church. The African American church has generated and retained a strong religious orientation in its members. Lincoln and Mamiya (1990) define this church as the black-controlled independent denominations that make up the heart of black Christianity. In their quest for both independence from white authority and religious freedom, African Americans began separate denominations and their own institutions of worship. In essence, the African American church became a symbol of freedom from white domination (Wingfield, 1988). The transformation from an agricultural to an industrial economy in part fostered the abolition of slavery in the country, as the need for certain types of black labor changed. The transformation did not, however, bring about a change in white racism and prejudice, as evidenced by the "Jim Crow Laws" and "Black Codes" that were prevalent during and after the period of reconstruction. The black church then served a different yet similar role. It was different in that it now ministered to a people who were in theory free from forced labor, but who were nevertheless subject to racism—discrimination, segregation, and intimidation. Its role was similar to the role played earlier in its response to the community's need for spiritual, emotional, psychological, physical, and moral support. The church became a buffer to those who had migrated from the southern to the northern and western states only to find themselves facing overt discrimination, residential segregation, overcrowding, and unemployment as they competed against European immigrants for scarce resources.

The African American church continues to address not only the religious and spiritual needs of the individual, family, and community, but also their social needs. It serves as a coping and survival mechanism against the effects of racial discrimination and oppression and as a place where African Americans are able to experience unconditional positive regard (Smith, 1985). It serves as a pseudofamily where its members can be nurtured and feel accepted. It is also the hub of their social and political activity and has been responsible for the formation of African American seminaries, colleges and academies, insurance companies, banks, and civil associations including the NAACP and the civil rights movement of the 1960s (Lincoln & Mamiya, 1990; Lum, 1992). It also provides support and space for civic activities, a broad spectrum of social and health services, and facilities for community events (Cnann, 1997). From its initial beginning as a visible institution in 1775, the African American church has grown to a membership of approximately 19 million individuals, representing seven major and a host of minor denominations (Birchett, 1992).

Continuing Need for Empowerment. African Americans, individually and collectively, have been relegated to a position of marginality and powerlessness by virtue of the country's socioeconomic and political infrastructure. They have been systematically denied equal access to resources and have endured the inferior treatment of minority status. This arrangement has had very deleterious psychological, emotional, and physical effects on the black community in terms of stress, stress-related disorders, and mental health problems that emerge as individuals, families, and communities attempt to cope with and often internalize their inferior status.

COMMON CHARACTERISTICS: COMMONALITY
OF CULTURES AND WORLDVIEWS

In order to meet their survival needs, African Americans have modified the models of social institutions of the larger society. This has resulted in an indigenous African American culture marked by distinct forms of family, community, and church. Their families and communities are characterized by strong ties to immediate, extended, and fictive kin and by egalitarian role sharing (Leashore, 1995). The commonalties in values and behaviors that, according to Turner (1991), constitute the Africentric perspective include a belief in a harmonious relationship between man, nature, and God; respect for the elderly; a consanguineal family structure; sharing of resources; antisuicide ideation; and mistrust of the medical community.

Belief in the Relationship Between Man, Nature, and God. A common thread among African people is their philosophical belief in the relationship between man, nature, and God. This relationship is a harmonious one in which God is viewed as being omnipresent, omnipotent, and omniscient and is looked to for assistance in all areas of life (Reese & Ahern, 1999). It is believed that God, all elements of nature, and humans are in a reciprocal relationship and that all are to be respected. The earth, sky, and other natural elements are entertained in a respectful manner, and great care is given to preserving the sanctity of life and all of creation and especially to showing respect for the African elders and ancestors.

Antisuicide Ideology. African Americans have lower suicide rates than whites (Stack & Wasserman, 1995). Among the explanations offered for this fact are (a) racism, (b) marital bonds, and (c) church attendance. Both stress and a survival solidarity are by-products of racism experienced by the African American community (Davis, 1980). Sometimes African Americans lower their expectations and aspirations regarding their occupations, which can "protect persons from the anomie associated with failure in the occupational system" (Swanson & Breed, 1976, p. 119). Stack and Wasserman (1995) found a low prosuicide ideology among African Americans who had spouses. Being attentive to the needs of a spouse decreases an individual's focus on his or her own problems, which may decrease the propensity toward suicide. The African American church has historically condemned suicide. African American clergy define suicide as an unforgivable sin that is not an imaginable solution to life's problems. Instead, clergy encourage African Americans to provide social support to each other in times of difficulty and to focus on an afterlife that will be free of present life struggles. A social audit conducted by the Gallup Organization in 1997 found that 92% of African Americans have an affiliation with a religious institution (Reese & Ahern, 1999). More than half of all African Americans attend church on a regular basis and are likely to encounter antisuicide sentiment there (Lincoln & Mamiya, 1990).

Belief About Death and Dying. Many African Americans believe that death is a means by which the individual is ushered into a better afterlife, namely Heaven. The afterlife is free of sickness, pain, sorrow, discrimination, racism, poverty, and other social injustices. It is a place where they can be recompensed for all of the hardships suffered while living on earth (Cooper-Lewter & Mitchell, 1992). The sick and dying persons receive social support from their family and community. A network is created for providing the needed assistance with activities of daily living, meals, transportation, and so forth. During the final hours of life, the dying person is often surrounded by family and friends, who may utter words of encouragement and consolation. Funeral services are often very different from those in the majority population. For instance, many African Americans do not consider funerals to be somber occasions but view them as "home-going" celebrations. Although there is sadness and grief over the loss of a loved one, the transitional service is often celebrated joyously with the belief that the deceased is in a better place and is free from the struggles of this world.

Respect for the Elderly. The elderly are held in high regard in the African American family and community. This results from (a) the acknowledgment of their having a collective history of lifelong discrimination; (b) the belief that offspring should provide in-home care when the need for assistance arises; and (c) the habit of allowing relatives and nonrelatives to live with them in times of family crises (Harel, McKinney, & Williams, 1990; Logan, Freeman, & McRoy, 1990). Grandparents, uncles, aunts, godparents, and non-blood relatives are also held in high regard. This is evidenced, for instance, by the use of surnames when elders are addressed or referred to by members of the African community. Second only to the church, the grandmother is probably the most important person within the extended family network (Paniagua, 1994). She frequently extends herself as a caretaker of grandchildren for working parents and provides economic assistance and much-needed emotional, social, and spiritual support to the family (Lum, 1986). It is often the grandmother who functions as the primary caretaker within the African American family.

Intrafamilial Roles and Relationships. Both the nuclear family, which includes the parents and children, and the extended family, which includes the parents, children, relatives, friends, and the minister, constitute the African American family (Smith, 1981). Thus, the concept of family in the African American community usually includes both biologically related and nonbiologically related individuals (Paniagua, 1994). The characteristics of this family are strong ties to the immediate, extended, and fictive kin and an egalitarian role sharing (Leashore, 1995).

> The deep sense of kinship has historically been one of the strongest forces in traditional African life. Kinship is the mechanism which regulates social relationships between people in a given community; almost all of the concepts pertaining to and connected with human relationships can be understood and interpreted through the kinship system. (Harvey, 1985, p. 13)

According to Aschenbrenner (1973), kinship bonds are foremost among the cultural values of African American families, with other values including (a) a significant value placed on children, (b) the support of guarding mothers, (c) an accentuation on stern discipline, (d) reverence for elders, (e) strong family bonds, and (f) the aim of spiritual independence. The manner in which these values are expressed in the African American community is often very different from the European community.

Fluidity of male and female roles is another characteristic that sets African American families apart from others. The father is not always the head of the family (Baker, 1988). Sometimes, the mother or grandparent operates as the head. Often fathers will perform tasks such as cooking, cleaning, grooming of children, and performing other household chores that by traditional European standards are usually ascribed to females (Hill, 1997). Additionally, older children often take on the parental role or function as caretakers for younger siblings. The parental role is also assumed by grandparents, aunts, and cousins

(Hill, 1997). African American mothers, usually out of necessity, have always contributed to the economic stability of the family by working outside of the home. It is not uncommon for women to also perform such tasks as home maintenance (e.g., painting and home repairs), yard work, and household budget management. There are different views of this gender role reversal.[2]

African American families have also demonstrated an egalitarian perspective in regards to male and female role performance. An analysis of the National Survey of Black Americans (Hatchett, 1991) revealed that most of the respondents, irrespective of socio-economic position, supported an egalitarian division of labor within the family. Most men and women (88%) strongly supported the idea that there should be no gender differences in the sharing of such tasks as child care and housework. Almost 98% of the respondents agreed that African Americans should spend more time in child rearing, and three fourths of them supported the idea that both men and women should work outside the home and contribute to the support of the family.

Extended Family Ties. When the circumstances of the family of origin so dictate, children are cared for by relatives or non-kin until the situation stabilizes, although it is not at all uncommon for children to be raised from birth through adulthood by extended family members. For instance, the African concept of children being raised by the entire village can be seen guiding the African American practice of informal adoption of children. Informal child adoption services are provided on both short- and long-term bases. In 1990 approximately 1.6 million African American children were being raised on an informal basis by extended family members (U.S. Bureau of Census, 1994). Children are not viewed as being disadvantaged because they are adopted, and adoptive parents rarely treat their biological children and adopted children differently.

Sharing of Resources. Within the African tradition, members are expected to share resources with family and friends. To do otherwise would be disrespectful. For instance, it is not uncommon for family members to borrow goods without repayment from relatives who are merchants. This giving away of their profits sometimes results in those merchants' losing their businesses (Ngwainmbi, 1999). The African value of sharing through communal economic and social support is still embraced and encouraged in many African American communities. It is reinforced through the teaching and practices of the African American church. One of the ways in which the concept of cooperative economics is practiced is through the use of *Susus*. Susus, as traditionally known in Caribbean countries, is a common mechanism for raising capital. "Susu is derived from the Yoroba word 'esusu' which roughly translates to 'pooling the funds and rotating the port'" (Huggins, 1997, p. 32). Jamaicans refer to this concept as "partners." This usually involves five or more extended family members or friends who, on a weekly basis for a specified period of time—usually for 2 to 4 months—pool a certain amount of money that can be used for rotating credit. The money is kept in an accredited financial institution. The total of the weekly contributions can range from $5,000 to $15,000. Each week one member of the collaborative group receives "a hand" or the full amount of the money pooled for that week. The practice continues until all members of the group have received a weekly pool. Susus are often used to secure home mortgages but may be also used for acquiring seed money.

Lack of Trust for Health Care Providers. Many African Americans approach the health care industry with caution and apprehension. Reese and Ahern (1999) found that it is not uncommon for African Americans to be fearful that they will "end up being a guinea pig in one of their experiments" (p. 554). "The Tuskegee Syphilis Study provided validation for common suspicions about the ethical even-handedness in the medical research establishment and in the federal government, in particular, when it comes to Black people" (Ruffins, 1998, p. 31). Between 1932 and 1972, 400 black men were withheld treatment for syphilis by the Macon County, Alabama, public health service. This was done despite the fact that penicillin had been developed as an effective cure for the disease. Of the 400 men involved in the experiment, approximately 107 died as a result of being untreated. Such experiments have generated conspiracy theories. The belief in these theories can have both positive and negative consequences. Such belief can serve to solidify the community and move it toward social action. Members of the African American community are admonished to remember the atrocities that were once experienced and to approach participation in clinical studies with skepticism. Thus, being encouraged to approach participation in research as a conscientious consumer and partaker is empowering. On the other hand, as a consequence of this belief, members of the African American community do not participate in legitimate research studies whose findings can potentially have a positive impact on their overall health. African Americans suffer from high rates of cancer, diabetes, and strokes.

DIVERSITY WITHIN: SUBGROUP AND INTRAGROUP DIFFERENCES AMONG AFRICAN AMERICANS

Within the overall commonality of ancestry, experiences, values, and worldviews, African Americans are a heterogeneous group. There are significant differences among and within their subgroups. Their heterogeneity is reflected in diversity across all spheres of life, including their religion and theology, family functioning, socioeconomic situations, acculturation, and political involvement.

Differences Based on When They Came to the United States. We have divided African Americans into three distinct groups—the U.S. African Americans, the Caribbean African Americans, and African immigrants—based on when they came to this country.

The U.S. African Americans are the descendants of slaves. The first Africans brought to this country as slaves arrived in Jamestown, Virginia, in 1619 under Dutch command. For centuries people of African descent would work as free laborers under the most barbaric conditions. Slavery proliferated throughout the United States as early colonies passed laws that supported the enslavement of African people.[3] They were forced into what Walker and Wilson (1997) refer to as "coercive acculturation," that is, taking on white culture and customs through a process called "seasoning," which involved being forbidden to speak their native tongue. Slaves were thus divorced from all identification with their homeland and disconnected from their African heritage in an effort to render them less threatening. States in the deep South were known to practice the worse forms of enslavement, as reflected in the type of work required of slaves and the kinds of punishments meted out to those who resisted.[4] Although the Emancipation Proclamation was signed by Abraham Lincoln in January 1863, it was not until the end of the Civil War that slavery came to an official end in the United States. Even a century and a half after the Emancipation Proclamation and the subsequent adoption of the Thirteenth Amendment of the U.S. Constitution, making slavery illegal, society at large is reluctant to treat African Americans as equal citizens. African Americans still struggle with many issues that threaten the viability of their community. The 1990 data reveal that 83.7% of African Americans reside in metropolitan areas, with 56.7% located in central cities. Fewer blacks (27%) live in suburbs, as compared to 50% of whites. Approximately 6 million African Americans live in poverty, with the poverty rate for African Americans standing at 33%. Fifty percent of African American youth between the ages of 16 and 19 are unemployed. For every dollar earned by whites, African Americans earn 56 cents, and the median net worth of white households is 10 times that of African Americans. Of African American workers, 70 to 75% are employed in either the service sector or in the area of production (Walker & Wilson, 1997).

The Caribbean African Americans represent those who originate from Cuba, Puerto Rico, the Dominican Republic, Jamaica, Barbados, Trinidad, and Haiti. Their presence in the United States population is partly a result of homeland economics (unemployment), political unrest, aspirations for personal growth, and demographic factors such as over-crowding. They tend to maintain their ties to the Caribbean region through visits to their ancestral homes and through other contacts with their extended familial social networks. This helps them to retain their own culture.

There is a lot of cultural variance among these African Americans depending on the local customs, languages, social status, and economy of the land they come from. Their immigration status—U.S. citizen, legal alien, or illegal alien—also influences the nature of their needs and the expression of their culture. So do factors such as the "sense of calling to return and share in the fate, life quality and needs of their ancestral homes" (Bryce-Laporte, 1972, p. 31) and the state of adaptation to this country of those who choose to make it their permanent home. What also differentiates the various groups of Caribbean people is their history and language as well as how they perceive their racial makeup. The variance in their dialects results from their regional history with colonialism. Haitians have been described as being black, whereas those from Spanish-speaking regions, namely the Cubans, Puerto Ricans, and Dominican Republicans, have been described as being more heterogeneous. Historically, Puerto Rican residents of the United States have been called citizens; Cubans have been referred to as refugees; and those from Haiti, the Dominican Republic, and the British West Indies have been labeled as immigrants. Between 1960 and 1995, 1.6 million Caribbean Africans migrated to and settled in the United States. They represent 7.3% of all black U.S. citizens who are foreign born (Anderson, Barrett, & Bogue, 1997). According to the 1990 census, there are 33,178 Barbadians, 520,151 Dominicans, 225,000 legal and an estimated 88,000 undocumented Haitians, over 2.7 million Puerto Ricans, 100,000 British West Indians, and 113,367 Cubans in the United States (U.S. Department of Commerce, 1997).

Between 1829 and 1970, approximately 1 million Caribbean people entered the United States (Dominguez, 1975). In 1924, national quotas for U.S. immigration were established. The subsequent passage of the 1952 Naturalization and Immigration Act spelled out which foreign nationals were candidates for special consideration. Exempt from national quotas were those whose birthplace was in Canada, Cuba, Haiti, the Canal Zone, the Dominican Republic, or any of the independent countries in South or Central America. In 1965 this Act was made more stringent, and an annual ceiling was placed on the number of people who could immigrate from these countries. Also contained in the 1965 Act was a work requirement such that anyone applying for permanent residence in the United States had to show that he or she was available and qualified to fill the available employment positions. In effect, the labor certification requirement was created to increase selectivity in immigration. Further legislation in 1973 restricted immigration from countries in the

Western Hemisphere to 20,000 per country. Despite these restrictions, there is a sizable population of individuals from Caribbean countries in the United States.

People from Tobago, Trinidad, Jamaica, Guyana, and Barbados constitute those from the British West Indies. They are the largest group of voluntary immigrants of African descent in the United States. With the cessation of U.S. slavery, a small number of individuals from these countries migrated to the United States in the early 19th century. They came in larger numbers after the first quarter of the 20th century, primarily because of problematic economic conditions in their homelands, caused by competition from imported labor, a growing population, seasonal unemployment, and devastating hurricanes that hit the area between 1910 and 1921. The population of the British West Indies is predominantly composed of blacks and mulattoes. These two groups make up 80% of the population. There are significant similarities as well as remarkable differences among African Americans from the Caribbeans.[5] "Caribbean immigrants have largely been ambivalent about identifying with African Americans" (Allen, 1995, p. 124).

Regarding African immigrants, two thirds of all the immigrants from the various countries of Africa have come to the United States since 1980. They are representatives of a continent that has 54 countries and a population of 500 million people, 80% of whom live in poverty (Ngwainmbi, 1999). They also represent a diversity of ethnic groups, whose francophone, anglophone, and lusocophone languages emerged according to the patterns of colonial rule (Gellar, 1986). According to Ngwainmbi (1999), there are approximately 1,000 language groups in Africa. Among African immigrants, there are often more differences than similarities. This is true even of those coming from the same country. Those differences emerge from the diversity of cultures, languages, religions, and traditions. Although we acknowledge the presence of many different groups of African immigrants, we have chosen to focus on four that are most represented in American society.

1. Nigerians. Nigerian Americans come from a country that, according to their country's 1991 census, has a population of over 88.5 million people representing more than 250 different ethnic groups. Although roughly 400 different languages are spoken in Nigeria, the chief ones are Yoruba, Ibo, and Hausa. Although Nigeria had been one of the suppliers of slaves, after emancipation the first documented Nigerian immigrants arrived in the United States in 1926. They came as students for higher education, with the intention of returning home. By 1944, the number of Nigerian students had risen to 44, and further immigration continued, particularly in the 1970s, when Nigeria experienced an oil glut that made it one of the wealthiest African countries. Subsequently, many more students had the financial means for foreign study and travel. According to the latest U.S. Census report, an estimated 91,688 people of Nigerian descent reside in this country. Education is highly valued in the Nigerian culture. Of the Nigerians who come to the United States, half of those aged under 24 years receive bachelor's degrees. Of those who were 25 or older, between 1980 and 1990, approximately 33% earned a master's degree, and slightly under 10% earned doctoral degrees (Sarkodie-Mensah, 1995). Nigerians often come to this country because of the climate, relatives living in this country, or their need to attend American universities and colleges. Nigerians can be found throughout the United States and are concentrated primarily in California, Texas, New York, Maryland, Illinois, New Jersey, and Georgia. Many Nigerian Americans have done very well socioeconomically. They have established themselves as entrepreneurs in the areas of foreign costume trade, travel, transportation, and life and health insurance. Bartholomew Nnaji is among the top three scientists in the world specializing in robotics; Hakeen Olajuwon, a member

of the Houston Rockets, has been credited as being the second-best basketball player in the world; and Tiyilayo Rachel Adedokum became a finalist during the Miss America pageant of 1993.

2. Yoruba. The Yoruba people comprise a sizable number and one of the largest ethnic groups of the Nigerian American immigrant population. They also came to study in the United States, with many choosing to attend historically black colleges and universities such as Morehouse College, Howard University, Lincoln University, and Wilberforce University. Many Yorubians have settled in the major urban areas, that is, New York, Chicago, and Washington, D.C. They are a relatively young population, with over 60% between the ages of 25 and 45 (Brandon, 1997). Most households have an average yearly income of just over $38,000, and roughly 6% have household incomes that exceed $100,000. Many maintain close ties with relatives in Nigeria and often return home. It is not uncommon for them to send financial assistance to their relatives in Nigeria.

3. Ghanaians. Millions of African slaves who were captured by Portuguese, Dutch, French, British, and German slave traders came from Ghana's Gold Coast. Ghana is known worldwide for its gold mines and for its export of cocoa, timber, and the Kente cloth that is so often worn by various Americans. Ghana's history is unique in that it was the first African country to gain independence. Prior to Ghana's independence, there was a small contingent of Ghanaians, perhaps only a few hundred, who immigrated to the United States and settled primarily in New York and Chicago. Unlike Nigerians, they did not come as students. They were angered by what they perceived as their country's slow advancement toward independence. They took jobs in factories, as blue-collar workers, and in the U.S. military. They were followed by several thousand who came to the United States in the 1960s after Ghana gained independence. Further immigration occurred in the 1970s and 1980s as a result of political unrest in Ghana. Represented among this second wave of immigrants were professionals such as doctors, lawyers, and academicians who sought employment opportunities in this country. Most of those who migrated in the 1990s were entrepreneurs and educators. The 1990 census records 20,889 foreign-born Ghanaians as U.S. residents, of whom 15,709 are noncitizens (Vecoli, 1995). These estimates may be undercounted by as much as 10 times. Most reside in urban areas, with approximately 75% living in the state of New York. California, Maryland, Virginia, and Washington, D.C. also have significant populations of Ghanaians. Like Nigerians, Ghanaian immigrants tend to keep close ties with their homeland and relatives and practice many of their traditional religious customs.

4. Ethiopians. Many of the earlier Ethiopians immigrants to the United States came as refugees because of the political unrest and violence in their country occurring under the Armed Forces Coordinating Committee, which governed Ethiopia between 1974 and 1991. Between 1976 and 1994 approximately 33,000 Ethiopian refugees resettled in the United States. Ethiopians constituted about 93% of all African refugees who came to the United States between 1982 and 1991. They settled primarily in Maryland, Virginia, Texas, and Washington, D.C. A 1995 estimate of the number of Ethiopians residing in the United States stood at over 100,000. The majority of Ethiopian Americans (almost 62%) are male. Many of the first refugee immigrants considered their stay in the United States as temporary but relinquished this idea as their country's political situation became worse. Some have been able to establish businesses, but many remain in lower socioeconomic situations.

When they arrive in the United States, most African immigrants experience a shift in their social status. These newcomers—legal and illegal immigrants and refugees—enter a culture with a distinct history of discrimination against people of African ancestry. They are subjected to the same discriminatory practices and prejudicial attitudes that black Americans face. As a result, many of those who are highly educated and would be among the middle class in their country of origin find themselves working in blue-collar and service positions. For the first time, they experience being members of a minority group and have problems locating employment commensurate with their educational and occupational abilities. They face discrimination not only from the majority white population but also from African Americans (Ross-Sheriff, 1995). Thus they suffer from "double invisibility" (Bryce-Laporte, 1972).

Differences Based on Religion. Most U.S. African Americans belong to the major African American Christian denominations; some African Americans also practice Catholicism, Judaism, and other religions. Theological differences sometimes create philosophical divisions regarding a national black agenda. Some denominations place more emphasis upon successfully making it to the next world. This focus has tended to de-emphasize such things as educational advancement, the development and retention of a healthy self-esteem, cooperative economics, and other areas necessary for people to live successful and productive lives in the present world. Other denominations, such as the First African Methodist Episcopalians, have historically placed great emphasis on educational achievement, cooperative economics, and educational ventures as means for socioeconomic mobility. There is no consensus among religious denominations, both major and minor, regarding a social, political, and economic national African American agenda for addressing problems of the African American community and the means by which this agenda can be achieved. Hence, African Americans do not all share the same religious views.

Among African Americans of Caribbean origin, Cubans come from the country that is the least religious (Skabelund, 1995). Although Catholicism is the most widely practiced religion among Cubans, many combine Catholicism with African religious practices, resulting in beliefs known as *Santeria*. Cubans are also Methodists, Baptists, Presbyterians, and Spiritualists. Spiritualists believe that people can communicate with the dead. A small number of Cubans also practice witchcraft, which they call *brujeria*. Jamaicans by and large practice Christianity. Although the Anglican Church is the official national church of Jamaica, many Jamaicans are Roman Catholics, and others belong to other Protestant denominations. A large number of Puerto Ricans are Roman Catholics, and Protestant and other Christian denominations are represented among the American Puerto Rican population as well.

Among African immigrants, almost half of Ethiopian immigrants belong to the Ethiopian Orthodox Christian Church. Many others practice Islam. Others follow traditional African religions such as animism. Animism is the belief that all things are reverent and are to be respected. Most Ghanaians adhere to traditional African beliefs and practices irrespective of what other religious affiliations they may have. Ghanaians traditionally believe in a Supreme Being who is the creator of all things. It is believed that the Supreme Being has bestowed different degrees of power upon both living and inanimate things. They use intermediaries—which can be inanimate or animate objects—and the spirits of their ancestors to communicate with their Supreme Being. It is believed that to attempt to do so on one's own would show disrespect. Half of the Nigerian population is Muslim, and approximately 40% is Christian. The remainder practice traditional African beliefs, although many Muslim and Christian Nigerians also incorporate traditional African beliefs into their worship practices. These religious differences are reflected in Nigerian Americans as well. It should also be noted that there are members within all of these groups who practice no religion at all, and some are atheist.

Differences Reflected in Ceremonial and Holiday Observances. African Americans differ in their levels of exposure to and embracing of the majority American holidays. Some African American, Caribbean, and African families celebrate Kwanzaa along with or instead of the traditional Christian celebration, and others do not. Kwanzaa is a spiritual holiday that was founded on December 26, 1966, by Dr. Maulana Ron Karenga, a political and cultural scientist. Kwanzaa is observed annually between December 26 and January 1. Dr. Karenga began Kwanzaa as a way of unifying the diversity of ideas and strategies to help African Americans in their struggle for social changes in the American society during the civil rights era of the 1960s. Kwanzaa was to be a mechanism for addressing three conditions affecting the African American community. The first was the economic exploitation of the African American community during the Thanksgiving and Christmas holiday season. The second was the absence of an African American national holiday. The third was the need of people of African heritage to reassess, reclaim, recommit, remember, resurrect, and rejuvenate many of the principles used by their ancestors. These principles had enabled them to endure slavery, racism, and oppression in America. Collectively, these principles are called Nguzo Saba and are designed to be a way of life that emphasizes the unity of the African family and community. The seven principles of Kwanzaa are *umoja* (unity), *kujichagulia* (self-determination), *ujima* (collective work and responsibility), *ujamaa* (cooperative economics), *nia* (purpose), *kuumba* (creativity), and *imani* (faith). Kwanzaa is not a religious celebration, as some believe. It is designed to help African Americans link their history to their present situations and circumstances and to help them address issues that are germane for their future.

Although Kwanzaa is celebrated by over 13 million people worldwide, not all people of African ancestry embrace it. Some people incorrectly assume it to be a religious holiday, others mistakenly believe it to be a substitute for Christmas, others do not celebrate it as a means of protesting its commercialization by capitalists, and still others have no objection to it but are simply not interested in observing it.

As with Kwanzaa, there are diverse holidays that are celebrated by different ethnic groups within the African American community. We will name a few. Cubans observe Liberation Day on January 1, which commemorates the 1958-1959 revolution; the anniversary of the attack on Moncada Garrison in Santiago de Cuba in 1953; and the beginning of the War of Independence from Spain, which is celebrated on October 10. Jamaicans recognize National Heroes Day on the third Monday in October and Boxing Day (derived from the British custom of giving small gifts in boxes to service workers and tradesmen) on December 26. Most West Indian Americans who formerly belonged to the Church of England changed their membership to the Protestant Episcopal Church once they arrived in the United States. However, they have continued the practice of giving alms to the needy during the West Indian Harvest Festival, at which time fresh produce is distributed to the less fortunate through the church. Puerto Ricans mark the end of the Christmas season by giving gifts to young children during the Day of the Three Kings on January 6. They also note the abolition of slavery on March 22, the discovery of Puerto Rico Day on November 19, and their Constitution Day on July 25. Ghanaians celebrate their country's independence day on March 6, and Nigerians observe Christian as well as Muslim holidays, such as Idul Fitr, which is a 3-day feast that occurs at the end of Ramadan. Ramadan is a month-long observance during which time participating Muslims abstain from food and water from dawn to dusk. During the evenings, families have dinner together.

Thus, there are numerous differences among African American ethnic groups in relation to their holiday and religious observances. Although many participate in various traditional religious and American holidays, such as Easter, Christmas, Independence Day, and New Year, they may also have their own celebrations that are particular to the countries they came from.

Differences Based on Socioeconomic Status. The U.S. African Americans differ from Caribbean African Americans and African immigrants socioeconomically. Upper-middle-class and wealthy African Americans are the offspring of former slaves who were accorded certain privileges by virtue of the type of work they were assigned and their physical characteristics (Graham, 1999). They are the wealthiest families in the African American community, although being wealthy does not guarantee inclusion within this group. Those who belong to this group have a history of family wealth and social relations that others with newly acquired wealth, such as athletes and lottery winners, do not have.

After being brought to this country as slaves, Africans were divided into those who were given the more desirable work assignments in the home of the plantation owner and those who worked outside as laborers. This created a caste system among the slaves, who in time began to believe that those who worked in the master's home were superior to those who worked in the fields. Moreover, as a result of established clandestine and forced sexual relations with female house slaves, offspring were born to the plantation owners. "While none of these illegitimate offspring had any more rights than the unmixed African slaves, they became a part of a growing phenomenon of lighter-complexioned house slaves who separated themselves even further from the field blacks" (Graham, 1999, p. 7). They were sometimes given preferential treatment, taught to read and write, and introduced to the customs and traditions of the white middle class. This caste system was further perpetuated after the passage of the 1780 Act for the Gradual Abolition of Slavery, which over the next 50 years allowed some African Americans to be freed. Many of the free blacks formed families and were allowed to work for wages and to buy property. "The nucleus of the black elite was formed around these families" (Graham, 1999, p. 8). Following the Civil War, African Americans began to attend colleges that were established by religious and abolitionist groups. Many of these individuals became a part of the Black upper-middle class, held political offices, and became successful professionals and entrepreneurs. Many of the offspring of the slaves who worked as laborers and field hands have remained members of the working class. They are now represented among the blue- and white-collar workers and middle-level managers. They are among those African Americans whose median family income is $21,548 but that ranges as high as $74,999 per year (Smith & Johns, 1995). The poor within the African American community have earnings at or below the poverty level.

The Africans who came to the United States from the British West Indies assumed major leadership roles in African American political and intellectual arenas. Their sense of class distinction was very developed, and they willingly became very involved in leftist politics. Many of them were among their country's middle-class population who came to the United States to seek advancement. They tended to be more represented in the professional, white-collar, and skilled employment sectors than were U.S. African Americans. They were often given jobs in areas that were denied to U.S. African Americans. On the other hand, they found racism and discrimination much worse in the United States than in the West Indies. They discovered that they could raise their socio-economic status through entrepreneurial ventures, so they took advantage of the retail and real estate opportunities in the urban areas and opened businesses. It is commonly believed that Caribbean immigrants earn more than native-born African Americans and that African immigrants are intellectually superior to both African Americans and Caribbean immigrants and have higher earnings than the other two groups (Dodoo, 1997). However, according to census data, although African immigrants are depicted as "one of, if not, the most highly educated of all immigrant groups" (Dodoo, 1997, p. 528), their earnings do not reflect this educational status. Using 1990 5% Public Use Microsamples, 14,347 African American men, 7,346 Caribbean immigrant men, and 1,973 African immigrants between the ages of 25 and 64 who were employed during 1989 were studied. It was found that 58% of African immigrants had college degrees (earned both in the United States and abroad), compared to 13% of the U.S. African Americans and 14.5% of Caribbean men; that the earnings of African immigrants and African American men are roughly equal; and that Caribbean immigrants earned roughly 8% more than the other two groups.

Differences Based on Sociopolitical Experiences. African Americans and African immigrants differ in their experiences in the political arena. As a result of the deculturalization that the U.S. African Americans suffered during slavery, they lost much of their African culture, traditions, and languages and have constantly struggled to retrieve and revive what was lost. African immigrants have not had this experience. Although the continent of Africa experienced colonization, Africans were able to retain their traditions and cultures. For instance, many Africans are multilingual and can speak their national language, various ethnic dialects, and other foreign languages, whereas most African Americans can speak only English.

In most African countries, the indigenous people are in ruling and leadership positions. They are by and large the policymakers and decision makers for their countries. Upon migration to the United States, they cease to be politically active. In 1994, 37% of all African Americans participated in the electoral process, down 2 percentage points from 1990 (Jacobs, Siegal, & Quiram, 1996). Low voter turnout may be a function of people's comfort with the way things are or a reflection of their cynicism about their ability to make changes in a system that they perceive as flawed. Nevertheless, African Americans have made advances in the number of elected offices held since the civil rights period. For instance, whereas in 1974, 964 African Americans held elected public offices in six states that had prior histories of severe discrimination against them, that figure had doubled by 1979. Nationally, African American elected officials rose from 82 in 1951 to 3,503 in 1975 (Kook, 1998). African Americans occupy positions as Supreme Court judges, mayors, senators, and congressmen and congresswomen.

Differences Based on Age. African American men represent 6.7% and women represent 9.6% of the elderly (those aged 65 and older; Daniels, 1998). They are different not only from the general population of the elderly but also from other African Americans in their history and social experiences. Many of them are the grandchildren and great-grandchildren of slaves. They were born before the Great Depression and have an intimate knowledge of racism, segregation, and discrimination. They had to develop a repertoire of survival skills to live in an inhospitable social climate. They developed their own methods for meeting their material, emotional, spiritual, and psychological needs. These included informal networks and formal social services that resembled mainstream services. For example, jitney service, an informal transportation arrangement, was developed in response to not being privileged to ride in taxicabs prior to civil rights legislation. During the presidency of Ronald Reagan, many social service programs were cut or reduced. Many of the programs affected were service programs for the elderly. Subsequently, many African American elderly looked to family, other relatives, and friends for support. They also relied on many of the self-help measures developed during historical periods of extreme hardship (Barker, Morrow, & Mitteness, 1998). Therefore, these elderly are different from those in younger generations in their past experiences and in their present responses to life's demands.

Differences Based on Sexual Orientation. The exploration of homosexuality among racial-ethnic minorities has only recently become an area of research, and the African American homosexual population has been given scant attention. In the past, even in large-scale studies, participation by members of the African American gay and lesbian community was low. For example, only 39 of the 1,930 gay men and 15 of the 1,549 lesbians studied by Blumstein and Schwartz (1983) were African American. Peplau, Cochran, and Mays (1997) conducted the first national large-scale empirically based study of relationships between 700 same-sex couples in the African American population. They studied a subset of 325 men and 398 women to determine the nature of gay and lesbian African American relationships. They found that female participants on average had their first same-sex experience at age 20. Eighty-five percent of the female participants identified themselves as lesbians, and 12% identified themselves as bisexual. All of the women indicated that they were in a committed relationship with another woman. Three hundred twenty-five of the African American male participants indicated that they were in a serious relationship with a man. The average age at which they first had sex with another man was 15. Most of the men indicated that they were gay or bisexual—84.6% and 10%, respectively. Partners were generally similar to each other in age, education, and employment, although interracial relationships were not uncommon. Thirty percent of the women and 42% of the men were in relationships with partners who were not African American. These findings are similar to studies on heterosexual relationships among African Americans, which report that African American men have higher rates of interracial relationships than African American women do (B. Greene, 1994). Nationally, 3% of African American women report having had non-African American sexual partners, and 18% of African American men report these experiences. African American gay men and lesbians' interracial relationships may be a function of their environment and the small number of same-race partners from which African American homosexuals have to choose. Most African Americans are urban dwellers. The urban African American homosexual community may be more tolerant in their views about interracial dating than the general public.

African American gay men and lesbians view inner qualities as attributes that they most consider when selecting a mate. Both genders place greater emphasis on a potential partner's intelligence, personality, and spirituality than on their material possessions. Eldridge and Gilbert (1990) report that gay men and lesbian couples usually enjoy high levels of love within their relationships and report being very happy. Peplau et al. (1997) reported similar findings. Although both genders of homosexual African Americans reported satisfaction with their relationships, lesbians reported more often that they were in love with their partners, and their relationships had greater closeness. The satisfaction with their relationships may have been a function of the degree of monogamy that existed within the relationship. Half of all the respondents indicated that their relationships did not include having sex with outside partners. Blumstein and Schwartz (1983) found that among white couples, only 36% of gay males thought that monogamy was an important element in their relationships. Not only do many gay men and lesbian women enjoy satisfying partnered relationships, they also tend to be very involved with their families of origin (Clarke, 1983). Although the African American community is generally homophobic, it is also at times very welcoming of the homosexual, as is the case in many family circles. Family ties tend to be very strong within the African American community. Rarely do families reject the person, but rather it is the behavior that they may abhor.

MAJOR NEEDS AND PROBLEMS
OF AFRICAN AMERICAN GROUPS

Needs Related to Poor Socioeconomic Status. Life for most African Americans can be viewed as a series of negative experiences. Approximately 31% of African American individuals and 29% of African American families are in poverty (Paniagua, 1994). One of the chief factors contributing to poverty is unemployment. Unemployment among African Americans stands at 10.5% (U.S. Department of Commerce, 1997). Between 1979 and 1982, the nature and number of jobs in both the public and private sectors were significantly affected as the United States suffered a major shift in the structure of employment opportunities. During the 1980s, the American industrial sector shifted from producing goods to trade and private services. The trade sector was one of slow growth, and African Americans were underrepresented in the service sector (Larson, 1988). Subsequently, this situation contributed to unemployment. Fifty percent of African American youth between the ages of 16 and 19 are unemployed. As mentioned previously, for every dollar earned by whites, African Americans earn 56 cents, and the median net worth of white households is 10 times that of African Americans. Furthermore, the majority of African Americans (70 to 75%) have been employed in either the service sector or in the area of production (Walker & Wilson, 1997). This situation worsened because of (a) the decrease in retail opportunities in central cities and the increase in such opportunities in suburbia, which is mostly populated by whites; and (b) the decline of old industries and the development of new "high-tech" industries. African Americans could not now find employment in the new industries, because they often lacked the skills for high-tech jobs. Unemployment further diminishes the African American men's ability as potential heads of households to provide for themselves and their families. Contributing to the decrease in marriage rates among African Americans and the increase in the female-headed family are the high unemployment rate and low earnings of young black males who have no post-secondary schooling (Horton, Thomas, & Herring, 1995).

Dropping out of high school continues to be a problem for African American youth. In 1995, their high school drop-out rate was 14.4% (U.S. Department of Commerce, 1997). The youth who drop out of school suffer both short-term and long-term consequences. Failing to complete their high school education places them at a disadvantage in providing for the basic essentials of daily living. In both the short and long term, their potential earning power will be decreased, and they will not have the credentials necessary for educational and economic advancement and competition in the job market (Gibbs, 1988).

Of all black families, 54% are headed by females (Tucker & Mitchell-Kernan, 1995). The effects of growing up without a father in the home may be far-reaching. A strong, stable family is most apt to meet the needs of African American youth for healthy development, such as physical and emotional nurturance, discipline, and spiritual growth. Although having a stable home does not ensure a positive environment, not having a stable home environment appears more likely to place African American youth at a high risk of exposure to the kinds of family instability and turmoil associated with deprivation (Hare, 1988).

For all Americans aged 12 and above, approximately 75 million report having used an illegal drug in their lifetime (Burston, Jones, & Saunders, 1995). Of those, approximately 10% are African American, but African Americans make up approximately 36% of U.S. citizens who are drug-dependent (Burston et al., 1995). As the dependency upon drugs progresses, individuals become more involved in the drug subculture and may isolate themselves from their families. This isolation may in turn cause family tension. Gross preoccupation with using drugs causes them to lose motivation for work and other types of activities. They may lose interest in physical appearance and may have a tendency toward suicidal ideation as their perception of self-worth and self-esteem changes.

Needs Resulting From the Societal Images of African Americans. African Americans suffer from negative imaging and labeling. The African American male continues to be viewed and related to negatively. He has been labeled as irresponsible toward his family obligations, lazy, nefarious, and prone to crime. Any demonstration of autonomous or aggressive behavior is feared, and he is still expected to be unassertive and unassuming. Further, feelings of despair may be brought on or exacerbated by the negative images that the African American male sees of himself. Historically, African American males have been imaged as felony-prone, violent, and unintelligent beings. According to Hutchinson (1996), this image has been perpetuated by the media and Hollywood. These negative descriptors "became a part of the psychological tools that were used to support European enslavement of Africans and are currently and prevalently used in the oppression of black people" (Moore, 1998, p. 41). Across socioeconomic, political, and class boundaries, negative descriptors of African American men prevail and continue to have an adverse effect upon their psychological well-being.

African American women are also affected by negative imaging. Like African American men, they are often devalued, stereotyped, and assigned negative roles. One such role, as identified by Abdullah (1998), is that of "mammy." Abdullah postulates that African American women have historically taken on this role as a coping strategy. The internalization of this image allowed them to survive the perils of slavery, physical harm, and other adverse situations and to prevent harm of their loved ones and families. They "were viewed as being non-threatening, nurturing, selfless people who demonstrated love and devotion to their oppressors and the oppressors' families rather than to self and family" (Abdullah, 1998, p. 197). They were expected to be a nurturer to others at the expense of their own and their family's needs and desires. This subservient role is sometimes seen in corporate America among African American women who hold clerical, managerial, business, and professional positions. It is asserted that some African American women still carry and execute the role of tough, nurturing, maternal figures. Even in employment situations where the environment is emotionally, physically, and psychologically undesirable, some African American women have appeared to

> internalize white racism, accept oppression, aspire to and emulate white standards of beauty, call the company her company, and invest her total energies in the profits of the company, only to return home exhausted with no quality time for family. (Abdullah, 1998, p. 199)

This phenomenon can be viewed as a mental health issue, in that "the current use of this coping strategy is related to sub-optimal functioning, thus depriving the woman of African descent of the true nature of her oneness with God, world view, cultural identification, and self-appreciation" (Abdullah, 1998, p. 196).

Needs of African American Women. The physical, psychological, and emotional strength often attributed to African American women may in part be a result of the internal and external resources they have developed as a result of being faced with numerous challenges. They have demonstrated their resiliency in dealing with a variety of issues and obstacles, irrespective of their socioeconomic status. Health issues have been an ongoing concern for African American women. African American women die at disproportionately higher rates from such causes as diabetes, cancer, cardiovascular diseases, and homicide than other women do. Other problems with which they struggle are domestic violence, substance abuse, addiction, HIV and AIDS, living in poor housing, limited economic mobility, and negative imaging.

Violent physical abuse and sexual abuse also affect large numbers of African American women. At any age, they are at much greater risk for rape and sexual abuse than any other group of women (White, 1990). African American girls between the ages of 9 and 12 experience a greater amount of sexual abuse and incest than do their white counterparts. Fullilove et al. (1993) and McCollum and Trepper (1995) have reported an association between early-life traumatic events and substance abuse in women. Eliason and Skinstad (1995) found an association between childhood sexual abuse and substance abuse. These experiences produce feelings of inadequacy, poor self-esteem, and helplessness.

Substance abuse remains a major issue affecting the health of African American women. Thirty-eight percent of all women who are heavy drinkers are African American. The use of crack cocaine is also more common among African American women than any other group of women (Davis, 1997). Davis (1997) asserts that racism and sexism, along with early-life traumatic events, may be precursors to substance abuse among this group. Traumatic events such as rape, incest, abuse, and other events may lead to the abuse of substances as self-anesthetizing and self-medicating mechanisms to decrease the emotional and psychological pain of the early-life stressful experiences.

Increasingly more African American women are contracting HIV and AIDS. In 1993 the Center for Disease Control reported that whereas adult women represented 16% of all AIDS cases, African American women represented 54% of cases among adult women. This represented a 151% increase from the figure reported in 1992. AIDS is now the second leading cause of death among African American women between the ages of 25 and 44 years (Warren, 1993). African American women, who are more likely to be infected with HIV and subsequently die from AIDS, are exposed to the virus by their own or their male partner's use of drugs. They, like all women, also have a shorter survival time than men after being diagnosed with AIDS. Generally by the time they do present themselves for treatment, they are in more advanced stages of the disease and have more symptoms (Raveis & Siegel, 1998).

HIV and AIDS are not the only areas in which African American women experience delayed treatment. Although the incidence of breast cancer is lower among African American than white women, they have a higher mortality rate because of late diagnosis. Many African American women are in more advanced stages of breast cancer when they seek treatment. Cultural beliefs and practices, such as use of home remedies and over-the-counter medicines, coupled with socioeconomic variables, are responsible for late diagnosis.

Needs of African American Men. The African American male is in a precarious position. Some people believe that conscious efforts are being made to extinguish him from existence. Theories of black male genocide abound, and issues regarding his survival have become so crucial that some call him an "endangered species" (Bowser, 1991). Whereas some African American men have resiliently overcome obstacles and roadblocks to their life and have risen to world renown in such areas as medicine, the arts, politics, religion, and business (Harel et al., 1990), most are marginalized. Marginalization is a problem linked to the underclass segment of American society. In this group are individuals who: (a) are chronically unemployed or do not have the skills necessary for labor market participation, (b) have ceased looking for employment, (c) participate in criminal behavior, and (d) have families who are impoverished and or are dependent on public welfare (Tucker & Mitchell-Kernan, 1995). The decline in the numbers of African American men from the productive spheres of American life is also a function of their high rates of mortality and the increased rates at which they are being institutionalized. Their rate of mortality is 795 per 100,000. As of 1990, they represented 47% of all those incarcerated throughout the nation. This figure represents a 6% increase since 1970. In 1995, 33% of African American men between the ages of 20 and 29 were under the supervision of the criminal justice system (Evans, 1998). African American men also represent approximately 29% of those institutionalized in mental hospitals. These rates of mortality, incarceration, and institutionalization in mental facilities are significant, because African Americans compose only 12% of the American population (Tucker & Mitchell-Kernan, 1995).

Marginalization leads to self-destructive behavior among African American men (Tucker & Mitchell-Kernan, 1995). Criminal activity may be one manifestation of self-destructive behavior. An example of this can be seen in the area of substance abuse and drug trafficking among African American males. From an economic perspective, drug trafficking is a very profitable venture. An individual can make as much as $1,200 or more per day by selling drugs. With the dismal reality of their employment situation, too often the minimum wage employment they may be offered cannot provide them a lifestyle above a level of subsistence. Thus, many become involved in illegal drug distribution for purely economic reasons. The African American male has a long history of suffering brutality at the hands of law enforcement officers. This is not a thing of the past:

> For the years 1920-1932, 54 percent of the 479 blacks killed by white persons in the South were slain by white police officers. Seventy five percent of the civilians killed by police in seven cities between 1973-74 were black males. (King, 1997, p. 83)

The incidents of police brutality continue to be as blatant and undeniable as the videotaped attack on Rodney King and as subtle as the phenomenon recently named "Driving While Black" (DWB). Recently the media has given attention to DWB, a situation resulting from racial profiling. In the absence of national figures, estimates compiled in relation to lawsuits filed by African American motorists in the states of Maryland and New Jersey show that African Americans are stopped and searched more frequently than white motorists. For instance, in Maryland over 75% of all drivers who were stopped on a section of Interstate 95 were African American, although African Americans represent only 17% of those who drive on that section of the highway. Similar incidents have occurred in Volusia County, Florida, where African Americans represented 70% of motorists stopped during a drug interdiction sting on Interstate 95, even though they were only 5% of the travelers on that highway. African Americans are only 13% of the people who use drugs in that county (Merida, 1999).

Reports of African American male motorists' being stopped by police simply because they fit a criminal or drug profile abound throughout the nation. Some of the reasons for DWB given by law enforcement agents are: because of the type of car blacks are driving; because they are seen driving in white neighborhoods; or because of minor motor vehicle incidents, such as failing to put on turn signals. Some African American men view these explanations as excuses used by police to investigate them. This form of psychological intimidation and harassment transcends class lines and has been reported by members of Congress, actors, prominent sports figures, lawyers, police officers, and members of the business community and their families. This unfair treatment often further polarizes African Americans and law enforcement agencies. A more serious consequence is that African American men are placed in danger of being seriously injured or killed if a mis-understanding should occur between law enforcement officials and them while they are being investigated.

The homicide rate for African American males has been steadily increasing since the 1950s. By 1980, the homicide rate for African American youth stood at 66 per 100,000, as compared to 10.4 per 100,000 for white males. African American teenagers have a homi-cide rate that is three to five times higher than that of their white counterparts (King, 1997). The likelihood that young African American males will be robbed or suffer aggravated assault is also greater than that of white teenagers. Eighty percent of the violent crimes committed against African Americans 12 to 19 years old are committed by African American teenagers, and in 90% of these cases the victim is male. Several explanations of this phenomenon have been presented.[6]

Needs of the Elderly. Although African American elderly are living longer, they are more likely to be infirm, to die earlier, to have chronic diseases at earlier ages, and to be more physically limited in these illnesses (Harel et al., 1990). As a result, as they age, they are not likely to be employed. This may have a direct bearing on their quality of life and financial standing. The poverty rate for elderly African Americans was over 2.5 times greater than that for whites, 25.4% and 9%, respectively. Their health status may be fur-ther compromised by poor insurance coverage. In 1995, according to the National Center for Health Statistics, 31% of African American elderly had Medicare only, and only 22% of African American elderly were covered by both Medicare and Medicaid (Begun, Jacobs, & Quiram, 1998). They are "a product of an underclass citizenship" (Begun et al., 1998, p. 36.) Many have not had the opportunity to participate in the decision and policy making that has a direct impact on their day-to-day lives. For a good portion of their lives they have experienced restrictions on social and economic mobility. The majority of them have not had significant input in the social structuring of their circumstances. As a result, they often have a limited impact upon their environment (Begun et al., 1998).

Needs of African Refugees. In 1993 there were approximately 5,698,450 African refugees throughout the world, of whom 2.25 million migrated to the United States (H. Green, 1994; Kamya, 1997). The experience of being a refugee is both alarming and unsought. Gavagan and Brodyaga (1998) have identified five transitional phases of the refugee experience. The first is the *crisis phase*, during which the individual, family, and community merge to pool resources and develop a plan in response to the crisis. The *migration phase* is the period in which people flee from their homes. Once situated in their new place of residence, they enter the *overcompensation phase*, "where they mobilize all their energies to enable them to live in a strange country. A *honeymoon phase* ensues, in which the refugees orient themselves to life's new challenges, and finally there may be a *resolution of personal problems* and an interval of intergenerational conflict. African refugees have special physical and psychological needs. Before entering the United States, they were placed in camps in countries bordering their lands of origin. While in these camps, they experienced a breakdown of their family structure as well as poor sanitation and nutrition, which often lead to a host of medical problems (Kang, Kahler, & Tesar, 1998). They may also have infectious diseases that are autochthonous to their country of origin. These conditions include various types of parasitic infections, malaria, and tuberculosis. Many refugees have been the victims of beating, torture, rape, and sexual abuse. As a result of family displacement and disintegration and as a result of often being witness to the torture, death, or both of family and community members, these refugees suffer from a number of mental health problems such as anxiety, posttraumatic stress disorder, and depression. They also have mental health problems related to poor self-esteem, which may be exacerbated for men by their inability to provide for their families as a result of their loss of traditional occupations (H. Green, 1994).

Women make up the majority of the adult African refugee population. They share many of the same traumatic experiences as men. Their experiences may be compounded by "gender-specific vulnerabilities such as pregnancy, childbirth, care of children, sexual violence and prostitution" (H. Green, 1994, p. 175). In the 26 African countries where female genital mutilation is practiced, 99% of the females are circumcised. Genital mutilation has been documented as causing a number of problems for women during labor and delivery (Lightfoot-Klein & Shaw, 1990). Additionally, they have many social issues. Many have come from countries where women assume subservient roles and have limited opportunities for redress and advancement. Spousal abuse may have been a common practice in their homeland. They may be at risk for abuse by their husbands, who are under stress because they cannot find employment and who may be partaking of the freedom of alcohol use within this country (Kang et al., 1998).

African refugee children experience the same trauma as adults. They often have poor physical health, dental problems, and poor growth and development. Many have themselves been the victims of torture. Others have been witness to the torture or death of their parents and to random acts of violence, or they may have been cared for by parents who, as a result of their own traumatic experience, were unable to parent properly. Approximately 50% of refugee children have been found to have serious psychiatric problems or conditions (Hodes, 1998), including posttraumatic stress disorder, depression, fear of separation, and somatic disorders. Additional stress is placed on these children as they adapt to a new culture, language, and school. Thus, African refugees face a myriad of challenges and have a wide range of physical and psychosocial needs. Their needs are compounded by the racism and discrimination that they face once they enter this country. For many, racial discrimination is a new experience because Africans dominated the economic, social, and political spheres in many of their countries of origin.

Needs of Sexual Minorities. African American homosexuals are double minorities. They are a minority by race and a minority as a result of their sexual orientation. Because family ties tend to be very strong among African Americans and because families rarely reject its members, many gay men and lesbian women enjoy satisfying partnered relationships and also tend to be very involved with their families of origin (Clarke, 1983). However, this is not true beyond the family. The African American community is generally very homophobic. African American homosexuals are often isolated and are not always accepted by members of the African American community. African Americans have a history of sexual racism that has a bearing on their views on homosexuality. During slavery African Americans were routinely sexually exploited and raped. In part as a result of a history of violent heterosexual and same-sex experiences, the African American community is described by many African American homosexuals as being extremely homophobic (B. Greene, 1994). A second factor influencing homophobia within the African American community is Christianity. Traditionally the African American church has denounced homosexuality as sinful and immoral. Of the estimated 33.5 million African Americans, approximately 19 million attend church on a regular basis (Lincoln & Mamiya, 1990). Those who participate in religious organizations are more likely to be influenced by religious beliefs regarding homosexuality. Thus the African American community has a tendency to shun homosexuals. African American homosexuals often do not have the multiplicity of social organizations that their white counterparts have. Opportunities to meet other same-sex, same-race individuals with whom committed relationships can be established are limited. This issue may be further compounded because African American homosexuals are not as open about their sexual orientation as white gay males and lesbians are. African American gay men and lesbian women are discriminated against in many of the same ways that other homosexuals are.[7]

A major problem experienced in the African American adolescent homosexual population is suicide. The rate of suicide of these youth is roughly two to three times higher than that of other youth. Approximately 34% of homosexual youth have attempted suicide (Fischer, 1995). Similarly, gay and lesbian elderly African Americans have many needs for which they may seek services from health and human service organizations. Many homosexual elderly have lived during the time of the Great Depression. This was an era in which sex was not openly discussed during their childhood. If they recognized themselves as having homosexual orientations, they would almost without question have no opportunity to discuss these feelings, because discussions about sex were generally considered to be adult topics. During the years of their most heightened sexual urges, usually between the ages of 20 and 30, they were often forced to suppress their homosexuality. As a result, many elderly homosexuals have lived lives in which they hid their sexual orientation by pretending to be heterosexual. Berger (1982) identifies this as *passing*. Elderly gay and lesbian African Americans have special emotional needs and needs for social support. There are limited opportunities for gatherings that provide formal emotional and psychological support. To illustrate, many elderly homosexuals who experience the death of a partner often find that bereavement counseling is not available to them through conventional funeral services. Depression can result if the person does not receive the needed support from family and friends or professional services. Out of fear of being identified as a homosexual, elderly gay men and lesbians often do not attend senior citizens or community centers that have been established for gay and lesbian elders.

Having HIV disease and AIDS raises socioeconomic issues for African American homosexuals. First, many physicians are still homophobic and refuse to treat gay and lesbian persons who have the disease. The issue of "freedom not to treat" among members of the medical community will be an ever-escalating discussion as the number of people with AIDS increases and as public pressure to meet the needs of people with HIV disease and AIDS is put upon members of the health care system. A second issue has to do with access to health care. Approximately 20% of people with AIDS have no health care coverage, and roughly 40% are covered by Medicaid.

SOCIAL WORK PRACTICE: GENERAL CONSIDERATIONS
FOR INTERVENTION WITH AFRICAN AMERICANS

In this section, we provide some general ideas and suggestions for intervention with African Americans.

Engaging the client and establishing a relationship is extremely important. Initially, it is not unusual for African American clients to show some nervousness or anxiety. This may be the result of uncertainty regarding the nature of the helping process or apprehension about the helper's ability to assist with the problem, or it may be because they have not voluntarily chosen to participate in the process. It therefore becomes incumbent upon you to create an atmosphere of warmth and an environment in which they feel relaxed, secure, and cared for. They need to know that you believe in their ability to participate in the helping process. You can convey that belief by demonstrating personal qualities that indicate that you believe in the client and are genuine and trustworthy. The principles of engagement suggested in Chapter 2 can easily be adapted for use with African American clients. The following are a few suggestions for doing so.

Eye contact and a smile followed by a "hello" after you give your name can go a long way toward helping the client to feel comfortable. Remember that the first contact should convey to the client that you not only are willing to assist as much as possible but also have positive regard for the client. The initial greeting can then be followed by an icebreaker in the form of small talk or inquiries about social events. Such light conversation also helps to put the client at ease.

The next major task is to set the stage for the parameters of the helping relationship. You can open the dialogue either by asking the client if there is any information about you or your agency that he or she would like to know or by electing to volunteer information about yourself. Among items that need to be addressed are:

1. the length of time of each unit or meeting of the intervention process overall;

2. an initial agreement regarding goals;

3. who will be involved in the process;

4. where the helping process will take place; and

5. in the case of a referral, how the client came to be referred to your agency or you.

The above discussion presupposes that the client (individual or family) comes to you for assistance. There are times when it is more appropriate to engage the client as part of in-home services or at a community setting. You will find the following guidelines helpful when the interaction takes place in the client's environment.

Before entering the client's domain, introduce yourself by full name while giving the client (and others, if any) eye contact. This is a very important point. Giving your full name helps to assure the client of your legitimacy and may serve to decrease any apprehension that the he or she may have to opening his or her environment to a stranger. Remember that effective communication takes place on both verbal and nonverbal levels, and thus, maintaining eye contact with an individual helps to improve the communication process. Giving the client eye contact as you introduce yourself will also help the client to gain a sense of your self-confidence, trustworthiness, and attitudes about working with the client (DuBrin, 1988).

Upon meeting the client, indicate what agency you are from. This will further legitimize you. Address the client or clients by surname, especially when addressing, acknowledging, and referring to an elderly African American person. It is customary for African Americans to acknowledge "elders" by using their surname. To do otherwise, unless given permission by the individual, would symbolize disrespect, whether intentional or unintentional.

Out-of-home placement as an intervention requires careful handling. Remember that the African American elderly have a special place in and have special expectations from their family:

> After slavery, the extended family was prevalent in the black community. Generally, the black household had twice as many relatives from outside the immediate family as did white ones. Egalitarian in nature, the family was marked by flexibility of roles, informal adoption of children, and care for the aged. Blacks seemed to have greater abhorrence of institutionalizing the aged than whites did. When aged blacks did not live with their children, several other members of the local community took responsibility for them. (Berry & Blassingame, 1982, p. 85)

Generally, African Americans do not consider caring for their elderly to be burdensome (Barker & Morrow, 1998). Being sensitive to this issue can prevent misunderstandings. If the ultimate service needed by the client involves a nursing home placement, you should approach the discussion of the idea of such placement with tact. Although this idea could be explored at a later time, approaching the subject before trust and a working relationship have been established can create a distance between the client or family and you.

The African American church is a significant resource. Be aware that the African American church can serve as an invaluable resource for psychological, spiritual, and social support. You can engage it as a potentially powerful source of help. African Americans are very religious people (Wingfield, 1988), and it has been widely documented that those who actively participate in religious activities usually report healthier life outcomes than those who do not (Billingsley, 1992). The theology of faith taught in the African American church emphasizes one's faith in God's ability to resolve problems, be they social, political, economical, physical, or mental. Therefore, many African Americans, particularly the elderly, tend to be reluctant to depend on external, formal, professional sources for assistance. Hence, you may encounter resistance on the part of the individual and family. For example, a client may be reluctant to seek medical services for an illness, insisting that God will heal the sick person, and the client may choose instead to use home remedies and folk medicine. In such situations, you may engage the pastor and members of the congregation in an effort to persuade the client or family to access the available medical services as a vehicle through which God heals.

Approaching the client from a holistic perspective is necessary. In order to be truly effective in your work with African Americans, consider the client from a holistic point of view. As suggested in Chapter 1, ideas drawn from the ecological-systems approach are helpful. Protection from life's stresses often comes from social affiliations with significant others in one's kin and non-kin social network. African Americans rely heavily on these networks, which often serve as support systems and buffers against stress. Consider the client's circumstance from a global point of view in order to fully appreciate the significance of both internal and external factors that may be affecting the person, family, or community.

Understanding their past experiences with the helping professions is important. Historically, the social sciences have negatively stereotyped African Americans (Douglass, 1993; Logan et al., 1990; Taylor, 1994), and most American social institutions have related to African American and other culturally diverse populations from a white Anglo middle-class orientation (Congress, 1994). According to Douglass (1993), the social sciences have been guilty of continuing erroneous assumptions and untruths about African American inferiority. The stereotypes of African Americans portray them as unmotivated for treatment, psychologically bankrupt, inarticulate, and hence not able to successfully engage in therapy. Such a view of a client becomes a self-fulfilling prophecy. These stereotypes have resulted from the lack of a conceptual understanding of African American culture. Read about and expose yourself to the experiences of African Americans in the society at large and at the hands of helping professionals.

It is wise to assume and deal with client mistrust. Remember that African Americans are often very suspicious of and reserved with those from different racial and cultural backgrounds. This may interfere with the helping relationship, and trust is vital to establishing a therapeutic helping relationship. White helpers are often seen as an extension of white supremacy and racism and are approached with caution or a "healthy paranoia" until they demonstrate an understanding of and appreciation for the African American culture and experience (Paniagua, 1994, p. 22). Clients may totally or partially withhold information that they feel to be of a private nature, or they may not be forthcoming with information if they think that your interpretation of such information could result in negative consequences. If you suspect mistrust on the part of the client, attempt to show an understanding of the historical context of the African American experience by fostering a dialogue that addresses the issue of differences between the client and yourself in terms of past and present encounters that have occurred between African Americans and others. Also, discuss cultural norms and values in relation to self-disclosure.

SOCIAL WORK INTERVENTION AT MICRO-, MEZZO-, AND MACROLEVELS: PRINCIPLES AND APPROACHES

Assessment-Related Practice Principles and Approaches

1. Include strengths and resources of African Americans in your assessment. Social workers often approach the African American client in terms of problems and base their assessment of the client on deficits rather than strengths. For instance, female-headed households are often characterized as pathological, and single African American mothers are rarely given credit for raising healthy children who go on to be productive members of society (Paniagua, 1994). "The worker must be careful not to portray a negative valuation of a family type of composition that is unfamiliar or different from the married-couple-with-children model" (McPhatter, 1991, p. 16). In this instance, the social worker should explore the families' coping mechanisms and support systems, both of which may reveal extraordinary survival skills. These and other skills are strengths that should be thoroughly assessed and used as tools for helping the client to problem-solve.

2. Make the assessment global in nature. You should explore the client's problem or problems from a systems perspective. General systems theory helps the helper to consider the client from a global perspective while considering the impact of other systems that operate on and affect the circumstances of the client. The client's circumstances must be considered from a global point of view in order to fully appreciate the significance of both internal and external factors that may be affecting the person, family, or community. Variables that are external and internal to the client should be explored as contributors to the client's problem:

> These factors include sources of stress, such as family finances and the degree to which the family is able to adequately meet food, shelter, and other instrumental needs; employment concerns; health-related issues; and neighborhood concerns, including how safe and connected the family feels in the neighborhood. (McPhatter, 1991, p. 14)

The client may be negatively affected by his or her physical and social surroundings. For instance, people who live in neighborhoods where loud music is played continuously or where being a victim of crime is a constant threat can be negatively affected emotionally or psychologically.

3. Consider the intragroup variances among African Americans. Intragroup differences exist among African Americans on a number of variables, such as by age cohort, geographic location and origin, and religious practices. For instance, there may be variations in beliefs concerning religious traditions and dress codes among African Americans who belong to the same religious denomination. Some may feel that women should not wear "men's apparel" such as pants, whereas others may not consider these to be relevant issues. It would be erroneous to assume that all or even most African Americans who share the same social or religious affiliations hold the same or similar points of view. "Not all individuals within a particular minority culture share similar values and expressions of behaviors" (Whitler & Calantone, 1991, p. 461). Before you can make a thorough assessment of the client's situation, you must understand the social context of the client's problem. Before this can occur, you must understand the client's cultural environment. This would include being knowledgeable about the client's culture, language, religious beliefs, customs, and historical background. All of these factors affect the client's perception of and response to the problem.

4. Assess the overall functioning of the community. This includes assessing the intellectual level of the community and the gaps in services that may exist. Assessing the intellectual level of the community will enable you to plan programs and services that are relevant and appropriate to the population. For instance, before providing an educational program to the African American community, you will need to assess the level of literacy within the population. Some elderly African Americans may not have completed grade or high school. They would be ill served by receiving information that was written for an audience with higher levels of educational experience. Conversely, it would appear demeaning to provide well-educated individuals with information that was written for an audience with limited educational experience.

5. Familiarize yourself with alternative ways of interpreting behavior. "The social worker must be well versed in alternative theoretical explanations to mainstream explanations of various cultural groups behavior and functioning" (McPhatter, 1991, p. 15). If the

African American client's behavior is not referenced against that of other African Americans, it may appear abnormal or deviant, when in fact it may not be. For example, spanking has been a traditional way in which many African Americans have disciplined their children, whereas the mainstream society now considers spanking a form of child abuse. Many African Americans would not consider disciplining children by hitting them on the hands or hind parts with a belt or "switch" (small hedge twig) to be abusive. The adage "spare the rod and spoil the child" is believed by many African Americans, especially among many of the elderly, to be an effective means of discipline. Norton (1978) suggested that social workers use a "dual perspective when working with clients who have different cultural and racial backgrounds." Norton goes on to define the dual perspective as "the conscious and systematic process of perceiving, understanding, and comparing simultaneously the values, attitudes, and behavior of the larger societal system with those of the client's immediate family and community system" (p. 3).

6. Base your assessment on facts. "Therapists need to approach diagnosis carefully because the client's presenting problems may not be the primary treatment issue" (Franklin, 1992, p. 354). For instance, the client may complain of somatic symptoms that may be the result of stress or other psychological issues. Sometimes social workers rush to judgment and make decisions about clients that can and do have dire consequences. Avoid making decisions based upon assumptions, stereotypes, or prejudgments. A good assessment of the African American client is based on solid evidence and information that has been well researched and verified.

7. Include all significant others in the assessment process. African Americans have a close kinship network that often includes people who are not related by blood (Paniagua, 1994). Often nonrelatives will "go for" brother or sister, aunt or grandmother, and so forth. These people, although not related, often play a very important role in the life of the individual, family, or community. Likewise, neighbors and others may be very active and helpful to you and the client. You should not overlook their significance while gathering data.

Intervention-Related Practice Principles and Approaches

The following practice principles and approaches are drawn from the experiences of several social service professionals and the author's own practice experience.

At the Microlevel.

1. Involve extended support systems in intervention. You will find the involvement of the client's extended support system helpful in several different ways. Members of the client's support system can be helpful in your information gathering, depending on the age and degree of literacy of the client. Therefore, a more accurate assessment and treatment plan may result by involving the client's significant others. They may also help to defuse misunderstandings or mistrust that the client may have toward you or toward the helping process. The client's problems may stem from a variety of sources, including poor interpersonal relationships. This issue can be better addressed if all involved parties are present.

2. Show respect for the client's worth and dignity. You can do this by showing an appreciation for the life experiences and wisdom of the client; recognizing the client's ethnic and cultural supports; and not talking to the client in a patronizing manner. Address the

issue of confidentiality, as this will allow the client the opportunity to decide what information to share with you, considering the limitations of confidentiality.

3. Empower the clients. African Americans need to value themselves and to consider themselves from a more positive point of view in spite of negative messages they constantly receive from mainstream society. You can encourage them to be more self-reflective and to increase their self-confidence and self-regard. Help them to grow in their assertiveness and ability to express their thoughts and feelings. Approach them from a strengths perspective that appreciates their culture, which in turn will help them to better appreciate themselves. For example, Abdullah (1998) observed, "The therapist must be able to appreciate the personal strength of Black women, who have historically survived the physical enslavement period, the psychological enslavement and the self-preservation strategies of survival through assimilation" (p. 203).

4. Establish effective communication. Sometimes helping practitioners assume that African American clients do not understand the context of what is being said and tend to talk to them in a condescending manner. There may be a tendency to oversimplify words and phrases when communicating with African American clients. The client may perceive this as demeaning and insulting. Decrease the likelihood of this occurring by carefully using appropriate communication techniques such as clarification and validation.

5. Do not discount clients' perception of the impact of racism and discrimination on their lives. Helpers sometimes tend to minimize this impact and do not believe that the client's problem is a result of racism or discrimination. They may unintentionally cause the client to perceive them as thinking that the client's problem is self-created or a figment of his or her imagination. This will impede the development of client-worker trust. You should thoroughly explore racism and discrimination from the client's perspective in order to make an accurate assessment.

6. Deal with the client's fear. Be cognizant that the client may have a fear of social service agencies and their staff, particularly white social workers. This fear may be the result of distrust for such individuals or of uncertainty about their intentions. The client's fear may also be the result of past negative experiences with helping professionals. For instance, the African American individual or family may have a prior history with child and youth agencies that involved the termination of parental rights, out-of-home placements, or allegations of abuse with ensuing investigations. The client's response to future social work intervention will depend on how the case was handled by the social worker and other human service agencies involved and the final outcome of the case. They may also have had negative experiences with social workers and agencies that were not culturally sensitive to their needs and issues.

7. Realize that African Americans have different communication styles. The words and phrases used by African Americans may have different meanings. For instance, the word *man* is synonymous with a police officer, *fat* may be used to denote something that is nice or exquisite, and the term *not down with that* means that something is not favorable. Failure to understand and validate the meanings of unfamiliar words and phrases can lead to misinterpretation of their stories and statements. However, be aware that not all African Americans use ethnic jargon or Black English. Do not attempt to use Black English or African American jargon as it can be viewed by the client as belittling. For instance, European American social workers who refer to African American clients as "soul brothers

or sisters" are sometimes perceived as being insincere. Most members of the African American community do not consider Europeans to be their "brothers" or "sisters." Therefore, in order to prevent misunderstandings, it is wise to stay away from the use of jargon (Brille, 1998).

8. Know that not all African American clients are welcoming of African American helpers. If you are an African American social worker, do not assume that all African American clients are going to gravitate toward you because you are an African American. For any number of reasons, there may not be a bond between a particular African American social worker and the African American client. These reasons may be as varied as the differences in values, beliefs, or experiences between the two and the client's unresolved issues around the experience of being abandoned as a child. Perhaps the client's parents were not available when needed. This experience might have caused a distrust for those who are responsible for caretaking. This distrust may extend to the social worker.

9. Know that many African Americans have a different sense of time. Be aware that African American clients may not in all cases be as conscientious of time commitments as expected. They may not always be on time for appointments and may not always complete assignments on time or within the designated time frame. You may need to allow extra time for some African American client appointments and should not be unduly upset when the client is late for an in-office appointment or is not prepared at the exact time of a scheduled home visit. This awareness may decrease the likelihood that you would abandon the scheduled appointment or think that there is a lack of commitment or involvement on the client's part.

10. Understand that materialism does not signify irresponsibility. Do not view the individual or family as having the wrong priorities when parents on a limited income make expensive material provisions such as designer clothing and technological devices for their children. Parents sometimes feel successful when they can provide for the material needs of their children. In such cases, the parents are not irresponsible but may be satisfying their own need to feel that they are good parents by fulfilling their children's wishes. However, in other cases, some parents may lack the wherewithal to provide for the emotional well-being of their children and may instead substitute material possessions.

11. Appreciate the diversity of family types among African Americans. Be cognizant of the differences in family structures in order to accurately assess the family system and appreciate its strengths and weaknesses. Logan, Freeman, and McRoy (1990) differentiate between three types of family structures within the African American community. They are (a) the *nurturing or well functioning family*, which has a high level of functioning and in which boundaries are well defined and are open for change; (b) *mid-range functioning family*, seen across all socioeconomic levels, which has well-defined but less flexible boundaries and tends to be less democratic in nature; and (c) the *dysfunctional family*, which does not operate cohesively and whose members lack self-direction and healthy out-of-family relationships.

12. Recognize the importance of family secrecy among African American clients. Most African Americans parents teach their offspring that personal issues related to family experiences are not to be divulged to outsiders. This may apply to extended family members as well. Therefore, reconcile yourself to the possibility that you may have

difficulty obtaining relevant information from family members and may in fact never be told detailed and in-depth information about family issues and secrets.

At the Mezzolevel. As pointed out in the preceding chapter, the focus of social work at this level can be on improving the responsiveness of your agency to the needs of special groups of clients. The following considerations will contribute to the effectiveness of its services for African Americans and their community.

1. Acknowledge the historical distrust of the European professional community. A historical understanding of the nature of race relations and experiences would help your agency to understand better any resistance or paranoia that might be encountered. One area of concern within the African American community that may have an impact upon its use of services has to do with the issue of participation in human experimentation.

2. Understand that there is a widespread belief in conspiracy theories. "Conspiracy theories are considered, by many, as not only common in the African American community, but just as pervasive among Black public officials, professors, and doctors as they are among average citizens" (Parsons, Simmons, Shinhoster, & Kilburn, 1999, p. 209). As mentioned earlier, African Americans have, without their knowledge and consent, been used as human guinea pigs in scientific and medical experiments by private and governmental organizations. A notable experiment occurred in the 1970s with funds from the National Institute of Health. Blood samples were taken from 7,000 young boys from the Baltimore area, 95% of whom were from underprivileged black families, without parental consent and under the guise that they were being tested for anemia (Washington, 1994). They were actually screened to identify those who had an extra Y chromosome. It was hypothesized that individuals with an extra Y chromosome were likely to become criminals in later life. Consequently, many of these young men were labeled as such. It is also believed that African Americans have been injected with cancerous cells and cancer-producing substances, forced to eat fecal matter, subjected to lobotomies, and injected with syphilis. Especially targeted were those individuals who were poor (Washington, 1994). Although many of these beliefs do not have a factual basis, some do, and they may account for low client participation in agency programs, services, and clinical trials.

3. Recognize the necessity of using African American religious institutions. As pointed out earlier, the black church serves as a pseudofamily where African Americans can be nurtured, feel accepted, and worship within the context of their culture. It operates as a forum for mutual aid and provides the community with a sense of hope. Worship services are a medium for the release of tension, frustration, and discouragement and are a source of encouragement and hope of freedom and a brighter day both in this world and the world beyond. Churches tend to be stable institutions with long roots in the neighborhoods they are located in. Your investigation of area resources through the church would likely reveal many services provided to members of the African American community. Collaborative efforts between churches and religious and nonreligious human service agencies are not uncommon. Not only do African American churches network among themselves, but they frequently work with local schools, police departments, hospitals, and welfare departments to provide services for their community (Billingsley, 1992).

The African American church provides its community with psychological, emotional, and material support. The church is second only to the family in its importance to the African American community, and McRae, Carey, and Anderson-Scott (1998) have identified the therapeutic and supportive contributions that the black church makes to the African American community. "Black churches provide an array of emotional and learning experiences and embody therapeutic factors that enhance group cohesion and promote empowerment and social change" (McRae et al., 1998, p. 780). According to Gilkes (1980), the black religious experience is therapeutic in that it allows for individual and collective articulation of suffering, location of persecutors, provision of asylum for "acting out," and validation of experiences. For instance, prayer meetings serve as mechanisms whereby members can receive mutual aid, help group members to adjust to life stresses, and provide a feeling of relief. Group solidarity and cohesion are fostered as people share their experiences with oppression, racism, prejudice, and other life problems that are often denied by whites. Not only are their experiences affirmed, but members also learn through testimonies how others have dealt with negative life situations.

The African American church is one of the few social institutions where African Americans are given status and placed in authoritative positions and where its elderly are afforded unquestionable respect. For instance, while at his job, the 60-year-old man who is employed as a skilled laborer would most likely be referred to or addressed by his first name by members of the dominant society. However, in the African American church, he would be referenced to or addressed by his surname and may hold a high position or office, such as chairman of the trustee or deacon board. As chairman of the trustee board he would be responsible for oversight of the church's finances and budget, which could exceed hundreds of thousands or even millions of dollars. The same would hold true for the African American woman. The woman known as Lilly or Daisy on her job becomes Mother Lilly Grose or Sister Daisy Johnson when she is at church and among her fellow church colleagues during her day-to-day interactions with them. She may be the Church Mother or director of the Women's Department, which may require supervision of the church's women's auxiliaries and could involve thousands of women. Thus the church serves as a place where race pride and self-esteem are enhanced. It would be a gross oversight for any therapeutic helper to fail to consider the importance of the black church when providing intervention.

4. Involve the African American minister as lay therapist. The African American minister is equally important as a source of help within the African American community. Neighbors, Musick, and Wiliams (1998) found that the African American minister often performs the role of counselor, diagnostician, and referral agent and is often sought as the primary source of help for advocacy, economic, and psychosocial, as well as religious, problems. Using data from the National Survey of Black Americans, which was compiled from the 1970 census, Neighbors et al. (1998) studied the interviews of 2,107 African Americans who were 18 years of age and older. They found that 21.1% of the respondents used clergy as their first source of help with problems; of that group, 50% sought help from no other source. Those who used their clergy as their primary intervention source were less likely than any others to seek professional help. Clergy were consulted by members on such issues as death and bereavement and during serious psychological crises, such as when a person experienced a nervous breakdown or psychosis. Many of the ministers often held very different views about the etiology and assumptions of life problems. Clergy tended to view problems with family relations as stemming from mental illness, sin, and being out of a proper relationship with God. It was not uncommon for clergy, especially older ministers, not to refer members for mental health treatment because many ministers did not agree with the Western ideas about the causation and treatment of mental health

disorders. The ministers more likely to refer members of their congregation to mental health services were younger and more educated (85% of ministers who held college degrees reported having made referrals for mental health services).

If a minister denounces a mental health service or another service, he or she may be very influential in deterring his or her congregation from using those services. On the other hand, if a pastor or minister embraces a particular mental health service or intervention, so will the majority of his or her congregation. Hence, do not take lightly the power of African American ministers to influence others. Congregations often turn to their minister before seeking help from others for assistance with marital, personal, financial, interpersonal, family, and other problems. Consider him or her a vital component in the intervention team. Work needs to be done to bridge the gap between the African American community and the health and mental health field, considering the level of distrust that exists among African Americans in relation to counseling services. Perhaps the African American minister can be a point of contact for a beginning to this process.

5. Include the African American community in program development. Agency directors and others responsible for program development should be careful to consult members of the African American community when making decisions regarding services that will be offered to them. Potentially successful programs have sometimes done poorly, and in some instances have been forced to close their doors, because of failure to consult with constituents beforehand. The services may be well conceptualized and well intended, but they may be viewed as irrelevant or as suspect by members of the African American community, which may result in their being underused.

6. Provide diversity training to social workers and other agency staff. This training should include not only exposure to theoretical material but also experiential learning using opportunities within the African American community. Social workers can gain a wealth of knowledge about the issues and concerns affecting African Americans and the means of addressing them by attending forums in which the issues are discussed. For instance, they should be encouraged to attend Black History Month programs, many of which take place in African American churches. Other avenues include housing development tenant council meetings, African American church services, NAACP meetings, and rites of passage programs.

7. Ask the clients for feedback on agency effectiveness. Agencies provide services but forget the importance of requesting client feedback, either formally or informally, as to how services are perceived by the constituents. You may unintentionally operate from the premise that if clients make no complaints, then all is well. This may be an erroneous assumption. For any number of reasons, African American clients may not volunteer suggestions and comments that could be very valuable to you. Remember that program evaluation should be an integral part of program operation. Clients not only can tell you what they need but also can identify community needs.

8. Be as comprehensive as possible in your scope of services. The needs of African Americans are as broad and diverse as they are. Between- and within-group differences mean that service providers will have to be creative in program development and service delivery. For instance, the Department of Aging may operate several senior citizens centers throughout a large metropolitan area. The programming at one center might include fund-raisers, such as bingo and dances, and other activities, such as trips to

gambling casinos, which may be well received by many African American seniors. Another senior center may find it necessary to eliminate these activities because a majority of the African American senior participants object to gambling and dancing for religious reasons. Instead, they may be more amenable to quilting, fashion shows, or bake sales as means of raising funds.

9. Interagency and intra-agency linkages should exist between those who provide services to African Americans. No agency, regardless of how comprehensive its services, can meet the needs of all members of the African American community. To identify gaps in services and to eliminate duplication of services, agencies should regularly communicate with each other.

10. Educate and utilize local community members as paraprofessionals. To the extent possible, African Americans who are indigenous to the area where your agency is located should occupy semiprofessional positions. They can assist you with program planning and development, give you access to members of the community, help you make connections with those who control or have access to resources, and encourage members of the community to use your services.

At the Macrolevel. Macrolevel social work interventions deal with social, political, economic, and environmental forces affecting the human condition and are aimed at changing laws, creating resources, and modifying public opinion in favor of the disadvantaged groups. Practice principles and approaches suggested in the preceding chapter are equally applicable to African American communities. The following are a few more.

1. Encourage and involve African American leadership. The mainstream media and the society at large often assume that many of the most vocal and visible African Americans, such as the Reverend Jesse Jackson, Reverend Al Sharpton, Honorable Louis Farrakhan, and others, are the ones who should be consulted regarding social policy in relation to the African American community. The African American community is not unlike the Jewish, Latino, Asian, or any other community in declaring individuals or certain persons as its official leadership. Before formulating policy, on all levels—local, regional, state, and national—policymakers should consult with the African American community as to who the leaders within the community are.

2. Explore the impact of social policy. Because social policies often have broader impact than originally intended, policymakers should consider the short- and long-term implications of their policy decisions on the African American community. The African American community's ability to access services is hampered when policies are too prohibitive. For instance, some policies regarding academic standards in relation to student athletes' eligibility for financial aid have disproportionately affected African American college students, some of whom are underprepared for the rigor of college studies. It is therefore necessary to garner as much feedback as possible from the African American community prior to policy development and implementation via such mechanisms as focus groups, surveys, and town meetings.

3. Encourage political activism. Members of the African American community often feel alienated from the political process. Some feel that their thoughts and opinions are not taken seriously. This is manifested, for instance, through low voter registration and

turnout. Involve your agency in identifying mechanisms for ensuring that the input and ideas of African Americans will inform the formulation of policy. Social workers should be active advocates for those within the African American community who are or feel disenfranchised, and social workers should encourage their participation in the political process.

4. Contribute to the public accountability of media and mass communication. Social work agencies should provide the media with accurate information about the African American clients that they work with. This will help to counter the dissemination of negative propaganda about and stereotypes of African Americans. The African American community continues to suffer from the effects of negative characterization, which adversely affects both the provision of health and human services to its members and the ability of the members to benefit from those services. Advocating for clients requires calling into question individuals and institutions that promote ideas and comments that are damaging to African Americans.

5. Strive for social change through community organization:

> To solve problems, people need to get some control over the concrete circumstances of everyday life. Organizing seeks to do this. The person who acts alone has very little power. When people join together and organize, they increase their ability to get things done. The goal is to strengthen their collective capacities to bring about social change. (Staples, 1984, p. 1)

According to Shulman (1999), communities provide many types of social support to their residents. *Personal-emotional support* is provided when neighbors acknowledge and make social calls to one another. This support helps to enhance people's feelings of connection and reduces the likelihood they will feel lonely and detached. *Instrumental support* involves neighbors' providing mutual aid for one another. *Informational support* involves the sharing of information between neighbors, such as community resources, and *personal social networks* are the networks that people form with central figures within their community who can either serve as a resource or connect the individual with needed resources. *Neighborhood social networks* involve all of the associations that neighbors develop between themselves. All of these support systems exist in the African American community.

There are several models of community organization. Choose a model that best fits the community you are working with. Consider every African American community in terms of its (a) community resources, (b) the individuals and groups who have influence and who are connected to or have access to resources, and (c) the manner in which members of the community interact. For instance, one community may have a large professional community that spearheads many social justice initiatives, whereas in a different community similar types of activities may be taken on by retirees and people who have limited formal education but who have many years of experience in social programming. As another example, an African American community may be extremely limited in the number and type of formal social services that it offers residents, yet it may have a wealth of informal networks and services of which residents can avail themselves. Approaching community organization within the African American community from a strengths perspective will enable you to discover the many ways in which many African American communities have developed adaptive mechanisms for meeting the needs of residents.

NOTES

1. According to King (1997),

African Americans are unlike those of any other ethnic and cultural group in this country. No other group was enslaved for centuries, systematically denied their basic human, social, and economic rights for almost 325 years, has experienced the poverty and economic deprivation that African Americans have experienced or has been and continues to be victimized by institutionalized discriminatory practices and policies in every arena of American life solely on the basis of an immutable attribute such as skin color. (p. 80)

2. Some social scientists have described African American men who perform traditional female functions as "henpecked." Others disagree and view this role flexibility as a strength of the African American family.

There is, from a European American perspective, a remarkable degree of overlap in the behaviors associated with the male role in European American culture; such behaviors are associated with both men and women in this community. For example, women as well as men are viewed as individualistic and non-conforming in their behavior. Both husband and wife have authority in the home; both are responsible for the economic support of the family; both take the initiative for forming and breaking up a marriage and both may find separation to their advantage. (Hill, 1997, p. 126)

3. By 1749 eight states—Connecticut, Virginia, Maryland, North Carolina, Pennsylvania, Rhode Island, South Carolina, and Georgia—had legalized slavery within their borders. By 1860, there were approximately 3,953,760 slaves: 1,982,625 male and 1,971,135 female (Walker & Wilson, 1997). The number of free African Americans, who resided primarily in urban centers, was nearly half a million.

4. We could find no estimates of the slaves who died as a result of punishment practices. Slave rebellions and antislavery initiatives were common. The Amistad Rebellion was the most notable uprising, and among the people who organized resistance movements were Nat Turner, Harriet Tubman, William Parker, Dred Scott, and Sojourner Truth.

5. Many Cubans, Puerto Ricans, and other people from the Caribbean and Latin America, such as Haitians, Dominicans, and Jamaicans, do not identify themselves as African Americans but rather as Hispanics. They use nonracial sources of identity such as culture, ethnicity, nationality, and class. They are likely to emphasize ethnicity, partly because racial mixing in their lands has made attempts to neatly categorize people based on skin color virtually futile (Payne, 1998) and partly because of the stigma attached to being black. In our highly racialized society, large numbers of Hispanics with some black ancestry have succeeded in defining themselves as Hispanics or Latinos, thus evading the one-drop rule (Davis, 1991). We have discussed the one-drop rule at some length in Chapter 7 and have provided more detailed information on Cubans, Puerto Ricans, and Dominicans in Chapter 3.

6. King (1997) asserts that African American youth violence stems from the inhumane treatment African Americans endured during the period of slavery, the impact of racism and discrimination, and the violent nature of the American society. During slavery, African boys and men were viewed as a threat to white supremacy and masculinity and were therefore treated more harshly than the African females. They were subjected to all types of physical punishment. Commonplace were lynching, castrations, mutilations, and beatings. Their castrated bodies were often burned during public displays. Lynchings continued well into the early part of the 20th century and on average occurred at a rate of 113 per year between 1885 and 1921 (King, 1997). The brutal way in which African American men were treated over hundreds of years may have become a learned response to

addressing conflict. Violent behavior among African American teenagers may also be a result of the influence of the violence that is a part of the American culture. All major sports, which have historically served as a mechanism by which many African American youth have been able to become upwardly mobile, involve some form of physical contact and aggression. The combination of seeing adults resort to violence as a means of dealing with anger, the influence of the media, and the violent nature of the American society affects the manner in which African American teenage boys respond to their own disappointments and frustrations. Racial discrimination causes many teenagers to witness the despair in many adult African American males when denied opportunities to achieve economic and social parity with their majority counterparts. "The emotional upheaval that they endure all too often leads to an obvious sense of personal devaluation, degradation, and a disrespect for their lives and the lives of their peers" (King, 1997, p. 85).

7. Homosexuals are often ostracized and restricted from participating in social interactions. Often partnered homosexuals are not invited to attend functions such as office parties and dinner affairs as a couple. They are often denied equal access to fair housing, employment, and membership in organizations. Discrimination in housing is particularly evident when gay men and lesbians attempt to rent apartments. They are sometimes denied housing by private owners or corporate landlords, who sometimes argue that a homosexual presence within a neighborhood will corrupt the morals of the children. There is no federal law prohibiting discrimination based on sexual orientation. Sexual orientation was not included as a protected classification under Title VII of the Civil Rights Act of 1964 (Blank & Slipp, 1994). Homosexuals are often denied, under other pretexts, promotions and high-level management positions for fear that they will not "represent" the company well. They are often not privy to spousal and other family-related work benefits.

5

Understanding and Working With Asian Americans

ASIAN AMERICANS: WHO ARE THEY?

In Chapter 1, we discussed the various groups to which the term *Asian and Pacific Islander American* applies. These Americans represent about 30 countries of Asia and almost as many islands in the Pacific. They are the fastest-growing part of the country's population. Our focus in this chapter is on Asian Americans. Whereas race separates African Americans from mainstream Americans, and the Spanish language and Hispanic culture distinguish Latino Americans from others, there is no apparent racial, language, or cultural unity among Asian Americans. All these factors—the racial, language, and cultural differences in various combinations—set this group apart from the mainstream Americans as well as from other minority groups. Some of the Asian Americans, such as the Chinese and Japanese, have been a part of this country for several generations, whereas others, such as the Vietnamese, Laotians, Hmong, and Cambodians, are among the most recent arrivals. Between 1980 and 1990, the numbers of Asian Americans in the United States grew by 108%, which is more than 10 times the rate of growth for the total population. Whereas the foreign-born constituted only 8% of the total U.S. population in 1990, 74% of the Asian Americans were foreign born. The different subgroups of Asian Americans are growing at different rates. Over the 10-year period from 1980 to 1990, the number of Japanese Americans grew by only 21%, as compared with the growth rate of 82% for the Filipinos, 104% for the Chinese, 124% for the Koreans, and 135% for the Vietnamese. All Asian American communities combined amount to approximately 4% of the U.S. population. Together, Asian Americans are projected to reach 10% of the U.S. population by 2050 (U.S. Bureau of the Census, 1991, 1992a, 1992b). They will be an important challenge to the commitment and resources of human service organizations.

A HISTORICAL OVERVIEW OF ASIAN AMERICANS: COMMONALITY OF EXPERIENCES

Asians have been coming to the United States in substantial numbers since the middle of the 19th century. A host of factors, including economic hardship and political instability in several Asian countries, pushed them out of those lands, and the wealth of this country and its need for manpower pulled them toward its shores. Despite their contributions to the economy of the country, the existing popular attitudes and prejudices toward nonwhite people were extended to Asians, making them victims of social and institutional racism. Governments at the local, state, and federal levels passed, implemented, and upheld the constitutionality of anti-Asian ordinances and laws. From time to time, the political needs and climate of the country also influenced the nature of the welcome and conditions of life for Asian Americans. All these elements of their history, to varying degrees, are still a part of their reality. The past affects their present and is reflected in their needs for human services. This section looks at the history of major Asian American groups from several thematic perspectives.

Socioeconomic and political conditions in their native lands force many Asians to emigrate. Chinese started coming to this country in noticeable numbers in the middle of the 19th century. Such factors as natural disasters, political instability, and economic hardship forced many of them to leave their country. By 1860, there were more than 30,000 Chinese in the United States. Most of them were from a particular part of southern China. Japanese Americans have been a part of the American social scene for as long as the Chinese Americans. In the 1880s, the emigration of Japanese to the new world was also partly the result of an economic crisis in their country. In the latter part of the 19th century, Asian Indians began to immigrate in large numbers to Canada and the United States (Chandrasekhar, 1982). Most of them were Sikh farmers from the Punjab province of India. The Punjab was annexed by the British in 1849, and that annexation created conditions conducive to emigration. The amount of land revenue was now fixed and had to be paid in cash instead of in kind as in the past.

> An increasing number of people mortgaged their plots to secure the cash for their tax obligations, but in time many lost their property. The result was a greater concentration of landownership, rising tenancy, and a higher rate of land dis-possession. Large number became migrant workers; others found employment in the British colonial army and police force. Since the British empire at its zenith stretched around the globe, these soldiers and policemen were often sent to other parts of the empire to keep law and order. In this manner, many Punjabis became worldly travelers, unafraid to try their fortunes in far-flung places. (Chan, 1991, p. 20)

After Canada made it virtually impossible for them to migrate to that country in 1908, Indians started coming to the United States directly.

The Philippines, a Spanish colony for over 300 years, became a possession of the United States at the end of the Spanish-American War in 1898. Some Filipinos had been fighting for independence. A segment under the leadership of Emilio Aguinaldo proclaimed themselves independent. The Americans refused to recognize their government. The Philippine-American War began and lasted several years.

> After the fighting was over, the first American civilian governor of the Philippines, William Howard Taft, began nearly half a century of avowedly benevolent despotism by proclaiming his concern for the welfare of the people of the Philippines, whom he described as our "little brown brothers." (Kitano and Daniels, 1988, p. 77)

Being U.S. "nationals," Filipinos traveled on U.S. passports and could enter this country freely. The first Filipino immigrants were students who were chosen, financed, and sponsored by the U.S. government so that they could learn skills necessary for the development of their country. These were followed by other students, who were not similarly financed and sponsored, and others who were driven by economic motivations.

Koreans were latecomers to this country.

> After being ravaged by Japanese invasions in 1592 and 1597 and by Manchu invasions in the 1630s, Korea sealed itself off from the outside world for almost two and a half centuries until the 1860s, when Western ships began to appear in Korean waters. (Chan, 1991, p. 12)

Koreans were legally forbidden to leave the country (Mangiafico, 1988). The history of modern Korea is a story of its powerful neighbors—China, Japan, and Russia—vying for influence and control over Korea as well as for political and military supremacy. Guided by international politics, Americans went to Korea in the 1880s and not only opened that country to American influence and interests but also encouraged Korean emigration to the United States. In 1882, the United States secured a treaty with Korea that called for free trade between the two countries and included the permission for Koreans to reside, to rent, and to purchase land in America. By the beginning of the 20th century, the economic and political situation in Korea worsened. There was a severe famine, an epidemic of cholera, heavy taxes, and government corruption; furthermore, the process of the country's being taken over by Japan had begun, a process that was completed in 1910. By 1905, over 7,266 Koreans had arrived in Hawaii (Kitano & Daniels, 1988).

Southeast Asian is the term used for immigrants from Vietnam, Cambodia, and Laos. Most of them have come here since 1975, after the collapse of the American-supported governments in those countries. They came here as refugees. Whereas immigrants leave their country willingly and come to another more or less prepared to make it their home, "becoming a refugee is a catastrophic life change. It is an upheaval of all that is known and familiar. It is a series of losses, which include country, home, family members, and friends. Previous support systems may be lost and earlier coping patterns may no longer be useful" (Fox, 1991, p. 55).

The United States and its wealth beckon and invite people from Asia. People from all over the world have been coming to this country to make their fortunes. For the Chinese, the California gold rush provided another incentive. The Chinese characters for California can be translated as "gold mountain" (Kitano & Daniels, 1988). The Japanese were enticed by labor contractors to come to the United States. Large numbers came to Hawaii as contract laborers. After the 1900 Organic Law made Hawaii a formal U.S. territory, the entry of contract laborers became illegal, and all contracts became null and void; at that time, labor recruiters from the mainland "descended on Hawaii to lure Japanese workers away with the prospect of higher wages. Railroad companies, lumber mills, and farmers in the Pacific Northwest and in California all desired Japanese labor" (Chan, 1991, p. 37). For the Asian Indians also, agents of steamships, labor contractors for railroad companies in Canada, and Indian pioneers in North America were actively encouraging emigration from India. The need for cheap labor in Hawaii and on the U.S. mainland and aggressive recruitment by labor contractors encouraged emigration from the Philippines also. However, the appearance of large numbers of Filipinos on the mainland is a post-World War I phenomenon. In 1884, an American medical missionary, Horace Allen, arrived in Korea, became instrumental in saving the life of a relative of King Kojong's queen, and managed to gain the confidence of the king. During the next two decades, he (a) paved the way for the arrival and work of many American Protestant missionaries in Korea; (b) acted as the intermediary between the governments of the United States and Korea as well as between private American citizens and the Korean authorities; (c) helped his friends gain lucrative concessions and franchises, including the Unsan gold mines; (d) persuaded the king to allow his subjects to emigrate to Hawaii; and (e) got his friend David Dashler the emigration franchise. The Hawaiian Sugar Planter's Association was interested in recruiting Korean workers, and the American missionaries worked to persuade members of their congregations to go to Hawaii, a Christian land (Chan, 1991).

Popular prejudice and discrimination against Asians dominate the social scene. Irrespective of their country of origin, Asians became the object of prejudice and discrimination. As their number increased, Chinese became increasingly unwelcome. Their skin color, language, dress, and hairstyle made them not only objects of curiosity but also victims of racism. Japanese were also subjected to humiliating acts of racial discrimination and mob violence. They were prohibited from entering into interracial marriages and owning property and were restricted from entry into skilled crafts by local trade unions. Hence, they turned to agriculture. Although there was an abortive anti-Japanese movement in the 1890s, the effective movement against the Japanese immigrants dates from newspaper agitation in 1905. The issue became notorious and a matter of diplomatic concern in 1906 as a result of the San Francisco School Board's attempt to force Japanese pupils to attend the long-established segregated school of Chinese (Kitano & Daniels, 1988). A number of first-generation Japanese immigrants, the *issei*, served in the American forces in World War I in the hope of becoming American citizens. They discovered that the promise of citizenship for service did not apply to "aliens ineligible to citizenship" (Dunn, 1975).

Asian Indians were initially employed in lumbering and railroad work, but they then turned to agriculture, first as laborers and later as tenants and proprietors. They also experienced legal and extralegal discrimination. Because of their beards and turbans, they were also visibly different from the larger society. From time to time, there were anti-Indian riots in Pacific Coast states (Balgopal, 1995b). In 1908, a mob attacked about 100 Asian Indian workers at Live Oak in California, robbed them of $2,500, drove them out of their camp, and set it afire (Mazumdar, 1984).

For Filipinos, "migration to the United States merely transferred their colonial subordinate position from their native land to that of the colonizer" (Pido, 1997, p. 31). Although considered nationals, they were neither citizens nor foreigners. They had some rights of citizenship but were denied the rights of franchise, property ownership, and the freedom to marry whom they chose (Ishisaka & Takagi, 1982). As their numbers grew, they became more unwelcome both at places of work and in the communities at large. Their numbers, visibility, and tendency to get involved in union activities and radical politics led to an anti-Filipino movement: "Beginning in 1929 there were anti-Filipino riots in Watsonville and other small central California cities. Civic organizations, such as the Los Angeles and Northern Monterey County Chambers of Commerce, deplored their presence" (Kitano & Daniels, 1988, p. 82). Most of the early Korean immigrants were Christians who brought their families or imported picture brides from Korea, had a sojourner's orientation, and were preoccupied with the happenings back home. Nevertheless, they and their children were experiencing the same difficulties that other Asian Americans had in this country.

The reception and experiences of the Southeast Asian refugees in the United States have been in some ways different from those of other Asian immigrants. They were admitted into the country under the refugee-related laws. In 1980, the Refugee Assistance Act was passed, which formulated an explicit policy for refugees: "It recognized the principle of asylum and regularized mechanisms for distributing federal aid to refugees and for reimbursing states, local governments, and private voluntary agencies for their refugee-related expenses" (Kitano & Daniels, 1988, p. 137). Welcoming Southeast Asian refugees seemed like the right thing to do for the government on humanitarian and moral grounds, particularly because these refugees were escapees from communism. However, government welcome did not equate to popular acceptance.

Local, state, and federal governments reflect the popular prejudice and legalize racism. As the Chinese started working in the gold fields, they came into conflict with white miners. The latter often chased them away or cheated them out of their claims. Mining camps passed resolutions to exclude them, and the state discouraged them by such measures as the Foreign Miner's Tax Law (Lyman, 1977). Under the laws of the land, the Chinese could not become U.S. citizens, bring their families into the country, or marry Americans. Many states passed discriminatory laws, and local authorities restricted their activities and living arrangements. Mob violence—resulting in murders, hangings, and burning to death of Chinese—was often the culmination of the hostile legislation and discriminatory practices. Their unwelcome was formalized by a federal law forbidding Chinese immigration altogether.[1] Not only were new Chinese barred from immigrating, but those already here were discouraged from coming back if they left the country.[2] They were not safe on the streets and had no protection in courts of law. Many men were forced to lead lives of involuntary celibacy, and many of the few women were forced into prostitution or polyandry. The lack of a stable family life led to widespread gambling, the use of opium, and other aberrations in them (Dunn, 1975). Their population of 125,000 in 1882 gradually dropped down to 61,639 in 1920 (Kitano & Daniels, 1988). The phrase "Not a China man's chance" was an accurate reflection of the harsh reality of the Chinese in this country.

The official discrimination against Japanese took a different form. The United States did not want to antagonize Japan, a rising military power. The laws affecting Japanese immigrants did not name them specifically. Negotiations with the Japanese government led to a "Gentlemen's Agreement" in 1907 whereby Japan would stop issuing passports to Japanese laborers. However, immigration of women continued, which nearly balanced the Japanese American sex ratio and led to a continuing increase in the Japanese American population. The Gentlemen's Agreement approach was again used in 1920 to stop female emigration to the United States. However, this was not enough to satisfy the people in the Western states. Therefore, the Immigration Act of 1924 barred the entry of "aliens ineligible to citizenship." Although this act also did not mention Japanese, it virtually ended Japanese immigration (Chan, 1991; Kitano & Daniels, 1988; Murase, 1995).

Following the example of California, many states passed laws that prevented aliens who were ineligible for citizenship from owning land. These laws were used against Asian Indians as well. Immigration officials used administrative regulations to stop and discourage them from entering the country. Their job was made easy by a clause in the 1917 Immigration Act: An unusual geographic criterion was used to exclude Indians, because their racial or ethnographic status was unclear.[3] Several of those who had lived here for years and had acquired American citizenship were denaturalized and deported, as illustrated by the 1923 case of *United States v. Bhagat Singh Thind*.[4] Like most other immigrants from Asia, most Filipinos were single men, but unlike others, "Filipinos actively sought white female companionship, and this overt sexuality enraged much white opinion" (Kitano & Daniels, 1988, p. 81). Laws in many states clearly forbade marriage of white persons with Mongolians, Negroes, and mulattoes. Because the racial classification of Filipinos was open to question, many county clerks were issuing marriage licenses to Filipino men and white women. Anti-Filipino groups sued Los Angeles County to end this practice, and in 1930, a superior judge prohibited the Los Angeles county clerk from issuing a marriage license to a Filipino-white couple. That prohibition was challenged in the county appellate court. Based on an exhaustive study of the 19th-century ethnologists,[5] the majority opinion of the court was that Filipino-white marriages were not illegal. The anti-Filipino forces took their demand to the state legislature, which amended the antimiscegenation laws to include Filipino-white marriages. Several other states followed the example of California. The right of Filipinos to enter this country freely ended with the passage of the 1934 Exclusion Act.

A combination of factors—the Japanese government's policies and practices in Korea and the U.S. immigration laws restricting the entry of Asians into the country—put a stop to the immigration from Korea. From 1924 to the end of World War II, practically no Koreans came to the United States. The treatment of Koreans already here was no different from how other Asian immigrants were treated:

> In eleven states, they could not buy, own, or lease land. Twenty-six states refused them old age pensions. New York's laws excluded them from twenty-seven different occupations. Fifteen states refused as late as 1950 to sanction marriages between Koreans and white persons. (Melendy, 1977, p. 138)

In a hostile social environment, Asians turn to their own communities for help and resources. The attitudes and behaviors of the general public toward Asians were marked by prejudice and discrimination against them in the social and economic realms of life. The country's political institutions, from the local to the national level, reflected and legitimized popular sentiment by passing and enforcing anti-Asian laws, ordinances, and regulations. In such an atmosphere, Asians could not seek and get help from social service agencies. They turned inward and depended on their own communities. For example, in the Japanese community, "[t]here evolved an extensive community infrastructure that comprised protective mutual aid associations, rotating credit unions, religious institutions, newspapers, language schools, and cultural and recreational groups" (Murase, 1995, p. 244). This was more or less true of most Asian groups. Their ethnic neighborhoods, such as Chinatowns, became sources of economic and social support.

World War II changes political conditions and the social scene affecting Asians. Things changed with World War II. The war efforts, the needs of the economy, and the role in the war of the native lands of Asians determined the treatment meted out to them. The lot of the Chinese in America improved, because China was an ally of the United States in the war. In 1943, "Congress rescinded the Chinese exclusion laws, set a quota to allow 105 Chinese immigrants to be admitted each year, and granted Chinese the right of naturalization" (Chan, 1991, p. 122). Many more than 105 came, under special legislation allowing for family reunification. An act passed in 1946 allowed Chinese alien wives of American citizens, native born or naturalized, to come here on a nonquota basis (Kitano & Daniels, 1988). The Chinese Americans became welcome in all kinds of jobs, including some in technical professions and skilled trades. They were also inducted into the armed forces. "The citizenship requirement for service was waived in some instances, while in other instances mass naturalization ceremonies were held before induction" (Chan, 1991, p. 122). They were no longer seen as "heathen, morally inferior, savage, and childlike" (Takaki, 1990, p. 217). A Gallup poll taken in 1942 found respondents characterizing the Chinese as "hardworking, honest, brave, religious, intelligent, and practical" (Isaacs, 1972).

On the other hand, the war brought Japanese Americans new indignities. Even before the outbreak of the war, Americans had begun looking on Japan with distrust and harassing Japanese Americans. That harassment took such sinister forms as federal agents closing Japanese Americans' businesses, the Treasury Department freezing their bank accounts, police authorities searching their persons and property without warrants, employers firing them in spite of unblemished work records, authorities canceling their business licenses, and even some hospitals refusing to accept them as patients. There was also physical violence against them, which resulted in injury, death, and destruction of property (Dunn, 1975). During the war, these indignities culminated in the placement in concentration camps of 120,000 Japanese and their children, two thirds of whom were American citizens by birth or naturalization.[6]

During the 1940s and 1950s, many Filipinos were recruited into the U.S. armed forces. The onset of wartime prosperity and the removal of Japanese Americans from West Coast agriculture created economic opportunities for Filipino Americans. The overglamorized media portrayals of all Filipinos as loyal friends of America and enemies of Japan made them, along with Chinese Americans, at least "assistant heroes" in the great Pacific war (Kitano & Daniels, 1988). In 1946, Filipinos became eligible for U.S. citizenship two days before the Philippines was granted independence.

On the East Coast and in Midwestern cities, there were smaller Asian Indian communities made up of merchants and middle-class professionals. Their presence, visits to this country of such famous personalities as Swami Vivekanand and Rabindernath Tagore, and world events created among Americans an interest in and political sympathy for India. Some Indians, most notably Jagjit Singh, a Sikh import merchant, took advantage of this and lobbied the United States Congress. These efforts led to the passage of the Immigration Act of 1946, which gave the right to naturalization and a small immigration quota to "persons of races indigenous to India."

Asian Americans in Post-World War II America. Immediately following the war, the condition of the Chinese Americans improved:

> The demographic changes of the 1940s were quite pronounced. Nearly 20,000 Chinese American babies were born during the decade: for the first time in history the most numerous five-year cohort of Chinese Americans was persons under five years of age. (Kitano & Daniels, 1988, p. 37)

The relaxation of the immigration laws and China's complex political status after the war—the three different political entities: the People's Republic of China, Taiwan, and Hong Kong—also helped.[7] They also benefited from the general postwar economic prosperity of the country. However, in 1949, the communists under Mao Tse-tung came into power in China, and the American image of China changed:

> Knowing that in the past attitudes toward China had quickly been translated into worse or better treatment for Chinese in America, many in the Chinese community were nervous about their possible fate after 1949. The nervousness increased when China intervened against American troops in Korea in late 1950. Many feared that Chinese Americans would be placed in concentration camps as Japanese Americans had been just eight years previously. (Kitano & Daniels, 1988, p. 41)

Hostility toward mainland China continued until President Nixon's trip to that country in the early 1970s. During the Cold War years, many Chinese Americans became suspect. Federal Bureau of Investigation (FBI) and Immigration and Naturalization Service (INS) agents often raided Chinatowns and harassed their residents. The Cold War affected Chinese Americans in other ways as well.[8]

For the Japanese Americans, the postwar years were harder. The federal government revoked the mass exclusion orders in December of 1944, but thousands of the internees had nowhere to go and were fearful of the world outside the camps. Those who had relatives in the Midwest or on the East Coast joined them. Others left the camps with nothing more than train fare to the locations where they had lived before the war:

> Those who still owned property found their homes dilapidated and vandalized, their farms, orchards, and vineyards choked with weeds, their personal belongings stolen or destroyed. Others with nothing left were sheltered for a time by churches and few social agencies as they looked for ways to eke out a living. (Chan, 1991, p. 139)

There were more than 500 federal, state, and local laws and ordinances aimed against the Japanese Americans in 1950 (Dunn, 1975). Besides causing physical and emotional discomfort and stress, their wartime experience had hurt them in other ways as well.[9] They worked hard at recovering from their losses:

> It meant extra work, overtime, and dependence on multiple family incomes and multiple jobs. Gardening was one popular field; professionals and businessmen mowed lawns on a part-time basis to accumulate the capital needed to buy homes, to start their own enterprises, and to finance education of their children, the Sansei. (Kitano & Daniels, 1988, p. 70)

They also took advantage of the changes taking place in the society. Less than 50 years after being the most hated minority group, they have become the model minority.

Prior to the war, most of the Asian Indians in the United States had settled in California and engaged in farming. Their number had stayed small. Their families had not come with or followed them to this country. Most of them married Hispanic women, mostly from Mexican and Mexican American migratory worker families. Prior to the passage of the Immigration Act of 1946, people from the Indian subcontinent could not legally immigrate to this country. The most impressive of Asian Indians to benefit from this act was Dilip Singh Saund, who, after he became a citizen, was elected to a local judgeship and in 1956 was elected to Congress—the first Asian American congressman. He was reelected twice. Great changes have occurred in the Asian Indian community since the passage of the Immigration and Nationality Act of 1965. Under the family reunification provision of this act, U.S. citizens and permanent residents could sponsor their immediate family members for immigration. People from all parts of the Indian subcontinent and its vicinity (India, Pakistan, Bangladesh, Nepal, and Sri Lanka) with their linguistic, religious, and cultural differences, are represented in that community. They are more or less evenly distributed throughout the country and reside in neighborhoods that reflect all socioeconomic levels. There are no Indiatowns, Little Nepals, or New Pakistans. Overall, their major characteristics include a high level of education, concentration in the professions, and a commitment to maintaining family connection both here and between the United States and their country of origin (Glazer, 1976). Their overall economic status has put them in the group of other Asian Americans whom the society at large chooses to label as a "model minority."

In the olden days, most Filipinos worked in agriculture in California, in fish canneries in Alaska, and in menial service jobs elsewhere. They tried "Uncle Tomming," which meant letting the white Americans feel superior and playing the role of an inferior "little brown brother" to their fullest advantage (Pido, 1997). When the 1965 immigration law did away with the quota system, the Philippines became one of the chief suppliers of immigrants to the United States:

> The Philippine government as well as its educational system are both modeled after those of the United States. Most educated Filipinos speak a fair amount of English, which is the medium of instruction in secondary and higher education in the country. (Chan, 1991, p. 149)

Filipinos who have come here since 1965 are a highly educated group. A large proportion of them are professionally trained, the majority as doctors and nurses. Some are able to continue their careers, and others settle for lower jobs. "Filipino lawyers may find work as clerks; teachers as secretaries; dentists as dental aides; and engineers as mechanics" (Kitano & Daniels, 1988, p. 85). World War II resulted in the freedom of Korea from Japan, but it also created two Koreas. The U.S. Army established a military government in South Korea, and the Russians occupied the northern part. A United Nations commission unsuccessfully tried to hold national elections. In 1948, South Korea approved a national constitution and elected Syngman Rhee as the first president of the Republic of Korea. In the North, the Communists established the People's Republic of Korea. Hostilities between the two Koreas led to the Korean War in 1950. The United States went to the protection of South Korea. Three years of fighting only reaffirmed the status quo— the reality of two Koreas (Melendy, 1977). Thousands of Americans fought in the Korean War, and after the war, the United States continued to station thousands of troops in South Korea (Chan, 1991). A wave of Korean immigrants, consisting of wives of American servicemen, war orphans, and students, arrived between 1951 and 1964.[10] Most Koreans have, however, come after the passage of the 1965 immigration law. As a group, they were highly educated: Many came with professional degrees. Nevertheless, they had difficulty in finding jobs commensurate with their skills. Although second- and third-generation Koreans have adjusted to American life and become successful businessmen and professionals, most newcomers have not reached the social and economic level to which they aspired. Failing to find employment in the areas of their training and expertise, many end up in the small-business sector.

With the takeover of China by Mao Tse-tung's forces in 1949 and the outbreak of war in Korea in 1950, Vietnam had become vital to American's security in terms of containing the spread of communism (Chan, 1991). On the emergence of South Vietnam under Diem, a staunch anticommunist, the United States assured him of its full support and showed this support with $100 million in aid. Later on, it agreed to help train the South Vietnamese army, raised the number of American advisers in South Vietnam, and started pouring in military assistance. Communist insurgent activities in South Vietnam by infiltrators from the North and by the South Vietnamese Communists, called Vietcong, began. In 1964, the North Vietnamese shelled the American destroyer *Maddox* in the Gulf of Tonkin. Within 5 days, Congress passed a resolution that gave President Johnson extraordinary powers to act as he saw fit in Vietnam. The United States became a major player in the war. By the end of 1967, there were half a million American troops in the country, and the United States was spending $2 billion per month on the war (Chan, 1991). The war went on until 1973 and cost over 50,000 American and several million Southeast Asian lives. Upon realizing that the war could not be won, the United States decided to withdraw, leaving the South Vietnamese to do the fighting. Within 2 years the Saigon government fell. Vietnamese refugees have come to the United States in two waves. In the first wave were military personnel, professionals, civil servants, farmers, and teachers, who were mostly educated and familiar with the English language and the American culture. The majority belonged to the middle and upper classes and were Catholic. The second wave consisted of those who left Vietnam after the fall of Saigon in 1975. Most of them were poorer, less educated, and mostly Buddhists.

Cambodia gained independence from France in 1954, and under Norodom Sihanouk's government, it declared itself a neutral nation. However, problems with the United States led to an increased dependence on Russian and Chinese aid. There was also increased cooperation with the North Vietnamese. By 1966, Cambodia was indirectly involved in the Vietnam War. Border areas of Cambodia became the targets of American-South Vietnamese assaults, because the North Vietnamese and the Vietcong were regularly using those areas for food and as a sanctuary from South Vietnamese and American air attacks (Kitano & Daniels, 1988).

> In 1970, General Lon Nol, with the approval of the United States, overthrew Prince Sihanouk's government. Relations with North Vietnam and the Viet Minh were broken off. Between 1970 and 1975 the United States dropped over half a million tons of bombs. The war created more than three million refugees. (Kitano & Daniels, 1988, p. 147)

In 1975, the Khmer Rouge came into power in Cambodia. The new radical Marxist regime led by Pol Pot began to purge Cambodia of all Western influences by rooting out all undesirable elements—intellectuals, government officials, and urban dwellers. In 1978, Vietnam invaded Cambodia and replaced the Pol Pot regime with a pro-Vietnam puppet communist government. In view of the traditional enmity between the Khmer and the Vietnamese, people anticipated more destruction and fled to Thailand. Over the years, millions of Cambodians have left their native land and become refugees.

Laos also wanted to be an independent, neutral country, but its geography made that impossible. The Ho Chi Minh trail, a major supply line for North Vietnam, ran the length of eastern Laos. In order to destroy that line, the United States dropped more than 2 million bombs on Laos between 1965 and 1973 (Chan, 1991; Kitano & Daniels, 1988). Moreover, as in Cambodia, when the Royal Laos Government came into power, the communist Pathet Lao, who were allies of the Vietminh in Vietnam, controlled half of the countryside. The U.S. Central Intelligence Agency,

> in violation of the agreements reached at the second Geneva Conference in 1962, which guaranteed Laotian neutrality, fought a war of its own against the Pathet Lao, using a mercenary army composed of 9,000 Hmong tribesmen led by General Vang Pao. (Chan, 1991, p. 154)

After the communists took full control of the country in 1975, the government adopted a policy of purging "cultural poisons" and punishing the traitors. Thousands of lowland Lao were sent to reeducation camps, and the highland Hmongs became the object of the government's ire.

By 1982, about 120,000 Laotian refugees had been admitted to the United States. The majority of them were Hmong (Wodarski, 1992a).

Relevance of the History of Asian American Groups for Social Work With Them. Social workers need to know that the past persists in the present of Asian Americans. As in the past, the socioeconomic and political conditions in Asian countries are forcing many of their citizens to look beyond their borders for better conditions of life promising economic prosperity, political freedom, and social stability. America and its wealth are still beckoning and inviting people from Asia. Changes in the immigration laws, however, reflect a different methodology for invitation. The U.S. manpower needs still determine the inflow of people from other countries. As in the past, the needs of the economy and the popular reaction to nonwhite immigrants often do not mesh. Public prejudice and institutional discrimination against Asian Americans, though not as blatant and rampant as in the past, are still a part of the reality of these people. Governments at the various levels are not as eager to accommodate and back the popular attitudes and actions as they were even half a century ago. Although there is no legal inequality and social segregation, Asian Americans continue to be treated differently because of their different appearance, lifestyles, and values. As in the past, the attitudes and behaviors of the mainstream Americans toward Asian Americans are influenced by what happens in and foreign policies of their countries of origin. For example, when the communists came into power in China, the American image of China changed. Many in the Chinese American community became nervous about their fate. When China intervened against American troops in Korea in 1950, many feared that they would be put in concentration camps, as the Japanese Americans were during the war. During the Cold War years, the FBI and INS agents often raided Chinatowns and harassed their residents.

Social workers should realize that Asian Americans still face extensive prejudice, discrimination, and denial of equal opportunity and that many are deprived of equal access to public services, including police protection, education, health care, and the judicial system. Hate crime incidents include physical attacks on and murders of Asian Americans, assaults on their homes and places of worship, racially motivated boycotts against Asian-owned businesses, and harassment of Asian American students on college campuses (U.S. Commission on Civil Rights, 1986, 1992). Although Asian Americans are acknowledged as people who work hard and want to excel, they are also viewed as "foreigners" who are taking jobs and other economic opportunities from "real" Americans. Even the highly qualified experience discrimination in the labor market. Furthermore, their image of success creates interracial tensions and conflicts between Asian Americans and other minorities (Balgopal, 1995a; David & Lin, 1997).

Because of their history (for those who have been Americans for generations), unfamiliarity with the American human services system (for those who are new to this country), mistrust of government and its officials (for those who have come as refugees), and cultural values that stress keeping personal and family problems within the family and that attach stigma to the experience of mental and emotional distress (for most), Asian Americans are reluctant to ask for and use help. An understanding of these factors should inform social work interventions with Asian Americans. Asian Americans need their ethnic communities as significant sources of emotional and practical help. As havens of social support, economic assistance, and political power, most of those communities either do not exist or have lost their vitality. Therefore, one of the foci of intervention with Asian Americans should be to revitalize those communities.

COMMON CHARACTERISTICS: COMMONALITY OF CULTURES AND WORLDVIEWS

The lands that Asian Americans or their ancestors came from have varied geographical conditions, histories, customs, languages, and religions. On the surface, they seem to have nothing in common among them. However, there are striking commonalities in their historical and contemporary experiences in this country as well as in their worldviews. The commonalities of their experience as Americans include (a) experiencing hostility from the larger community, which has taken the forms of prejudice, economic discrimination, political disenfranchisement, physical violence, immigration exclusion, and social segregation; (b) living in a state of ambivalence—lauded as a "successful minority" while simultaneously being subjected to continuing unfair treatment (Chan, 1991); (c) being stereotyped, sometimes as a "problem minority" and at other times as a "model minority"; (d) being perceived as "perpetual foreigners"; and (e) struggling to realize the American dream. The reasons for the discrimination, inequality, and maltreatment experienced by Asian Americans have been analyzed from several different perspectives.

> Marxists claim that Asian Americans have suffered because they were part of the proletariat; scholars and activists who consider racism as the most fundamental issue employ race as a central category of analysis; while those with an international perspective emphasize the link between the national subjugation of certain Asian countries and the maltreatment of their emigrant abroad. (Chan, 1991, p. 81)

The truth is that they were maltreated because of all these reasons. They were unwelcome because of class, race, and nationality simultaneously:

> The law relating to Asian Americans was often as discriminatory as that relating to Blacks. Perhaps it was less ambiguous, less confusing, because it was more evenly administered from place to place. There was no "north" for the Asian American to escape to. (Dunn, 1975, p. 101)

White America created its own definitions of the Asian identity, which varied from time to time and from group to group, with varying effects on the Asian Americans' perceptions of themselves.

Worldviews result from people's experiences as well as from cultural beliefs and values. Here, we identify the common cultural values of Asian Americans.

Family-Centeredness. In most Asian societies, family, not the individual, is viewed as the basic unit. Family members are socialized to think of the family's needs, prestige, stability, and welfare as more important than the individual's aspirations, comfort, health, and well-being. The family's structure, the roles of its members, and the rules of relationships are prescribed and rigidly followed. Families are patriarchal, patrilocal, and patrilineal. The man—the father—is the head of the family and the main provider. His authority is not questioned. The woman leaves her family of origin after her marriage and becomes absorbed in the husband's family. She is the main nurturer and caretaker. Because of patrilineage, the birth of a son enhances the status and security of the mother. Sons are valued more and are given higher status than daughters are. Preserving the prestige of the family and its lineage is seen as the most important duty of family members. They are expected to excel in things that will bring honor to the family and to avoid behaviors that reflect poorly on it. Problems originating within or outside the family are kept within the family, lest negative information outside the home bring disgrace to the family (Lum, 1986). In a discussion of the difficulty in convincing Asian refugee victims of rape and sexual abuse to seek help, Mattson (1993) said, "[I]t is as if the whole family has been raped, and the woman brings further shame to the family as well as to herself if the crime is publicized" (p. 161). A strong sense of obligation pervades the life of family members:

> Parents are considered by their children as the greatest obligation because parents were the ones who brought them into the world and cared for them when they were helpless. Hence, regardless of what parents may do, the child is still obligated to give respect and obedience. (Ho, 1987, p. 25)

Family harmony is stressed, and control of emotions is emphasized. A clear definition of members' roles helps to minimize conflict within the family (Balgopal, 1995a).

Intrafamilial Relationships. Asian families are different from mainstream American families in the relative place of different family members and their roles and responsibilities, as well as in the family's patterns of communication and control. The father's position is supreme, and he has the final say in all major decisions. If his parents are available, he consults his father and acts on that advice. The wife's position is lower than not only her husband and his parents but also her oldest son, because he will become the head of the family after his father's death. In arguments between his wife and his parents, the man is expected to side with his parents. In parent-child relationships, the father makes and enforces family rules. There may not be extensive two-way communication between the father and children. There is a stronger emotional bond between the mother and the children, who rely on her to be not only the link of communication with their father but also someone who intercedes on their behalf. Love and affection are not openly displayed in the Asian family. Both parents usually show no hesitancy in pampering an infant publicly, but after these early years, "the child quickly becomes incorporated into his or her role in the family structure and learns to live by the more rigid guidelines and expectations of the family and the society" (Ho, 1987, p. 28). In general, the communication between parents and children is one-way, with messages flowing from parents to children in the form of directives.

Because the oldest son is the most desired child, he carries more responsibilities than his siblings. He has authority over the siblings, but that authority carries the burden of being a role model for them. He is expected to provide guidance to his younger siblings. Daughters are socialized as caretakers of the household. Older children are

> encouraged to set a good example for other siblings in gentleness, manners, and willingness to give up pleasure or comfort in favor of someone else. To show respect to the older siblings, the younger siblings use appropriate kin terms of address between brothers and sisters in different age groups. (Ho, 1987, p. 29)

Sibling rivalry and aggression are discouraged. Overall, a member's status determines his or her role within the family. Everyone is expected to meet the appropriate role obligations, which for those with lower status involve obedience, submission, and respect. The idea of shame rather than the concept of punishment guides the family in keeping its members within the societal norm. Children are not encouraged to become independent at an early age, and grown sons are expected to stay on with their parents. Individualism is equated with selfishness (Ryan, 1985).

Extended Family Ties. In the traditional Asian culture, great importance is given to maintaining a wide network of kinship. Individuals are expected to treat other relationships as secondary to the needs of the kinship relationships. Network ties are maintained by a common domicile or by frequent visits (Ho, 1987). Referring to the Chinese extended family, Ishisaka and Takagi (1982) observed,

> Whether represented by lineage membership or, as in the U.S., by the bonds of blood assumed on the basis of common surname, kinship is basic to the definition of the relationships that are important in everyday life and to an individual's prerogatives. (p. 129)

For the Hmong, the extended family is the whole clan. Families belong to one of the 18 clans, all of which are represented among the Hmong refugees in the United States. The clan helps in several ways. Its leader is recognized as the head of all the families in the clan; identification with the clan serves the psychological and sociological need for belonging; and it provides for group decision making and problem resolution. In the United States, the clan leaders also function as liaisons between Hmong and non-Hmong communities and as arbitrators in resolving intraclan and interclan conflict (McInnis, 1991). The extended family among Filipinos is a wider group in a different sense:

> Rather than reckoning family membership only by patrilineal descent, Filipino families tend toward bilateral equality in family relationships, with the relatives of both parents being incorporated into the extended family. Relatives acquired by marriage play roles of importance equal to those related by blood ties. An additional source of members is the *"compadrazgo"* system, in which friends and allies can be recruited to serve as godparents to children. Thus incorporated into the family network, the godparent also assumes the responsibilities and obligations attendant to the role. (Ishisaka & Takagi, 1982, pp. 141-142)

Similarity in Religious Beliefs. Buddhism, Confucianism, and Hinduism are the main religious systems that have dominated the society of almost every Asian country. These systems are markedly different from Christian theologies. Buddhism does not have a "god," does not define human beings as having a soul, and does not acknowledge any supernatural power or force that can help mankind. Its core consists of four "noble truths"—that (a) human existence is suffering and unhappiness, (b) this unhappiness is caused by selfish cravings and ignorance, (c) selfish cravings and ignorance can be destroyed, and (e) this can be done by following the eightfold path. Thus this religion urges the individual to take responsibility for his or her behavior and to actively strive to change behavior, while recognizing that one is a part of a larger whole (Burtt, 1959; Enos, 1997). "Buddhism teaches compassion, a respect for life and moderation in behavior. Self-discipline, patience, modesty, and friendliness in relationships, as well as selflessness, are qualities which are highly valued in Buddhist canon" (Ishisaka & Takagi, 1982, p. 129).

Similarly, Confucianism is a way of practicing a righteous lifestyle. Confucian ideals are loyalty, filial piety, chastity, heroism, selfless friendship, and the man's duty to use his talents to serve his family and country (Dunn, 1975). The emphasis is on the concept of piety, which means that the living are linked with their ancestors as well as with the societal institutions. They are challenged to live a good and virtuous life. Confucianism's core beliefs are in humans' (a) ability to achieve self-understanding by looking inward and introspection; (b) ability to appreciate the feelings, needs, and desires of others; (c) ability to acknowledge their limitations while demanding the most of themselves, and (d) understanding that changing the world requires a collective action (deBary, 1959). Spiritual fulfillment is to be sought through harmony in the five basic relationships: those between a ruler and his subjects, father and son, husband and wife, elder and younger siblings, and friends. These relationships demand loyalty and respect (Ishisaka & Takagi, 1982). The doctrine of the mean is emphasized, which recommends the middle way, the path between life's extremes (Ryan, 1985).

Unlike Buddhism, which has no god, and Confucianism, which is more a philosophy of life than a religion, Hinduism believes not only in God but also in His numerous incarnations in the forms of many gods and goddesses, as well as in the human soul. Hinduism teaches that all human beings are godlike and have divine nature and that the individual self or *atman* is a part of the cosmic absolute or "Brahman." For the individual's perfection and the creation of a perfected and harmonious world, the divine nature of human beings needs to be expressed. However, individual suffering and societal injustices are explained by the theories of *karma* and *dharam*. One's *karma* or deeds in the past life determine one's status and position in this life. *Dharam* is a human quality that is conducive to happiness and, ultimately, to *moksha* or salvation. One develops this quality by controlling one's anger and practicing harmlessness, benevolence, truthfulness, cleanliness, purity, and devotion to God (Thangavelu, 1980). One's *karma* and *dharam* determine one's place in the society, which is organized on a caste system.

Ideas drawn from Buddhist and Confucian thought, combined with indigenous folk religions, give people in many Southeast Asian countries their cultural beliefs and values. For example, Japanese religious traditions consist of Buddhism, Confucianism, and Shintoism, which is the indigenous religion of Japan. Japanese households typically have two altars, one each for Buddhist and Shinto devotion. *Shinto* literally means "the way of god," and primitive Shinto centered on the animistic worship of natural phenomena—the sun, mountains, trees, water, and rocks (Kumagai, 1995). There are three basic types of Shinto shrines. One type is found at scenic places near mountains, seas, and waterfalls. The legendary figures in ancient myths are deified in shrines of the second type. The third type of shrines is for the worship of ancestral spirits by each family or clan (Ito, 1998). Shintoism thus has a pantheistic orientation and includes elements of nature and ancestor worship (Rarick, 1994). There is a remarkable similarity between the Japanese Shintoism and some of the Hindu religious practices. Hindus also have deified elements of nature, such as the sun, moon, fire, and rain, as well as mythological heroes, and they worship these deified elements. Buddhism was a revolt against the Hinduism of the time of Gautama Buddha, the founder of Buddhism. The Buddha did, however, accept the basic Hindu philosophy and metaphysics but prescribed a different methodology to attain *moksha* or *nirvana*. Hinduism incorporated the Buddha's teachings into the Hindu belief system, made him a Hindu god, and drove Buddhism out of India. There is thus an underlying commonality among these religions. The beliefs and values of these religions have had an impact even on those professing imported religions.

Of the imported religions, Christianity and Islam are the most prominent. Whereas there are small Christian communities in most Asian countries, Islam is the dominant religion in Bangladesh, Indonesia, Malaysia, and Pakistan, and many other countries also have large Muslim populations. Followers of Islam are called Muslims. The Qur'an is their holy book. It contains the basic beliefs of Islam and also provides specific guidelines for daily living. "It forbids the eating of pork, the drinking of liquor, and gambling and provides guidelines for marriage and divorce" (Locke, 1998, p. 217). It also spells out the Five Pillars of Faith, the essential religious practices: (a) *Shaheda*, the confession of faith that there is no god but God and that Muhammad is the messenger of God; (b) *Salet*, prayer that must be performed five times each day—at dawn, midday, afternoon, sunset, and evening; (c) *Zaket*, money given in charity for the poor and needy; (d) fasting for the whole month of Ramadan; and (e) *Hajj*, a pilgrimage to Mecca undertaken at least once in lifetime. Most Muslims adhere strictly to their religious practices and visit the mosque every Friday for communal prayers. The family is considered a key social unit in which each member is valued and plays a special role. Loyalty to one's family takes precedence over personal needs. The Qur'an stresses that parents must be well cared for in their old age. Piety, love, and mercy in marriage are emphasized. Sexual fidelity is demanded. The best believers are those who are good to their wives. Among all lawful things, divorce is considered as the most hated by God. Fathers retain custody of their children after divorce unless otherwise arranged. Compassion, goodness, and piety are important values. A person's dignity, honor, and reputation are of major importance. Humans are unable to control all events in their lives and must acknowledge their dependence on God (Ahmed, 1992; Locke, 1998; Mahmoud, 1996).

Other Cultural Values. Cultural values that more or less affect most Asian Americans' response to the demands of life and are likely to have a bearing on social work interventions include:

1. acceptance of suffering in life as inevitable,

2. a sense of fatalism,

3. self-effacement,

4. avoidance of shame,

5. filial piety,

6. respect and loyalty for all authority,

7. obedience to rules and roles,

8. middle-position virtue,

9. an awareness of social milieu,

10. restrained modes of emotional expression, and

11. use of indirect methods of communication. (Browne & Broderick, 1994; Kitano, 1990)

Carr-Ruffino (1996) has discussed the commonality of cultural patterns among Asian Americans in terms of the concepts of *the group, harmony, modesty, education, status,* and *customs.* They are socialized to see the group as the most important part of the society: valuing group recognition and reward, emphasizing a sense of belonging to the group, and extending strong family ties to other relatives and close friends. They are expected to put group harmony first by avoiding personal conflicts and by being flexible, deferring, and complying with others' wishes. They are expected to show modesty by avoiding statements perceived as boasting or self-congratulatory, being reticent to talk about themselves and their accomplishments, and avoiding drawing attention to themselves. They place unique emphasis on education, seeing it as a moral virtue and an investment in family status. They value a sense of order, propriety, and appropriate behavior between persons of varying status based on occupational position, education, wealth, and family background. They respect seniority and the elderly. Among the typical customs, Carr-Ruffino (1996) has mentioned the gesture for beckoning someone to come (by holding out the arm with the palm down); meals as being more ritualistic, communal, and time consuming; and colors and numbers having different meanings.

Their belief in the inevitability of suffering in life, fatalism, filial piety, and middle-position virtue, as well as their acute awareness of one's social environment, tend to blind Asian Americans to the fluidity of social situations. Because open expression of emotions is discouraged, emotional difficulties and problems often manifest themselves through physical complaints and illnesses. Subordination of the individual to the family and the larger group creates intrafamilial and intragroup discord. The individual's failure to live up to the familial expectation leads to guilt and suffering on his or her part and a sense of being let down and shame on the part of others.

The previous discussion on the cultural commonalities among Asian Americans should be viewed only as background information. It should not lead to rigid categorization and the expectation that individual and group behaviors will neatly reflect these values.

DIVERSITY WITHIN: SUBGROUP AND INTRAGROUP DIFFERENCES AMONG ASIAN AMERICANS

Despite the common characteristics of most Asians Americans presented earlier, a closer look reveals significant differences among the various Asian American groups. Some of these can be traced to the differences in their national and ethnic origins, whereas others can be explained in terms of many other variables. A brief profile of each of the major Asian American groups is presented in the endnotes of this chapter.[11-16] This section brings out the differences among and within these groups.

Differences Based on National-Ethnic Variations. The differences among Asian Americans from different countries can be quite marked, because of the variations in their history, geography, stage of economic development, and degree of exposure to Western culture and the English language. There are also subcultural differences among people from the same country. For example, persons from India may speak different languages, profess different religions, wear different dresses, eat different foods, observe different customs, and have different worldviews. However, there is likely to be much more in common among Indians than between Indians and others. For instance, there is hardly anything in common between Hmong from the highlands of Laos and Parsees from Bombay, India. Hmong lived in the hills of Laos, isolated from the rest of the country. They have a culture distinct from that of the larger Laotian society. They had no written language until about 30 or 40 years ago, when missionaries went to their villages. They believe in evil spirits as the cause of illnesses and other forms of human suffering, and they trust their shamans for help with their problems (Kitano & Daniels, 1988). On the other hand,

Parsees are unlike the majority of Indians. They are not Hindus and do not subscribe to Hindu beliefs and values. They are a highly Anglicized, modernized, and educated group. The tasks of learning and mastering the English language, understanding and adapting to the American culture, and acquiring and refining the skills to survive in American society are vastly different for the Hmong and the Parsees. Chinese Americans are a good example of intragroup differences. They may be (a) individuals with a family history of several generations in the United States; (b) immigrants and their children; (c) migrant students, sojourners, and others who have chosen to stay on; or (d) refugees from countries such as Vietnam, Hong Kong, Malaysia, and Singapore. Hence, besides the between-group differences, there are also within-group variations in cultural orientation status among these people (Dana, 1998).

Differences Based on Socioeconomic Status and Situations. There are differences among Asian Americans in terms of their educational level, economic status, and social situation. The range of these differences is very wide, with the extremes being overrepresented. On the one hand, 39.1% of Asian Americans 25 and older have 4 or more years of college education (compared to 21.5% for the total population), but on the other hand, the percentage of those with only 0-4 years of elementary education (5.3%) is more than double that of the total population (2.4%). Similarly, on the one hand, the overall median family income for Asian Americans ($42,245) is higher than that of the total population ($35,353), partly because Asian American families have more earners per family. On the other hand, one out of every five (20.5%) year-round full-time Asian American workers earns less than $15,000, and roughly one out of eight (12.2%) lives in poverty.

Whereas only 8% of the total U.S. population is foreign born, the foreign-born make up 74% of Asian Americans (U.S. Bureau of the Census, 1992a, 1992b). The present picture of Asian Americans is dominated by immigrants who have come since 1965. Unlike their predecessors, these immigrants have included large numbers of white-collar professionals, most have come as families, and many women have come as principal immigrants. Espiritu (1996) has divided the contemporary Asian Americans into three categories: *highly educated, the disadvantaged*, and the *self-employed*. The highly educated are both men and women. A vast majority are immigrants. Many of these are in professional occupations more or less appropriate for their education and skills, although a few are in executive and management positions. Generally, they earn less money than their white counterparts. Some have failed to find appropriate professional positions and have ventured into business or gone into blue-collar jobs. In general, women make less money than men and encounter the "glass ceiling" more often than men. The *disadvantaged* group is made up of those who have limited education, occupational skills, and proficiency in speaking English. Almost all are immigrants who came as relatives of pre-1965 immigrants and refugees. Even working full-time year-round, a large portion of this group earned less than $10,000 (Ong & Hee, 1994). "The typical pattern of a dual-worker family is a husband who works as a waiter, cook, janitor, or store helper and a wife who is employed in a garment shop or on an assembly line" (Espiritu, 1996, p. 72). The *self-employed* group has emerged in response to the problem of underemployment, misemployment, and discrimination in the labor market. This group includes both the disadvantaged and the highly educated. Most are in labor-intensive marginally profitable businesses (Ong, 1984). Koreans are in the grocery business, dry-cleaning services, and the sale of Korean imported goods. Chinese run garment factories, restaurants, and gift shops. Indians are in hotel and motel and in the retail sales of Indian groceries and imported goods. Cambodians have found a niche in the doughnut business. Most of these businesses are surviving because of unpaid or minimally paid labor of spouses, children, relatives, and other disadvantaged workers (Espiritu, 1996).

Differences Based on Levels of Acculturation. Based on the level of acculturation, there are generally three types of families: (a) recently arrived immigrant families, (b) immigrant-American families, and (c) immigrant-descent families (Ho, 1987). For the recently arrived immigrants, factors such as the reason for coming (i.e., immigrant vs. refugee status), their residence (in ethnic vs. mainstream neighborhood), and assets on arrival (command over the English language and other marketable skills) create different patterns of acculturation. Most respond to being here in the ways identified by Shon and Ja (1982) as:

1. cultural shock and disbelief at the disparity between what was expected and what actually exists,

2. disappointment at what exists,

3. grief at the separation from and loss of what was left behind,

4. anger and resentment,

5. depression because of the current family situation,

6. some form of acceptance of the situation, and

7. mobilization of the family's energy and resources.

Specific reactions of individual families, however, involve varied combinations of these responses and different degrees of intensity. Within a family, responses of individuals vary. The immigrant-American families have foreign-born parents and American-born children. In the beginning, parents tend to cling to their traditional values and selectively adopt American values on the basis of their functional utility. Even after years of stay and increasing acculturation, influences of their original cultural heritage persist, whereas their children are acculturated faster. The values of the family's subsystems clash, as do those of individuals within these subsystems:

> Members of subsystems between wife and husband, parents and child, and siblings may share different values and goals conflicting with those set previously by the parents or grandparents. Some children may not know or speak their parent's native language, making communications and negotiation among family members nearly impossible. (Ho, 1987, p. 35)

The immigrant-descent families consist of second-, third-, or even fourth-generation American-born parents and their children. They are acculturated to the mainstream American values, speak English at home, and live outside the ethnic neighborhoods (Ho, 1987). There may still be traces of the old culture indirectly influencing the life and behavior of individuals and a periodic urge to learn about their roots and cultural heritage. Connor (1974) studied acculturation and family continuity in three generations of Japanese Americans and concluded that even the third-generation Japanese Americans retained many of the characteristics common to the traditional family system.

Differences Based on Immigration Status. As stated earlier, 74% of all Asian Americans are foreign born. Many of them are recent arrivals. They all experience situations peculiar to new immigrants from non-English speaking parts of the world, including problems of adjustment; lack of social support; deficiency in English language facility; and unfamiliarity with the American social, economic, and political systems. However, there are marked differences between immigrants and refugees. Those who have come as refugees have also problems resulting from (a) losses of their country, home, family members, friends, and a sense of connectedness; (b) the experience of physical and psychological trauma including torture, starvation, and illnesses; and (c) an uncertain present. War and violence have virtually destroyed their old ways of life. Their past and their ways of life are also devalued in the new country; the need to learn a new language, customs, and skills is overwhelming; and older people among them are confronted with the prospect of dying as strangers in a strange land (Kemp, 1993). Poverty among many refugees is a part of their reality. A survey of 739 Hmong, Khmer, Laotians, Chinese-Vietnamese, and Vietnamese in San Diego, California, found 75.8% of them living under the poverty level, with the range from 93.7% of Hmong living in poverty on the one extreme to 57.1% of Vietnamese on the other (Rumbaut, Chavez, Moser, Pickwell, & Wishnik, 1988).

Differences Based on Gender. We have discussed the patriarchal, patrilineal, and patrilocal families in most Asian cultures, pointed to the clearly prescribed and rigidly enforced gender-based roles of family members, and highlighted the differences in the positions of men and women. Despite their culturally conditioned role expectations, the conditions of life and socioeconomic forces in a new environment change people and their institutions. Asian Americans are no exception. Theoretically, migration should lead to an improvement in women's status as the family moves away from the traditional environment and as women participate in wage employment, gain more control over family income, and have greater say in family decision making. However, Asian American families do not present a clear picture of such improvement. Migration seems to produce contradictory outcomes, so that women's position improves in some ways and worsens in others (Morokvasic, 1984), and their within-family status rises some times and patriarchy reasserts itself at other times.

There are varied gender-based differences in the three groups of Asian Americans mentioned earlier. Men from the highly educated professional group are more willing to participate in the household work than are those from the working and small-business groups. There is also variance in the degree of egalitarianism within the family based on subcultural differences. The relationship between Filipino men and women is more egalitarian, and the difference in status between the two is much less than that between men and women in the Chinese, Indian, Japanese, and Korean groups. However, in general, women perform more household work than men in most Asian American households, and most men consider housework as women's work.

Most women from all socioeconomic groups work to supplement the family's income. In the larger job market, the Asian American woman has the disadvantage of being both a minority and a female. Most men view a woman's work on a job outside or in the family business as an extension of her family obligation. The persistence of the traditional division of labor, the need to do wage work as well, and the lack of appreciation by their men generates resentment in these women. This, in the context of their increased independence and contribution to the family's economic well-being and the larger society's emphasis on individualism, creates tension. On the other hand, men in underemployment or misemployment job situations have another unpleasant dimension of life to contend with. The negative image of the Asian American man constructed and propagated by the society at large adds to his anger and frustration. The loss of status and power of many Asian American men in both public and domestic arenas puts pressure on the family and leads at times to verbal and physical abuse and divorce (Luu, 1989).

Differences Based on Age. Older Asian Americans, particularly the first-generation immigrants, have a host of problems. Most cannot work because of age, disability, or lack of occupational and English language skills. Their acculturation difficulties cut them off from the larger world. Older women, the grandmothers in multigenerational households, share the household work, provide child care, and help in the socialization of children to the family's ethnic culture. However, their presence adds to the complexity of the family dynamics. Unlike older women, older men do not have much to contribute to the family's well-being, and there is low intergenerational solidarity. Therefore, they do not know how to fit in to the new world of the Asian American family. They want to retain the benefits of patriarchy, and they expect the same commitment, devotion, and subservience from their wives and obedience from their children that most Asian cultures prescribe. The struggle involved in the accommodation and adjustment to the realities of American life, viewed as a loss of power and status, is frustrating and painful for most of them.

Differences Based on Self-Perception. Self-perception determines how people view their reality and deal with life and its demands. A number of factors create and feed individual and group self-perceptions. Lee (1992) has identified the following nine self-images of the Chinese immigrant groups:

1. Refugee image—mentally retreating from political oppression and planning to return for revenge and revolution

2. Victim image—feeling victimized by events

3. Face-saving image—failing in business, marriage, or family in the country of origin and dreaming of rebuilding the business or family in this country

4. Sojourner image—suffering from past family, business, or professional failures and maintaining a neutral stance in this country

5. Betrayal image—feeling cheated by friends or business associates for investing money in business ventures in the United States

6. Opportunistic image—maintaining a detached attitude toward the social and political world around and being unwilling to commit to the well-being of the American or Chinese community

7. Crusader image—glorifying the virtues of Chinese culture or anticommunism and building psychological defense for justifying an existence in this strange land

8. Pioneer image—overcoming frustrations and miseries of this country and striving to contribute to its well-being

9. Participant image—adapting to the American way of life and becoming a part of American social, economic, and cultural community

The presence of these and other differences highlights the need for individualizing the client system—a person, family, group, or community—and ensuring that no Asian American group is reduced to a set of traits.

MAJOR NEEDS AND PROBLEMS OF ASIAN AMERICAN GROUPS

In our discussion of the commonalities and differences among Asian Americans, we have alluded to their needs and problems. This section elaborates on those.

Needs Related to Adjustment to a New Environment. For the newcomer, immigrant, and refugee alike, adjustment to a new environment is stressful. Besides the uncertainty, language deficiency, and financial insecurity, this experience involves *desocialization* and *resocialization* (Nah, 1993). Desocialization brings loss of roles, functions, values, old ways of life, status, and support systems. Resocialization involves changes in the traditional roles and relationships. Both tend to create problems. For example, economic necessity demands that all adult members work, which challenges the traditional hierarchical structure and roles of the family. As the head of the household, the man's inability to provide for his family single-handedly wreaks havoc with his self-image. Because the wife also works, she cannot be a subservient wife to her husband and a nurturing mother to her children. In the job market, many newcomers are employed in positions where their educational and experiential assets are ignored or devalued and where their lack of language facility is generalized to all dimensions of their ability. Nevertheless, their presence threatens several groups, both the "once-hads"—the nativists—and the "never-hads"—the disadvantaged (Kitano & Daniels, 1988, p. 154). That threat occasionally leads to outbursts of racially motivated violence, making a difficult environment hostile as well.

Needs Related to Adjustment to Downward Socioeconomic Mobility. Many of the recent immigrants and refugees who have a high degree of facility with the English language and employable skills experience downward socioeconomic mobility. A recent study of 196 Afghan refugee families in the San Francisco Bay area (Lipson, Omidian, & Paul, 1995) found that whereas in Afghanistan 29% of the men were professionals (professors, judges, high government officials) and 50% were in skilled jobs, sales, minor administration, or business, the corresponding numbers in similar positions in the United States had fallen to 8% and 27%, respectively. Earlier, a survey of Filipino immigrants had found that 20% of men and 34% of women had held professional or technical positions during the year just prior to their immigration but that these proportions had declined dramatically after 2 years in the United States for both men (9%) and women (15%). On the other hand, whereas only 6% of men and 9% of women had held service jobs before immigrating, these figures had increased considerably 2 years later for both men (33%) and women (24%) (East-West Population Institute, 1990). The same is true for many other Asian Americans. Those in professions occupy less desirable positions. For example, many Asian American physicians are employed by county and state hospitals as emergency room doctors—positions shunned by the majority doctors—earning less income than other doctors in private practice (Cho, 1997).

Needs of Those Experiencing the Glass Ceiling. Asian Americans have collectively established themselves as a stable, "overachieving" minority whose contributions are acknowledged in business, academia, medicine, science, and the arts but who are given limited access to the society's reward and recognition system (Mohan, 1997). Thus, those who seem to have moved into the mainstream, to have succeeded in attaining middle-class status, and to have adopted the American middle-class culture and norms also experience a lack of upward mobility. In the words of Mohan (1997), "[T]hey are servants of an organizational culture that needs them for particular roles and positions to a certain level. Beyond this functional necessity, their existence is a meaningless presence under the fabulous glass ceilings" (p. 122). They bear the pain of exclusion and exploitation stoically. Nevertheless, their success generates jealousy and resentment in others, and they are subjected to discrimination and racism. From time to time, both the newcomer and the third- and fourth-generation native-born experience anti-Asian sentiment expressed in the form of violence, vandalism, harassment, and intimidation.

Needs Resulting From the Societal Images of Asian Americans. The society at large constructs different images of Asian American men and women, sometimes positive and at other times negative, but always aimed at defining, maintaining, and justifying white male privilege. Living or fighting those images strains the life and resources of Asian Americans and their communities. Yoon (quoted in Espiritu, 1996) found a group of Asian American women at a college campus describing Asian men as "too passive, too weak, too boring, too traditional, too abusive, too domineering, too ugly, too greasy, too short, too ... Asian." Espiritu (1996) concludes that "[p]artly as a result of the racist constructions of Asian American womanhood and manhood and their acceptance by Asian Americans, intermarriage patterns are high, with Asian American women intermarrying at a much higher rate than Asian American men" (pp. 97-98).

Needs of the Poor Asian Americans. Although some Asian Americans are doing very well economically, there are many more who are poor. As compared with 6.9% of white families and 9% of white persons, 11.9% of Asian American families and 14.1% of Asian American individuals are below the poverty line. Like other poor, they experience the deprivation and degradation that poverty brings. Most work in minimum-wage jobs, and many hold more than one job. They live in crowded quarters in run-down neighborhoods. The conditions of their lives leave little time and energy to learn new skills, master the English language, explore opportunities for social and economic progress, and be exposed to the finer elements of the American culture. The need for social support forces many to live in ethnic neighborhoods where most of their interactions are with fellow ethnics. They continue to be cut off from the mainstream and to lead marginal lives. However, most Asian American poor believe in the American dream of success, wealth, and happiness and are willing to make the needed efforts and sacrifices to realize that dream. But the stereotypical view of the poor is imposed on them, whereby negative qualities are attributed to the poor, and then those negative attributes are used as justification for treating them negatively (Dhooper, 1997a).

Needs of the Elderly Asian Americans. The elderly Asian Americans are also a varied group with some common as well as unique needs. Beckett and Dungee-Anderson (1992) have divided them into categories: (a) retired single males, mainly Chinese and Filipinos, who never married because of immigration restrictions; (b) elderly females, mainly Japanese, who came here as picture brides; (c) immigrants and Americans born during the early 1900s; (d) parents who accompanied their children to America during the last two to three decades; and (e) persons who came with their families as refugees. Most of these elderly either did not work, did not work long enough, or held low-income jobs and are therefore eligible for minimal or no social security retirement benefits. Overall, they have a low economic status with a large proportion in poverty. For example, 36% of the Vietnamese elderly were under the poverty line.

The respect for the elderly is a common cultural value among people from Asian countries, and this respect is shown through the fulfillment of their tangible and intangible needs. This expectation of the Asian American elderly, particularly the foreign-born, acquires a special significance in view of the social conditions or inadequate resources of their families. The extended families that they nurtured are largely absent here, and even members of the immediate family tend to become independent of each other. The youth-centeredness of the American culture and the general indifference of the larger society toward the elderly make it harder for Asian American families to meet the needs of their elders. Moreover,

> Increased mobility and the contingencies of the American economic system promote independence and living apart. With the break of close ties comes the loss of the father's position as the patriarch and the mother's position as the emotional center of the family. This loss of authority and respect is more painful when the aging parents realize and blame their inability to function in the new society. (Miah & Kahler, 1997, p. 83)

Aging is a multidimensional phenomenon. The aging-related biological, cultural, economic, psychological, and social needs and conditions of the many Asian American elderly are compounded by the state of their uprootedness. They lack social support systems and cannot use the formal human services.

Needs of Asian American Women. There are marked differences among Asian women based on the level of acculturation, socioeconomic status, and subgroup variations. In her study of acculturation among Asian American professional women, Chow (1982) found four types:

1. The traditionalist, who is low on American values and high on Asian values. Her self-worth is defined by obedience to parents and by bringing honor to her family and ethnic group. Tension results from feelings in conflict with traditional expectations and from difficulty in dealing with the larger society.

2. The assimilationist, who is high on American values and low on Asian values. She tends to question the traditional values and defy parental authority. She defines her self-worth in terms of acceptance by Caucasians but suffers from feelings of guilt, self-denial, and self-hatred.

3. The pluralist, who is high on both American and Asian values. She tends to incorporate the useful aspects of both the minority and majority cultures and to balance her responsibilities at home, at work, and in the community. This requires continuous attempts to reconcile the two cultures.

4. The ambivalent, who is low on both American and Asian values. She tends to reject both cultures and is relatively isolated from both her ethnic group and the larger society. She derives little meaning from either world and experiences anomic feelings.

Generally, Asian cultures reinforce traditionally "feminine" characteristics—submissiveness, passiveness, altruism, adaptiveness, and timidity—and discourage independence, assertiveness, and competition, which are considered "masculine" traits (Fong, 1997).

Socioeconomic status also creates different sets of needs. "Working class women, including those who are less visible (such as women in Asian enclaves, Indochinese refugee women, and wives of U.S. servicemen) are clearly disadvantaged, with their needs and wants often ignored or inadequately addressed" (Fong, 1997, p. 97). Their problems emerge from their lack of English language proficiency, low level of education, low-ranking and low-paying jobs, low self-image and prestige. Educated and professional Asian American women experience the same problems in the larger society that their male counterparts do. Like women in the society as a whole, Asian American women, irrespective of their educational and economic status, are likely to be victims of domestic violence. There may be intergroup variations in the severity of this problem. According to Rhee (1997), wife abuse is much more prevalent in the immigrant Korean population than in other ethnic groups. However, the contributing factors that he has identified—high level of male domination in immigrant families, immigration stress and adjustment difficulties of men, and heavy drinking—operate in other communities as well.

Needs of Asian American Refugees. All the difficulties, needs, and problems that we have identified among Asian Americans thus far are equally parts of the reality of Asian refugees. In a sense, those needs and problems are compounded by their traumatic past, precarious present, and uncertain future. These put them at a high risk for serious psychiatric disorders and social dysfunctions. Their major mental health problems include anxiety, depression, and posttraumatic stress disorder. Thus, they require mental health and social services. They may also have serious physical health problems, which can be attributed to several factors, such as:

1. their premigration physical trauma, lack of medical care, starvation, and malnutrition;

2. diseases and high-risk health behaviors common in their native lands that they brought along;

3. physical effects of acculturation-related stress;

4. diseases related to the American life conditions and style; and

5. the lack of fit between their needs and the health care system's resources. (Dhooper & Tran, 1998)

Frye (1995) has classified their health problems into (a) initial concerns, (b) subsequent concerns, and (c) emerging conditions. The *initial concerns* centered on the high prevalence of tuberculosis, parasitic diseases, hepatitis B, severe anemias, malnutrition, and malaria. Tuberculosis continues to be serious problems among Indochinese refugees (Hann, 1994). The risk of perinatal hepatitis B transmission is 16 times as high for Asian infants as it is for the total U.S. population (Mayeno & Hirota, 1994). Overall, these problems have lost their prominence. The *subsequent concerns* focused on physical sequelae of malnutrition, disabling skeletomuscular and arthritic conditions, chronic pain from gunshot wounds and amputations, sensory-cognitive impairments, and sudden unexpected nocturnal death syndrome. The *emerging conditions* include hypertension, chronic gastric pain, chronic headache, diabetes, and nonspecific fatigue and dizziness, along with other harmful conditions of life that these refugees share with other Americans. They brought some of these conditions with them and acquired others as a result of acculturation. Examples of the former are smoking and eating foods high in sodium; examples of the latter include eating more meats, fats, proteins, and refined sugars. A host of factors—some patient-related, some health care system-related, and others social environmental—make it extremely difficult for these refugees to deal with their health problems.

SOCIAL WORK PRACTICE: GENERAL CONSIDERATIONS FOR INTERVENTION WITH ASIAN AMERICANS

In this section, we provide some ideas, insights, and suggestions that should inform social work intervention with Asian Americans.

A Pervasive Sense of Powerlessness Among Asian Americans. We have alluded to the status role reversal and downward social mobility of most new Asian immigrants and refugees and to many Asian Americans' experience of being denied occupational roles and rewards for which they are educationally and experientially qualified. Then there is the myth of the "Model Minority," which creates the belief that Asian Americans have their own resources to overcome adversity and succeed despite societal prejudice and discrimination. This myth has resulted in the denial of their vulnerability and need for services. There is thus a pervasive sense of powerlessness among Asian Americans, which tends to feed their cultural belief in "fate." Therefore, you should use empowerment-oriented approaches in working with Asian American individuals and communities. These should be geared toward: (a) helping individuals to acquire appropriate tangible resources and develop intangible assets such as a positive self-concept, hope and high morale, cognitive skills, interpersonal communication, and American problem-solving skills, health and physical competence, and supportive social networks; and (b) educating communities on how civil, political, and legal systems work and are influenced and how social institutions and service organizations can be made responsive to human needs (Dhooper, 1991, 1997a).

Family—A Source of Both Strength and Strain for Asian Americans. Traditionally, the family has been the hub of Asians' life and a bulwark against stress. However, devoid of resources of the larger kinship system, in its nuclear form, the family does not have the same vitality and resources. Nevertheless, Asian American families deeply care for, are concerned about, and are willing to invest in the well-being of their members. View the family as a resource and involve it in your intervention with the individual. The head of the family can be a source of useful ideas and can help in the acceptance and utilization of health and human services by family members. Remember that the family can also be a source of strain for many Asian Americans. Its structure, roles, rules, and the expectations from its members put strain on individuals, who are torn between the conflicting pressures of the traditional family and American culture. There is usually a discrepancy in the level of acculturation between parents and their children. "The children's greater receptivity to the ideas of individualism, independence, and assertiveness and attitudes in relation to authority, sexuality, and freedom of individual choice becomes problematic particularly for the newly arrived and first-generation immigrant Asian-American families" (Dhooper, 1991, p. 70). The individual is beset with feelings of alienation and a lack or conflict of identity, and the family is faced with marital and intergenerational conflict (Sue & Morishima, 1982). At the same time, there is a taboo against taking personal and familial problems outside the family. Make efforts to understand the dynamics of the Asian American family situation while keeping in mind that shame and guilt are important elements of the situation. Because structure is the essence of these families, structural and strategic-structural forms of family therapy have been found to be effective with them (Jung, 1984; Kim, 1985).

Consciousness of Being Different From Mainstream Americans. Earlier, we have discussed the relevance to the present situation of Asian Americans of their history of popular prejudice and discrimination, institutional racism, and discriminatory immigration and naturalization laws. Many Asian Americans use denial as a defense mechanism, denying the existence of racism against them. At the same time, they are conscious of being different from mainstream Americans, of being perpetual foreigners, an image that is constantly reinforced by the larger society. This creates a complex client situation. You should make constant efforts to acknowledge your own biases, prejudices, and concepts of what is normal and healthy; to accept the validity of clients' perspectives on their lives and situations; and to consider them as culturally equal to you (Dhooper & Tran, 1987). Encourage clients to accept their unique values and traditions and to take pride in their culture and its positive aspects (e.g., the family's place in the individual's well-being; importance of education, self-control, and religious faith); explore with them how these assets can be used for dealing with the problem.

Reluctance of Most Asian Americans to Ask for Help. Most Asian Americans are not likely to ask for help easily on their own:

> Those who have been here for generations are used to fend for themselves, turn inward for strength and/or seek solace and support from their families, and those who are new may not know of and/or feel comfortable in asking for help. For many Asian Americans new to this country social work is an alien concept. (Dhooper, 1997a, p. 38)

You should reach out to them in creative ways in order to deal with their culture-based barriers. They are also conditioned to control their feelings and to have a low level of emotional expressiveness. Most have difficulty in acknowledging the problem and coming out and talking openly about it. In the first encounter with Asian American clients (particularly those who are new to the American culture and service system), use culturally sensitive approaches to engaging them; putting them at ease; building a relationship with them; generating in them trust and faith in you; letting them disclose the problem at their pace; and encouraging them to share their interpretation of the nature, manifestation, and etiology of the problem. Many clients will only hint at the problem or will bring it up indirectly while talking in general or about other people.

> Allow the client to lead you into problem-area disclosure. Look for verbal and nonverbal cues from the client. Let the client state the problem area in his or her own words, then restate and clarify what the client is saying. (Lum, 1996, p. 165)

It is all right to assume that the client is looking for a solution to the problem and affirmation that he or she is not crazy, and that the client feels embarrassment over having to seek help and confusion or puzzlement over how therapy can be helpful (Root, 1985).

Need to Adapt Social Work Intervention Strategy to Asian Americans and Their Needs. Most Asian Americans do not believe in psychiatric dynamics and psychological explanations of behavioral difficulties. Instead, social, moral, and organic explanations are used (Ho, 1987). In general, Asian Americans tend to experience stress psychosomatically, so that many of their emotional and psychological problems are expressed as somatic complaints. Therefore, focus on the physical illness and rule out the possibility of an organic cause of the complaint. Using a therapeutic approach that focuses on external stress, emphasizes direct problem solving, and suggests active problem management is more effective with this group of clients (Kim, 1985). Similarly, "they find loosely targeted and abstract long-term goals incomprehensible, unreachable, and impractical. They prefer structured and goal-directed work with clear, realistic, concrete, and measurable objectives" (Ho, 1987, p. 49).

In some Asian American cultures, priests, indigenous healers, fortune tellers, and the like have significant influence on people's ability to deal with their difficulties. View these as parts of the client's social support system. Their collaboration can improve the likelihood of the client's cooperation and the success of intervention. Also, view special prayers for and wearing of an amulet or talisman by the client as psychological supplements to the social worker's counseling, educational, and resource mobilization activities.

Respect for authority is a cultural value in most Asian cultures. Therefore, try to convey an air of confidence. When asked, do not hesitate to disclose your educational background and work experience. "Asian/Pacific American clients need to be assured that their therapist is more powerful than their illness or family problem and will 'cure' them with competence and the necessary know-how" (Ho, 1987, p. 46).

In general, a concrete, tangible, problem-focused and result-oriented approach is needed for effective work with Asian Americans, irrespective of the level of intervention—whether you are working with individuals, groups, organizations, or communities.

Special Sensitivity for the Needs of Asian American Refugees. Premigration stresses continue to predict depression and anxiety for years in Asian refugees, although there are unique intergroup and intragroup differences (Chung & Kagawa-Singer, 1993). In working with these refugees, your approach should be informed by sensitivity for their experiences. A confrontational approach in which "identification and dissection of the psychological trauma is encouraged, and introspection is expected to be followed by verbalization" (Frye & D'Avanzo, 1994, p. 94) is antithetical to many Asian cultures. In her discussion of working with Southeast Asian refugee women, Mattson (1993) suggested,

> The professional should ask only as much as is needed to obtain a history and then follow the woman's lead about how much other information to try to elicit. A history of sexual violence is rarely offered directly by a refugee woman. The history of rape trauma is usually revealed through a veiled account of personal injury, through the comments of family members or friends, or by considering the likelihood of such an event occurring. (p. 162)

Conditioned by their experience in their native land and in other countries as refugees, many of them have a deep mistrust of government officials, representatives, and workers. Because of this mistrust, most are hesitant to express their needs and ask for services. Therefore, reach out to them with genuine concern, sensitivity, and understanding.

SOCIAL WORK INTERVENTION AT MICRO-, MEZZO-, AND MACROLEVELS: PRINCIPLES AND APPROACHES

The many commonalities and yet significant differences among Asian Americans that we have discussed earlier point to the difficulty in grasping the reality of individuals, families, and communities. Those similarities and differences will play out in unique ways in specific situations. Problems are experienced by people in a social context and cannot be completely understood independently of the dynamics of the total situation. Hence, there is the need for an assessment of clients and their situations as the basis for intervention. In this section, we are presenting ideas and suggestions that will help improve the fit between your professional resources, skills, and services and the needs of Asian American clients.

Assessment-Related Practice Principles and Approaches

1. Make the assessment comprehensive and multidimensional. Only a comprehensive and multidimensional assessment can lead to the most appropriate intervention. In Chapter 2, we recommended a system-oriented approach to assessment. Table 2.1 gives a list of systems that should be explored, as they account for the complexity of life and its social environment. We have also given suggestions for modifying that list for assessing families and have presented ideas for assessing communities. Because many Asian Americans hesitate to disclose their problems, a review of the various systems will reveal areas for further exploration and can lead to the "discovery" of problems. Whenever appropriate, supplement this review and exploration with group-specific questions. For example, in order to understand the problems of Asian American refugees, you can explore the following areas, as suggested by Ishisaka, Nguyen, and Okimoto (1985):

a. Family life and experiences during childhood

b. Life experiences before the client became a refugee

c. Reasons for escaping, the escape process, losses, and expectations

d. Life in refugee camps, attitude about camp life, and problems of sustenance

e. Sponsorship to the United States, expectations of life in the new land, experiences with culture conflict, survival problems, and coping strategies

f. Family-life adjustments necessitated by residency in the United States

g. Current concerns and expectations for the future

h. The client's present understanding of adjustment problems

2. Do not assume the cultural identity of the client-system. The effects of culture on people's attitudes, perspectives, and behaviors persist for generations in both obvious and indirect ways. However, the extent of those effects is determined by the level of acculturation. Looks can often be misleading. Make efforts to understand the cultural dimension of the client's life by exploring "what," "how," and "how much" being an Asian means to the client, that is, assess the client's cultural identity. The use of such instruments as SUINN-LEW Asian-Identity Acculturation Scale (SL-ASIA; Suinn, Rikard-Figueroa, Lew, & Vigil, 1987) can be helpful in this assessment.

3. Do not assume that the client's ethnicity and culture uniformly pervade all dimensions of life. Not only are there degrees of identification with one's ethnic group, but there are also differential effects of that identification on different aspects of life. Therefore, it is unwise to assume that the client's cultural identity necessarily has a bearing on the problem or its situation.

4. Do not assume how the client's culture helps or hinders the problem. The client's cultural perspective and values may explain the "why" of the generation or persistence of the problem or the "how" of its elimination. Encourage the client to provide the cultural explanation of the problem if considered relevant for its solution.

5. Assume the pervasive role of the family in the lives of its members. The history, culture, and even contemporary needs of Asian Americans point to the importance and special meaning of the family for its members. As pointed out earlier, it is both a source of support and of stress for the individual. Explore thoroughly the familial dimension of the client's life.

6. Examine the role of symptomatology in the problem expression. Most Asian cultures discourage owning and talking about problems, particularly emotional and mental health conditions, that are likely to bring shame to the family. People therefore tend to somaticize their emotional problems. Carefully explore their physical health and complaints and make an effort to relieve the symptoms of the problem.

7. Recognize that most Asian Americans may have difficulty talking about their problems. This may result from the cultural prohibition on taking personal problems outside the family, the cultural emphasis on privacy and self-control, or an uneasiness in talking to a stranger. Use a manifold approach that consists of building relationship and trust, assuring the client of confidentiality of information shared, and asking questions with genuine interest and concern. Many clients find it easier to answer questions than to volunteer information.

8. Explore the social and spiritual support resources of Asian American clients. Most clients have access to both informal and formal sources of support within their ethnic community. Some may choose not to use those resources for fear of shame, stigma, and gossip. However, you should explore those resources and encourage the client to evaluate the pros and cons of using them.

9. Make the assessment process a multipurpose activity. Exploring the client's psychosocial systems should not be a mechanical exercise. Structure and conduct it so that it helps in building a trusting relationship with the client, is therapeutic for the client, facilitates acknowledgment of the problem or problems, and leads to planning for intervention.

10. Make assessment the basis for client strength- and empowerment-oriented intervention. This is particularly relevant for work with Asian Americans and can be accomplished through the following methods:

a. Viewing and labeling problems as unmet needs and looking for strengths in the situation. Relabeling-reframing by emphasizing the positive is consistent with the Asian cultural emphasis on respect and compassion for others (Ho, 1987).

b. Conveying a genuine belief in the client's ability to deal with the problem situation. This will kindle or increase hope in the client that the situation can change for the better.

c. Highlighting the present and potential pluses in the situation. These pluses may include the individual client's understanding, motivation, experience, and capability; the family's concern, adaptability, resources, and social supports; and community leaders' concern, commitment, and resourcefulness.

d. Looking for positive cultural strengths in the client's background. These may include commitment to the family, respect for the elderly, a holistic view of life, religious faith, middle-position virtue, and an emphasis on balance or equilibrium in life.

e. Emphasizing the environmental and societal conditions that may be creating or contributing to the problem. Doing so will reduce self-blame and a sense of worthlessness.

f. Actively involving the client in assessment. This will give the client ownership of the assessment process and product.

11. Be cognizant of the complexity of using a translator-interpreter in communicating with Asian American clients. Just anyone who is bilingual will not do as a translator or interpreter for most Asian American clients. The status hierarchy within the family and community and the people's fear of "losing face" and of gossip in the community make it unwise to use many members of the family and the community as translators and interpreters. Using children as translators for their elders exposes them to adult problems and weakens the strong sense of hierarchy and authority within the family (Frye, 1995). You may find foreign students attending a nearby college an excellent resource for interpreting and translating (Kulig, 1994).

Intervention-Related Practice Principles and Approaches

At the Microlevel. The following principles and approaches are built on ideas from the work of several human services professionals as well as the senior author's personal and professional experience.

1. Observe the formalities of the communication protocol even beyond the initial contact. The extent of this observation would be determined by the client's level of acculturation. In general, until you have been inducted into the client's extended family system as an informal member, it is wiser to deal with the individual client or family formally. This involves addressing the client appropriately; showing respect; asking questions at a pace comfortable for the client; treating the family head with extra consideration and regard for his position (displayed through formality, politeness, and avoidance of direct eye contact); showing a genuine desire to understand and appreciate the client's culture and condition; and acknowledging the tendency of Asian Americans to not disagree with those in authority. Such cultural sensitivity on the part of the professional is appreciated by these clients. At the same time, most want to see the human side of the professional also. Thus, make sure that within the formality there is room for purely social conversation and self-disclosure, which will help reduce the client's anxiety and uncertainty.

2. Accept the validity and value of the client's perspective on life and its problems. Our theories and explanations of human needs and problems are not helpful if they do not make much sense to the client. Client empowerment-oriented interventions should be premised on the client's ownership of the problem, agreement with the social worker's problem assessment and intervention plan, and willingness to actively pursue the solution. You should creatively incorporate the client's perspective into your intervention with Asian Americans.

3. Acknowledge your own biases and prejudices in viewing and treating these clients. Social workers are trained to value self-awareness, but they are not free from biases that the larger society constantly reinforces. Negative views about the different Asian American groups abound. Therefore, get in the habit of periodically reflecting on your

views of these clients and attitudes toward them. You should aim at considering them as culturally equal to you.

4. Encourage these clients to acknowledge and accept their values and traditions. This will be a welcome step in strengthening your relationship with the client, increasing his or her trust in your concern and commitment to help, and enhancing his or her motivation for solving the problem.

5. Choose concrete problem-focused interventions. Remember that with most Asian Americans, particularly newcomers and first-generation immigrants, the probability of the client's cooperating, actively working on the problem, and not dropping out prematurely is high if the focus of intervention is on the problem and not on the person or his or her personality.

6. Mix and match the therapeutic approaches for maximum impact. Because most Asian Americans are eager to resolve their problems and get on with their lives, you will find that a brief but focused intervention is more effective with them. "The therapeutic approach which focuses on external stress (vs. internal conflicts), emphasizes direct problem-solving technique, suggests active problem management (vs. process-oriented discussion), and offers external resolution (vs. internal resolution) can be more effective with Asian American families" (Kim, 1985, p. 342).

7. Emphasize environmental factors contributing to the problem and external sources of stress. Identifying external sources of the clients' problems and the resulting stress over which they have little control will reduce the degree of self-blame and guilt. You should also acknowledge that discrimination against Asian Americans is real and that many of their needs and problems can be attributed to the consequences of a racist society.

8. Make the intervention comprehensive and multipronged. A unidimensional thrust of social work intervention with Asian American clients is not likely to be valued by them. Most are conditioned to expect better results from a combination of many approaches. For example, in the indigenous systems of medicine in many Asian countries, a physician prescribes not only the appropriate medicine but also changes in diet and lifestyle. Creating a multidimensional approach will require that you play several professional roles, such as teacher, counselor, advocate, support person, and so on.

9. Take an active and direct role in working with Asian Americans. You are likely to be viewed by these clients as an authority figure, one who is an expert, has clout, and is resourceful. They expect you to take an active and direct part in their struggle with the problem. A passive and nondirective approach may be misinterpreted as lack of concern.

10. Involve the family, and build on its internal resources. Assume the family's concern for the client and its willingness to help, and explore its assets. Intrafamilial relationships may seem like enmeshment from a non-Asian perspective. Do not view this as pathological dependency.

11. Utilize the cultural value placed on the extended family and the large social network. The degree of acculturation and the nature of the problem may determine the extent to which the larger social network will be involved and approached for help. However, view the extended family as a potential resource. Encourage the client to talk about and decide if and how the extended social support system can be mobilized for help.

12. Use the client's cultural beliefs and values as strengths in the problem solution. In all cultures, there are beliefs and counterbeliefs, as well as values and their countervalues. You should creatively use your knowledge of the clients' belief system as an asset. For example, the belief in the inevitability of suffering in life can be countered by the value placed on one's duty toward one's family. Thus, reducing suffering will be seen as improving the person's ability to carry his or her familial responsibilities. Similarly, a client's guilt can be neutralized by the cultural belief in fate.

13. Supplement the usual intervention approaches with the client's culture-specific strategies. Western methods of intervention, including psychotherapeutic approaches, may not be effective because of the client's different worldview. Yamashiro and Matsuoka (1997) have discussed the differences between Western and Eastern psychologies and how people from Asian cultures react to and process experiences differently. Creatively mixing your approach with the client's culturally conditioned ways of dealing with problems will yield better results. The client's ways may include relaxation, meditation, special prayers, and the involvement of an indigenous healer.

At the Mezzolevel. As pointed out in the preceding chapters, the focus of social work at the mezzolevel can be on improving the responsiveness of human service agencies to the needs of these groups. You, as an agency director, program planner, and quality assurance and service utilization manager, will find the following principles and approaches helpful.

1. Recognize the historically and culturally based resistance of Asian Americans to seek help. A recent nationwide study found that in all states and territories except Colorado, Asian Americans and Pacific Islanders underutilized formal mental health services (Matsuoka, Breaux, & Ryujin, 1997). Yamashiro and Matsuoka (1997) have analyzed the help-seeking behaviors of these people from such different perspectives as human ecology, worldview, sociohistory and cohort mentality, acculturation, sociobiology, and social learning. Familiarize yourself with such analytical approaches, enhance your understanding of these client groups, and make that understanding the basis for service planning and delivery. For example, changing names of services, for example, from "Mental Health" to "Family Outreach," will destigmatize those services (Hogan-Garcia, 1999) and address the Asian American bias against mental illness.

2. Make outreach an important element of the services for Asian Americans. Because of cultural, historical, practical, and other reasons, many Asian Americans do not avail themselves of much-needed services. Consider reaching out to them an important part of your agency's activities. Outreach should be aggressive and should use creative approaches and multiple media. Messages should be in the group language as well as in English and should be conveyed through personal contact, written literature, radio and television, and videotapes. A survey in California revealed an association between smoking and rental of videotapes. This led health agencies to the practice of inserting anti-smoking messages on Cantonese and Filipino tapes (Chen, 1993).

3. Hire bilingual and bicultural social workers. Besides helping to create a climate of familiarity, these workers can assist in understanding Asian American clients' needs, nuances of behaviors, and problem symptoms, and in devising more effective interventions. They can also function as consultants to other service personnel and as a bridge to the ethnic communities.

4. Train agency social workers and other service providers to be culturally sensitive. Given the vast diversity within the Asian American group, it is unlikely that any agency will have bilingual and bicultural personnel corresponding to clients from all Asian American subgroups. The next best thing is to train service providers to recognize clients' fears, appreciate their beliefs and perspectives, and respond to their needs and problems effectively.

5. Seek the opinions of clients on how the agency is meeting their needs. This can be done by asking clients to (a) describe their best and worst experiences with the agency and its personnel; (b) list what they like and dislike about the agency, its policies, programs, and personnel; and (c) give suggestions about how the agency can improve its services. This should be done periodically.

6. Seek the advice, opinions, and suggestions of leaders of the communities served. Community leaders can be a source of information about, understanding the needs and problems of, and access to the community and its members. This can also be an indirect response to the general sense of powerlessness in most Asian Americans. Approach them as advisers and consultants. Their input can help in making the agency's policies and protocols more responsive to client needs and situations, and they can provide ideas for program activities that can increase the acceptance of agency services by individuals and community.

7. Make the agency's policies and procedures reflect its commitment to culturally sensitive services. This is an effective way of ensuring the delivery of effective services. Requirements of the agency's policy and procedures and policy-driven structural changes can ensure greater and more uniform compliance than dependence on the service providers' sense of responsibility alone.

8. Train and utilize indigenous community members as paraprofessional staff. Every agency has tasks that require the services of paraprofessionals. Whenever possible, paraprofessional positions should be filled with indigenous members of ethnic communities. This will help in improving the agency's service delivery, acceptance, and image in the community.

9. Explore establishing parallel services that accommodate unique aspects of client needs. Depending on the size of the Asian American community that your agency serves, you should explore various ways of providing client-oriented culturally competent services. The provision of parallel services can be one such way. Such services can become either the hallmark of an agency's main service site or the characteristic of its satellite office in the ethnic community.

10. Make agency services as comprehensive as possible. In many Asian cultures, life and its needs are not compartmentalized. For example, the separation of health and mental health in this country does not make sense, and specializations within medicine and health care are confusing to many newcomers. Social work's "bio-psycho-social" perspective and its simultaneous focus on person and environment are truly needed in working with most Asian immigrants and refugees. These perspectives, combined with an understanding of their cultural values, will lead to truly comprehensive services. Families of many refugees are truncated and incomplete. Given the importance of family in their lives, it is not enough to help refugees with the grief over their losses. Social work intervention should include the facilitation of searches for their missing family members and

family reunification. Similarly, many newcomers do not have adequate life skills for survival in America. Teaching them those skills should be built into the intervention plans.

11. Social work agencies specializing in serving Asian Americans should be multiservice. This principle is particularly valid for working with Asian Americans who are new to the country and its culture. Chow (1999) has described the experiences of three multiservice centers in Chinese immigrant communities in Chicago, Los Angeles, and New York. In view of the cultural barrier of shame and "saving face," these centers do not focus on helping clients with their problems but emphasize meeting the normative needs of the people living in the community. They provide multiple services. Their approach is based upon a model named DECENT. Each letter of the name stands for an aspect of the philosophical rationale and thrust of their activities: Developmental, Educational, Comprehensive, Empowerment, Networking, and Teamwork.

12. Social work agencies serving Asian Americans should be committed to interagency communication, cooperation, and coordination. No agency, including multiservice agencies specializing in serving Asian American clients, is likely to have all the answers and resources. Therefore, they should be closely linked with all health and human service organizations. Make sure that your agency actively cooperates with others and coordinates its services with theirs.

At the Macrolevel. As pointed out earlier, macrolevel social work interventions should deal with changing social, political, economic, and environmental forces that adversely affect the human condition, through changes in laws, creation of resources, and modification of public opinion. Social work agencies serving large numbers of recent Asian immigrants and refugees should undertake advocacy on behalf of those clients and their communities. Most of them do not know how the large American systems function and how they are responsive to public opinion, pressure, and lobbying on behalf of special causes and groups. Here are a few suggestions.

1. Social work agencies should provide Asian American communities with empowerment-oriented educational and organizational services. These should be aimed at (a) teaching them about their rights and how the political system works, (b) generating or reviving their faith in the general fairness of the American societal institutions, (c) identifying their leaders and educating them in the American approaches to problem solving, (d) helping their leaders to organize their communities to deal with their needs and problems, (e) assisting them to become politically visible, and (f) aiding them to build coalitions with others.

2. Social work agencies should educate and influence the society's elites about the plight and problems of Asian Americans. Elites control power and resources in the country. Their opinions, values, and priorities determine public policy and government's response to human needs. The elite should know that contrary to the myths about them, Asian Americans require help to become model U.S. citizens, and that many of their problems are the result of societal and structural factors rather than personal deficiencies. Elites can be approached and educated. There are many time-honored methods of doing so, "including one-to-one lobbying; collecting and presenting signed petitions; initiating and managing letter writing, phone call, and telegram campaigns; mobilizing groups to appear at public hearings; preparing and presenting statements at public hearings; and suggesting the wording of proposed law" (Dhooper, 1994, p. 159).

3. Social work agencies should undertake ongoing public education about Asian Americans. Minorities in general and newcomers in particular are at the mercy of the goodwill of the general public. Public education is extremely important for the well-being of vulnerable groups. Social workers know the realities of their Asian American clients and can take on leadership roles in supplying facts about their lives and needs. They have the characteristics and skills—the abilities essential for publicity work as identified by Nolte and Wilcox (1984)—and they can help in projecting "an image of Asian Americans as hardworking, honest and loyal Americans despite their non-white features and accented English" (Dhooper, 1997a, p. 36).

4. Social work agencies and personnel should treat the media as a special resource. The media have tremendous impact on the opinions, attitudes, and behaviors of the public and politicians alike. The media should be wooed and treated as allies, because they are also in the business of informing, educating, and serving the public. They are always looking for reportable news. Social work agencies should consider most of their activities as worthy of coverage by the media. Establishing and maintaining contacts with the media; supplying newsworthy stories; and becoming a reliable source of accurate facts about human needs, problems, and situations and a source for ideas for improving human conditions are simple approaches to dealing with the media. Such media-related activities on behalf of Asian Americans will go a long way to helping them.

The macrolevel social work activities suggested in this section and others are very important in view of the increasing anti-immigration sentiment and attacks on affirmative action.

NOTES

1. In addition to discrimination from individuals and local and state governments, Chinese immigration was eventually forbidden by federal laws—starting with the Chinese Exclusion Act of 1882, which barred the entry of Chinese laborers for 10 years and prohibited the naturalization of Chinese immigrants as U.S. citizens. In 1892, the Greay Act extended these provisions for a further 10 years, and in 1898, the act was extended to Chinese immigrants seeking to enter the Hawaiian Islands. Finally, in 1904, the Chinese Exclusion Act was extended indefinitely (Mangiafico, 1988, p. 116).

2. In 1888, Congress passed the Scott Act making it impossible for Chinese to return once they left the country. "The Scott Act, which went into effect immediately, abrogated the reentry right of an estimated 20,000 Chinese laborers with certificates in their possession, including 600 who were en route across the Pacific" (Chan, 1991, p. 55).

3. According to Chan (1991),

Anthropologists classified some of the inhabitants of the Indian subcontinent as "Aryans," but no one was sure whether Aryans were Caucasians and whether the latter referred only to whites. ... An imaginary line was drawn from the Red to the Mediterranean, Aegean, and Black seas, through the Caucasus Mountains and the Caspian Sea, along the Ural River, and then through the Ural Mountains. All people living in the areas east of the line—which came to be called the "Barred Zone"—were denied entry from then on. Asian Indians were of course among those excluded. (p. 55)

4. Thind had lived in the United States since 1913, had served in the U.S. Armed Forces during World War I, and had received his citizenship papers from the U.S. District Court in Oregon in

1920. But Thind was known for advocating independence for India—something that the federal government found embarrassing, given the close relationship between the United States and Great Britain—and immigration officials looked for a pretext to deport him. The bureau of immigration took him to court in an attempt to "denaturalize" him. The U.S. Supreme Court upheld the federal agency, arguing that whereas Thind, as a native of India, might indeed be an Aryan ethnographically, he was nonetheless not "white" (Chan, 1991, p. 94).

5. The court "declared that since the most influential writer of the day divided *homo sapiens* into five racial groups—Caucasian (white), Mongolian (yellow), Ethiopian (black), American (red), and Malay (brown, the category to which Filipinos belonged)—Mongolians and Malays were obviously not synonymous" (Chan, 1991, p. 60).

6. During the first few weeks of the war, a few thousand so-called enemy aliens—Japanese, Germans, and Italians—were interned, and all had a hearing eventually. Thus, in the beginning, aliens of Japanese, German, and Italian ancestry were treated alike, but shortly thereafter, Japanese and their American-born children were singled out for discriminatory treatment. That involved herding and sending to relocation centers the entire population of Japanese Americans living in the so-called "military areas," which included the entire state of California, most of Washington and Oregon, and part of Arizona. The explanation for the relocation was that they could not be kept under watch, because "the Occidental eye cannot rapidly distinguish one Japanese resident from another" (Chan, 1991, p. 124).

7. The Immigration Act amendments of 1965 replaced the quota system with a system of preferences that favored persons with close kin in the United States and those who had professional and entrepreneurial skills. That law allowed up to 20,000 visas for preference immigrants from each country each year. Thus, 20,000 Chinese could come from the Republic of China, another 20,000 from Taiwan, and 600 from Hong Kong, a British colony until 1997. The immediate relatives of U.S. citizens were not counted under these limits (Mangiafico, 1988).

8. The sympathies and loyalties of Chinese Americans were divided between the China represented by Taiwan and the China of the mainland. However, slowly, most Chinese Americans—including many refugees from communist rule—have come to support or at least be reconciled to the People's Republic of China (Kitano & Daniels, 1988).

9. They could not retain their family structure and norms—particularly the authority of the father and culturally determined intergenerational relationships—in the face of several powerful factors. These included the lack of privacy, the communal duties, the dependency on the government (rather than the head of the household) for providing necessities, younger children's preference for eating meals with their friends and running around out of the sight and control of their parents, and older children's acquiring independence and power because they could earn salaries for the work they were doing or become ward leaders (Dunn, 1975; Uchida, 1982).

10. Several thousand Korean women came and are probably scattered all over the country. Similarly, over 6,000 orphans—both biracial, who were the children of American fathers and Korean mothers, and full Korean—were adopted by American families between 1955 and 1966. The adoptive families were white middle-class Protestants living in rural and small urban communities (D.S. Kim, 1977; Kitano & Daniels, 1988). Barring a couple of studies, there is nothing in the literature about the experience of those women or children in the United States.

11. Chinese. There are approximately 1.25 million Americans of Chinese descent. There is significant diversity among them, which is attributed to several factors. One is the time of their arrival. There are those whose families have been in the United States for several generations. There are also those whose parents or grandparents came under the relaxation of immigration restrictions after World War II. Then there are those who themselves or whose parents came as a result of the changes in the immigration law in 1965. The second factor is the difference between the native-born and the foreign-born. The native-born tend to be college educated, have middle-class occupations, and live outside the inner-city Chinatowns. Many of the foreign-born are poorly educated and deficient in English, live in Chinatowns, and work in low-wage service trades and sweatshop

manufacturing plants (Kitano & Daniels, 1988). The third factor is where they came from. The places whence they came can be in mainland China, Taiwan, Hong Kong, or another Southeast Asian country. There are marked differences in their command over the English language and sociodemographic characteristics. The fourth factor is the difference in the dialects spoken by them:

> The early immigrants, originating in a locale of Kwantung Province, were most speakers of Cantonese and Toisanese. The more recent arrivals are largely Cantonese- and Mandarin-speaking. With the arrival of a large number of ethnic Chinese from Southeast Asia, there have arrived a significant number of Fukienese-speaking refugees (Ishisaka & Takagi, 1982)

Differences in educational attainment, occupational skills, and income constitute a fifth factor responsible for their diversity. The degree of acculturation is still another factor responsible for the stratification of the Chinese American community.

12. Japanese Americans. There are about 850,000 Japanese Americans in the country. They are the slowest-growing Asian American group, which partly reflects a low rate of immigration from Japan. A large part of this population is made up of the survivors and descendants of the original Japanese immigrants (Ishisaka & Takagi, 1992).

> By almost any standard, Japanese Americans are firmly established as middle-class Americans. Their mean income is higher than that of white Americans; they are among the highest educated of all racial and ethnic groups; they are overrepresented in the professions; the vast majority live in white neighborhoods; and currently over half of all new marriages involving Japanese Americans are with white Americans. (Murase, 1995)

They have maintained their ethnic identity despite being culturally assimilated into the life of the larger community.

13. Americans of Indian, Pakistani, Bangladeshi, Sri Lankan, and Nepalese origin. These sub-groups together are estimated to number at least 1.2 million and are among the fastest-growing immigrant groups. Balgopal (1995b) has classified all the Asian Indians into six groups: (a) Punjabi farmers, who came here between 1895 and 1920; (b) scholars, who came as students for graduate work between 1947 and 1965; took positions in academia, research, and industry; and stayed on; (c) professionals in science, medicine, engineering, and business, who immigrated because of their technical expertise; (d) refugees from African countries such as Uganda who were of Indian origin and had settled in those countries; (e) Caribbean Island Indians, who have immigrated since 1965 for economic reasons; and (f) extended family members of all the above who have come since 1965. Like the Punjabi farmers of the past, some Punjabis are in farming on the West Coast. Scholars and professionals hold positions in the professions and in business. The refugees have established themselves in various businesses. Those from the Caribbean Islands had marginal educational and technical backgrounds and are in low-paying jobs. Those who came as members of the extended families of others are not as well placed. The median income of those who came between 1987 and 1990 is one fifth of that of those who came before 1980, and their unemployment rate is twice that of those who came before 1980 (Melwani, 1994).

14. Filipino Americans. Filipino Americans are distributed across all income and occupational groups and are in varied living arrangements (Lott, 1997). Kitano and Daniels (1988) have divided them into four groups: (a) the first generation, (b) the American-born second generation, (c) the post-World War II veterans, and (d) the newly arrived. The first-generation Filipinos are mostly men, old-timers who came here in the 1920s and became U.S. citizens in the 1950s. Many Americanized their names but experienced little acculturation and integration into the larger society. They are found in

dingy hotel rooms in large and small towns of California and Hawaii. Those born and bred in America also lack social acceptance. Many have low education, income, and self-image. Most of them have no ties with the Philippines. Most have been victimized "by the model minority stereotype of Asian Americans that essentializes the latter as academically gifted, over-represented in higher education, having relatively high occupational and income status, and able to succeed through their own individual and family efforts and sacrifices" (Okamura & Agbayani, 1997, p. 189). The war veterans came here in their adult years. Their life in the United States has been marginal, both economically and socially. Many have retained close ties with their motherland and live within their own cultural network.

They are of the conviction that Bataan and Corregidor will always be there, that the ties of friendship between the Philippines and the United States will be special and lasting; and that ultimately, the Philippines will forever be part of the American entity. (Munoz, 1971, p. 160)

This sentiment is also shared by those who had worked in the army depots and navy installations in Guam and elsewhere. Those who came as students, tourists, and immigrants before the Immigration Law of 1965 have worked in hospitals, schools, factories, gas stations, and restaurants. The new immigrants form the bulk of the Filipinos. Overall, they have done well. They brought professional degrees and skills; had attitudes not conditioned by an experience of overt racism and discrimination imposed by law; and came at a time of favorable social, economic, and historical conditions.

15. Korean Americans. The 1990 census puts their number at 798,849. They are a highly urban population and are scattered all over the country. In areas where there is no large Korean community, the family is looked up to for support and strength. The majority of Koreans are in small businesses:

Many of the small-business enterprises are run by immigrants with considerable educational or professional backgrounds, but difficulties with English have forced them to take a different path. They may start by taking menial jobs, scrimping and saving enough to buy a gas station, liquor store, convenience market, or laundromat. Stores that sell wigs and the "mama and papa grocery" are also popular. (Kitano & Daniels, 1988, p. 112)

Most of these businesses are in poor black and Spanish-speaking neighborhoods and are often a source of tension between Korean merchants and neighborhood residents. These businesses also require the whole family and extended family to struggle for long hours 7 days a week under poor working conditions. Even families not in their own business find that wives and children must also work, which affects the family roles, rules, and dynamics and creates problems. Spouse abuse is a serious problem in the Korean community.

16. Southeast Asian. According to the 1990 census, there are more than 1 million Southeast Asians, who constitute about 13% of the total Asian American population. Sixty percent are from Vietnam, and the others are from Laos and Cambodia. These people came here as refugees. Unlike other Asian Americans, they had no indigenous Vietnamese, Laotian, and Cambodian communities to look to for support and guidance (Wodarski, 1992a). The government policy was to scatter the refugees across the country so that their large numbers would not increase competition for jobs and create feelings of resentment and animosity in the larger communities. That policy did not work. Many refugees moved away from their sponsors to areas where others like them were concentrated. In many states, their visibility in large numbers has brought out the anti-Asian biases and prejudices in other Americans. Even after years of resettlement, their past traumatic experiences continue to assert themselves and to make their present precarious and uncertain. Their physical and psychosocial needs are much more intense.

6

Understanding and Working
With Native Americans

NATIVE AMERICANS: WHO ARE THEY?

Native Americans, or "Indians," are the original inhabitants of this country. Prior to the Columbus expedition to North America in 1492, there were an estimated 10 million Native American people in what is now the United States. Some researchers place this estimate at between 800,000 and 9 million (Trimble, Fleming, Beauvais, & Jumper-Thurman, 1996). It has been suggested that Native Americans may have inhabited the Western hemisphere between 25,000 and 75,000 years prior to the Viking settlement or the Spanish Conquest (Lewis, 1995). By 1850 their numbers had declined to approximately 250,000. "Over fifty tribes are known to have become extinct" (Lewis, 1995, p. 216). Over time their numbers slowly increased, so that by 1960 there were approximately 650,000 Native Americans in the United States. This increase has been attributed to a decrease in infant mortality, improved census collection methods, the resumption of tribal roles, and a public attitude of tolerance that led many to claim Native American ancestry. In 1998 their population stood at 2.3 million, which is less than 0.9% of the total U.S. population. Only the Cherokee, Navajo, Chippewa, and Sioux tribes have populations that exceed 100,000 individuals (Begun, Jacobs, & Quiram, 1998).

The average age of Native Americans is approximately 45 years (their median age is 26), which is 7 years younger than the average age for all U.S. citizens (Begun et al., 1998; Hodgkinson, 1992). Because they are often counted in the census as "other," it is difficult to obtain accurate information regarding their labor force participation. Approximately 70% of Native American males and 55% of Native American females are actively involved in the labor force, compared to 74% of the overall U.S. male and 56% of the overall U.S. female population (Begun et al., 1998). Native Americans are attending college in increasing numbers. Whereas in 1976 only 2,662 of them took the Scholastic Aptitude Test, by 1986 there were more than 90,000 Native Americans attending institutions of higher education (Carnegie Foundation, 1990). Half of the 103,000 Native Americans who attended college in 1990 were enrolled in 2-year colleges, and the other half were enrolled in 4-year institutions (Hodgkinson, 1992). Although these figures are encouraging, the number of Native Americans who attend professional school has declined over the past few years by 22% (Carnegie Foundation, 1990). This helps to explain why most Native Americans are employed in low-paying occupations such as sales, service, and clerical positions. Only 17% of Native American men and 15% of Native American women occupy professional and managerial positions. Those who seek middle-class positions often move away from the reservations. Others are establishing new businesses on reservations and in rural areas. Native Americans owned 17,000 business in 1987, which generated $800 million (Hodgkinson, 1992).

A HISTORICAL OVERVIEW OF NATIVE AMERICANS: COMMONALITY OF EXPERIENCES

In common with African Americans, Hispanic Americans, Asian Americans, and many other people who are labeled as minorities, Native Americans have a history of white domination and oppression (Gibson & Ogbu, 1991). However, many facts and factors distinguish them from other minority groups, such as: (a) the fact that they are indeed the first inhabitants of North American land, (b) the manner in which Anglican Protestants colonized them, (c) their lack of interest in integrating with the larger society, and (d) their desire to remain a separate nation (a nation within a nation). Deculturalization and attempts at assimilation were the mechanisms used by the U.S. government to conquer the nations of the American Indians (Spring, 1997). It was expected that through the process of cultural genocide, Native people would be separated from their language, religion, dress, judicial system, jobs or vocations, customs, and culture, and that through assimilation they would relinquish their land and natural resources. The goal of the earlier English settlers was to civilize them by replacing their culture with that of the white Anglo Protestant culture. Some assumptions underlying deculturalization were that Protestant Anglican culture is superior to other cultures and that the political institutions of the United States far outweigh those of other nations. Another assumption was that the American government had a responsibility to raise the Native people to the level of the rest of society. Native Americans were to be acculturated through (a) federal "franchising on Indian nations given to anxious Christian denominations; (b) through a cultural unraveling, imposed educational system designed to separate child from family and instill non-Indian values; and (c) through federal efforts to break up tribal land holdings, turn Indians into individual landowners, and impose taxes on their land" (Harjo, 1993, p. 200). Other commonalities among Native Americans include the following.

Popular prejudice and discrimination against Native Americans have dominated the social scene. During the 17th and 18th centuries, the English colonists brought to the United States beliefs about the superiority of their culture. This was the era of English colonialism, which spread throughout the world. The English felt justified in their colonial expansion because they perceived that such expansion was a vehicle for dispersing European forms of civilization. Believing themselves to be a genetically superior race, they perceived the North American Indians to be savages who could not be tamed, even though these people provided the newly arrived Europeans with resources and advice for their adjustment to their new environment. The idea of living in a multicultural society was unthinkable for the European Americans, some of whom entertained ways of eliminating the Native people. Many believed that whites should be the chief residents of America. Among them were such well-known personalities as Benjamin Franklin and Thomas Jefferson (Spring, 1997).

Government policies and activities reflect and accommodate the popular prejudice against Native Americans. Earlier immigrants from Europe believed in the Protestant work ethic. This ethic promoted the idea that the condition of the poor and disadvantaged was a result of their own irresponsibility and innate negative attributes. They needed the assistance of "more capable others." Native Americans were viewed from such a perspective, and many initiatives to remove, displace, and deculturalize them began. The 1790 Naturalization Act denied citizenship to Native Americans; furthermore, they were forced to attend segregated schools; laws forbidding interracial marriages were enacted; and attempts to transform the Native American family from an extended to a nuclear structure were begun (Gibson & Ogbu, 1991). Also passed in 1790 was the Indian Nonintercourse Act, which made void any transaction for Native land absent of approval by the U.S. Congress. President George Washington erroneously thought that this act protected Native Americans from being defrauded of their land. Others felt the only way to conquer the Natives, thereby allowing for land expansion, was through the act of genocide. Some settlers promoted the idea of genocide on the belief that Native Americans "did nothing to enhance the productive capabilities of the land" (Martinez, 1996, p. 51). However, the U.S. military realized that genocidal efforts would exact too great a toll in military casualties. Instead, the government devised plans for peaceful means of land expansion through the acculturation of Native Americans. Europeans espoused individualism, capitalism, and the Protestant work ethic via the introduction of the European system of barter and trade and replaced the Natives' use of fishing and hunting with agriculture and husbandry. It was hoped that these initiatives would result in a total transformation of Native American thought "regarding the economy, government, family relations, property and manipulate desires regarding consumption of goods" (Spring, 1997, p. 13). During the early part of the 19th century, many Anglo Americans believed that Native Americans could only be successfully civilized through education. However, they were really concerned about the acquisition of land, especially that which lay west of the Mississippi and in the southern region of the country (Champagne, 1993). This land was thought to be rich in minerals and other natural resources. The U.S. government took the position that education, not trade and agriculture, was the means by which the Natives would be acculturated. The passage of the Civilization Act of 1819 and the creation of the Office of Indian Affairs provided the auspices under which the educational initiatives would occur.

Initially begun as educational experiments funded through the Civilization Act of 1819, schools were developed as mechanisms for cultural transformation. Native male children were taught reading, writing, and math; female youth were taught domestic roles; and adults received instruction in agriculture with Presbyterian, Methodist, and Baptist missionaries serving as their primary teachers.[1] Under government auspices, the missionaries were to educate Native people by divorcing them from their religious beliefs, ceremonies, and practices. These missionaries also discouraged the Native Americans' use of their native tongue. English was espoused as the primary language in order to further demolish Native culture.

Native Americans are forcefully removed from their land. The Civilization Act of 1819 and subsequent school initiatives were not totally successful, in that many of the Native American tribes located in the western and southern regions of the United States would not sell or relinquish their land. They did not believe in the government's promises to allow tribal control over their land. In 1830 the Indian Removal Act was passed, whereby territory west of the Mississippi River was exchanged for that east of the river, with provisions for the government to handle Native American resettlement. What ensued was one of the most devastating acts against humanity, which later became known as the Trail of Tears (Spring, 1997). Between 1831 and 1833, an estimated 70,000 to 100,000 Native Americans from the Cherokee, Choctaw, Chickasaw, Creek, and Seminole tribes were forced to march to Oklahoma (Lewis, 1995; Snipp, 1997). Thousands died from disease, starvation, and exposure to the elements. They were also subjected to military roundups, in which families were forced into military forts while their homes were burned and looted and their livestock dispersed and displaced. Once established in what was called the "Indian Territory," the Native people established their own family-centered, segregated schools, many of which were very successful. The Natives became bilingual, and some tribes reported close to 100% literacy. In their own schools, Native American students could be given culturally relevant material that fostered a healthy environment and that promoted the Indian way of life. Some of the graduates of these schools were sent East to receive college educations.

As a result of a growing European American population and further expansion into western land (once thought to be uninhabitable by whites)—with the prospect of getting rich from gold findings—the issue of Native American resettlement resurfaced. The government responded by passing the General Allotment Act of 1887. It established reservations and allotted pieces of land to individuals. It was hoped that Native Americans would embrace the European concept of rugged individualism and give up their belief in communalism. As a result of the General Allotment Act, land owned by Native people declined from 138 million acres to 48 million acres between 1887 and 1934. Almost 20 million of the remaining 48 million acres was wasteland and unusable. The government's need for containment and control of Native people was the rationale for this program. Impediments to Native American self-governance and self-determinism were pervasive. Native Americans were to remain on the reservations until they could show that they had become civilized. Boarding schools were established by the government for children, who at early ages were taken from their families and tribes in order to separate them from their customs, traditions, and language. Parental visits were not permitted during the school year. While they were in these government-run boarding schools, students were taught that their culture was deviant and void of morals. School activities were designed to instill in them allegiance to the U.S. government. Government-run high schools also had the same foci and goals as the boarding schools.

Native American parents did not support these schools because of the racial, ethical, and philosophical differences between them and Europeans. Differences abounded regarding the issue of social productivity and formal education. These efforts were destructive to the autonomy and motivation of Native children as revealed by the 1926 Merriam Report by the Institute for Government Research (Ambler, 1996). The report discussed the deleterious effects of removing these children from their families and cultures. These findings were supported by another study done in 1969 for the U.S. Senate Subcommittee. That study found a general atmosphere of disregard for and discrimination against Native Americans in off-reservation towns where numerous Native American students were being educated in public schools. These attitudes continued to prevail. This is reflected in the fact that nearly one fourth of all public school teachers surveyed in the 1960s indicated a preference for not teaching Native Americans. As a result of the 1926 study, the government's educational practices regarding Native Americans began to fade, and a shift toward cultural immersion became vogue. It was recommended that more funding be given to Native American education and health services and that these services be placed under tribal authority. As a result of the Great Depression, the impact of the Merriam report was curtailed, because government interest shifted to national issues.

In a hostile environment Native Americans advocate for themselves. Native Americans still continue to attempt to gain control over the education of their children. As a result of various education reform acts of the 1970s, tribes are increasingly gaining control in this domain and are attempting to diminish many of the negative effects of being forced to participate in an education system fraught with institutional racism. The reform movement is directed at enabling public schools to be more sensitive to Native American students and their culture. Perhaps one of the most relevant among these reforms is the American Indian Education Act of 1972 (Pub. L. 92-318). Under this act, provisions were made for funds for special programs for Native American children who attended reservation-based schools. Funds were also given for Native American children who attended urban public schools.[2]

Successful attempts are also being made to rectify some of the injustices perpetrated upon Native American people. One example is the Native American Graves Protection and Repatriation Act of 1990 (NAGPRA). This Act was passed to protect the cultural property rights of the indigenous people. Cultural property refers to items that were considered to be sacred and those that were used in various ceremonies (Ambler, 1996). It also includes such things as songs, family stories, and the actual ceremonies that are part of the Native tradition.[3] Many Native American tribes are taking active roles to secure their artifacts and the remains of their people from museum holdings. In the state of New York, a 1972 moratorium prohibited the excavation of Native burial places, and during the 1990s the Smithsonian Institution promised to give human remains and other artifacts back to the Native people (L. Hall, 1997b). The passage of NAGPRA made provisions for Native Americans to become the stewards of their cultural property by assuming positions that enable them to direct the education of museum staff and to have leadership roles in establishing guidelines for tribal research.

COMMON CHARACTERISTICS: COMMONALITY OF CULTURES AND WORLDVIEWS

The literature repeatedly points to certain elements that are characteristic of either Native American cultures or experiences. Many Western intellectuals have very little experience with traditional Native American ways, as few have actually lived or been employed in Native communities (Martinez, 1996). As a result, many of the cultural characteristics have sometimes been taken out of context and misunderstood. Native Americans are extremely different from each other in terms of how they practice their culture, but there are certain features about them that are nearly universal to all.

Beliefs Pertaining to Religion, Spirituality, and Disease. It was not until the passage of the American Indians Religious Freedom Act of 1978 that Native Americans were permitted religious freedom in the United States. Prior to that time, they were considered heathens and were often arrested and imprisoned for practicing their religion. Religion is a universal concept among Native Americans. When they refer to the universe they include the world, god, the self, and others. Their religion embraces many gods or spirits, but there is usually one great god or Great Spirit to whom reference is made. Faith, an outgrowth of their religiosity, is a harmonizing force that gives purpose and significance to their culture, life, and land (Kasee, 1995). They believe in the reincarnation and infinite existences of their spirits and consider the elements and forces of nature such as the rain, sun, lightning, water, and fire as objects of worship. They believe that the natural world is controlled by the supernatural through spirits. From their perspective, every sphere of life is governed by religion. God and nature are inseparable, and being in disharmony with God will cause disharmony with nature, which will have a negative impact upon the self.

Although many Native Americans have come to accept Christianity, Locke (1998) noted that the single religion most widely practiced among them is the Peyote Cult, which operates under the auspices of the Native American Indian Church. This is the chief religion of the largest number of Native Americans who reside between the Mississippi River and the Rocky Mountains. Members of the Peyote Cult consume portions of the peyote cactus during their religious services. Subsequent to the ingestion of the plant, visions and hallucinations occur. Singing, praying, and testimonials are given during their services. In recent years, this cult has gained increased recognition and popularity as a result of Native American nationalism and the Pan-Indian movement.

"Basic to the concept of the treatment of disease among many American Indian tribes is the idea that humans are made up of body, mind, and spirit" (Williams & Ellison, 1996, p. 148). Illness is a sign of disharmony in these three spheres. Traditionally, various healing ceremonies and practices are performed by medicine men, medicine women, and shamans (of both genders). The type of ceremony practiced and medicine used varied. Among the Washo tribe, for example, the shaman would often wash the patient's body, pray, sing, or attempt to suck the object out of the body. The Eastern Cherokee healers would recite sacred formulas, use plants for medicinal purposes, and use dreams to identify the illness. Some tribes believed in self-exploration through dreams, others resorted to herbal medicine, and others believed in incantation and exorcism. The use of traditional medicine is still prevalent among Native Americans to varying degrees. However, the number of medicine men and women and shamans has somewhat declined.

Emphasis on Harmony With Nature. Native Americans do not view the world environment from a dichotomous perspective as do Europeans. Subsequently, they do not divide the world between humans and nature. As Martinez (1996) explains, Natives view the world from a "Kin-centric" perspective, in which the natural and human worlds are one. Thus, they believe that the relationship between nature and man should be reciprocal. As man took care of the environment, the environment would thrive and replenish itself, thus providing for the sustenance of man. For this reason, Native people practice various ceremonies designed to renew the world. Within their culture, plants and animals are respected and cared for. Among the Cherokee people, for example, plants are viewed as being in union with humans, and spirits protect humans from animals who would punish them for their demise. "Plants and animals, like humans, are part of the spirit world. The spirit world exists side by side with and intermingles with the physical world" (Garrett, 1999, p. 95). They believe that misuse of plants will cause the spirit of the plant to return and tell others how they were misused or abused. Native Americans have an ethical regard for nature and take personal responsibility for care of their surroundings. They believe the destruction of their environment will lead to starvation or genocide (Martinez, 1996). Some refer to their surroundings as the "natural community" and consider plants and animals as relatives.

The Concepts of Sharing and Respect for the Individual. Another common belief among Native Americans is that the most respected among them are those who share and extend the most to others. Emphasis is placed on the value of giving and on generosity. "People are judged by their contribution to the group rather than by individual achievement" (Dykeman et al., 1996, p. 350). The needs of others and of the community take precedence over individual needs (Benjamin, 1995). "In the Indian tradition, receiving was not stigmatized, and needy people were seldom divided into the categories of deserving and non-deserving" (Williams & Ellison, 1996, p. 148). The Native American values of sharing and communalism are in direct opposition to the individualistic orientation of mainstream society. Natives have potlatches and giveaways in which personal belongings are often given to or shared with others, particularly the less fortunate. This value serves to enhance their informal support systems and to promote group solidarity.[4]

The Desire for Sovereignty. Unlike many other U.S. minorities, who struggle for integration, Native American groups seek to be autonomous and to be recognized as nations within this nation. They wish to have control over the preservation of their land, their traditions and customs, and what they consider to be their legal rights. To be given sovereign status would mean that, barring congressional approval, federal and state laws would not apply to Indian reservations. Their experience with the U.S. government is quite unique in that throughout their history they have agreed to over 600 treaties and have given away hundreds of millions of acres of their land. As of 1996, their land mass of 138 million acres in 1887 had been reduced to 50 million acres (Harjo, 1993). They lost much of their land as a result of flooding projects conducted by the Army Corps of Engineers, of being forced by the Bureau of Indian Affairs (BIA) to put their land up for sale on the open market, and of being required to relinquish their land for welfare repayments and tax defaults. Much of the land that has been left for Native American occupation is desert and is not fit for cultivation.

All Native American groups were subjected to policies and practices aimed at acculturating and assimilating them into American culture and society. Perhaps one of the most notable of these initiatives was the Wheeler-Howard or Indian Reorganization Act of 1934. This act has been problematic for most Native nations. Although all Native people were given some degree of autonomy over self-governance, the Wheeler-Howard Act requires that the Native people practice a type of government that combines forms of American corporate and government systems, as opposed to practicing their native traditional government.[5] A persistent issue with which they struggle with the U.S. government is whether they should be forced to assimilate into the American mainstream or whether they have a right to be recognized as a sovereign nation (Goodluck, 1993).

Extensive Experience With Racism. Native Americans were subjected to colonization both structurally and culturally. Structural colonization of Native Americans occurred as their political control and decision-making authority were usurped. Examples include being forced from their land and not having their tribal governance policies recognized by the U.S. government. Cultural colonization occurred through the numerous ways that Native Americans were forced to suppress their culture and values and to replace them with those of the dominant society. These included the unfair requirements of educational programs that destroyed their community identity (Lewis, 1995). One of the responsibilities of schools was to expose Native American children to the curriculum of the larger society, which would give them skills needed to be successfully competitive. However, many children were exposed to a curriculum that "allowed for only two choices: acculturation and rejection of their own culture or continued marginalization" (Benjamin, 1995, p. 208).

A History of Slavery and Oppression. Native Americans have also experienced slavery. Many of them were sold into slavery by European settlers as part of the transatlantic slave trade in 1524 (Locke, 1998). They were oppressed by those settlers because of their inability or unwillingness to take on European values and culture, about which they had little knowledge or experience. Toward the end of the 1700s, their numbers had been reduced from approximately 2.5 million to 250,000, in part from disease, slavery, and policies that were designed to ensure their extinction. Whenever their land was found to be rich in minerals and other natural resources, they were forced to relocate to other areas. They have been placed on reservations on land that is barren and virtually useless for industrial or agricultural purposes. Disagreements still abound regarding reservation boundary issues. These issues have often been settled to their disadvantage, in part as a consequence of inaccurate information given them at the time of treaty negotiations. As Lewis (1995) indicates, the term *treaty* implies equal bargaining status. It is clear that linguistic differences and cultural factors placed the Native people at a disadvantage to fully understand the meaning and relevance of many of the treaties that were made. Further, the meaning of the treaties would often change during the final phase of the treaty-making procedure and during the period of discussions on ratification.

Native Americans are people who live in the shadow of a history that has by and large been presented from a European perspective. They are aware that their customs and traditions are not reflected in this country's policies and practices. Hence, for those who struggle with living between American and Native cultures, life becomes very difficult.

DIVERSITY WITHIN: SUBGROUP AND INTRAGROUP DIFFERENCES AMONG NATIVE AMERICANS

Despite the commonality of cultures and experiences of Native Americans, there are significant differences among them based on a number of factors.

Differences Based on the Definition of a Native American. A Native American has been referred to as an Amerind, Amerindian, Indian, American Indian, Native American, Native American Indian, or an Indigenous American. There are different views about the appropriateness of each of these names. Trimble et al. (1996) consider *American Indian* to be an ethnic term that has been imposed upon this group of people and that actually has very little meaning. Dykeman et al. (1996) suggest that "there are no 'general' Indians" (p. 338). The term *Indian* is thought to have been coined by an Italian sailor who arrived in the United States by accident while trying to reach India. The term became part of the English vocabulary as a noun to refer to Indians who reside in Mexico, Brazil, Central America, Canada, and in the United States. It has also become an acceptable term among the indigenous people. Some in the United States prefer the term *Native American*.

There are also various definitions of who a Native American is. According to one Native American Indian law program, there are 52 legal definitions of the Native American (Locke, 1998). The Bureau of Indian Affairs' (BIA) definition is used by government agencies to determine the eligibility of Native Americans for government assistance and services. The Bureau defines an Indian as a person who "1) is an enrolled or registered member of a federally recognized Indian tribe or; 2) is at least one-fourth Indian or more in blood quantum and can legally demonstrate that fact to the BIA officials" (Locke, 1998, p. 60). The American Indian Education Act of 1972 identifies students as Native American "if they are members of a nation, band, or group of Indians or a terminated group or if they are Alaskan Native or who have one parent or grandparent who was a member of any of these groups" (Franklin, Waukechon, & Larney, 1995, p. 186). Harjo (1993) proposes that being an Indian is a state of mind or being in relation to the universe and therefore cannot be defined. During the civil rights movement, many non-Indian people in the "hippie movement" dressed themselves in Indian attire and incorporated elements of Indian culture into their worldview. Many Americans began to practice various Native American rituals and developed an interest in Native American folkways, art, and ceremonies. Others took advantage of race-based educational scholarships that became available by claiming Native American ancestry. During the 1990 census, "over 5 million Americans indicated on the Census forms that they were of Indian descent" (Hodgkinson, 1992, p. 3). The United States Census Bureau accepts self-report as a satisfactory proof of a person's racial-ethnic status. Thus, there is no universally accepted definition of who a Native American is and what it means to be one. The U.S. Census Bureau reports more than 500 tribes and over 187 Native American languages (Trimble et al., 1996).

Differences Based on Tribal Affiliation. More than 500 Native American tribes exist today. Some of these are recognized by the federal and state governments, and others are not. Approximately 40% of the total population of Native Americans live in the states of Arizona, New Mexico, Washington, and California (Locke, 1998). Over 50% of the total population resides in urban environments, and the 52 million acres of land that have been designated as reservations are home to approximately 637,000 Native Americans. We are describing the most distinct historical experiences and current situations of the eight most widely known tribes. The absence of attention to others does not reduce their significance.

1. The Apaches. It is generally agreed that the Apaches might have been among the last groups to make the trek from the Siberian peninsula to Alaska. They did not arrive in the southwestern part of the United States until the end of the 14th century. By the mid-16th century, at the time of their first encounter with Spanish explorers, they (and the Navajos) were well settled in the area known as the Grand Apacheria, which consisted of the areas of central Arizona, central and southern Texas, northern Mexico, and eastern Colorado. The area was split between the Plains Apaches, who resided in the eastern part, and the Western Apaches, who resided in the area west of the Continental Divide.

Presently, the Apache tribes are federally recognized and have both tribal and nontribal governments. The tribal governments are found in Arizona, New Mexico, and Oklahoma. The tribe has three reservations in Arizona.[6] They did not succumb to the U.S. government's attempts to terminate their tribes through various policy initiatives during the 1950s. However, as a result of the government's assimilation policies, including English-only school instruction, 80% of Arizona Apaches were speaking English in 1952. As a result of their self-directed efforts in the education of their people, now the public schools at the San Carlos and Fort Apache reservations are known to have outstanding bilingual and bicultural curricula. Similarly, the Apaches have not entirely lost their customs and traditions. One of their longest-lasting customs is a rite of passage ceremony called the Changing Woman, which is held during the summer for girls who reach puberty. This 4-day event is open to the public and is generally well attended by non-Native people as well. The family serves as the hub of cultural and political activity among the

Apache people. They still operate within a matrilineal extended family system in which the grandmother plays a very significant role. Spousal abuse is almost totally unheard of.

A large number of Apaches rely on agriculture for employment. The unemployment rate among all Apaches stands at 50% (Birchfield, 1997a). This situation has been helped somewhat by several tribal entrepreneurial initiatives,[7] including ski resorts and lumber mills. Apaches are represented among all professions and are most noted as superb professional rodeo performers. World-renowned Apache sculptor Allan Houser (1914-1994) is noted for 60 years of work in the mediums of wood, bronze, marble, and stone. His works include a bronze sculpture that was presented to Hillary Clinton and several pieces that are among collections of the British Royal Collection; at the New York Metropolitan Museum of Art; and at the Linden Museum in Stuttgart, Germany.

2. The Cherokees. The Cherokee nation is located primarily in the northeastern part of Oklahoma, on land that has not been designated as a reservation but of which parts are under tribal jurisdiction. The United Keetoowah Band of Cherokees, who reside in this area, has been given federal recognition as a tribal government. The Eastern Band of Cherokees live on a reservation in North Carolina, and there are various other groups elsewhere in the country that assert that they are Cherokee tribes or bands. The 1990 census estimated the Cherokee population at 308,000. Of all Native groups, they have the largest tribal affiliation (Franklin et al., 1995).

The Cherokees often refer to themselves as the "Original People." They originally took up residence in the southeastern part of the United States in what is now the states of Virginia, Alabama, Georgia, Kentucky, North Carolina, South Carolina, and West Virginia. In 1803, Thomas Jefferson, then president, began plans for their removal to land west of the Mississippi River. He signed a covenant with the state of Georgia for their immediate removal. This did not actually occur until several years later. Under an executive order of Andrew Jackson, the Cherokees were forced to relocate from their homes in 1838. They were placed in overcrowded, unsanitary holding camps until this process was complete. More than 20,000 Cherokee people were made to march, of whom an estimated 4,000 died from exposure to the elements, disease, and other hardships on what came to be known as the "Trail of Tears." Once settled in the west, the Cherokees divided into two groups, based on whether they had agreed to or opposed the removal; the former group was known as the Treaty Party, and the latter was known as the Ross Party (after Chief John Ross, who had led the opposition to the "Removal Process." This division led to a civil war within the tribe in 1843. Ultimately, both groups made peace and rebuilt their nation by establishing new homes, schools, and churches. Their peaceful existence was short-lived, however. Various members of the Treaty Party joined forces with the U.S. Confederacy during the U.S. Civil War. Those who followed Chief John Ross refused to do so, but after the war the whole tribe was punished by the government and was forced to give up more of their land. They (along with the Choctaw, the Chickasaw, the Creek, and the Seminole Nations) became part of the land that the government called "Indian Territory." For 100 years following the U.S. Civil War, the U.S. government continued to decrease the power of this group, and in 1907, despite their opposition, their new territory was coupled with the Oklahoma Territory to become the state of Oklahoma.

The original family structure of the Cherokees was matrilineal. As a result of intermarriage with whites, this structure was drastically changed.[8] Cherokees bowed to pressures to become "civilized." They began building dwellings modeled after the homes of the white settlers, rewrote their constitution, and set aside a significant part of their budget for education. They employed faculty from northeastern universities and missionaries to teach them. Beginning in the late 1800s, they were so successfully acculturated and assimilated into American society that they "became white" (Conley, 1997). However, they were able to maintain several of their traditions and customs.

Prior to the time when the state of Oklahoma either closed down their schools or took them over, Cherokees had established very successful school systems that produced many college graduates. In the state-run schools, Cherokee children were routinely placed in classes for slow learners, and high school students were discouraged from applying to college. This situation has slowly improved. The Cherokees once again have become involved in their children's education by taking control of the Native high schools and establishing preschool programs. Although unemployment among them is high, their nation has undertaken economic ventures in the areas of nurseries and meat processing, which employ approximately 1,300 people (Conley, 1997).

3. The Choctaws. Prior to the settlement of Europeans in the United States, the Choctaws owned more than 23 million acres of land in what is now Mississippi, Alabama, and Louisiana. Their first contact with Europeans occurred around the mid-16th century through a Spanish expedition conducted by Hernando DeSoto. The explorers demanded women and resources, which resulted in a battle in which many lives were lost. French explorers and settlers who arrived after the Spaniards benefited from the forced free labor of members of this tribe who were sold to them as slaves by English slave traders. The Choctaw still maintained hospitable relations with the new Europeans and served as scouts in the Revolutionary War as allies of the United States. After the war, they gave Americans permission to build roads through their land. As a result, they encountered many more Europeans. They all demanded land. In 1805, the nation was again pressured to relinquish their land and to relocate to land west of the Mississippi River.[9] Many Choctaws now reside in their original homeland in east-central Mississippi as well as in the area west of the Mississippi River. They are found in heaviest concentrations in Oklahoma, Louisiana, and Alabama.[10] Each Choctaw nation has its own constitution and its particular governmental jurisdiction. The Choctaw Nation of Oklahoma and the Mississippi Band of Choctaw Indians are the largest, and they are the only bands that the U.S. government formally recognizes.

Originally matrilineal, Choctaws have assimilated to the present-day male and female role expectations, but women still provide much of the leadership within the family and in the community. Recently, Choctaw tribes and reservations have taken advantage of entrepreneurial activities. On Choctaw reservations there are corporations such as General Motors, a greeting card company, an enterprise that produces electrical parts for automobiles, and a company that builds radio speakers for cars. Combined, these companies employ over 1,000 Choctaw people. Perhaps the biggest industry to have a positive effect on their economy is gambling. The Choctaw bingo facility in Durnatto, Oklahoma, is well known.

4. The Creeks. The Creeks originally settled in the present-day states of Georgia and Alabama. Their confederacy was made up of about 50 local tribal towns or villages, each of which operated autonomously (Champagne, 1993). Creeks traditionally lived in clusters of residences called towns.[11] Overall, the Creeks had amicable interactions with the

Europeans. They became allies of the English and fought against the French and Spanish in the Queen Anne's War of 1702, and a group of them traveled to England in the 19th century to sign a treaty with King George II. It was not uncommon for Creek women to marry Europeans and other traders, for whom they often served as translators. Creeks also have a history of close relations with African Americans, although because of economic reasons or coercion by Europeans, they participated in the transatlantic slave trade and were often employed to recapture runaway slaves.

In the early 19th century, they numbered approximately 22,000. By 1839, their numbers had decreased to less than 14,000 as a result of the hardships they suffered on the Trail of Tears during their forced removal to Indian Territory. Their number further decreased to 10,000 as a result of the Civil War. According to the 1990 census, there were 43,550 Creeks in the United States. They rank 10th in population among all Native American tribes (L. Hall, 1997a).

The Creeks were among the earlier Native American tribes to copy the ways of the Europeans. L. Hall (1997a) noted that the introduction of alcohol to Creeks proved to be very damaging to them because water had been their main beverage, even for special occasions, and they had no experience with intoxicating drinks. Alcoholism became their major problem. They also suffered from measles, smallpox, and other illnesses they acquired through contact with the Europeans. Their assimilation was also enhanced by the U.S. government through its "liaisons," who encouraged them to adopt European customs and practices. However, many Creeks considered assimilation threatening to their worldview.[12] Some of their cultural beliefs have survived. Two of their basic beliefs are that material possessions are to be shared and that food is not to be stored but consumed and replenished daily as needed. They also viewed land ownership from a communal perspective that served to unite the people and promote solidarity. However, the Dawes Act of 1887 dissolved all communal property, and land was appropriated to individuals for their singular use. The Creeks' civilization was based on a matriarchal system of clans. Adultery was forbidden, and harsh penalties ensued for those found guilty. Child rearing was primarily left to females, and rites of passage were conducted for both males and females once they reached puberty. Creeks viewed physical illness as resulting from something evil placed in the body by a spirit, and they dealt with illness via medicine men. Today, health care issues not adequately addressed through the Indian Health Service continue to be of concern for this nation. Prior to white settlement, they fared very well from agriculture and hunting on Creek land. After white settlement they were pushed into overcrowded areas, and with ensuing land cessions, they experienced a collapse of their economy. The U.S. government promised them various compensations for their land, most of which they never received. A high unemployment rate is their major concern, and the issue of their right to self-determination remains a key area of contention between the Creeks and the U.S. government. The Muskogee Creek Nation of Oklahoma has been vigorous in its quest to become a sovereign nation. They seek to regain and control land that once belonged to the tribe. Most notable among the Creeks are Will Sampson, an actor who appeared in *One Flew Over the Cuckoo's Nest*; Gary Fife, the National Public Radio news producer; and Allie P. Renolds, a former pitcher for the Cleveland Indians baseball team.

5. The Iroquois. The Iroquois Confederacy or League is a consortium of five tribes—the Onondaga, Mohawk, Cayuga, Oneida, and Seneca. It was established between the mid-14th century and the beginning of the 17th century. It is an association of tribes that share a common linguistic heritage. They lived in the northeastern part of the United States.

They refer to themselves as the *Haudenosaunee* ("people of the longhouse"), signifying the structure of the dwellings in which they lived and the extended family arrangements that were a part of their culture. As many as 50 people inhabited each such house.

The Iroquois have a significant place in U.S. military history. They fought in the 1754 French and Indian War and in the American Revolutionary War. These wars and the retaliatory raids by the American forces resulted in the loss of many of their lives and the destruction of many of their villages and fields (L. Hall, 1997b). In the mid-1900s, a sense of togetherness developed among the Iroquois people as a result of their disputes with the New York State Power Authority and the U.S. Army Corps of Engineers over various energy projects that had been proposed. The Iroquois Nation operates now as a more cohesive unit as it seeks to settle disputes with various government agencies on land use issues. This Native American Confederacy continues to struggle with some of the same socioeconomic and political issues their ancestors faced. They continue to strive for a sovereign status. Protecting their land against environmental pollution is an ongoing issue. So is the issue of who (the tribe or the government) is to control the very profitable legal gambling operations on their reservations. Their value of land as sacred and their reverence for the earth are major sources of contention between them and non-Natives. However, many are now private owners of land, which is in contradiction to the historical concept of communal land holdings. Many have relinquished the traditional extended family longhouse in exchange for small individually owned farms. The Iroquois people have not resisted adaptation to social changes and technological advances, but they refuse to relinquish their culture (L. Hall, 1997b).

Mental and physical illnesses are addressed by tribal medicine men and women trained in the use of herbal therapy and folk remedies. They also rely on spiritual healers and dream interpreters. In their society, women serve as clan mothers and are responsible for choosing men to serve as tribal chiefs. Many Iroquois have converted to Catholicism, and others belong to the Methodist, Baptist, and Quaker religions. There has also been a revival of their traditional religious practices, called the "New Religion." The New Religion denounces witchcraft and abortion and focuses on abstention from alcohol and the practice of many of their ancient beliefs.

The Iroquois are primarily urban dwellers. Approximately half of those who do not live in urban areas live on reservations. It is common for those who live and work in urban areas to return to the reservations on the weekends. Many Iroquois men work in construction, as ironworkers, in factories, and in the retail industry. Iroquois women are primarily employed as domestic workers in non-Indian homes. Some Iroquois are in professions, and some occupy positions as academicians and scholars at major U.S. colleges and universities and have made significant contributions in the areas of visual and performing arts and literature. It has been said that the U.S. Constitution was fashioned after the Constitution of the Iroquois Confederacy and that their form of government served as the model for the U.S. democratic structure. Their estimated population of 49,000 gives them the eighth-highest census among Native Americans.

6. The Navajos. The Navajos are thought to be the last people to cross the Siberian peninsula into Alaska during the Ice Age. The Navajo Nation occupies an area equivalent to the size of New Hampshire, Vermont, and Massachusetts combined. They are the largest reservation-based Native American nation. "More than 200,000 Navajos live on the 24,000 square miles of the Navajos Nation" (Birchfield, 1997c, p. 954). At the beginning of the 19th century, they resided in the area that is now New Mexico. Their

stability and peaceful living changed after claims to their land were made by the U.S. government after the Mexican-American War. This situation became even worse after the American Civil War, when much of their land was destroyed by the forces of Colonel Kit Carson during an attempt to gain control of Navajo land. Approximately half of the Navajo Nation acquiesced to the U.S. forces and were subsequently trekked 370 miles to a concentration camp at the Bosque Redondo on the Pecos River. Several hundred Navajo people died of starvation, from freezing cold, from diseases, or from being shot by soldiers during the Long Walk (Birchfield, 1997c). As many as 2,000 died from smallpox in a 1-year period. They were imprisoned for 4 years. They began their long journey home in 1868 after signing a treaty with the United States. That treaty reduced their homeland by 90%.

Navajo people now reside in the states of New Mexico, Utah, and Arizona. According to the 1990 census, they have the fourth-largest population among Native Americans. The majority of the reservation does not have telephone service and electricity. They operate under tribal governmental units called chapters, of which there are over 100. Most of the chapter revenues come from profits generated from mineral leases (Birchfield, 1997c).

More than most Native American groups, the Navajos have been able to maintain their traditional customs, language, and cultural identity. Many adults still use medicine men called *Hataali* to deliver health care. Many of the modern health care facilities on the reservation are now administered by the Navajo people and include space for traditional medicine men, who practice under the auspices of the Navajo Medicine Man's Association (Birchfield, 1997c). Many Navajos have converted to Christianity, and many combine traditional practices with Christianity. Approximately 25,000 Navajos are members of the Native American Church.

In the mid-19th century, compulsory school attendance was mandated by the federal government, leading to an increase in the number of schools on the Navajo reservation. Up until the end of the 19th century, those schools were run by missionaries whose primary objective was to assimilate the Navajo people into the mainstream culture. During the mid-20th century, the Navajo people began to take more control of the education of their people through contract schools that were directed by the community. In 1969 the first community college to be administered by Native Americans was founded by the Navajo people.

The Navajo Nation still relies on agriculture as a major source of their revenue, although federal and tribal governments provide the largest number of employment opportunities. The Navajo Nation has several enterprises in the areas of parks and recreation, tourism, coal mining, fishery and wildlife, health services, and law enforcement. There is a tribally operated electronics plant at Fort Defiance, Arizona, and a sawmill located at the Navajo Forest Products Industry that employs Navajos. Despite these enterprises, unemployment remains an issue for the Navajo people. In 1990, the unemployment rate for Navajo people was 36%.

7. The Sioux. Perhaps the best-known Native Americans are the Sioux. This nation comprises the Dakota, Lakota, and Nakota people who live in the upper Great Plains area. White settlers going west in search of gold traveled through the Sioux homeland. With them came many contagious diseases. As a result, the population of Sioux people declined by approximately half (Birchfield, 1997d). The number of Sioux residing in Texas was also decreased when Texans, hostile to the indigenous people, drove almost all of them out of the state. From the later part of the 19th century on, the Sioux held the U.S. government in contempt, viewing the American system as corrupt and untrustworthy.

The Sioux nation benefited from the 1960s civil rights movement. It gained attention to its concerns and needs. In 1979, they were granted the right to practice their religion openly without fear of legal reprimand. Most Sioux people reside in the midwestern and western regions of the country. They have tribal governments that have federal recognition in Nebraska, Minnesota, North Dakota, South Dakota, and Montana. Sioux also reside in Canada.

Sioux live in family units of small groups of 30 or more households called *tiyospaye*. These households are populated by individuals who are blood kin and who provide economic, emotional, and social support for each other. Fraternal societies known as *akicitas* were an element of the traditional Lakota community of Sioux people. The fraternal structure provided role models for young Sioux males. The Sioux are also widely known for their Sun Dance ceremony, which occurs yearly during the month of March at Pine Ridge, and for their Sweat Lodge (Birchfield, 1997d). The Sweat Lodge serves to cleanse individuals from spiritual, emotional, psychological, and physical conditions and is sometimes partaken of by non-Indian people as well.

Most of the reservations upon which the Sioux people live are located away from industrial urban areas. As a result, many of these areas have the highest national unemployment and poverty rates. There has been some out-migration of the Sioux people to areas where employment opportunities are greater. The Sioux Nation is perhaps remembered most for the massacre the Sioux experienced at Wounded Knee, in which 153 unarmed men, women, and children were killed by the U.S. Army on the Pine Ridge Reservation on December 29, 1890.[13]

8. The Yupiat. Having originally migrated from Asia, the Yupiat settled in what is now known as Alaska. They are among the Native people who reside in that state and number approximately 21,415 (Kawagley, 1997). As is the case with other Native Americans, the Yupiat were affected by the diseases brought on by their encounters with European settlers, and many of them died or suffered residual effects of these diseases. Much of their folk medicine was ineffective in curing the new diseases that they encountered. They suffered and continue to suffer psychological damage as a result of deculturalization. The Yupiat taught their children about the importance of a harmonious relationship between the spiritual, natural, and human worlds. They believed that all of creation was to be respected and that a natural balance existed between living creatures. As a result of this worldview, the Yupiat Americans de-emphasized materialism and emphasized enjoying life to its fullest devoid of the acquisition of wealth. They struggle with preserving their original ceremonies, as many of these observances were passed down through oral traditions. With a dwindling number of elderly people, many of their practices are in danger of being lost. Their ceremonial practices place emphasis on "centering or balancing within oneself and with the world; reciprocation to the plants and animals that must be killed in order to live; and expression of joy and humor" (Kawagley, 1997, p. 1422).

The Yupiat's value on child rearing is similar to that of the African community. Although the father is considered to be the head of the household and the mother performs domestic roles, they value the contribution of all members of their community to child rearing. They are experiencing increasing elementary and high school drop-out rates. Many of those who do matriculate through colleges and universities do not return to their homeland. Those who do return make contributions to their communities as teachers and counselors. As with other Native American communities, the Yupiats are beginning to take initiatives toward developing and administering their own educational institutions.

Many of them are presently advocating for educational reform. They want the American educational system to become culturally sensitive by embracing their languages, ways of solving problems, and worldviews. Lacking marketable skills and being noncompetitive in today's labor market, many of them live at or below the poverty level. Unemployment is well over 75% in some villages, and over 50% of those in some villages receive some form of assistance from the government.

Differences Based on Level of Acculturation. Native Americans are heterogeneous and diverse. Various degrees of acculturation are evident among and within different tribes. Some have totally assimilated into the mainstream, whereas others have retained their native language, beliefs, ceremonial practices, values, and customs. More than 500 tribes have been documented, which means that there can be no "absolute universal cultural norms" among them (Dykeman et al., 1996, p. 338). Most present-day Native Americans are the products of interracial marriages between Native Americans and people of Hispanic, African, and European descent. It is estimated that over 60% of Indians are of mixed blood. Some Native people do not recognize these individuals as being "pure Indians," although there is no precise definition of the word "Indian." Whether or not one has pure Native lineage does not guarantee that the traditional way of life or cultural practices are being followed or even ascribed to. As a result of intermarriage, the physical characteristics of the Native American people have also changed. Originally, there were likenesses among them in terms of their hair and eye color and skin tone. Now there are substantial differences in their physical features. No longer do all Native Americans fit the stereotypical image of an Indian, a person with dark skin and long dark hair.

Differences Based on Language. Native American languages have been labeled as primitive languages. Lord (1996) rebutted that, arguing that there are no primitive languages, only "languages with varying emphasis" (p. 48). Initially, there were upward of 2,200 different languages spoken by Native Americans (Trimble et al., 1996). Today, over 300 North American Native languages exist, of which 210 are still spoken. Because of Eurocentrism, until the 1960s, Native Americans were forbidden to speak their native tongues, which were not taught in school. Parents were instructed to discourage their children from speaking their native tongue at home. As a result, for example, 90% of school-age Navajo children do not know how to speak their language. The loss of Native American languages is further compounded by the influence of the media and an ever-increasing global community (Lord, 1996). On the other hand, many Native Americans are rediscovering their native languages. Different languages of the various tribes add to the differences among them.

Differences Based on Geographic Residence. Their residential location, in terms of on the reservation or off the reservation, as well as rural or urban, creates differences among Native Americans, even those belonging to the same tribe. Native American migration to urban areas has been generational. Most often, movement from rural to urban areas is a slow process that takes many generations to achieve. Their migration to cities and urban areas was facilitated by the Relocation Program, which began in 1950. This effort was an attempt to rectify the government's "Indian problem" by forcing them to assimilate into mainstream society, with the ultimate goal of making them vanish (Steiner, 1971). Native Americans were encouraged to leave their reservations to seek employment opportunities in heavily populated urban areas. Provisions were made for vocational training and job placement at no cost to the trainees and their families. However, under the auspices of the BIA, those who relocated were purposefully separated from associations with their tribes. Initially an estimated 50,000 Native Americans participated in the program (Steiner, 1971). This program proved to be terribly harmful to the vast majority of them.

Many who relocated did so to become a part of the mainstream, and others relocated to seek employment in hopes of improving their economic situations. They settled in large numbers in Chicago, San Francisco, Los Angeles, New York, Cleveland, Denver, Detroit, Minneapolis, and Seattle. They called their new places of residence "The Cement Prairies" (Steiner, 1971, p. 178). Most found the transition from rural to urban environments difficult. Having received no formal orientation to urban life, they could not easily adjust to the fast pace, the infrastructure, the impersonality, and the social isolation of the city. The settlement allowances provided by the government were woefully inadequate, and many were left destitute after relocating. The boarding homes to which the participants were assigned were often poorly run, underfunded, and located in ghetto areas. The employment that the Natives secured was often short-lived and paid low wages. Many Native people were unprepared for living in the city and for the demands of the urban work environment, such as fixed working hours and days. As a result they fell to the lower strata of society. They were subsequently offered secondary education courses designed to orient them to employment and city living. In most cases, these courses also did not prove successful.

Subsequently, many Native Americans formed their own grassroots organizations and centers where fellowship with relatives and tribesmen provided mutual aid and emotional and psychological support and protection. These centers also provided a forum through which they could learn to function in their new environments and to sustain their cultural values and traditions. They held Potlatch dinners, tribal dances, and powwows while simultaneously learning vocational skills and learning about issues related to housing, social welfare, and employment. Although many eventually assimilated into their urban environments, others, longing for their relatives and traditional ways, chose to return to their native reservations.

Many Native Americans who presently move to urban areas do so for some of the same reasons, namely, in hopes of bettering their economic situation; some hope to make enough money to eventually return to their homelands and live under more comfortable circumstances. An established Native presence within the urban community and Native residents within the area are important to them. Almost half of Native American people live off the reservation (Kasee, 1995). According to the 1990 census, approximately 1.4 million people who claimed Native American status lived in areas other than reservations (Lewis, 1995).

Differences Based on Socioeconomic Status. Three socioeconomic classes of city-dwelling Native Americans have been identified by Wax (1971). At the upper end of the economic ladder are those who identify themselves as Indian when it is to their advantage to do so, such as when there is a need to claim their heritage in order to benefit from land distribution of a tribal estate. These have usually severed both social ties and memberships in Native American organizations and may be several generations removed from their traditional customs and tribal heritage (Franklin et al., 1995). Some within this class view those who remain on the reservations as regressive, and they choose to have little to no association with them or with those who rank among the lower socioeconomic classes. Those who are at the lower end of the socioeconomic ladder have a high incidence of unemployment, poverty, encounters with the judicial system, and poor health. They are often transient and have had experiences with discrimination, which further compounds their situation. These experiences cause them to retreat from interactions with formal social service systems. They tend to settle in cities near reservations, such as Gallup, New Mexico; Rapid City, South Dakota; and Scottsbluff, Nebraska (Wax, 1971). They are often underrepresented in the census data because of their transient nature. Those who are among the stable working class are often active in Native American institutions where Native Americans are numerically represented. They often are active in churches, various Native American social agencies, and powwow groups. Of the three groups, this group is most likely to maintain strong familial ties with and to frequently visit those who remain on the reservations and in rural areas. Among all socio-economic classes of Native Americans who become urban dwellers, there tends to be a clustering together by residential areas and the building of institutions that enable them to have "a meaningful existence" in their new places of residence (Wax, 1971).

Differences Based on Age. Native American elderly, those aged 65 and above, are more traditional in their philosophy and values and have a deeper understanding of racism and oppression against Native people as a result of having a longer history of experience with these forces. Some of them were children when in 1901 the BIA sanctioned field agents to alter Native customs. "Forbidden were the wearing of long hair by males, face painting of both sexes, and wearing Indian dress" (Hirschfelder & Kreipe de Montano, 1993, p. 22). Many were teenagers when the federal government terminated its special relationship with Native tribes, thereby ending federal assistance in education, housing, health, welfare, and other programs and subjecting their land to taxation. The elderly have been the vanguards of their culture and have passed down their traditions and cultural beliefs throughout the generations. Through the elderly "traditional values are sustained. ... The ancient languages are spoken and taught, traditional ceremonies are observed and baskets are woven" (L. Hall, 1997b, p. 755). As such, they are held in high regard by their people and are treated respectfully. "Generally Native American traditional values consist of sharing, cooperation and a deep respect for elders" (Garrett, 1999, p. 87).

Differences Based on Gender. Native American societies were largely matriarchal, and women traditionally occupied positions of authority. The Native American woman had and still has a great deal of input into the affairs of her community. Her role in family, community, and tribal affairs was much more assertive than that of her European American counterparts, many of whom participated in activities designed to place her in a subordinate position (Kasee, 1995). In many Native tribes, the clan "was led by the clan mother, who was usually the oldest woman in the group. In consultation with the other women, the clan mother chose one or more men to serve as clan chief" (L. Hall, 1997b, p. 758). Native American women were taught to be modest in their attire and character. They were instructed to have a modest disposition in order to represent themselves, their family, and their tribe or clan in a respectable way. Of chief importance to Native women is the spirituality and spiritual well-being of their families and tribe. Many Native American women have chosen not to become involved in the American women's movement but instead focus their energy on maintaining traditional tribal ways. "Similarly, Indian women are prone to say that their preeminent concern is with community survival—treaty rights, the protection of native resources, and child welfare—rather than with making common cause with other women in the struggle for equality" (Evans, 1996, p. 688). Native American women occupy positions of power, because they often have the responsibility for appointing the tribal chiefs and leading the tribe in day-to-day affairs. Historically, if a Native man did not properly fulfill his role as tribal leader, the female clan leader had the authority to remove him from that position (Hagan, House, & Skenadore, 1995).

The mother, grandmother, or female members of the tribe often decide who will marry the tribal daughters. They are responsible for teaching the young girls and women of the tribe. The term *grandmother* does not necessarily indicate blood relations but rather is often applied to a number of women who are either elders or medicine women (Bataille & Sands, 1984). To be labeled grandmother signifies that the individual is considered wise and therefore is to be treated with respect. Among the Mesquakie Natives, a woman could not become a medicine woman until she had passed the childbearing age. This shows the reverence and credibility afforded the aged. Among the Mesquakie people, mothers continue to play an active role in the lives of their daughters. Bataille and Sands (1984) cite the case of a Mesquakie mother who played an important role in her daughter's decision not to be sterilized after the birth of her third child.

There were gender role differences among tribes. For example, among the Yupiat people, the father headed the household, and the mother performed domestic duties such as food preparation and caring for the plants and animals. Presently, this tribe is experiencing many of the domestic problems, such as divorce and single parenthood among teenage girls, that are prevalent in the dominant society. In the Navajo tribe, men who marry move into the household of their wife's extended family. The traditional clan system is giving way to Chapter Houses, in which people are included as family based on local residence. Men still maintain head-of-household positions, and the women concern themselves with domestic roles. Women who earn college degrees are encouraged to use their education for the betterment of Native people. With the help of Native American men, they "have maintained the mechanism both for adaptation and for encouraging the continuity of traditional cultures in the modern age" (Evans, 1996, p. 688).

Native American men have figuratively and literally been fierce and brave warriors and the protectors of their women, children, and culture. They have sustained their culture and history through oral traditions and the preservation of rituals. Historically, Native boys were guided and directed by their elders. They learned various aspects of their culture through folk tales and stories that were intended to shape and build their character and to serve as "disciplinary tools instead of physical punishment" (Thom, 1992, p. 21). Young men were prepared for adult responsibilities through rites of passage such as vision quests. Vision quests had several purposes. "He may want medicine power to protect him and make him successful in battle. He may be in search of power to use for curative or healing purposes. Or he may be seeking the answers to a question" (Thom, 1992, p. 22). He was prepared to hunt game in order to provide for the sustenance of his tribe and family. He was taught to share his major kill among his people to demonstrate the values of sharing and generosity. Native American men participated in many games and sports, such as the hoop and pole game and lacrosse. These activities were more than physical exercises. They were designed to develop their survival skills and began as religious rites. "In the past, and to some extent today, games were played to honor the dead, comfort the bereaved, placate spirits, influence weather, heal the sick, and to end misfortune" (Hirschfelder & Kreipe de Montano, 1993, p. 123). Native men are the traditional healers of their tribes and serve as shamans and medicine men who "divine the future from information and power received while dreaming" (Hirschfelder & Kreipe de Montano, 1993, p. 166). As medicine men, they address a variety of physical illnesses ranging from broken bones and fevers to poisonous snake and insect bites. They are known for their powwow or war dances, which have their origins among the warrior societies of the Great Plains.

Traditionally Native men were assigned occupations that benefited their tribe, such as civil policemen, camp movers, horse trainers, and so forth. Once Europeans moved them to reservations, many of their traditional occupations were no longer needed. Today, agriculture is the backbone of the economy of reservations. Many Native American men work in livestock and other aspects of the agricultural industry. Those who live in urban areas have become famous as construction and ironworkers. In these positions, they "walk steel girders high in the air unhampered by any fear of heights" (L. Hall, 1997b, p. 760). Historically, Native American men have been supporters of the U.S. military and have fought in every American war since the American Revolution.

Differences Based on Sexual Orientation. Native American culture does not view heterosexuality and homosexuality as dichotomous categories. Native Americans generally do not dichotomize the world into categories such as good-bad, positive-negative, and homosexual-heterosexual; rather, they consider experiences and life from the perspective of what is appropriate or inappropriate according to the particular situation (Green, 1987). More than half of the 225 Native American tribes present at the time of European colonization condoned male homosexuality, and about 17% accepted lesbianism (Eitzen & Zinn, 1997). Understanding the Native Americans' view of sexual orientation is necessary to understanding their ideas about gender and sexuality.

It was not uncommon for Native American people to consider themselves as being multiple-gendered. This was far different from the way in which Europeans classified their sexual orientation. For this reason, Native Americans were considered to be deviants by the early European settlers, and they often experienced physical punishment and even death. "Queer Indians have been the target of homophobic and racist genocidal campaigns since conquest" (Gould, 1997, p. 34). Subsequently Native Americans developed a code of secrecy regarding discussion of their sexuality. Although sex was not openly discussed, it was understood among Native people to be a natural part of the human experience. There are 168 Native American languages that have terminology for people who are considered to be neither male nor female. In colonial times Native people believed that gender roles were not necessarily tied to physical anatomy, and persons who claimed multiple genders or who assumed different gender roles were accepted. *Berdache* is the term most often applied to Native Americans who fit this description. It was first ascribed to Native Americans by French fur traders, who found that Native American cultural standards for gender roles were different from those of Europeans. For instance, cross-dressing, in which people adopt the sexual identity of the opposite sex, has been known to exist in Native American societies. This phenomenon was not exclusive to men. Native American women also engaged in this type of behavior and often performed activities that were usually carried out by men, such as hunting, engaging in warfare, and taking a wife (Gould, 1994; Greenberg, 1988). These women were accepted by the Native community and were sometimes given high status. Actually, *berdache* is a Persian word that defines a male sex slave, and the term has really been used incorrectly to denote this class of Native people. Although many *berdaches* engaged in homosexual and heterosexual relationships, some chose to remain celibate. Among the Native people, the practice of *berdaches* was usually accepted, although their acceptance varied from tribe to tribe. In many instances these persons were highly regarded and were given or assumed active positions as tribal healers or spiritual vanguards. *Berdaches* were often taken as second wives by tribal chiefs, and single *berdaches* sometimes engaged in serial homosexual relationships with heterosexual men (Hurtado, 1996).

Many present-day Native Americans do not identify with the terms *gay*, *lesbian*, or *bisexual*. Rather, they view themselves as being *Two-Spirited*, which denotes a positive attitude toward homosexuality. The term signifies that homosexuality can be a spiritual choice. The individual has the spirit of both genders but does not necessarily share the experiences and worldview of a homosexual person. Native Americans consider the term *gay* as a noun used to denote the person, but the word *Two-Spirited* is used as a verb and deals with the individual's conduct and intercommunications. In Native American culture, a person's sexual orientation is not necessarily lifelong or fixed. As the person moves across the life span, his or her sexual orientation may change. Hence, Two-Spirited people may be heterosexual, homosexual, bisexual, or asexual at any period in their life. Native Americans demonstrate a greater appreciation than Europeans for self-determination and the individual's choice regarding sexual expression (Green, 1987).

MAJOR NEEDS AND PROBLEMS
OF NATIVE AMERICAN GROUPS

Needs Related to Poor Economic Conditions. Native Americans have been subjected to horrible conditions, which in turn have had a bearing on their current socioeconomic, environmental, and mental health status. Of all Americans, they are the most economically disadvantaged and perhaps the most misunderstood. The overall picture of their health is worse than that of the general population of this country. They have the highest rates of diabetes, fetal abnormalities, cirrhoses of the liver related to alcohol consumption, homicides, and fatal accidents (Schinke, 1996). In a study that focused on the underreporting of mortality rates for Native American children in the state of California between 1979 and 1993, it was found that 4.1 times more Native American children died than were actually reported because of racial misclassification (Epstein & Moreno, 1997). This study concluded that in less than one third of deaths among Native American children in California are children identified as Native American on death certificates.

The average income, education level, and standard of living of Native Americans are the lowest of all groups (Locke, 1998). American Indian youth have the highest school drop-out rate and are referred for special education more than any other group (Dykeman et al., 1996). In 1987, the drop-out rate for Native American students (35.5%) was higher than that of Latino (27.7%) and African American (22.2%) students (Franklin et al., 1995). It is estimated that 40% of Natives between the ages of 18 to 24 are high school dropouts, compared to 17% of whites (Carnegie Foundation, 1990).

The land upon which their reservations have been placed is mostly desolate. The reservations' employment and educational situations are tenuous. Although unemployment, as high as 70% depending on the location, is a major concern for both reservation and urban Natives, generally those who reside on reservations have poorer economic, health, social, and life satisfaction indexes than those who do not (Schafer & McIlwaine, 1992).

Hodgkinson (1992) reports that between 17 and 47% of Native Americans who reside in the 10 states with the largest number of Native Americans live in poverty. Over 28% of all Native Americans have incomes that fall below the poverty line, whereas only 13% of the general population of the United States is so affected (Schinke, 1996). Forty-five percent of those who reside on reservations live below the poverty line (Franklin et al., 1995). Their reservations are generally located in isolated locations where accessibility and transportation become issues. The reservations have a poor skilled labor force and are generally devoid of capital resources. The minimal numbers of industrial jobs available on reservations are low-wage positions. These factors contribute to their unemployment rate. The preceding factors also result in unfavorable housing situations and poor nutrition, which in turn cause health and related problems. In 1980, Native Americans were many times more likely to have tuberculosis than any other American population and had a dysentery rate that was 70 times higher than that of white Americans. Many Native Americans exist and manage to thrive under conditions that would be judged substandard by others (Schafer & McIlwaine, 1992). There is no reason to believe that their situation has improved significantly.

Needs Related to Substance Abuse. Alcoholism and drug abuse continue to be the biggest social problems among Native Americans. It has been estimated that approximately 80% of the men and between 35 and 55% of women suffer from alcoholism. They have a 33% higher rate of alcoholism than any other ethnic group. Among their youth, it is estimated that 25% of males and 14% of females ingest alcohol on a weekly basis by the time they have reached the 12th grade (Schinke, 1996). Approximately 75% of all Native American deaths and accidents are associated with alcoholism, and 8% of suicides are attributed to alcohol abuse. Compared with men between 25 and 34 years of age in the general population, Native American men are 2.8 times more likely to die as a result of motor vehicle accidents, are 2.7 times more likely to die from other types of accidents, and have suicide and homicide rates that are 2 and 1.9 times higher, respectively (Schinke, 1996).

The socioeconomic and health problems that threaten their community may have several causes. The marginalization and alienation they have experienced since the days of European settlement in the United States have had negative psychological impacts upon many members of these groups. They have been made to relinquish the traditional components of their way of life via armed conflicts, boarding schools, and the influence of missionaries, and all of these have been well documented as contributors to the etiology of many of the social pathologies they experience (Kasee, 1995). Many of the experiences that Native American children had with the American educational system during the period from 1568 to the mid-20th century have become stories that are sometimes used by parents to frighten children into good behavior.

Acculturation also helps to explain the incidences of their morbidity, health issues, and their socioeconomic status. Although the level and impact of acculturation varies individually and by region among the Native people, many experience dissonance between theirs and the majority culture. The use of alcohol and other substances, suicide, and risky behaviors may emerge as coping mechanisms that further threaten the viability of the various groups (Schinke, 1996). Historically, Native Americans used various types of psychoactive substances during ceremonies and spiritual observances. Many tribes became socialized to the euphoric effects of these substances, and patterns of use resulted. Social influences such as peer pressure may also contribute to their use of alcohol and other substances, because the refusal of such when offered may be considered discourteous. Kasee (1995) suggested that the loss of many of their traditional forms of religion has been a major factor contributing to the increase in their substance abuse. Finally, Lewis (1995) opinioned that the incidences of suicide and alcoholism among Native Americans may be rooted in colonial interference by Europeans, which resulted in "an erosion of genuine native leadership; a decay of traditional institutions; and an individual social weakening" (p. 223).

Needs Resulting From the Societal Images of Native Americans. Since the 19th century, Native Americans have been negatively stereotyped and labeled by others. For example, Thomas Jefferson Morgan, a widely known educator of his day, described them in the late 19th or early 20th century as "speaking an alien language, habitually idle, listening to stories of war and bloodshed, laboring without a system, obeying without question the word of their chiefs, gratifying their passions, living in hovels, and practicing a religion that was mere superstition, legends, and 'meaningless ceremonies'" (quoted in Harmon, 1990, p. 98). As recently as 1969, these attitudes were pervasive. A U.S. Senate Subcommittee found that individuals who were not of Native American descent but who lived near reservations often identified American Indians as lazy, exotic, unclean, drunkards, and beastly (Gibson & Ogbu, 1991). Such images may have been fostered by educational and media-related material that portrayed Native Americans in negative terms. "The popular American media image of Indian people as savages with no conscience, no compassion, and no sense of the value of human life and humanity was hardly true of the tribes—however true it was of the invaders" (Allen, 1986, p. 193). These people tended to overlook historical and environmental factors that contributed to the plight of Native Americans and to put the onus for the improvement of their situation on them. Thus, the Native American worldview was considered inferior in terms of both its moral and its cultural value.

Needs of Native American Women. "The central issue that confronts American Indian women throughout the hemisphere is survival, literal survival, both on a cultural and biological level" (Allen, 1986, p. 189). A common concern for Native American women may be the changes that are taking place within the family as a result of out-marriages. These marriages often result in changes in family structures, from matriarchal to patriarchal, as these families adopt non-Indian family patterns. Within these new family structures, traditional customs and practices cease, leading to further acculturation, which for many is not a welcome event. Critical issues of concern that in part developed as a result of European-Native American marriages are domestic violence and imbalances in gender roles, for which assistance with empowerment becomes crucial.

Child sexual abuse is a concern of Native American women. In the vast majority of Native American tribes, child sexual abuse is a taboo. The offender is usually banished from the group if found guilty. Between 1986 and 1989, Schafer and McIlwaine (1992) investigated child sexual abuse on the Hopi and Navajo reservations of Arizona. They found that the topic of sex was not freely discussed in either the family or school environment and that parents or significant others may place pressure upon the victim of abuse to deny the allegations for fear of damage to their reputation. As younger generations become acculturated to the majority society, they often lose their traditional customs and historical identity. This in turn causes a breakdown in family structure as a result of the decline of the support that has typically been provided by the extended family. Sometimes child abuse is the end result of this process. Some parents of the abused children and others within the tribal community would not cooperate during the investigation of an alleged abuse because: (a) the perpetrators had developed a good rapport with the community, and (b) they feared losing respect within the community. The victims were often labeled as deviant and felt ostracized, and follow-up services for the victims were often inadequate because of limited resources. It should be noted that many Native American youth attend boarding schools, and research suggests that male youth who reside in institutional settings have an increased risk of being sexually abused (Schafer & McIlwaine, 1992).

Alcohol and substance abuse are the most significant health problems in Native American communities (Weaver, 1999b). In a substudy of a research project conducted by the National Cancer Institute, the incidence of the use of tobacco, including smokeless tobacco, was studied among 614 Cherokee women ages 18 years and older who resided in western North Carolina. The study found that the use of tobacco in this population was six times higher than that of the general population of women in that region. They also found (a) that this group's use of smokeless tobacco was highest among the oldest and youngest participants of the study, a finding similar to national data; and (b) that the number of those who smoke and have regular monthly intakes of alcohol was consistent with that of other populations. As discussed earlier, the Native American community has a very high incidence of substance abuse, particularly alcohol. Nicotine is also a drug. High incidence of tobacco use places Native American women at risk for nicotine addiction and an array of negative health issues, including various types of cancers (Hagan et al., 1995).

Diabetes is a serious health problem for Native Americans. "Fewer than 50 years ago, diabetes was almost nonexistent in the Arctic, U.S. Southwest and the Pacific Islands" (Ponchillia, 1993, p. 333). As Native Americans took on Western eating habits and lifestyles, they experienced an increase in the rate of non-insulin-dependent diabetes, which is "skyrocketing at the fastest growing rate in the world" (Ponchillia, 1993, p. 334). The two Native groups with the highest rates of diabetes in the world are the Pima Indians of the southwestern United States and the Nauru of the Pacific. Native Americans are eight times more likely than whites to develop diabetes-related end-stage renal disease, and they more frequently experience complications and early death as a result of the disease. It is anticipated that the rate of diabetes among Native people will continue to increase due to issues of poverty, poor access to health care, and cultural beliefs. Many Native groups perceive illness to be a natural consequence of one's having transgressed a rule, and they believe that the type of illness is related to the nature of the violation. For instance, blindness caused by diabetes may be interpreted as the result of having looked at something forbidden. This view of illness has hindered many from considering the complications of diabetes as a direct result of the disease and has been detrimental to prevention and intervention.

Needs of Native American Men. Native American men still suffer from stigmatization and negative valuation by American society:

> Evidently, while Americans and people all over the world have been led into a deep and unquestionable belief that American Indians are cruel savages, a number of American Indian men have been equally deluded into internalizing that image and acting on it. (Allen, 1986, p. 193)

Their internalization of negative images about themselves may be a causal factor in their participation in self-destructive behaviors such as the abuse of alcohol and drugs. Herring (1990) asserts that many of the areas of special need facing Native Americans, such as substance abuse and poverty, are the consequences of their struggle with acclimating to European American culture.

Related to the use of drugs among Native men is HIV-AIDS. "The rate of HIV/AIDS is increasing more rapidly in the Native American population than in any other ethnic group in the United States" (Weaver, 1999b, p. 28). Variables that contribute to this fact include poor health outreach by health officials, beliefs of Native Americans about HIV-AIDS, and the general public's perception of Native people. Many non-Natives do not consider the variations among Native people and view them as rural residents whose primary drug of choice is alcohol. This stereotypical description fails to consider urban Natives who may use drugs and thereby become susceptible to HIV-AIDS through needle sharing. "Seroprevalence data indicate that 33% of Native Americans with HIV/AIDS have risk factors associated with IV drug use" (Weaver, 1999b, p. 33). Many Native Americans do not view HIV-AIDS as a disease that affects them because they generally come from small communities (Weaver, 1999b).

Needs of the Elderly. Many of the needs of Native American elderly are related to their socioeconomic and health status. Because Native Americans were granted U.S. citizenship in 1924, the elderly are entitled to receive social security and other benefits through social programs. Many of their social security benefits may be low, because many have not worked in occupations in which their salaries contributed to their social security earnings. "In general the reservation group is poorer, supports more people on its income, has fewer social contacts, lower life satisfaction, and poorer health" (Locke, 1998, p. 62). As with all Native American age groups, the elderly suffer from diabetes, substance abuse, heart disease, and other life-threatening conditions. Traditional beliefs about the cause and cure of illness may be contributing factors to chronic health conditions.

Needs of Native American Sexual Minorities. Native American homosexuals have needs related to social isolation, discrimination, and internalized homophobia. Many Native American gay and lesbian people become the brunt of satire, sarcasm, and jokes and are subjected to discriminatory practices and prejudice. Many experience pejorative verbal abuse, some have been physically attacked, and others have been murdered as a result of hate crimes. They are seen as a threat to the macho male image of American culture. Lesbians, described as an invisible minority, have not experienced the level of physical attacks that gay men have. Several studies point to the increase in hate crimes against the gay community. The rate of violence against gay men and lesbians is four times that against any other group (Eitzen & Zinn, 1997). According to the National Gay and Lesbian Task Force,

> More than one in five gay men and nearly one in ten lesbians have been punched, hit or kicked; a quarter of all gays had had some object thrown at them; a third had been chased; a third had been sexually harassed and 14% had been spit on. (Mohr, 1998, p. 462)

Gay hate crimes make up 11.6% of all hate crimes committed in this country ("The Hate Debate," 1998). Native American gay and lesbian people are often viewed with contempt, considered sinful, and thought to be people who may have a tendency toward certain types of criminal behavior, such as pedophilia.

> What all share in common, at least in the United States, is an experience of living in a society which has oppressed gay men and lesbians and has generally failed to recognize and affirm

loving relationships and emotional ties between people of the same gender. (Slucher, Mayer, & Dunkle, 1996, p. 118)

Gay men and lesbian women suffer the brunt of ideological oppression. In the United States homosexuality is considered to be deviant behavior. Only 41% of people surveyed in a 1992 poll conducted by *Newsweek* agreed that there is nothing wrong with people living a homosexual lifestyle. Labeling homosexuality as deviant serves to reaffirm heterosexism and allows discriminatory practices against homosexuals. Many Native people have internalized homophobia as a result of the influence of Christian missionaries and from having attended federal boarding schools. This is especially evident among those who reside on reservations. Sears (1991) found that they are less accepting of the *berdache*.

Needs Based on Culture-Related Disorders. Dana (1998) included syndromes such as spirit intrusion, soul loss, rootwork, ghost sickness, and taboo breaking as culture-bound disorders that were identified among Native people. Further identified were problems in living that were directly related to Native American culture, such as "[m]arginal cultural orientation status, damaged sense of self, relationship problems, chronic alcohol/drug abuse and lack of skills" (Dana, 1998, p. 114).

According to Trimble et al. (1996), spirit intrusion, soul loss, ghost sickness, and taboo breaking are groups of dispositions or manifestations that appear in numerous tribes. Soul loss refers to the lack of a soul and has been commonly reported among Cheyenne, Mojave, and Seminole people. It is characterized by repeated fainting; withdrawal; and preoccupation with ghosts, spirits, and suicide threats. Spirit intrusion means that the individual has been made sick by a spiritual force. This has been reported among the Eskimo and Tenino people and manifests as feelings of dependency and discouragement and as hallucinations. Taboo breaking occurs when a norm, such as those related to sexual behaviors and murder, has been broken; this disorder has been documented among the Navajo and Dakota. These people report tissue edema, mild weight loss, and variations in their moods. Ghost sickness refers to sicknesses that a person experiences as a result of witchcraft. It is common among the Navajo tribe and is characterized by confusion, loss of appetite, and delusions. Although only small numbers of firsthand accounts of these manifestations have been reported, psychosomatic conditions have been attributed to all four of these conditions. Because cultural differences in the causes of illnesses and disease have not been thoroughly explored, even the best-intentioned professionals have labeled these behaviors pathological.

Problems in living reported in Native American people include problems of (a) lifestyles, (b) cultural confusion, (c) self-esteem, (d) relationships, and (e) poor skill development. Problems with lifestyles and cultural confusion occur when the Native American has internalized racism and is confused as to role expectations in relation to the dominant culture. Self-esteem issues arise from having experienced various types of abuse, poor parenting, and institutional care. Unemployment and poor health care services contribute to poor self-esteem. Relationship problems cover all areas of social interaction and have an effect on the soundness of the individuals and family. Poor skill development involves deficient academic and life skills, which render the individual inadequately prepared to be economically competitive. Dana (1998) noted that overriding feelings of loss of identity and forced assimilation and acculturation contribute to problems in living among Native Americans. These problems, along with poor socioeconomic conditions, often lead to early death among Native people.

SOCIAL WORK PRACTICE: GENERAL CONSIDERATIONS FOR INTERVENTION WITH NATIVE AMERICANS

The Issue of Client Trust. Before any intervention can take place within the Native American community, trust must be established between you and the client, particularly if you are of Anglo ancestry. The history of Native American-European immigrant relations has been and to some degree remains tumultuous. For this reason, trust, which is such a vital component of any phase of the helping relationship, is even more significant with Native Americans. "American Indians value trust and understanding more than any other attributes in social workers, counselors, and psychologists" (Dykeman et al., 1996, p. 337). Although some Anglo therapists are capable of delivering "acceptable services," more often than not therapeutic intervention provided by persons of European descent has been scrutinized, justifiably, because of European Americans' lack of cultural sensitivity and understanding and for patronizing behaviors that sometimes characterize their approach. Trust can be developed and continued to the extent that the helper: (a) is open to having new experiences; (b) takes an active role in learning about Native American cultures through literature review, having direct contact with Native American people, and participating in cultural immersion activities; (c) is open to challenge research and intervention methods based in European ideology; and (d) is able to communicate genuineness, sincerity, and warmth to the client by words and deeds (Dana, 1998, p. 139).

Diagnostic tools and interventions should be culturally relevant. Native Americans experience many of the same mental health problems as other populations. The type and degree of problem appears to be associated with the population's degree of acculturation (Dana, 1998). "American Indian children and their families are an extremely vulnerable population and are at greater risk than other ethnic groups for developing serious psychosocial problems such as alcoholism, substance abuse, low self-concept, suicide and other psychiatric disorders" (Franklin et al., 1995, p. 183). It is often assumed that all Native Americans exhibit the same symptomatology of problems, that Caucasian intervention methods are suitable for everyone, and that all people who reside in the United States wish to take on the culture of American society. Traditional diagnostic instruments such as the *DSM-IV* (1994) often overlook Native American problems that are culture-specific. Measurement and assessment instruments and interview techniques that have not been developed locally and that do not use vocabulary common to the community and individuals for whom intervention has been designated are questionable unless they are culture-specific and have been developed with the collaboration of those who live in the local community.

In a 1983 sample of Native Americans who used a mental health service in Billings, Montana, the majority of cases were given diagnoses other than mental health diagnoses. The major psychiatric diagnoses were related to alcohol dependency, depression, adjustment reaction, and personality disorders. A little less than half of those who visited the mental health facility received no diagnosis. They were identified as having problems associated with family situations and with other non-mental health areas. This suggests that service providers may have found their assessment tools inadequate to render a correct diagnosis. Hence, cultural variables may be confounding factors to mainstream diagnostic classifications (Dana, 1998).

Native Americans respond to white society in various ways. Hodge (1981) reported that based on their Indian identity Native Americans respond to white society in three ways.

He separated them into three groups: *bicultural, traditional*, and *marginal*. Native Americans who are bicultural typically copy the dominant culture in such areas as formal education, the acquisition of wealth and material goods, and social activities. They have bought into the American work ethic and work very hard to obtain social status. Although they adhere to their cultural heritage, they involve themselves within the American political and economic systems in an effort to bring about change. They work toward breaking through racial barriers and place value on being successful and achievers. The traditional Native Americans have mistrust for white society. They typically avoid interaction with whites and use the acquisition of wealth as a way of escaping white oppression. While maintaining their cultural identity, they work toward making changes in their life situations. They have a realistic perception of racism and the barriers caused by it. Actions that they sometimes take to overcome the racial barriers are often viewed by others as being aggressive. The marginal Native Americans have established a mutual aid system amongst themselves upon which they rely for the interchange of goods, emotional support, and other services. They do not subscribe to competing with the dominant society and do not feel that they have any influence on the majority system. They rely upon the government for financial and housing assistance, are relatively low postured in society, and have come to be viewed by some as having learned to be helpless (Locke, 1998). Sociocultural stress becomes problematic for them, because they are not fully accepted by either the dominant or traditional cultures. Marginal Native Americans are also often among the middle-class socioeconomic group. Middle-class Native Americans are more likely to adopt a Western-oriented lifestyle. "A relatively high level of formal education, greater generational removal from the reservation, a low degree of encapsulation within a family social network, limited traveling to and from the reservation, and previous experience with Western health care in the immediate family" are factors that can be used by therapists to identify persons who have been acclimated to health norms of the Western society (Williams & Ellison, 1996, p. 149).

The bicultural Native Americans are most likely to receive maximum benefit from mainstream interventions because they have assimilated into American society. The marginal Native Americans respond to mainstream interventions that are coupled with traditional elements of Native culture. This approach works well for them because the marginal Native people have integrated some of the majority population's values and beliefs with their own. Culture-specific interventions have been found to work best with the traditional Native Americans, because they are not as accepting of mainstream interventions. For example, "[h]ealth care for traditional American Indians must operate from an Indian value orientation" (Williams & Ellison, 1996, p. 148). Illness may be viewed by the traditional Native persons as a result of their inability to sufficiently accomplish traditional role expectations. Intervention will need to focus on both restoration of the person's physical health and restoring harmonious relationships within the individual's social and spiritual spheres.

Mainstream interventions need to be adapted to Native American cultures. Dana (1998) suggested that many of the major mainstream interventions can be adapted and used within the context of different settings and cultures. That is to say, psychoanalysis; gestalt therapy; transactional analysis; marital, reality, and family therapy; and others can be changed to work for Native American people. What makes the adaptation of these interventions most effective is the inclusion of input from those within the local community before their application. The local community should be empowered to give definitions and suggestions for interventive methods for their immediate problems. It is only after a general consensus has been reached regarding the problem and its solution that intervention should begin, and then with the involvement of tribal personnel. Treatment modalities that correspond to the cultural choices of the client should be substituted for those that are Anglo oriented. For example, when working with school students, the social worker may employ the use of an art therapy group instead of individual talk therapy. Art therapy has been found to assist students in disclosing their concerns about family and peer relations through "more culturally relevant expressions" (Dykeman et al., 1996, p. 345).

Trimble et al. (1996) give an example of how this can be done. They applied a cognitive-behavioral approach to bicultural provision in working with drug abuse among Native American adolescents. Parts of life skills training from the majority population were coupled with Native American local cultural lifestyles. An intervention that reflected traditional Native American values and lifestyles was developed. Anglo and Native American professionals used small groups to teach Native American youth to use "inner speech" as a coping and problem-solving mechanism. A 6-month follow-up indicated that the incidence of alcohol, marijuana, and inhalant use was lower for those who participated in the group compared to those who did not. In a second example, a family-systems model of family therapy was applied to a tribal setting. Families who were experiencing problems were identified by local mental health personnel. Services were subsequently provided by the Indian Health Services using a combination of mainstream interventions that were modified to Native culture. Favorable outcomes were reported. Schinke (1996) and Goodluck (1993) point to several considerations that need to be made when providing intervention services to Native American populations:

1. Services need to be combined with culture-specific intervention and a culture-specific delivery style, that is, the avoidance of eye contact and confrontation and recognition for the respect of social status, age, and secrecy in personal affairs.

2. Those who are within the informal support network of the Native American community should be included.

3. The local community should be included in each phase of the helping process. This serves to enhance group cohesiveness, which in turn fosters strength and encouragement.

4. Clients should have the opportunity to be referred to healers that have been approved by their culture whenever they so desire.

5. The therapist should be aware of the differences that exist in communication styles between types of clients, that is, the traditional client is likely to avoid eye contact and may not disclose personal or disturbing thoughts (Trimble et al., 1996).

6. Intervention should focus on restoring harmony between the spiritual and physical well-being of the client.

7. Illness should be understood from the client's definition, and intervention should be developed in accordance with the client's definition.

Although it has been suggested that the client may find support through the inclusion of other significant Native Americans while engaged in the helping process, Schafer and McIlwaine (1992) caution that the presence of other Native persons may in fact cause the client to be more inhibited and cautious. Because the tribal group and reservation milieu are "closed community environments," personal information is often disseminated throughout the community through informal communication networks (Schafer and McIlwaine, 1992, p. 159). Confidentiality therefore becomes a major point of consideration, and the therapist will need to weigh the cost versus benefits of such an arrangement and make adjustments if needed.

To be sure, for many Native Americans, especially those who have traditional backgrounds, the counseling sphere is a novel situation. "As a group or community, Indians have little direct experience in dealing with the outside world, nor do individuals have a real understanding of mainstream society" (Lewis, 1995, p. 223). Often the family, community, or client will approach the helper with caution or hostility, and sometimes they may test the helper's genuineness. "Social workers must be prepared to address these issues while designing interventions for clients who may distrust the very agency they have come to for help" (Williams & Ellison, 1996, p. 147). Given their overwhelmingly negative past and present experiences with the American people and government, it is not difficult to understand their distrust of non-Native people. Nevertheless, with patience and a positive attitude, the counselor can establish a trusting relationship with these clients.

SOCIAL WORK INTERVENTION AT MICRO-, MEZZO-, AND MACROLEVELS: PRINCIPLES AND APPROACHES

Before goals can be discussed and a plan of action can be made, a thorough assessment of the client's situation must be conducted. Without an accurate assessment, there would be no order to the helping process, and our efforts would be purposeless.

Assessment-Related Practice Principles and Approaches

1. Make the client a participant in the assessment process. Assessments are best when they have allowed for maximum client involvement. When clients are given maximum involvement in this phase of the process, they are motivated to work harder toward problem resolution. Make the assessment a collaborative process between you and the client.

2. Use nontraditional approaches with Native Americans. Most often, clients are asked to come to the agency to receive services. Sometimes a better assessment of the clients' situations can be made when you visit their environment. You will gain a much better understanding of the dynamics of their life situation by actually seeing their living arrangements and community and, if appropriate, talking with their significant others. Native American clients may also feel more comfortable with you when you interact with them in their settings.

3. Refrain from being too verbal, and allow for silences. Making a proper assessment of the Native American client requires you to have containment skills. This involves "patience, the ability to tolerate silence, and listening—all skills that require social workers to be less verbally active than they might be with clients from other cultures" (Weaver, 1999a, p. 222). A common belief among Native Americans is that it is wise to hear all that a speaker has said and then give deep thought to the content before making a response. This belief has grown out of their experiences with being deceived by government agencies and others. Often, you will need to refrain from being overly verbal and be willing to be quiet and listen attentively.

4. Recognize Native Americans as individual cultural beings. It would be incorrect for you to apply general concepts regarding Native people to any particular indigenous person. There is no one way or general way of being Native. Each person embraces his or her culture in a different way. Explore and appreciate the uniqueness of the client as a part of your assessment.

5. Make the assessment as inclusive as possible. The assessment of Native American clients should go beyond gathering demographic data and asking them to explain the nature of their problem. In addition to the review of systems suggested in Chapter 2, explore such areas as: (a) the role of religion in their life, (b) their view of therapeutic services, (c) the behavioral norms of their community, (d) the degree to which they have assimilated into the mainstream culture, and (e) specific tribal beliefs. The use of cultura-grams will also be helpful.

6. Explore the role and significance of the extended family. It is not uncommon for grandparents, aunts, uncles, and non-kin to be very active in the life of Native American clients. "One of the greatest strengths common to American Indian cultures is the extended family" (Dykeman et al., 1996, p. 339). For instance, children are often cared for on an informal basis by extended family or close friends of the family. It is important to know the extent to which extended family serves as a support network and is willing to provide additional support.

7. Remember that American Indians do not self-disclose readily. Anglo therapists often view a client's reluctance to self-disclose as problematic and a form of resistance. Generally, Native Americans do not readily reveal information about themselves. For instance, Gilliland (1992) noted that American Indian students took longer than other students to reveal their family or school problems to a counselor. Be patient and establish a trusting relationship with these clients.

Intervention-Related Practice Principles and Approaches

At the Microlevel. You will find the following helpful in working with Native Americans.

1. Strive to become as culturally competent as possible. Show an appreciation for Native American culture, and be supportive of the value and belief system of Native people. Goodluck (1993) suggested that for effective work with Native Americans, you should be knowledgeable about U.S. American history and the history of Native American tribes, the value systems of Native American tribes, Native American kinship and clan structures, mutual aid systems, Native American religions, and U.S. government and tribal laws. According to Locke (1998), Native Americans with greater degrees of cultural com-mitment prefer counselors who, besides their expertise, are more nurturing and who pro-vide conditions that will facilitate the helping process. This will require your willingness to learn about the cultural identity of the individual and of the family or group that he or she belongs to. This is important in view of the inter- and intratribal differences and levels of acculturation. Enhance your competence by having as many participatory expe-riences with their culture as possible.

2. Remember the importance of silences during the interviews with Native American clients. "Quiet time at the beginning of a session gives both counselor and client a chance to orient themselves to the situation, get in touch with themselves, and experience the

'presence' of the other person" (Garrett, 1999, p. 91). Demonstrate good communication skills, respect for the client, and understanding as you yield the urge to converse in order to break silence.

3. Be cognizant of your choice of words. When communicating with or about Native Americans, your choice of words needs to be taken into consideration. Negative attitudes and beliefs about Native American people still abound. Racism is evident in imaging and everyday speech, even within the helping professions. Even social work terminology and jargon are not bias-free. Historically, when Native Americans and whites were at war over the Native land, military successes by the U.S. government were often hailed as victories. In contrast, when Native Americans were successful in defending their homes and families, their killing of enemy whites in the process was recorded as massacres.

4. Explore client strengths that can be used as catalysts for change. Encourage Native American clients to discover the possibilities for change that emerge from within the framework of their cultures. Capitalize on their positive inner and environmental resources.

5. Involve traditional Native American practitioners in your intervention. Western therapeutic interventions may not always be appropriate or applicable for Native Americans. Include elements of their culture in intervention. "The ability of social workers to integrate Western medicine and psychological skills with traditional arts and beliefs is of primary importance. Such an ability requires trust in another mode of healing" (Williams & Ellison, 1996, p. 150). Traditional-indigenous healers, that is, medicine men and women, spiritual leaders, and so forth, should be involved in conjunction with culturally competent nontribal personnel. Give attention to the importance of ceremonies and rituals, such as the Sweat Lodge, among traditional Native people.[14] Folk tales and legends can also be used to promote healthy choices.

6. Seek to empower the Native American client. Native Americans individually and collectively have been relegated to a position of powerlessness by virtue of the socio-economic and political infrastructure in the United States. They have been systematically denied access to resources and have endured the inferior treatment of minority status. This has had deleterious psychological, emotional, and physical effects on their community in terms of the stress, stress-related disorders, and mental health conditions that evolve as individuals attempt to cope with and sometimes internalize the concept of inferior status. Use empowerment-oriented interventions with them. Empowering the Native American community involves a threefold process: (a) helping individuals to gain control over their personal lives, (b) helping individuals to conduct themselves in a manner that will afford them more positive and fruitful results, and (c) enabling both the individual and the community to acquire resources and skills for environmental structuring and restructuring.

7. Be cognizant of the cross-cultural differences among Native Americans. There are hundreds of Native American tribes representing hundreds of different languages, customs, and traditions. Not all Native Americans have strong cultural affinities, and each person experiences the culture in a different way. "The historical traditions, beliefs, and behavioral norms of the community being served, determine an Indian client's degree of assimilation into the dominant culture" (Williams & Ellison, 1996, p. 147). In order to provide effective intervention, explore the differences in values, beliefs, and traditions that exist between and within groups.

8. View the client as an individual and not as a case. In an attempt to minimize subjectivity, social workers sometimes objectify the client. This can cause clients to feel alienated, and they may perceive that you view them as merely a statistic in your caseload. Consider the client as an individual who has feelings and emotional needs and for whom seeking treatment may have been a difficult task.

9. Encourage the client to take pride in his or her identity. Promote pride in the Native American's ethnic identity through the use of positive image forms (arts and crafts, posters that depict positive role models, etc.) in an effort to increase the client's self-esteem and motivation.

10. Consider humor as a counseling strategy. Humor is an indirect way of communicating emotional messages that might be unacceptable if conveyed directly. "Native American Indians use humor's ability to erase, cleanse, or change what was embarrassing, oppressive, sorrowful or painful" (Herring & Meggert, 1994, p. 68). Learn appropriate uses of humor that are still used among traditional Native cultures. Metaphors can also be a valuable counseling strategy when working with Native American adults. When working with Native American youth, you could use storytelling and story-related activities, imagination and imagery, puppets and clowns. "Story reading serves to stress print as a means of preserving information and culture as well as a means of extending self. A clown puppet can allow for poking fun at stressful situations" (Herring & Meggert, 1994, p. 72).

11. Self-reflect on stereotypical ideas and negative perceptions that you may hold about Native Americans. Everyone in this society is exposed to the pervasive negative information about minorities and groups different from the dominant society. You may genuinely feel that you have no biases or prejudices against Native Americans. Negative beliefs and feelings may not surface until you have direct contact with them. Get in the habit of continuously self-reflecting on your attitudes and beliefs about Native people, and be willing to take necessary steps to change any negative attitudes.

At the Mezzolevel. As an agency administrator and program planner, you will benefit from the following suggestions.

1. Employ Native American social workers when possible. These individuals can serve as role models for Native American clients and can give valuable input on policy and procedural issues that arise regarding Native American constituents. Native American social workers interested in contributing to the development of competent social work professionals can also serve as agency field supervisors for social work interns. "It is critical to train indigenous social workers to provide care in their home communities" (Weaver, 1999a, p. 220).

2. Situate services within the Native American community. Services may need to be relocated and delivered in the local community, thereby fostering connections to informal supports. Additionally, clients often feel better connected with and have easier access to agencies that are located within their community.

3. Provide for cultural sensitivity training to agency personnel. Because of the breadth of diversity within Native American culture, agency personnel should receive sensitivity training. All agency employees who have direct contact with Native American clients should receive *ongoing* diversity training. Make every effort to have diversity training

provided by representatives of the Native American population or persons who have had direct practice experience with Native American individuals, groups, and communities. Encourage the employees to avail themselves of experiential opportunities with Native Americans for their personal growth and development. These can include powwows, Sweat Lodges, ceremonies, celebrations, and social events that are open to the public.

4. Solicit feedback from Native American clients. The client is in the best position to tell you which agency services are working for them and which are not. Regularly ask the client, family, and Native American community for suggestions pertaining to how agency services can be improved. "Interventions that involve Indian planning and implementation have the best chance for succeeding because they are likely to be more culturally appropriate" (Williams & Ellison, 1996, p. 150). Also encourage client feedback regarding their perception of how they are being dealt with by non-Native agency personnel.

5. Empower Native Americans to serve as a community resource. Your agency can serve as a valuable educational resource to the wider community by providing Native Americans with forums for providing community education. Create opportunities for Native Americans to give on- or off-site public presentations by which members of the wider community can be educated on Native American values, traditions, religion, ceremonies, intergroup differences, issues, concerns, and other facets of their life.

6. Be instrumental in your agency's participation in Native American-based research. "Taking the less arduous route of writing descriptive, non-analytical history—that has been the traditional method for the majority of scholars who study Indians—will continue to have serious repercussions on American Indian history" (Mihesuah, 1996, p. 25). Agencies that have a Native American clientele are in a good position to do strengths-based and solution-focused research with this community. Not only can agencies be valuable to the Native population as a result of the counseling and tangible services they provide, but they can also contribute to the social work knowledge base by conducting agency-based research.

7. Spearhead a movement toward human service agencies' forming partnerships with Native American initiatives. Collaborations between service agencies serving Native Americans are perhaps the best way to provide well-rounded comprehensive services in their communities. Social service agencies should partner with schools, Native religious institutions, grassroots organizations, and other entities to ensure that as many facets and issues as possible that are pertinent to this population are addressed. Often valuable resources are lost or underutilized when an agency attempts to operate without meaningful input from the other institutions within the community that work with Native Americans.

At the Macrolevel. As a member of the professional community, you can involve your agency in macro level interventions with far-reaching impact. You will find the following suggestions helpful.

1. Social work agencies should advocate for a positive societal image of Native Americans. Social workers often hold leadership positions as agency directors and supervisors and are very influential in political and social arenas. They often have direct access to policy and decision makers such as legislators and media personalities. They should use

these positions and their influence as opportunities to advocate for correcting inaccurate and stereotypical information about Native American history and culture.

2. Social workers should advocate for the inclusion of Native American studies in school curricula:

> The Native American experience, in any fair and substantial sense, has been omitted from the curriculum of schools in America and, without it, neither Native American students nor other ethnic groups are educated for the hard realities of their time. (Reid, 1993, p. 10)

One objective of the American education system should be to prepare students to be leaders in both their communities and the wider society. As leaders, they can advocate for social change and work to address many of the ills that affect Native Americans. Effective leadership should be based on a person's understanding of his or her past and present situation. Additionally, "one way of minimizing anti-bias in curriculum materials is to use Native-American controlled publishers and media distributors whenever possible in exploring American Indian and Alaska Native themes with students" (Almeida, 1996, p. 7). Native and non-Native students will not be adequately prepared for leadership roles if they have not had curricular exposure to accurate information regarding the Native population.

3. Social workers should encourage Native American parental participation in their children's education. "Parent involvement is an essential element in Indian educational programs. All educators recognize the family as an influential factor in the growth and development of the child" (Reid, 1993, p. 12).[15] Native American parents and teachers need to work collaboratively toward the education of Native children. Parents can become involved in the decision-making process and overall scope of services delivered by the educational system. Their participation has a reciprocal benefit. They will learn about the roles of social workers, counselors, and administrators involved in their children's education and have an opportunity to educate these people about Native Americans.

4. Social workers should advocate for social justice. Native American history is replete with instances of atrocities visited upon the indigenous people. They still suffer from discrimination and unfair treatment. As social work professionals, you have committed to embrace the tenets put forth in the NASW Code of Ethics. Part of this Code is concerned with social justice, and it advocates for fair and equal treatment for all members of society. You should take every opportunity to combat the oppression of Native Americans and call into question every instance of unfair treatment of them.

5. Social workers should engage in research collaborations with Native American researchers. Most of the research that has been conducted on Native Americans has been done by non-Native people and has tended to view them from a pathological perspective. "This significance, at least in part, explains the labeling of Native Americans as 'culturally deviant' by social and mental health academics" (Herring, 1990, p. 137). Social workers are committed to issues of social justice, self-determination, and empowerment. Because you hold these values, you are in a position to conduct solution-based research in conjunction with members of the Native American research community. Who better to report their story and to research issues that affect their community than members of the group so affected by the problems and topics under study?

6. Social workers should empower Native American communities to care for themselves. You should remember that social problems are not confined to urban areas and that "undervalued groups reside in all areas of the United States and are by no means restricted to urban areas" (Delgado, 2000, p. 4). Many Native Americans are not urban dwellers. When you engage in community organization with Native American groups, the ultimate goal of your efforts should be to empower them to care for their own needs. "It is urgent that we find ways to strengthen those characteristics of communities that enable them to care for their members, especially those who are most vulnerable to dramatic shifts in national policy" (Delgado, 2000, p. 5). Community organization involves assessing the strengths and resources of the Native American community, helping them to utilize those strengths as mechanisms for change, and encouraging inter- and intracommunity collaborations. Some Native American communities may for historical reasons be hesitant about community initiatives that are established by non-Natives or those outside of their environment. Because you have the skills and knowledge to negotiate with and navigate through social agencies, you should use these skills to encourage partnerships between the social work profession and Native American community leaders for the ultimate goal of improving the overall functioning of their communities.

NOTES

1. The missionaries embraced the American perspective that was to become known as manifest destiny, which asserted that the Anglo-Saxon culture was to be the central worldview and that it was the will of God that Native American tribes should be managed by the U.S. government (Spring, 1997). Various churches were assigned to different reservations. Christianity was incorporated into the school curriculum because it was believed to have civilizing qualities for those who were considered heathens by the American public.

2. Drawing on past experience, the curricula of these schools incorporated material that was culturally relevant and aimed at increasing self-esteem and pride in the student. Specifically, Native American history, language, culture, mentoring programs, and academic support services and intervention were to be incorporated into the school milieu. A current concern among Native Americans involves the persistent presentation of erroneous information on Native American history in many new textbooks. Much of the textbook terminology used in reference to Native Americans remains racist. The American tradition of giving special attention to Native American history only during Thanksgiving or Native American awareness days is drawing increasing criticism from members of that community.

3. Native Americans have a history of general distrust of researchers, anthropologists, archaeologists, and museum curators. For centuries researchers have made false statements and vilified the Native American culture, which many Native Americans feel has served to confuse their youth and the general public. Untold numbers of Native American artifacts, including skeletal remains, were stolen for profit. This contributed to the loss of their culture (Ambler, 1996). The majority of unearthed human remains are those of Native Americans (Harjo, 1993). These artifacts have often been kept in museums and universities but have not always been treated with respect. These events, coupled with past governmental prohibitions on their use of their languages and ceremonial practices, have caused many to practice their traditions underground.

4. For example, among Native people it is not uncommon for personal vehicles to be shared or to be offered for communal use. Educational attainment is often viewed as a mechanism through which individuals can contribute to the good of the community, and it is not unusual for those who attain advanced degrees to return to the reservation to assist with the education of others.

5. According to Birchfield (1997a), this Act was little more than a measure to allow for governmental access to the mineral and timber supplies located on tribal property. What resulted was exploitation of these resources, in varying degrees from tribe to tribe, with little recognition of the Native opposition to these practices.

6. The San Carlos reservation in eastern Arizona has a population of 6,000, which is under tribal authority and is run as a corporation. The Fort Apache Reservation is located in eastern Arizona and is home to over 8,500 Apaches, and the Camp Verde Reservation, which has a smaller population of 1,500, is situated in central Arizona. There are other Apache reservations located in New Mexico. The New Mexico Jicarilla Reservation has an annual income of $11 million as a result of oil and gas reserves that were discovered on the southern part of the reservation after World War I. The Mescalero Reservation is located in southeastern New Mexico, where many residents are employed in the tourism industry.

7. These include the development of a timber company at the Fort Apache reservation in Arizona, which employs approximately 400 Apache people. A ski resort and museum are managed by both the Jicarilla and Mescalero Apaches, and several campgrounds are owned and maintained by various tribes. Tourism provides a stable economy for some of the reservations. An ongoing issue between the Apache people and the U.S. government involves a settlement of $10 million for land that was wrongfully taken from them. The Jicarillas filed for compensation under the Indian Claims and Commission Act of 1946, but the U.S. government has rejected any attempts by the Apache people at negotiations toward the resolution of this issue.

8. White men insisted on keeping the European gender role structure, in which men are labeled the heads of the household, and women take on the surname of the husband. These ideas were supported by the missionaries who worked with the Native people.

9. Even under such pressure, they remained cordial with the U.S. government. They aligned themselves with the army of Andrew Jackson and fought with him at the Battle of New Orleans. In spite of their allegiance, in 1816, the government demanded more of their land, and in 1820 the Choctaws gave in to these demands. Finally, under the presidency of Andrew Jackson, they were forced in 1830 to cede their remaining land and to move as a nation to the western region of the United States (Champagne, 1993).

10. In 1944, the BIA purchased 16,000 acres of land in Oklahoma, which was to be divided among the Choctaw people. Instead, within approximately 20 years, most of the newly purchased land had passed from Native to white ownership. It was not until the early 20th century that the Choctaw received any settlement for the sale of their land, and it was not until 1949 that they received cash awards for the sale of the mineral resources that accompanied the sale of their property (Birchfield, 1997b).

11. Every town was unique in terms of its ceremonial practices and the traditions that were practiced. Individual identity or affiliation was not with a person's family of origin but rather was based upon the particular town in which one lived. Children were viewed as being a part of the town in which their parents resided. Creeks divided their nation into two categories, the upper and lower communities, which were then designated as red or white towns. Towns designated as white were known as peace towns in which persons could find refuge or in which councils would establish guidelines for peace and conduct business related to laws concerning tribal governance. Red towns were war towns in which all facets of issues related to war were handled: As well as diplomatic and foreign relations issues, problems or questions were given attention (L. Hall, 1997a). Towns were further divided by their geographical location into upper and lower towns, each of which had a red or white town (Champagne, 1993).

12. Under constant barrage by many whites and the government, many Creeks adapted some of their traditions to fit the American way of life. Some joined various Christian denominations and gave up practicing their religion, and others made the church, instead of the town center, their focal point for gathering and conducting business. The Creeks of Oklahoma were often negatively viewed by white citizens who were opposed to sharing in social and political activities with this group. As

a result, the Creeks seldom interacted with whites, and when they did, it was generally out of the necessity for commerce.

13. A contemporary issue for which they are seeking redress occurred in May 1973 on the Pine Ridge Reservation after a 71-day siege by the federal government. For more than 2 years, persons of Native and non-Native descent who resided on the Pine Ridge Reservation and who supported the American Indian Movement (AIM) were under surveillance and police patrol. It was reported that unmarked FBI agents were following a red pickup truck occupied by two men, one of whom they thought to be a fugitive. The truck actually contained explosives that were being delivered to an encampment of a small number of AIM members. Shots were fired between the two parties. Frightened by the shots, members of the encampment armed themselves and returned fire. A third FBI agent arrived on the scene and radioed the incident to the patrols. Members of AIM proceeded to the vehicles to find two FBI agents lying dead by their vehicles and one Native American killed. A barrage of FBI agents soon appeared and descended upon the reservation. A nationwide search was conducted for the red pickup, which was never found. Charged in the incident were three men who had been at the encampment on the day of the altercation. The trial was held in a different juris-diction under a judge who was sympathetic to the government. During the trial, FBI agents changed their stories to indicate it was a red and white van for which they were looking instead of a red pickup truck, as had originally been reported. Two of the defendants were acquitted, and one, Leonard Peltier, received two life sentences. Evidence that would have shown that Leonard Peltier had not fired the fatal bullets was held to be inadmissible. The documentary *Incident at Oglala: The Leonard Peltier Story* gives evidence that had the defendant received a fair trial, he would have been acquitted as the other two were (Birchfield, 1997d).

14. According to Hagan et al. (1995),

A sweat lodge is a squat enclosure that contains, at its center, heated rocks on which water is poured to make steam. Participants sit in the dark enclosure and with the steam. This, in addi-tion to ceremonial activities provides spiritual cleansing. (p. 126)

15. In an era of anti-affirmative action initiatives, researchers and social scientists are not opti-mistic regarding the future of professional roles for people who are members of ethnically diverse populations (Garrison, 1993). Although the number of minorities is expected to increase over the next few decades, researchers "do not expect a promising employment future for ethnically diverse populations in general, and for African American and Native American populations in particular" (Garrison, 1993, p. 161). Before individuals can occupy professional positions, they must be well educated and have adequate job preparation. In her study of gifted programs offered in 53 elemen-tary schools in a midsized Pacific Northwest city, Garrison (1993) found that Native American students were underidentified to receive gifted services, were underenrolled in advanced-level classes, and had lower grade point averages than gifted students who were of European American descent. Income was found to be a contributing factor to the Native American students' low perfor-mance. This study has implications for the Native American community, because many of them have incomes that place them below the poverty line, thus depriving them of the resources (such as home computers and access to personal tutorial services) that would assist in making them academically competitive. Not being equipped with the educational skills required in the workforce places many members of the Native American community at a disadvantage.

7

Understanding and Working
With Biracial/Mixed-Race
Americans

BIRACIAL/MIXED-RACE AMERICANS: WHO ARE THEY?

Biracial/mixed-race Americans are those whose parents are of different racial groups. People of mixed racial heritage are not a recent phenomenon. The purity of races is a myth. Biological and historical evidence points to the total inaccuracy of the idea of a pure race (Porterfield, 1978). Throughout human history, whenever there was contact between people of different racial groups, there was also sexual intermixing. There were no pure whites who came to America from Europe, nor were there any pure blacks brought here from Africa. Nevertheless, the beliefs in the superiority and inferiority of races and in the idea that racial mixture results in inferior offspring have persisted and colored peoples' attitudes and behaviors. In the words of Spencer (1997),

> In the United States the powerful have done such a thorough job at sewing the idea of race into the social fabric of the nation, that Americans have always treated race as though it were something that defined the very nature of people. Americans have especially treated race as though it defined the essence of black and white people, who generally have been viewed as opposites during the course of their shared history in the New World. (p. 1)

Thus, in the highly racialist American society, the world is viewed as only white and black or white and nonwhite. However, the rigid social boundaries between blacks and whites and an elaborate ideology to enforce this separation did not keep the two from crossing the color barrier. Similarly, there has been an extensive intermingling of white and Native American blood since the appearance of the white man on this continent. There has also been intermingling between Indians and blacks, although different patterns emerged in different parts of the country and at different times.[1]

Also, despite widespread opposition to Asian-white mixing, there were marriages between Asians and other Americans resulting in Asian-white and Asian-other biracial children throughout the country. Asians have mixed with others in Hawaii since the first Asian came there to work. Moreover, when America got involved in the global and regional wars beyond its borders, American men and Asian women came together on the soils of several Asian lands, and those unions resulted in biracial children. The provisions of the War Brides Act of 1945 (passed to facilitate admission of European spouses and children of members of the U.S. armed forces) were extended in the 1950s to the Chinese, Japanese, and Korean spouses and children of military personnel.

Thus, throughout the history of this country, there have been mixed-race people, but they were forced to identify entirely with the community of their nonwhite parent. What is new is that today the mixed-race Americans do not want to disown either side of their heritage. These new biracials are asserting an integrative multiracial identity "not to reflect internalized racism but to strive for a sense of wholeness" (King & DaCosta, 1996, p. 239). To what extent they are finding that sense of wholeness is hard to say.[2]

Most of those who identify themselves as black-white mixed-race are first-generation individuals who do not want to disown either side of their heritage. According to the U.S. Census, in 1992 there were about 246,000 married couples in which one partner was African American and one was white.[3] Many of these interracial couples bring their black and white backgrounds to the identity of their children. The carriers of this new identity are primarily these first-generation individuals, but this group also include a smaller portion of "multigenerational" persons who have been blended for several generations. Although viewed by the general society as black, they have resisted identifying solely with the black community. These "new" biracials are seeking to affirm an integrative identity that has both the black and white communities as reference groups or a pluralist identity that blends aspects of black and white communities but is neither (Daniel, 1996).

Among the Asian Americans, historically, Asian-white combinations have predominated, with far fewer Asian-Hispanic, Asian-Black, and other people of color combinations. This has changed over the last couple of decades. The number of biracial and multiracial Asian Americans can only be surmised from the rapid rise in the Asian American population and by the growing rate of out-marriages within that population. Although there are intergroup differences, the rate of out-marriages in the Asian American community is significant.[4] Moreover, if many of the international marriages involve military personnel, given the high proportion of soldiers of color in an all-volunteer service, many more of the unions will involve two people of color than was true in the past (Thornton, 1992). Who are the Asian American biracials? The question of identity of Asian American biracials is a complex one, because there are significant differences in their acceptance among the different subgroups of Asian Americans.

The majority of Hispanic Americans is made up of Mexican Americans. Over centuries, a complex interplay of race and culture has thoroughly homogenized the population of the old and present-day Mexico.[5] The same is true of most other Hispanic groups.[6] Our focus here is on the products of unions between Hispanics irrespective of their racial heritage and whites and nonwhites in today's American society. Gilbertson, Fitzpatrick, and Yang (1996) found that there is considerable intermarriage among all Hispanic groups along with intermarriage with non-Hispanics (over 50%) among second-generation Cubans, Mexicans, Central Americans, and South Americans. In 1992, nearly 26% of 4.45 million couples were exogamous relationships and about one fourth of Latino babies had a non-Latino parent (O'Hare, 1992; Snipp, 1997). A recent analysis of 1990 Census Bureau data by Reynolds Farley (1991) shows that among Hispanics between the ages of 25 and 34 born in the United States, about 31% are married to whites. Although "Latino, and especially Mexican Americans, have been conditioned by their history, however imperfectly and unevenly, to accept racial ambiguity and mixture as 'normal'" (Fernandez, 1992, p. 139), there are significant differences among the various Hispanic American groups in their attitudes toward assimilation into the mainstream culture and toward interracial and interethnic marriage.[7] Rose (1984) has discussed the complexities of biracial and bicultural Hispanic families, particularly when couples come from different Spanish-speaking countries. There is a paucity of research on the reality of biracial products of unions between Hispanic Americans and others.

A Fall 1993 *Time Magazine* survey on interracial families revealed that 70% of Native Americans married out of their communities ("Face of America," 1993). The Native American is defined in different ways.[8] Many Native Americans make a distinction between full-blood and mixed-blood Indians among them. How well are the mixed-blood accepted as Indian, and how well do they fit into the world of the Native Americans? There is not a lot of literature on mixed-blood Indians. On the one extreme are those who share the opinion of Clifton (1989) that Indianness is an ethnicity, not a race, and that one can be culturally an Indian irrespective of the proportion of Indian blood in his or her veins. On the other extreme are those who subscribe to the notion of blood quantum and vehemently define Indianness by blood quantum. Generally, identity is tied to cultural attributes such as reservation community ties and phenotypicality ("looking Indian") in addition to blood quantum. A great significance is attached to being a full-blood Indian or appearing to be so. Concerns are often raised about the authenticity of the mixed-bloods. They are viewed dubiously by those who claim to be full-blood Indians. Individuals deal with this problem of identity in different ways. Some defer to full-bloods as being "more Indian," others insist on being recognized as Native, and still others become indifferent and stop worrying about it (Wilson, 1992).

The black-white/black-other biracial persons are shunned by the white community and are encouraged by the black community to identify with it, provided they do not assert their other racial identity. Similarly, the Native American-white/Native American-other biracial persons are ignored by the white society and accepted into the Native American community to the extent that they can prove their Indianness. The identification of the Asian American-white and Asian American-other biracials with the larger white or black society, Asian community, or neither is dependent on several factors. The literature provides some glimpses of their experiences. Most biracial children face many challenges, because their identity is questionable, and they struggle to bridge a cultural gap both at home and outside (Sinha, 1996). The dynamics of cultural differences between ethnically different parents can make that struggle more confusing and difficult.[9]

However, biracial/mixed-race people are now engaged in the process of self-definition and self-validation. They have formed several local and regional organizations such as I-Pride (Interracial/Intercultural Pride) in Berkeley, California; Multiracial Americans of Southern California in Los Angeles; the Biracial Family Network in Chicago; the Interracial Club of Buffalo, New York; Interracial Connection in Norfolk, Virginia; Interracial Families in Pittsburgh; Interracial Family Alliance in Houston; and Project RACE (Reclassify All Children Equally) in Roswell, Georgia; as well as the national AMEA (American Association of Multi-Ethnic Americans). There is also an organization called Interracial Lifestyle Connection, located in Fort Smith, Arizona, which functions as a correspondence club for interracial people to develop friendships and to meet for interracial dating (Daniel, 1992a; Spencer, 1997).

The American civil rights movement created the opportunity for minority groups to declare what names they wanted to be known by. Those who used to be called Negro or colored proclaimed themselves black, Orientals became Asian, and American Indians became Native Americans. Feelings of group pride, solidarity, and empowerment surrounded these new names (Helms, 1990; Weisman, 1996). The process of self-validation for biracials also involves choosing their own name and proclaiming it as a significant activity. We will end this section by introducing the reader to the various terms used for racially mixed people. Some of these are generic, whereas others refer to specific groups of biracial individuals. Some are imposed on these people and rejected or grudgingly accepted by them, and others are the reflections of their self-identification. Understanding these terms is important in the context of the movement of mixed-race groups alluded to above. Generic terms for mixed-race individuals include the following:

- Bicultural/intercultural/multicultural.
- Interracial.
- Half-breed.
- Mixed/mixed-race.
- *Melange* is a new term used for individuals of mixed racial heritage with no racial designation.
- *Multiracial* refers to individuals who have two or more racial heritages.
- Rainbow.
- Racially/culturally blended.
- *Transracial* connotes movement across racial boundaries and is used in the context of interracial adoptions.

The group-specific terms include the following:

- *Mulatto* and *mulatta* refer to those who have varying fractions of African and European heritage.
- *Mestizo* and *mestiza* refer to those of Indian and Spanish ancestry.
- *Hapa* or *Hapa haole* refer to persons of half Asian (Chinese, Japanese, Korean, Filipino) and half Caucasian ancestry in Hawaii.
- *Cosmopolitan* refers to persons of multiracial ancestry—Polynesian, Asian, and European—in Hawaii.
- *Eurasian* refers to those of Asian and European heritage.
- *Afroasian* refers to people of African and Asian heritage.
- *Amerasian* refers to racially mixed Asians and covers both Eurasians and Afroasians.

The term *mulatto/a* is derived from the Spanish word *mulato* for mule, a hybrid between a donkey and a horse. Many racially mixed persons do not view this as a positive designation. In the same category are terms like *half-breed*. Similarly, *mestizo/a* is not commonly used by young multiracial people. However, because of shared Spanish ancestry, the term is sometimes used for biracial Filipinos. *Hapa* or *Hapa haole* is also used for those of Asian and Pacific Island origin mixed with European heritage (Root, 1996).

A HISTORICAL OVERVIEW OF BIRACIAL/MIXED-RACE AMERICANS: COMMONALITY OF EXPERIENCES

Throughout human history, there has been sexual intermixing between different racial groups.

> Ever since the existing human species diverged into its four or five existing varieties of sub-species, there has been a constant opposite movement at work to unify the type. Whites have returned southwards and mingled with Australoids, Australoids have united with Negroids, and produced Malanesians, and Papuans, and these, again, have mixed with proto-Caucasians or with Mongols to form the Polynesian. The earliest types of White man have mingled with the primitive Mongol, or directly with the primitive Negro. There is an ancient Negroid strain underlying the populations of Southern and Western France, Italy, Sicily, Corsica, Sardinia, Spain, Portugal, Ireland, Wales and Scotland. Evidences of the former existence of these Negroid people are not only to be found in the features of their mixed descendants at the present day, but the fact is attested by skills, skeletons, and works of art of more or less great antiquity in France, Italy, etc. ... There are few Negro peoples at the present day—perhaps only the Bushmen, the Congo-Pigmies, and a few tribes of forest Negroes—which can be said to be without more or less trace of ancient White intermixture. (Harry H. Johnston, as quoted in Reuter, 1918)

In an impressive review of the European image of the non-European from the ancient to modern times, Henriques (1975) has shown that the color prejudice, as we know it, did not exist in ancient Greece and Rome. He mentions Herodotus's opinion of the Ethiopians as "the tallest and handsomest men in the world" (p. 10) and quotes the following poem of Asclepiades as reflecting an appreciation of the beauty of blackness:

> She waved her branch, fair Didyme,
> And waving stole my heart away;
> And now like wax in fire, see,
> I melt in swift decay.

> If she is black, what's that to me?
> This charcoal too is black, but yet
> No rose more red can ever be
> When once alight 'tis set. (quoted in Henriques, 1975, p. 10)

The acceptance of miscegenation as normal is illustrated by a quote from Josephus about a story of Moses, who during the Israelite captivity in Egypt had become a general of an invading force of Egyptians against Ethiopia:

> Tharbis was the daughter of the Ethiopians [that is to say of their king]: she happened to see Moses as he led the army near to the walls, and fought with great courage ... she fell deeply in love with him; and upon prevalency of that passion, sent to him the most faithful of her servants to discourse with him upon their marriage. He thereupon accepted the offer, on condition she would procure the delivering up of the city; and gave her the assurance of an oath to take her to his wife ... No sooner was the agreement made, but it took effect immediately; and when Moses had cut of the Ethiopians he gave thanks to God, and consummated his marriage, and led the Egyptians back to their own land. (quoted in Henriques, 1975, p. 11)

In the early Christian Church, no distinctions were made in terms of skin color or ethnicity. Distinctions emerged out of the confrontation between Europeans and a North African people, the Moors, who dominated Spain for 800 years and pushed into other parts of Europe.

> What is of great significance is that this was the first time that the West had been exposed on such a scale and time dimension to people alien in religion, culture and appearance, and that this experience was one of subordination. (Henriques, 1975, p. 14)

On the one hand, there was the process of miscegenation between Moors and Europeans, and on the other, Moors were looked down upon. Europeans who traveled to distant lands for trade and colonization intermixed with local people. The Portuguese in Brazil, Africa, and the Far East freely entered into sexual liaisons and marriages with local women, but they preferred concubinage to marriage. However, there is a difference between the Anglo-Saxon view of miscegenation and that of the Latin people of Europe. "The main European view of the non-European in the sixteenth and seventeenth centuries was that of creatures which personified many of the European's own evil characteristics. Othello and Cleopatra stand out as magnificent exceptions" (Henriques, 1975, p. 21). The early English settlers in North America, unlike their European counterparts from Spain and Portugal, became averse to racial mixing. They did not have white blood any purer than that of other Europeans, but they had an attitude of superiority essentially because of social legitimacy and status positions. They did not want sexual relations between "superiors" and "inferiors" to undermine the power base of the "superiors" (Porterfield, 1978). The presence of marriage partners of their own community helped them in this. This historical overview of mixed-race people in the United States is organized around the following themes.

Exploitation of the nonwhites included sexual exploitation. "Black-white miscegenation dates back to the early colonial period; it became widespread and took place within the socioeconomic context of southern American slavery under thoroughly unequal and brutally coercive circumstances" (Williams, 1996, p. 195). The following examples illustrate the sordidness of that context.

> Approximately a century and a quarter ago, a group of slaves were picking cotton on a plantation near where Troy, Alabama, is now located. Among them was a Negro woman, who, despite her position as a slave, carried herself like a queen and was tall and stately. The overseer (who was the plantation owner's son) sent her to the house on some errand. It was necessary to pass through a wooded pasture to reach the house and the overseer intercepted her in the woods and forced her to put her head between the rails in a old stake and rider fence, and there in that position my great-great-grandfather was conceived. (quoted in Frazier, 1966, p. 53)

The punishment for refusal and resistance was severe.

> Thomas James, Jep's second son, had cast his eye on a handsome young negro girl, to whom he made dishonest overtures. She would not submit to him, and finding he could not overcome her, he swore that he would be revenged. One night he called her out of the gin-house, and then bade me and two or three more, to strip her naked; which we did. He then made us throw

her down on her face, in front of the door, and hold her whilst he flogged her—the brute—with the bullwhip, cutting great gashes of flesh out of her person, at every blow, from five to six inches long. The poor unfortunate girl screamed most awfully all the time, and writhed under our strong arms, rendering it necessary for us to use our united strength to hold her down. He flogged her for half an hour, until he nearly killed her, and then left her to crawl away to her cabin. (John Brown, as quoted in Henriques, 1975, p. 63)

The rape and sexual exploitation of black women on southern plantations by their white masters and plantation overseers are an undisputed part of the history. What is not as easily accepted is that black men were also sexually abused and exploited by white women:

The passionate gyneolatry of the Ante-Bellum South has obscured the fact that white women of the planter caste, and others of a lesser status, made a considerable contribution to the pattern of intermixture. Such women appear to have been just as susceptible to the sexual attractions of the Negro as their husbands. (Henriques, 1975, p. 69)

This was true not only of married women but of unmarried women as well. However, the code of the South refused to recognize that a white woman could give herself freely to a black man. Sexual intercourse, therefore, could only be an act of rape (Henriques, 1975), for which black men were severely punished.

The sexual exploitation of Indians took place in different ways. A pattern approximating to the custom of sexual hospitality occurred in some areas. The white man, on arriving for a stay in an Indian settlement, would approach the parents of a girl and seek her domestic and sexual services. After making the arrangement, he would set up his hut, and the girl would live with him during his stay (Henriques, 1975).

There is little doubt that the white man, through alcohol and the satisfaction of his lust, managed to achieve the debauching of the Indian over a period of time. ... What is surprising is that men of integrity and honour—it was not merely the agent or trapper who succumbed to the flesh—could treat Indian women much in the same way a sailor treats a whore in any port in the world. (Henriques, 1975, pp. 58-59)

In the earlier days, racism did not seem to be a factor in the English bias against sexual mixing with Indians. "Perceived as darker than Europeans, Indians were considered White people whose exposure to the sun and custom of painting the body with ocher and other natural dyes explained their various hues" (Wilson, 1992, p. 117). Although many found many things wrong with the Indians, others advocated marriage as the best approach to dealing with them. In the words of a colonial aristocrat,

The Indians are usually tall and well proportioned, which makes full amends for the darkness of their complexions. Added to this, they are healthy and strong with constitutions untainted with Lewdness (unlike the Anglo-Saxon), and not enfeebled with luxury. Besides morals and all considered, I can't think the Indians were very much greater heathen than the first adventurers, who, had they been very good Christians, would have had the Charity to take this only method of converting the Natives to Christianity. For, after all that can be said, a spritly lover is the most prevailing missionary that can be sent among these or any other infidels. Besides, the poor Indians would have had less reason to complain that the English took their Lands, if they received it by way of a marriage with their daughters. Had such affinities been contracted in the beginning, how much bloodshed had been prevented, and how populous would the country have been, and consequently, how considerable. Nor would the shade of the skin have been any reproach at this day; for if the Moor may be washed in three generations, surely the Indian might be blancht in two. (William Byrd, as quoted in Bassett, 1901, pp. 8-9)

In 1784, Patrick Henry presented a bill to the Virginia Legislature providing that,

> every white man who married an Indian woman should be paid ten pounds, and five for each child born of such a marriage; and if any white women married an Indian she should be entitled to ten pounds with which the county court should buy them livestock; and once each year the Indian husband of this woman should be entitled to three pounds with which the county court would buy clothes for him; that every child born to the Indian man and white women should be educated by the state between the ages of ten and twenty-one years. (J. F. D. Smyth, as quoted in Henriques, 1975, p. 58)

Such ideas and proposals were, of course, not palatable to Indian haters, and the actual laws on the books, with some exceptions,[10] prohibited both marriage and fornication of white men and women with Negro, mulatto, and Indian men and women. "Rejection of intermarriage with the Indian co-existed with unrestrained promiscuity with Indian women" (Henriques, 1975, p. 60).

There is a strong desire to cross the racial boundary. In the North, along with slavery existed the institution of indenture, which applied mostly to whites but to some Indians as well.

> White men and women from England, Ireland, and Scotland were bought and sold in the same markets with black men and women and bequeathed in the same wills. They were subjected to similar working and living conditions after their arrival in America. As indentured servants bound for five or seven years, whites worked in the same fields with black servants and lived in the same rude tenant huts. A deep bond of sympathy developed between these indentured servants and blacks who formed the bulk of the early population. They fraternized during off-duty hours and consoled themselves with the same strong rum. And in and out of wedlock, they produced a numerous mulatto brood. (Porterfield, 1978, pp. 2-3)

This similarity of life conditions led to interracial marriages as well as illicit sexual relations between members of not only white and black groups but also between Indians and whites and Indians and blacks. In Chapter 5, we have described how Filipino men married white women because many antimiscegenation laws specifically forbade only marriages between whites and Mongolians, Negroes, and mulattoes.

Interracial mingling through sexual liaisons and marriage was not a social phenomenon only of the lower classes. The upper-class, powerful, and famous also crossed the racial line.

> Concubinage in most Southern cities was a luxury of the idle rich. In New Orleans, Charleston, and several other cities, there were organized systems of concubinage. Needless to say, some of the most prominent men of the South patronized the system. (Porterfield, 1978, pp. 6-7)

It is widely believed that such social stalwarts as Thomas Jefferson, Patrick Henry, Alexander Hamilton, Benjamin Franklin, and George Washington associated with Negro women and fathered mulatto children. Recently, DNA tests performed on the descendants of Thomas Jefferson and of his slave, Sally Hemmings, have offered compelling evidence that Jefferson fathered at least one of her children. However, well-to-do and powerful people stopped short of marriage (Porterfield, 1978).

Popular attitudes and public laws discourage interracial marriages. Antimiscegenation laws in various states were aimed at discouraging marriages between whites and non-whites, because marriage signifies equality. The earliest such law was enacted in Maryland in 1661, and it prohibited marriage between whites and blacks. Under that law, if a free-born white woman intermarried with a Negro slave, she would have to serve her husband's master as long as the slave lived, and her children would also be slaves (Porterfield, 1978). Such laws were extended to marriages between whites and other nonwhites.

> The range of non-Caucasians with whom the Caucasian may not mingle his seed is very wide—Mongolians (Mississippi), Chinese and Japanese (Georgia), Malayans (Maryland), Asiatic Indians (Virginia), Mulattoes (Delaware), Ethiopians (Nevada prior to the repeal in 1962), Koreans (South Dakota prior to repeal in 1957), Mestizos and half-breeds (South Carolina). One wonders if there were any practical grounds for this highly idiosyncratic choice—was there a period when Maryland was subjected to a sudden invasion of Malayans bent on destroying the racial purity of the State? Did an expedition of Ethiopians ever penetrate the fastnesses of Nevada there to rape and pillage? The truth may be that legislators merely thought of ethnic groups they actively disliked. The racist path is unpredictable. (Henriques, 1975, p. 34)

Despite the anti-Asian immigration laws, which continued until the 1960s, Asians from various countries came and made this country their permanent home. Most of these were men whose families were not allowed to come along or follow them. At the same time, laws in several states prohibited sexual mingling and marriages between Asians and local Americans. The depth of public sentiment regarding miscegenation between Asian and whites is reflected in the following quotes, one from a politician and the other from a minister. In 1878 at the California constitutional convention, John F. Miller proclaimed,

> Were the Chinese to amalgamate at all with our people, it would be the lowest, most vile, and degraded of our race, and the result of that amalgamation would be a hybrid of the most despicable, a mongrel of the most detestable that has ever afflicted the earth. (as quoted in Takaki, 1989, p. 101)

At the height of anti-Japanese movement in the beginning of the 20th century, Ralph Newman, a white minister said,

> Near my home is an eighty-acre tract of as fine land as there is in California. On that tract lives a Japanese. With that Japanese lives a white woman. In that woman's arms is a baby. What is that baby? It isn't white. It isn't Japanese. It is a germ of the mightiest problem that ever faced this state; a problem that will make the black problem in the South look white. (as quoted in Spickard, 1989, p. 25)

The society at large continues to view interracial marriages with disfavor. The Gallup Poll has, over the years, surveyed black and white Americans about their attitudes toward interracial marriage. There has been some change in those attitudes. Whereas in 1968, 72% of Americans disapproved of interracial marriage, the corresponding figure in 1991 was 42%. The public disapproval at times takes the form of threats of physical harm and actual attacks on interracial couples and biracial children. Root (1996) discussed her 1990 survey of a sample of junior college students in Hawaii, which is heralded as the state with the most positive attitudes toward racial mixing. She asked respondents to write down words that referred to someone who is racially mixed. The survey generated a list of about 30 words, the majority of which biracial persons will find derogatory, words such as *mutt, mongrel, Heinz 57,* and *poi dog.*

White supremacy dictates the societal approaches and policies toward nonwhites. American society has used the "one-drop rule" to define a black person and to separate black from white. It is also known as the "one black ancestor rule." Anyone with one drop of black blood, that is, with one black ancestor in his or her family line as recalled by the white community, is considered black, irrespective of all other characteristics, including skin color. Some courts have called it the "traceable amount rule," and anthropologists call it the "hypodescent rule," as it assigns racially mixed persons the status of the subordinate group (Davis, 1991). Elaborate classifications of black-white mixed-race persons were created.[11]

It seems that blackness was viewed as impurity and whiteness as purity and that any impurity introduced into purity was seen as making the whole thing impure. Whites chose to preserve their purity and supremacy by relegating the tainted ones to a lower caste (Poussaint, 1984). Thus, black-white mixed-race persons were forced to identify themselves as black. Despite the illogic of the one-drop rule, which says that a white mother can give birth to a black child but a black mother cannot give birth to a white child (Payne, 1998), it was applied very rigidly and taken to even nonsensical extremes.

> It is perhaps most poignantly illustrated by the story of an actress in Mississippi in the 1920s, who was to be charged with contravening the state's miscegenation laws by taking a blond, blue-eyed white lover. Just as the sheriff was about to arrest them both, the boy used his knife to prick the woman's figure and then sucked and swallowed some of her blood. The couple was allowed to go free because, as the sheriff had to admit, in Mississippi one drop of Negro blood made anyone a Negro. (Wilson, 1987, p. 26)

The one-drop rule served the interest of the majority community. It ensured the supply of slaves. Because interracial liaisons were prohibited, the offspring of those liaisons were illegitimate in the eyes of the law, and in many states, even in the North, they could not inherit property (Fernandez, 1996).

> The 18th-century law makers discovered that if legislation and public pronouncement against miscegenation were relatively unsuccessful at controlling the sexual impulses of the European population, specially males, there was little harm done so long as white domination was preserved by disowning the offspring of blended descent. (Daniel, 1996, p. 125)

Englishmen had no problem in abandoning their centuries-old traditional custom whereby children took their father's ancestry.

All mixed-race individuals—mulattoes, quadroons, octoroons, and others—were commonly called "mulattoes," and mulattoes were classified as black and thus slaves. Laws dealing with Negro slaves added "and mulattoes" to make clear that mixed blood did not confer exemption from slavery (Jordan, 1968). However, mulattoes were considered intellectually superior to blacks with darker skins and were sometimes treated less harshly.

They were often given better positions, such as being house servants instead of manual field laborers. There were variations in the treatment of mulattoes in different states.[12] They were also used to spy on other slaves and to forewarn owners of possible slave revolts. Some mulattoes gained freedom and tried to gain a special class or caste status.[13] Their efforts were successful only to the extent that they suited the economic and social interests of the majority community.

> Mulattoes were visible evidence of the mixing which had long gone on in the shadows of black/white relations. As such, they were a powerful source of guilt, for they physically contradicted white notions about the crucial importance of maintaining racial purity. In this sense, white attitudes about the mulatto reveal an uneasiness which haunted white self-perceptions. Perhaps, after all, the white man was not really that different from the Negro he so disdained. (Mencke, 1979, p. xi)

Economic and power considerations triumphed over others.

> In the American colonies, the need was for plantation labor and the urge was for occasional sex partners with whom one could act out all one's sexual fantasies, since black women were defined as lascivious by nature. By prohibiting racial intermarriage, winking at interracial sex, and defining all mixed offspring as black, white society found the ideal answer to its labor needs, its extracurricular and inadmissible sexual desires, its compulsion to maintain its culture purebred, and the problem of maintaining, at least in theory, absolute social control. (Nash, 1974, p. 290)

These considerations were augmented by the "scientific" theories and evidence of the inferiority of blacks supplied by the scientists of those days.[14] However, the white attitudes toward mulattoes changed the attitudes of mulattoes themselves.[15] Between 1850 and 1915, mulattoes went from trying to assimilate into the white world to building their own world within the black community as they went from being partly accepted by whites to being rejected outright (Williamson, 1984).

Laws of the land change and legitimize interracial marriages. The constitutionality of antimiscegenation laws was questioned several times in state courts; 29 states had such laws as recently as 1960. In view of the Fourteenth Amendment to the Constitution of the United States, the question was raised whether or not state laws prohibiting intermarriage denied to colored people the equality guaranteed by the Constitution. State courts held those laws valid. In the case of *Naim v. Naim*, the State Court of Virginia in 1955 gave its opinion that it was a proper function of the State "to preserve the racial integrity of its citizens ... to prevent the corruption of blood, [the creation] of a mongrel breed of citizens [and] the obliteration of racial pride" (as quoted in Henriques, 1975, pp. 26-27). In another case (involving the marriage of two native-born Virginians, Richard Loving, a white man, and Mildred, who was part black and part American Indian) that ultimately went all the way to the U.S. Supreme Court, the trial judge stated his opinion in 1959 thus:

> Almighty God created the races white, black, yellow, malay and red, and he placed them on separate continents. And but for the interference with his arrangement there would be no cause for such marriages. The fact that he separated the races shows that he did not intend for races to mix. (*Loving v. Virginia*, 1968, p. 3)

In 1965, in the case of *Jones v. Lorenzen*, the Oklahoma Supreme Court was forced to uphold the state's antimiscegenation law because such laws had not been found unconstitutional by higher courts (Henriques, 1975; Porterfield, 1978). In 1967, the U.S. Supreme Court in its decision (in *Loving v. Commonwealth of Virginia*) did consider the constitutionality of one such state law and declared the Virginia law illegal, thereby overturning all state laws against interracial marriages (Henriques, 1975; Porterfield, 1978). People were freed from the constraints of law on their choice of marriage partners. "Not only could people marry across artificially maintained community boundaries, they and their families could now also live and travel where they pleased without the fear of the law" (Fernandez, 1996, p. 24).

Since 1967 there has been a steady rise in interracial marriages. Earlier (in Chapter 1) we have given various estimates of the population of mixed-race Americans. A more accurate picture will become possible in the future. A recent decision of the federal government will allow Americans to choose more than one racial category when describing themselves on the census and other forms. The new policy was in place for the 2000 census ("Census Will Let Americans," 1997). It is very likely that the population of biracial individuals will continue to rise, forcing the society and human services to acknowledge and accommodate their reality. The following quote from Root (1996) has captured the race-related change that U.S. society has experienced over the last 50 years.

[T]he third quarter of 20th-century history includes the dismantling of Jim Crow laws: desegregated schools were legally mandated with the 1954 decision in *Brown v. Board of Education*, public and private access to stores was assured, workplace affirmative action (though under reconsideration now) began in the 1970s, and integrated housing was spawned by the Fair Housing Act. The second reconstruction of civil rights resulted in the Civil Rights Act of 1964 and the Voting Rights Act of 1965. Discriminatory restrictive quotas for immigrants from "nonwhite" countries were replaced with the Immigration Act of 1965 (though, this too is being threatened). The repeal of anti-miscegenation laws in 1967 with the *Loving v. Virginia* Supreme Court decision removed a major barrier to racial mixing, which is one official marker for the start of the biracial baby boom. The fourth quarter of the century has concerned itself with the societal interpretations and adjustments to these attempts at deep structural change. (p. xxvii)

COMMON CHARACTERISTICS: COMMONALITY OF CULTURES AND WORLDVIEWS

Because we have included among biracial Americans individuals from varied racial and cultural heritages, it is hard to talk about their common characteristics. Many variables influence the reality of their lives. Answers to several pertinent questions and the various combinations of those answers suggest all kinds of experiences of biracial individuals and their families. Some of these questions are the following:

1. Which parent's culture dominated the family of the biracial individual? That determines the culture the child would identify with primarily.

2. If one of the parents was white, was that parent the father or mother?

First, race and sex intersect to determine the parent's potential earning ability. Whether it is the mother or father who is Black or Asian, for instance, can alter economic prospects.

Second, because household members perform different roles in socialization, whether the mother or father is a member of a racial minority will alter the cultural milieu for the child and family. (Chew, Eggebeen, & Uhlenberg, 1989, p. 67)

3. Where did the family live during the biracial person's childhood, in terms of the size, type, and dominant culture of the community? Experiences in a small town are likely to be quite different from those in a metropolitan area, and those in a predominantly white neighborhood will be different from those in an ethnic enclave.

4. What role did the extended family on both sides of the family play in the life of the biracial person? Some families are supportive, understanding, and warm, whereas others are cold, indifferent, and disowning.

5. What was the perceived acceptance of the biracial person? This may be marked by a lack of coherence and stability and by vulnerability to situational variables.

However, U.S. society continues to be highly racialized, and it is necessary that one be assigned to a sociopolitically defined racial group in order to be socially recognized as a functional member of the society (Williams, 1996). That assignment is not on a rational and just basis. "Multiracial people are constantly being shoved into one of the existing monoracial categories. Most of the time, it is the 'most' subordinate of the multiracial person's racial groups that he or she is pushed into" (Nakashima, 1992, p. 175). Therefore, it is possible to identify some commonalities among biracial persons. These include the following.

Exposure to Social and Institutionalized Racism. Because biracial persons do not belong to a "pure" race, they are viewed as belonging to neither of the races of their parents. Most experience "hypodescent," that is, being classified as the racial group that is lower in social status and economic opportunities and resources. Thus they experience social and institutional racism. Social racism involves negative attitudes that individuals and groups have toward biracials, which often result in overt acts such as name calling, social exclusion, and violence. Institutional racism is reflected in practices based on institutional policies and procedures that exclude or otherwise put biracials at a disadvantage. The literature provides ample examples of their experience. Weisman (1996), who is of Jewish and black heritage, speaks of being stoned, spit on, shot at, and told to "get out" of the all-black neighborhood where she had lived all her life. In her words, "I knew that I wasn't white. I never had any desire to be white. I knew that whites would probably view me as a Negro. But trying to be a Negro among Negroes was a constant struggle" (p. 153). Spencer has given several other similar examples. Valverde (1992) has given an insightful account of the experience of Vietnamese Amerasians—children of Vietnamese mothers and American fathers in Vietnam. They were ostracized as worthless half-breeds because they looked different in a physically homogeneous society and because they were fatherless in a culture that strictly observes patriarchy, and a person's identity and self-definition are derived through patriarchal lineage. They were also subjected to communist persecution because of their mothers' involvement with Americans. These children were known as "doi-doi," meaning "children of the dust." They were outcasts who were hated because they were a permanent reminder of the enemy of Vietnam that had killed millions of Vietnamese. They were forced to learn how to beg, steal, lie, fight, and form gangs in order to survive (Nwadiora & McAdoo, 1996). Amerasians were ignored by the U.S. government until the passage of the Amerasian Act of 1982 and the subsequent Homecoming Act of 1988. Since then, thousands of Amerasians have immigrated to the land of their fathers. Their experience in the United States has not been qualitatively different from that in Vietnam. Being culturally Vietnamese, they tend to congregate in areas with large Vietnamese communities, whose members carry the same stereotypes of Amerasians as found in Vietnam. They are seen as illegitimate, the products of "sleazy" liaisons:

> Because the community assumes that Amerasians' mothers were cheap bar girls, they place the same stereotype on Amerasian girls and women. Thus Amerasian women, on top of having to deal with racism and classism, also have to deal with sexism. (Valverde, 1992, p. 158)

Some opt to fit into mainstream society but find stereotypes as well as adaptation problems too hard to deal with.

A Sense of Being Different From the American Mainstream. Most biracials are phenotypically ambiguous individuals; that is, they do not fit the typical image of persons belonging to different races. They are asked the question, "What are you?" and are forced to respond to comments such as "You don't look Chicano," "You don't talk black," or "You don't act Asian" (Williams, 1996). This happens so often that they may feel doubly "othered" (Bradshaw, 1992). These experiences create and reinforce the feeling of not belonging:

> While some biracial individuals may seem successful in either the dominant culture or the minority one, an inner feeling of not belonging may concurrently exist. This is especially likely when both the majority and the minority communities insist on rigid classification based on biases in favor of racial purity. (Bradshaw, 1992, p. 81)

According to a participant in the study by Motoyoshi (1990), she is made to feel more Asian with whites and more white with Asians. This being on the margins of two groups is not a pleasant experience. Internalized marginality can adversely affect the person's self-esteem and emotional health. Parents and extended family can be extremely helpful in preparing a biracial individual to deal with the ills of societal prejudice. However, there is a large discrepancy between how one is perceived and treated within the family and in the larger society (Bradshaw, 1992).

The Urge to "Pass" as What They Are Not. Passing is the term used to describe an attempt to achieve acceptability by claiming membership in a desired group while denying one's biracial heritage. Because societal opportunities and rewards are generally given on the basis of one's race rather than ability or need, many biracial individuals feel a strong urge to pass as monoracial, as members of a "pure" race. Those who cannot pass as white pass as Latino or as members of Asian or Native American groups—groups that they perceive as more privileged in the social hierarchy of races. Historically there have been several forms and degrees of passing.[16] Passing has its positive and negative consequences. "While passing is an attribution externally made, it is internalized negatively. This denigrating attribution can be made by the majority, dominant group or the minority group" (Bradshaw, 1992, p. 79). The majority group may resent the individual's attempt to gain false status, and the minority group may resent his or her renouncing membership in the lower-status group. Although passing may open more doors to opportunities and prosperity, it means denying an aspect of one's racial heritage. It may also mean saying farewell to family and friends. It invariably invokes feelings of disloyalty and incongruity and causes pain to the one who passes and to those he or she separates from. Haizlip (1995) has detailed the pain her mother experienced when her mother's siblings decided to break all ties with their sister and pass in the white world.

Lack of Biracial Role Models. At least one of the parents of biracial individuals is a member of a racial minority and has experienced racism. The other parent, if he or she is white, is also forced to have a taste of racism:

> The White partner of an interracial union may have his or her first experience of being a target of racism when the couple "goes public" on their relationship. The birth of their first child often heightens the societal prejudices that the White parent feels over the public reaction to this interracial baby. (Wehrly, 1996, p. 9)

Despite this, most biracial individuals do not have biracial role models within their families. Outside the family, most tend to relate to other biracial and multiracial individuals if available. Many of the persons interviewed by Funderburg (1994) talked of the dearth of role models and people who can truly understand their biracial perspective. The intrapersonal conflicts suffered by interracial persons cannot be completely understood by their parents or monoracial friends (Wehrly, 1996). The local and regional organizations of interracial individuals that we have mentioned earlier are a recent phenomenon, and it may be that many biracial persons are not benefiting from these organizations.

The Feeling of Specialness Expressed as Heightened Self-Awareness or Self-Consciousness. According to Bradshaw (1992), specialness, experienced as positive or negative, tied to their experience of self is an important issue for all biracials. This specialness is different from the idea of uniqueness, which emphasizes a sense of individuality within a context of belonging, because "the state of belonging from which a secure sense of individuality can emerge is tenuous" (Bradshaw, 1992, p. 84) for the biracial. This specialness can be misunderstood or misconstrued by others, including monoracial parents, teachers, and clinicians.

DIVERSITY WITHIN: SUBGROUP AND INTRAGROUP DIFFERENCES AMONG BIRACIAL/MIXED-RACE AMERICANS

As is true of any large group, variations in the experiences and situations of subgroups create intragroup differences. Biracials, despite commonalities, also have significant differences.

Differences Based on Different Combinations of Part-White Heritage. Part-white biracial persons experience differential acceptance in different communities. Based on their personal experience or general expectation, most part-white biracials assume that white communities will reject them, but in reality there is differential acceptance of them. As compared to black-white biracials, Asian-white biracials have more access to white communities than black-whites because of their more ambiguous physical appearance (Bradshaw, 1992). Most of them have difficulty being accepted in the nonwhite community that represents the other half of their heritage. They are seen as inherently "whitewashed" and are harassed for their light skin and other Caucasian features. For those whose parents come from two nonwhite groups, the situation may not be any better. They may experience oppression from the group having the higher social status (Root, 1990). However, there are likely to be differences in the intensity of these experiences, and the possession of different attributes affects the degree and ease of acceptance. Nakashima (1996) has identified some of those attributes:

> In many Asian American communities, physical appearance plays a very important role in the level of acceptance a mixed-race person experiences. Also, having an Asian surname, which suggests patrilineal Asian heredity, seems to be an advantage. In many Latino communities, where racial phenotype varies greatly, language is considered an important indicator of legitimacy. In the African American community, which also claims a wide range of physical types, a person's lifestyle and cultural behavior are given considerable weight. (pp. 84-85)

Groups that recognize their own multiracial background, such as Filipinos and Chicanos, are much more willing to accept biracial and multiracial individuals. In many Asian American communities, generally white-Asian biracials are more easily accepted than black-Asian biracials.

Differences Based on Different Combinations of Part-Black Heritage. Black-white biracials experience greater difficulty in dealing with both communities. In the past, society at large not only has applied the one-drop rule to black-white biracials—treating them as black and forcing them to identify with the African American community—but has also considered them dangerous (Berzon, 1978).

> Most whites believed that the mulatto's admixture of white blood left him with many of the natural aspirations of the white man—aspirations which were often stifled by the strictures of American race relations. His consequent discontent drove him into the role of an agitator, dangerously fomenting unrest among the mass of blacks who otherwise instinctively recognized the superiority of the white race and submitted to its dominance. (Mencke, 1979, pp. 129-130)

They were resented by the blacks as well. In a discussion of the difficult experiences of mulattoes at the end of the Civil War, Haizlip (1994) observed,

> Negroes were especially conflicted about the living, breathing visible evidence of plantation owners' power. Shamed by their own helplessness, they could not divorce natural sympathy for the victims from anger at those who, after all, possessed the former oppressors' blood. (p. 56)

Now many black-white biracial individuals are identifying themselves as blended and do not want to disown either the white or black part of their ancestry. A distinction is made between multigenerational and first-generation blended individuals. In the former group are those who have parents or several generations of ancestors who have been designated socially as black but have multiple racial-cultural backgrounds and who have resisted identifying solely with the African American community. In the latter are individuals whose blended identity is based on having parents from more than one racial-cultural group and concrete and immediate experience of those backgrounds in the home and or extended family (Daniel, 1996). The majority of these mixed-race persons have been born in the post-civil rights era, which is marked by relatively more tolerance for cultural diversity and during which period it became legal in all 50 states to marry interracially. "As such, many mixed-race people have been raised in intact families, with access to and personal knowledge of all sides of their cultural heritage" (King & DaCosta, 1996, p. 237). Despite significant changes in the society, the white community, by and large, ignores them, and the black community considers them as betraying it in order to escape the stigma attached to blackness. Williams (1996) quotes a 21-year-old black-white biracial woman:

> Well, when white kids find out that my dad is black, then I am suddenly treated differently, needless to say I went from being one of them to being a nigger (excuse my language). Then, black people totally distrust me, you know? If I claim I'm black, I have to prove myself and some blacks even laugh at me, like I'm a white girl trying to be black. But, if I don't wear a shirt that says, "I'm black and proud" all the time, then I'm a sell-out, Oreo, wanna-be trying to pass cuz I'm ashamed of being black. (p. 205)

The current situation of black-white biracials can be summed up as "the possibility of affirming differences (pluralism) while nurturing commonalities (integration) appears ever more elusive in the schizoid racial/cultural maze of contemporary black and white relations" (Daniel, 1996, p. 123). Their task of "broadening the prevailing notions of what it means to be African American, so that identifying with one's nonblack heritage does not preclude identification with one's black heritage" (King & DaCosta, 1996, p. 239) is indeed a difficult one.

Williams (1992) studied 43 Amerasians—29 Eurasians and 14 Afroasians—who had spend at least 6 years of their adolescence in Japan. They had lived as military dependents on U.S. bases and had not directly suffered institutionalized Japanese racism. In the public, Japanese people were either disgusted by or envious of their physical appearance. Because most Afroasians were aware of Japanese and American societies' different views of black and white Americans, they tended to identify easily as being "American minority" members (Williams, 1992). Twine (1996) has given the example of a 26-year-old, brown-skinned daughter of a Chinese father and an African-descent mother who did not know anything about her mother's family until recently. Her father had kept her African ancestry hidden by prohibiting her mother from ever talking about her multiracial heritage. There is some truth in the statement of Nakashima (1992) that "multiracial Asian Americans, especially when they are part Black, are generally considered 'outsiders' and have very limited entree into Asian American communities, except for those who have become respected or well known for some reason (the 'claim-us-if-we're-famous' syndrome)" (p. 176).

Differences Based on the Needs of the Ethnic Community Associated With a Person's Heritage. The ethnic community's needs determine the level of acceptance of biracial individuals. Once one of the largest Asian American communities, the Japanese American community, is shrinking in numbers. Because of very low immigration, very high outmarriage, and low birth rates, that community is at the risk of dying out. Therefore, many Japanese American leaders are willing to entertain the idea of redefining "Japaneseness" and expanding the definition of a Japanese American so that part-Japanese biracial individuals can be included as full members of the community (O'Hare & Felt, 1991). Several elements, such as biological heritage, cultural membership, behaviors, attitudes, and values, constitute an ethnic identity, and a community can choose to emphasize some elements and de-emphasize others. In the words of Mass (1992),

> If the Japanese American community welcomes and accepts interracial Japanese Americans as part of the community, not only will it be unnecessary to worry about the end of the Japanese American community, but interracial Japanese Americans will be affirmed and strengthened in their Japanese American identity and in their ability to experience the best of both worlds. (p. 279)

In response to the need of the Japanese American community, some of the multiracial Japanese Americans have organized themselves into a community group called HIF (Hapa Issues Forum). They want to join and transform the Japanese American community into a more inclusive one (King & DaCosta, 1996). With other communities, acceptance of mixed-race persons remains a micro-issue.

Differences Based on Gender of the Biracial Person. Gender adds another dimension to the reality of biracial individuals and creates differences in their life experiences. We have discussed the biracial person's feeling a sense of specialness and being ambivalent about it, sometimes experiencing it as positive and at other times as negative. That ambivalence affects males and females differently. The specialness of biracials in the eyes of others is initially related to the ambiguity of their racial feature and subsequently to their racially mixed heritage. They are often regarded as an object (e.g., exotic) or a curiosity (e.g., "I have never seen a biracial person up close"). This may make them feel hurt, angry, and negative about themselves. On the other hand, a similar experience may make them feel important because of the extra attention they receive. However, if for some reason their appearance or experience is no longer perceived as special, they are likely to feel deflated and devalued (Root, 1997). Societal stereotypes can easily supply reasons for devaluing mixed-race people. They are seen as the product of immoral unions between immoral people and are therefore expected to be immoral themselves (Nakashima, 1992). Thus,

> attention that is removed from intrinsic qualities of the individual and is based instead on projected qualities, superficial characteristics, or mere unusualness is at best fickle and at worst demeaning and alienating. This kind of attention, if internalized, comes at the very high cost of the individual's sense of identity. (Bradshaw, 1992, p. 83)

Women are much more vulnerable to ill effects of these experiences because of the extraordinary value that the society places on women's physical appearance. They may feel alienated, anxious, and depressed and fall prey to such unhealthy practices as eating disorders, cosmetic dieting, and elective cosmetic surgeries (Root, 1997).

Many biracials grow up with experiences of being stared at and of being asked questions about their looks, name, parentage, family experience, cultural difference, and so on; experiences that make them objects of curiosity, pity, or fear; and experiences that set them apart from others without any logical reason or rhyme. Root (1997) quotes a light-skinned Eurasian woman describing her high school experience as being "liked by everyone and dated by no one" because she was seen as "a person of color" by whites, "not really Japanese enough" by her Japanese classmates, and "not a person of color" by black friends. Racially mixed women whose life experiences have reduced their uniqueness solely to their appearance may be starved for social acceptance. They may be more likely to accept relationships in which partners objectify them (as exotic) and seek to "possess" them. They feel emotionally unfulfilled. In fact, many of them are vulnerable because of their social, political, and economic powerlessness.

We have earlier given the example of the difficulties experienced by Eurasian women from Vietnam in the larger American society. Among the Hispanic groups, the LatiNegra is worse off than her male counterpart. Having a LatiNegra daughter-in-law is often viewed as marking the decline of the family's status and class and as reducing their opportunity to improve the race (*adelantar la raza*). From infancy, the LatiNegra learns to associate her blackness with negative attributes. Throughout her life, she frequently hears parents and family members making racist-sexist remarks about LatiNegras. Latino families may not be able to adequately buffer LatiNegras against racism of the larger society and the *racismo* of the Hispanic community. Whereas her parents (one or both of whom may not be considered African Latinos) may be able to teach her how to cope with ethnic discrimination and prejudice as a Latina, they cannot teach her the coping mechanisms to deal with racial prejudice and discrimination as a black woman (Comas-Diaz, 1996).

MAJOR NEEDS AND PROBLEMS
OF BIRACIAL/MIXED-RACE AMERICAN GROUPS

The social environment of most biracial and multiracial persons puts extra demands on them and in the process creates several layers of needs. Besides the basic human needs that they share with everyone else, they have needs similar to those of many minority groups in our society. They also have another layer of needs that results from their particular mixed-race status. The lack of societal response to these needs creates problems.

Needs Related to Mixed-Race Status. In many ways, by and large, the society does not acknowledge the existence of mixed-race persons. If it were to recognize them, they would be placed at the lowest rung of the socioeconomic ladder. Building on the Sandoval (1990) four-tier model for examining the development of social oppression by gender and racial group social status, Root (1992) has come up with the following hierarchy: At the top are the white males. White women occupy the second tier. Then come men of color. Women of color are at the fourth tier. Racially mixed men and women occupy the fifth and sixth tiers, respectively, because they "experience a 'squeeze' of oppression *as* people of color and *by* the people of color. People of color who have internalized the vehicle of oppression in turn apply rigid rules of belonging or establishing 'legitimate' membership" (p. 5). Thus, biracial people are different not only from the mainstream society but also from other minority groups in that they suffer from all the ills of a minority and more. They do not belong to the first four legitimate social tiers and are not acknowledged in their own right.

Society cannot free itself from the habits of its past. It still pressures biracials to choose one side of their racial heritage. Historically, most biracial people were the result of interracial unions of whites with Africans and Native Americans, who were outside the mainstream society and body politic and had no rights of citizenship. They were raised in the community of the nonwhite parent and were not a part of the white society. Approaches like the one-drop rule were used to ensure that biracial and multiracial persons stayed outside the mainstream society. Beginning in 1850, the U.S. Census did employ the term *mulatto*, and in the 1890 census the terms *quadroon* and *octoroon* were used, which may appear as an acknowledgment of mixed-race people. However, these biracial people were included as types of black or colored people and not as either types of white or an independent population category (Fernandez, 1996). Even today, mixed-race people are not acknowledged as an independent group, and they are ignored, rejected, resented, and discriminated against by the mainstream as well as minority communities. Those who are part white, even when they look white, are not easily welcome in the "pure" white community, and the belief that "minorities are more accepting of biracial children" is a myth (Wardle, 1992). Most nonwhite racial communities view biracials as harbingers of doom to their racial and ethnic continuity and solidarity. They believe that membership within the group is exclusive and that alliances with another group "dilute" the affiliation with the group (Hall, 1996). When they are accepted, it is done grudgingly. As stated earlier, part-black biracials are accepted in the African American community only if they accept black-only identity. Similarly, different Native American tribes accept mixed-race individuals differently, many just tolerating their claim to be Indian. Different Asian American groups also treat biracials differently: Some accept them, others tolerate them, and others ostracize them. Many part-black Hispanic biracials, particularly females, are forced to marry African Americans and into the African American group to the exclusion of their Latino identification.

Thus, prejudice and racism that biracial persons are subjected to emanate not only from the larger white society but from minority communities as well. A recent example illustrates the attitude of many in the general public toward biracial persons. The principal of a local high school in Alabama told students that the school prom would be canceled if attended by interracial couples. When questioned by student Revonda Bowen about how this would apply to her, as her father is white and her mother is black, he said that his rule was aimed at preventing "mistakes" like her. Perceived as the results of mistakes, many biracials find themselves on the margins of the society. Marginalization is also reinforced by the long-held belief that mixed-blood individuals are maladjusted and tormented souls (Spickard, 1989). This marginalization by the society affects even their basic needs. Graham (1996) has given examples of situations in the fields of education, employment, health, and housing in which biracial individuals are doubly disadvantaged. The following is one of those examples. Because most medical institutions do not allow for "multiracial" as a race code for their records, the records on mixed-race patients are not accurate. That inaccuracy can result in inappropriate treatment of mixed-race persons. In the words of Graham (1996),

> It is much more likely for people of the same racial or ethnic background to match as bone marrow donors, because human leukocyte antigens (HLA) follow racial background ... No donor drives have been directed toward multiracial people, as they have with other racial and ethnic groups, therefore the donor pool for our children is inadequate. ... How many multiracial children will suffer or die as a result of inadequate medical classification? (pp. 41-42)

Needs of Biracial Children and Adolescents. Many multiracial children face discrimination from people of all races, which leaves them feeling like outsiders everywhere (Sullivan, 1998). The same is true of adolescents. "Biracial children and adolescents are particularly vulnerable to differential treatment by their parents and relatives, social rejection by their peers, and ambivalent attention in their schools and communities" (Gibbs, 1989, p. 327). A study by Chauce and her colleagues (1992) found that whereas biracial adolescents are similar to monoracial adolescents of color in term of life stresses, psychological distress, behavior problems, and self-worth, they may be facing more stress because they must deal with nonacceptance and racism from multiple sources. In an in-depth study of 61 black-Japanese American families, Thornton (1983) found that 91% of the offspring of these interracial marriages had faced a racial identity crisis in their lives and that almost half felt that they were disliked by both blacks and Japanese. Many of these children and adolescents continue to deal with issues of their heritage throughout their life. They need help in dealing with issues related to their ambiguous ethnicity, in defining their identities, and in developing a greater sense of their racial roots and pride in all parts of their racial heritage.

Needs of Mixed-Race Families. The mixed-race families are as varied in their structure and resources as families in the general population. These families have the extra task of raising biracial children, a task for which they may be ill equipped. Couples may have diverse worldviews, producing strains that affect the development of a shared family identity and their ability to meet the psychological needs of their children. Barn (1999) explored the situation of white single mothers of mixed-parentage children in Britain and identified factors that necessitate the admission of those children to the public care system. These included "family relationship breakdown," "physical abuse and neglect," "mother's mental health," "child beyond parental control," in addition to financial and material hardship, absence of the father, lack of social support, and family's experience of racism.

Needs of Biracial Homosexuals. Communities of color have a different attitude toward homosexuality. Gay people of color may face criticism regarding suspicion that homosexuality is a sort of foreign, white American problem. Mixed-race women who are lesbians have special needs. Their need for acceptance and belonging is often ignored. Besides the mainstream society's racism, sexism, and heterosexism, many lesbians of color face the additional stress of coping with the gay and lesbian community's racism, plus the heterosexism, sexism, and internalized racism of their own ethnic community (Kanuha, 1990). Thus, they exist in a triply marginalized space. They are "suspicious of any kind of identity politics based on single-group membership, whether based on race, gender, or sexual orientation" (Allman, 1996, p. 287).

Needs of the LatiNegra. Like other mixed-race women, the LatiNegra is considered an unusual sexual being. There is also the perception that she has no control over her sexuality and can engender the same effect in her sexual partner; on the contrary, she may have an inhibitory effect. Identity issues plague her:

> Like other mixed-race women, LatiNegras do not necessarily identify racially with their physical appearance or with the way they look (black). They are caught between three diverse (and sometimes, antagonistic) worlds—black, Latino, and white—and racially excluded from all. Their marginality binds them in a conflict of racial loyalties without a satisfactory resolution of their racial identity. (Comas-Diaz, 1996, p. 185)

SOCIAL WORK PRACTICE: GENERAL CONSIDERATIONS FOR INTERVENTION WITH BIRACIAL/MIXED-RACE AMERICANS

In this section, we provide some ideas that should inform social work assessment and intervention with biracial and multiracial individuals and families.

Issues of identity affect the life situations of biracial and multiracial individuals. As pointed out earlier, some studies have found biracials to be as socially adjusted as members of non-white monoracial groups. We have also seen that in their adjustment to the social world, some resort to passing, others use situational ethnicity and maneuver different communities and situations to their advantage, and some are able to belong to both communities of their heritage, but many are plagued by a sense of ambiguity. In our highly racialized society, people are made acutely aware of racial differences on a daily basis. The societal messages to and about biracial/mixed-race people now are not qualitatively different from what they have historically been. Nakashima (1992) has summarized the ideas that feed those messages:

> It is "unnatural" to "mix the races"; that multiracial people are physically, morally, and mentally weak; that multiracial people are tormented by their genetically divided selves; and that intermarriage "lowers" the biologically superior White race ... the people of mixed-race are socially and culturally marginal, doomed to a life of conflicting cultures and unfulfilled desire to be "one or the other," neither filling in nor gaining acceptance in any group, thus leading lives of confused loneliness and despair. (p. 165)

It is healthier for biracial persons to embrace both (or all) parts of their identity than to cling to one and pretend that the other does not exist (Spickard, 1997), but their social environment does not allow this to happen easily. We have discussed the rule of hypo-descent being applied to these persons by not only the larger white society but also other racial groups. A child's identity depends on a secure sense of who he or she is, and that sense has to be fostered and supported by the family, child care programs, schools, and the community. Generally, the good work done at home is not reinforced outside the family. Poussaint (1984) studied a group of 37 biracial undergraduates. Some of his findings include: (a) the feeling of paranoia or being special; (b) the feeling that they were always looked at or scrutinized because of their biraciality; (c) the feeling that they did not belong to one or the other group; (d) people acting surprised or titillated that they were from a mixed union; and (e) other youngsters, both black and white, teasing them. Spickard (1997) has described the experience of a young lady whose father was Japanese and whose mother was Jewish; she had grown up in a Jewish neighborhood without an exposure to the Japanese American community until she went to a large university.

> I met more Asians my first year [in college] than I had ever known. When one Japanese American called me on the phone to invite me to join a Japanese American discussion group, I was very excited. I went to the group meeting a few times, but my "white-half" began to feel uncomfortable when the others began putting down Whites. (p. 50)

For most biracials, questions of "who they are" and "where they belong" are seldom far from the surface.

Self-concept and self-esteem of biracial-multiracial individuals are assaulted. Self-concept is what one thinks one is like, and self-esteem is whether one likes or dislikes oneself and how much. One's self-concept, self-esteem, and self-worth are tied to cultural pride and identification. There is thus a relationship between one's self-concept and racial identity. For the biracials, there is no group history to relate to and no group to belong to. Historically, interracial families and biracial individuals were encouraged not to acknowledge their blended heritage. "They were programmed to think that their births should have never happened and they possessed a trait making them different and strange. Thus what ultimately developed was a shame-based perception of self" (Brown & Douglass, 1996, p. 326). One's self-concept is made up of *personal identity* and *reference group orientation*.

Personal identity is believed to be made up of various facets of the self excluding factors pertaining to racial-ethnic group membership, whereas reference group orientation is seen as a pattern of behaviors, interests, and values associated with a particular racial group. Adoption of a reference group orientation that requires denial or distortion of one's self, one's racial heritage, or both puts the individual at risk for developing a negative self-concept (Helms, 1990). The relationship between personal identity and reference group orientation has not been subjected to extensive empirical research. A study by Field (1996) involved 31 biracial adolescents and two comparison groups, one of 31 African American and the other of 31 Caucasian adolescents. The three groups were matched on age, gender, socioeconomic status, and demographic location. This study found that self-concepts of biracial adolescents were as positive as those of their monoracial peers. However, "biracial adolescents who adopted a white [reference group orientation] might have greater difficulty developing a positive self-concept than biracial or black peers who adopt either a black or bicultural orientation" (Field, 1996, p. 222). Body image also feeds one's self-concept. Because mixed-race individuals often look physically different from whites, blacks, and others, these differences and lack of physical group identification may affect their body image. However, "[t]he journey toward attractiveness may be easier for men because the criteria for male attractiveness varied tremendously" (C. C. I. Hall, 1997, p. 88). There is not much research on the body image of biracials reported in the literature. C. C. I. Hall (1997) explored the body images of black-Japanese biracial men and women and found them overall satisfied with their body and body parts. Nevertheless, biracial children must cope in a society that has white standards of beauty.

Many biracial-multiracial persons experience rejection, marginalization, and complex forms of discrimination. We have mentioned the plight of Amerasians being rejected in Vietnam, Japan, and elsewhere in Asia. The rejection and ill treatment of biracial people is not an attribute only of Asian societies. Boushel (1996), who reviewed research on the experience of vulnerable and poor multiracial families and their children in Britain, observed, "In addition to verbal abuse, the families experienced racist attacks by both adults and children, including spitting, punching, shoving and kicking by white youth and men, and arson, vandalism and written abuse" (p. 309). Rejection and being marginalized by one or both communities of their parentage is the experience of many biracials in this country. Marginalization is a process by means of which some people (and ideas) are "ignored, trivialized, rendered invisible and unheard, perceived as inconsequential, de-authorized, 'other' or threatening" (Tucker, 1990, p. 7). White society forces white-other biracials into the other community and the other community forces them out to its periphery.

Cose (1997) has provided an example of how our societal institutions rigidly guard their traditional views on biracial people. Susie Phipps needed a birth certificate in order to apply for a passport. She was 49 years old then and had lived her entire life as a white person, but her birth certificate said she was black. In her own words, "My children are white. My grandchildren are white. Mother and Daddy were buried white. My Social Security card says I'm white. My driver's license says I'm white. There are no blacks out where I live, except the hired hands" (quoted in Davis, 1991, p. 11). Her attempt to change that designation led her to court. A genealogist who testified for the State of Louisiana calculated that she was 3/32 black, and the state law decreed that a person who was as little as 1/32 black could not be considered white. In 1985, the Fourth Circuit Court of Appeals upheld the ruling of the lower court that she must accept the legal designation as black. In 1986, the Louisiana Supreme Court declined to review the decision, as did the

U.S. Supreme Court later on. "Thus, both the final courts of appeals in Louisiana and the highest court of the United States saw no reason to disturb the application of the one-drop rule in the lawsuit brought by Susie Guillory Phipps and her siblings" (Davis, 1991, p. 11).

Being nonwhite and being perceived as such (even when they look white), biracial individuals share the experience of members of nonwhite communities in being discriminated against by the larger white society. But for them, white society is not the only source of prejudice and discrimination. Many minority communities also shun them, reject them, and discriminate against them. While discussing employment-related problems of biracials, Graham (1996) gives the example of an engineer who worked for a government contractor. "He had requested a multiracial classification on his employment records. The employer refused, giving 'government requirement' as the reason. The company solved its problem: They hired him as black and fired him as white" (p. 42).

Parents, extended families, and other social systems of biracial persons are of questionable help. The parents of biracial individuals care about them and wish them well. These parents face the same tasks that monoracial parents of children of color do. These tasks include making their children feel secure and loved and preparing them for the harsh reality of racism in the society. However, unlike other parents, parents of biracial children cannot completely share the experiences of their children: They do not know what it is to be mixed, and many are confused about the identity of their children. White parents of interracial children cannot give them skills to cope with racism (Shackford, 1984). According to Ladner (1984), parents of black-white biracial children tend to deal with the issue of racial identity of those children in one of three ways:

1. Parents emphasize the humanity of their children ("my child as a human above all else"), ignore race, and consider color as totally irrelevant. They refuse to face the reality of how the society categorizes their children.

2. They claim to socialize their children to have a biracial identity. How this is done sometimes becomes problematic, as reflected in the following quote from a white mother, provided by Ladner.

> I am proud of that part of my child which is white. Why can't I teach my child to be proud of being white just as much as I am told I must teach him to be proud to be Black? I have nothing against teaching him Black pride, but I am a White person. I'm not going to try to be Black. In this racist society, I'm not even permitted to feel good about being white and teach my child that it's okay that he has a part of whiteness in him as well. (quoted in Ladner, 1984, p. 7)

3. They teach their children that they have a black identity. Many of them immerse themselves in black communities, with the white parent trying to be black. The task of raising biracial children for single parents can be even harder.

Extended families may be understanding, warm, and supportive or distant, indifferent, and antagonistic. Despite the several educational and support groups (mentioned earlier), most interracial persons and families may feel alone, isolated, and overwhelmed. Beyond the informal social world, most societal systems, including child care organizations and schools, either ignore the existence of biracials or assume that they belong to the racial-cultural group of their minority parent (Wardle, 1993). When biracial children open story books and texts, they find no families like their own (Shackford, 1984). As Wardle (1993) put it, "Biracial children are not accepted by many components of the community: newspapers, magazines, churches, TV programs—including children's programs like *Sesame Street*—movies, children's books, and single race families in the neighborhood" (p. 46).

SOCIAL WORK INTERVENTION AT MICRO-, MEZZO-, AND MACROLEVELS: PRINCIPLES AND APPROACHES

The ideas and approaches we have suggested for social work assessment and intervention in Chapters 2 through 6 are equally valid for working with biracial/mixed-race clients, because the realities of their lives and situations are similar to those of monoracial people of color in the U.S. society. However, they suffer from all the ills of minority groups and more. They experience oppression *as* people of color as well as *by* people of color. They are often on the margins of both communities of their parentage and hence must deal with nonacceptance, rejection, and racism from multiple sources. In view of this, we are presenting and reiterating some helpful ideas for assessment and intervention.

Assessment-Related Principles and Approaches

1. Make the assessment comprehensive. Only a comprehensive assessment can provide a solid basis for effective intervention. It should lead to an understanding of the person, problem, situation, and the dynamics of interaction among these elements. You will find the systems approach suggested in Chapter 2 helpful for this.

2. Make the assessment process a multipurpose activity. Structure the assessment interview with the client system so that it helps in building a trusting relationship with the client, is therapeutic for the client, encourages the acknowledgment of the problem by the client, and leads to joint planning for intervention.

3. Explore the racial-cultural identity of the client-system. Remember that biracialism is not a singular phenomenon. Numerous factors shape the specific experiences of an individual biracial person. Generally, the experience of racism for biracials is likely to be worse than that of most monoracials, because race has been constructed around the idea of "either-or." They are caught between categories that do not fully describe their identity (Standen, 1996). Other external factors also may force them to deny a part of their heritage and to choose one racial-ethnic group. According to Brown and Douglass (1996), once they can celebrate and embrace their total identity, they experience a greater physical and psychological comfort with themselves and acquire an improved capacity to navigate the varied terrain of race and ethnicity. On the other hand, Standen (1996) is of the opinion that identifying oneself as a biracial is not always a sign of healthy self-acceptance: "Sometimes it is indicative of a new 'forced choice' dilemma. Rather than having to choose between their dual heritages, biracial people are put into a position that accuses them of being in denial for not accepting a biracial identity" (p. 247). Nevertheless, identity issues, especially of children and adolescents, should be attended to. Set the stage for that work through assessment.

4. Explore how biracial clients use their identity and how they feel about it. Keep in mind that biracial individuals negotiate their social environment in different ways. They may use their identity as fluid and express it differently depending on the situational

context. Standen (1996) found his biracial Korean-white subjects taking on the identity of Korean, white, Asian, Asian American, Korean American, or *hapa* in different situations. Nevertheless, they felt alienated. Mass (1992) studied white-Japanese biracial and monoracial Japanese American college students. Overall, biracials showed less identification with being Japanese. Most of those who had spent their childhood in Japan were called foreigners and treated as outcasts by the Japanese. When they moved to America, they felt out of place in the small midwestern and southern towns of their fathers. A strong sense of being different dogged them. Williams (1992) studied 43 Amerasians—29 Eurasians and 14 Afroasians—who had spent most of their adolescence in Japan. In the public, Japanese people were either disgusted by or envious of their physical appearance. Their bilingual ability also influenced their self-perception. Many learned when to keep quiet about their knowledge of the "other" language and when to disclose it. Sometimes they pretended that they could not speak either language.

5. Explore the vulnerability of mixed-race clients. Remember that these clients are more vulnerable to stress than their monoracial counterparts. Discussing Latinas, Vasquez (1994) noted that their chronic exposure to racism can lead to powerlessness, learned helplessness, depression, anxiety, and posttraumatic stress disorder. The lives of most Hispanic American-other biracial persons are even more complex and possibly more vulnerable. Multiracial women are characterized as vulnerable "in the sense that they are mentally, emotionally, morally, and socially weak, powerless, and tormented, and very often the product of sexual and racial domination" (Nakashima, 1992, p. 169). Root (1997) advises that a therapist working with biracial women

> should also consider whether a history of sexual abuse, rape, or emotional abuse may account for her vulnerability to these relationships, as these experiences also objectify an individual and may result in the acceptance of unhealthy relationships for fear of being otherwise undesirable, unacceptable, or alone. (p. 165)

6. Make assessment the basis for client strength- and empowerment-oriented intervention. You can mix and match creatively the approaches suggested in Chapters 2 through 6 for this purpose.

Intervention-Related Practice Principles and Approaches

At the Microlevel. Identity development is a central human task on the journey to adulthood. Most mixed-race individuals are likely to need help in resolving conflict about their biracial-multiracial identity. We have drawn on the summary of suggestions provided by Deters (1997).

1. Be aware of your own opinions and biases about interracial marriages, racial identity of biracial persons, and your own personal identity, and be aware of internalized racial and ethnic stereotypes. This will help to maintain objectivity by curbing prejudicial tendencies, will distinguish dysfunctional from normative behavior, and will empower clients (Root, 1994). McRoy and Freeman (1986) found biases of social workers to interracial children reflected in either their overemphasis on children's racial background or their denial that the children's racial heritage had anything to do with the children's behavior. A firm sense of one's own racial-ethnic identity is especially important for white workers, because whites do not think of themselves as having a racial identity (Wehrly, 1996).

2. Understand, be sensitive to, and address the following:

    a. Most biracials have a sense of being "different" and "special," but not in a positive way.

    b. Biracial children feel torn between selecting one parent's racial identity over the other's and may feel like a traitor to the parent they do not choose to identify with (Winn & Priest, 1993).

    c. Many adolescents feel that their parents did not prepare them for the realities of racism.

    d. They need help in beginning to view the world in less dichotomous terms, contrary to the stance of others around them.

    e. Many have a sense of not really belonging anywhere and feel lonely, confused, and victimized (Wehrly, 1996).

Listen to these feelings of loneliness, confusion, and victimization; help clients look for advantages of being biracial-multiracial; and help them develop a greater sense of their racial roots and pride in all parts of their heritage.

3. Use a nonoppressive theoretical perspective in working with biracial-multiracial clients. You can draw helpful ideas from feminist theory for this perspective. This involves conscious and concerted effort to separate pathological from nonpathological behavior in assessing your clients (Deters, 1997).

4. Mix and match therapeutic techniques in order to attain the best fit between the client's needs and your intervention. Ramirez (1999) has recommended an approach to multicultural psychotherapy that employs strategies ranging from an intensive study of the client's life history and use of insight to a cognitive behavioral approach.

5. Refine the following therapeutic skills for work with biracial adolescents:

    a. Develop a working relationship with extra sensitivity to the racial factors that may influence that relationship.

    b. Allow clients to ventilate feelings about their biracial identity, and validate the normality of those feelings.

    c. Help them identify and refine coping skills that are independent of their racial status.

    d. Provide support and help them build self-esteem.

    e. Help them see the link between their confusion over their identity and confusion in developmental tasks and in other areas of behavior. Of particular importance can be conflict about sexuality, autonomy and independence, and educational and career aspirations.

    f. Encourage them to explore both sides of their heritage and to form a positive sense of identification with all their roots (Gibbs, 1989).

The use of such tools as genograms, eco-maps, and the cultural continuum can be a helpful strategy.

6. Involve the families of biracial children and enhance their ability to meet the needs of those children. Some helpful suggestions include the following:

a. Explore the parents' need to feel comfortable with their own racial heritages and the impact of these on the family constellation. Communication within the family often needs improvement (Gibbs & Hines, 1992).

b. Help parents understand that they cannot completely share the experience of their children but that they can provide an environment in which family members talk about issues related to their children's identity, and one that allows children to raise questions, express anger, and work through feelings.

c. Encourage them to openly deal with racism and its effect on children's feeling that their family is not normal. (Sometimes living in a racially mixed neighborhood makes a significant difference.)

d. Expose them to the available helpful literature, such as the guide by Wright (1998) that teaches parents and educators of biracial children how to reduce the impact of racism on a child's development and emotional health.

e. Give them ideas and encouragement to assert themselves in dealing with educational and other service systems for understanding and accommodating their children's needs.

f. Assist them to improve their informal social network by forming a support group. Brown and Douglass (1996) have described the process of forming a multiracial support group.

g. Attend to the possible difficulties of interracial marriage and be extra sensitive to the situations and needs of single-parent families.

At the Mezzolevel. The focus of social work activity at this level can be on the local institutions and organizations that biracial children must belong to or associate with. Most important of these are child care programs and schools. You can function as an enabler of multiracial families and biracial individuals by communicating and negotiating with these organizations or by being an advocate on their behalf. The purpose of this work will be education and sensitization of school and agency personnel about the needs of biracial children and clients and about changes in their policies and procedures for better response to those needs. In his discussion of the needs of biracial children and interracial families, Wardle (1993) has also listed a number of school and classroom activities and specific teacher behaviors that will go a long way to correct the present picture.

The multicultural approaches used in schools are *cultural understanding, cultural competence,* and *cultural emancipation* (McCarthy, 1993), but in their impact they do not adequately challenge racism. To bring about significant institutional changes, you should involve communities of color. These communities have learned how to cope with common experiences of racism. "In addition, they offer youths standards of beauty, emotional expressiveness, interpersonal distance, degree of extraversion, and comfort with physical intimacy that is often quite different from the white norm. These are standards by which the individual might find affirmation" (Field, 1996, p. 225). The relevant professional roles that you will play include educator, negotiator, and advocate.

At the Macrolevel. At the community and societal level, there is ample room for significant work. A few macrolevel dimensions of the difficulties and problems of biracial-multiracial people include the following:

1. Racism, in its manifold manifestations of prejudice and discrimination, continues to dominate the consciousness of Americans, divide the country, vitiate the social climate,

and deprive the economy of untapped human capital. In the social pecking order, biracial-multiracial people often find themselves at the bottom of the ladder.

2. The rule of hypodescent, which forces biracials to deny and disown one half of their heritage, is still the societal approach to treating biracials; this approach wreaks havoc with their identity and places them on the periphery of even the racial group that they are expected to belong to.

3. The demographic changes affecting race relations in this country include increases in the proportion of people of color in the population, in the percentage of people of color who are not black, and in the number of biracial-multiracial people. These will challenge our color-conscious remedies for social problems and increase the potential for interracial conflict (Ramirez, 1996).

You can contribute to the elimination or alleviation of these problems. You can combine your intimate understanding of the realities of these clients and your community organizational and advocacy skills to improve the critical insights of biracial-interracial people into the contradictions and discontinuities of the racial order. You can thus be an invaluable ally to the emerging multiracialist movement, which aims to fight unjust racial hierarchies and safeguard the interests of biracial-multiracial individuals. Glass and Wallace (1996) have presented a number of principles and approaches to challenging race and racism that you can incorporate into your repertoire.

Racially mixed people want their existence to be recognized to the same extent as that of other groups. Their invisibility does no good, either to them or to the society at large. You should have no difficulty in seeing the validity of their demand, both from a philosophical perspective and in terms of client-level practice considerations. You should add your voice to the demand of biracial-multiracial people for dignity, equality, and fairness. Ramirez (1996) has proposed three approaches to the reform of the present race-conscious remedies to the country's social problems: (a) continue government-sponsored racial preferences and affirmative action programs, but create dispute-resolution mechanisms for interracial conflict and discern a method for acknowledging multiracial identity; (b) embrace a color-blind tradition, flatly prohibiting any distinctions made on the basis of race or ethnicity; and (c) construct policies that confront problems stemming from race without relying upon racial classification (p. 59). Although the first promotes equality of results and the second ensures equality of process, they can still be problematic. The third is a more eclectic paradigm. You should participate in the policy-level discussions of and search for solutions for this vital issue.

NOTES

1. The coming together and marriage of blacks and Indians in the New England colonies was not uncommon. There was no basic antipathy between Negroes and Indians regarding marriage. They both suffered the same servile status, which must have constituted a bond between the two groups. This community of feeling was assisted by the imbalance of males and females amongst black slaves (Henriques, 1975). There were many tribes in Virginia, the Carolinas, Tennessee, and elsewhere that had virtually become black because of miscegenation between Indians and blacks. At one time, there was a general fear of Indians and Africans' uniting against whites. The most effective way to deal with that fear that the whites discovered was to create suspicion, hatred, and hostility between the two. They started using Indians as slave catchers and using African soldiers against

tribes resisting colonization. Eastern state legislatures continually passed laws aimed at discouraging the existence of Black-Indian communities (Perdue, 1979). Several tribes, such as Cherokees, Chickasaws, Choctaws, Creeks, and Seminoles, not only learned the white man's attitude toward the Negro but also adopted slave holding. They would capture slaves in raids on white settlements and resell them. However, intermarriages between Indians and blacks were not uncommon (Perdue, 1979). The Cherokee and the Chickasaw remain exceptions to the general configuration of sexual relationships between Indian and Negro. Where white influence did not extend, as amongst the Seminole in Florida, both sexual and social relationships of the two groups are characterized by loyalty (Henriques, 1975). The Cherokee law (under the constitution adopted in 1839) forbade intermarriage. However, illegal sexual liaisons and marriages between Cherokees and blacks continued (Littlefield, 1979; Perdue, 1979).

2. Cunningham (1997) explored racial identity formation in light-skinned blacks. This group encounters prejudice from the dominant white culture but also experiences subdued rejection from the black community. Her subjects were men and women who identified strongly with being black. None expressed a desire to reject their black heritage, but they were often conflicted about the option of passing for white in situations where racist comments are made.

3. The number of these marriages has been rising since the *Loving v. Virginia* decision. The growing population of black-white mixed-race persons born from these marriages since 1968 is estimated to be between 600,000 and several million (Funderburg, 1994; Gibbs & Hines, 1992). Both blacks and whites who intermarry tend to have higher socioeconomic status (Heaton & Albrecht, 1996).

4. Kitano and Daniels (1988) gave the example of Los Angeles County in 1977, where the rates of out-marriages were 60% among the Japanese, 49.7% among the Chinese, and 34.1% among the Koreans. Hence, the Asian American biracials are the products of unions between Asians and white Americans as well as of those between Asians and nonwhite Americans; they result from unions that began abroad, that took place here in the past, and that are happening now.

5. Among the processes that accomplished this homogenization are: (a) Hispanicization, that is, the partly coerced, partly voluntary adoption of the colonial version of Spanish culture by the indigenous and African population; and (b) mestization, that is, the genetic mixture of the three main human stocks present in New Spain—the African, the European, and the Indian. Culturally, modern Mexico is a mixture of indigenous and nonindigenous elements, but the Spanish element is clearly dominant. Biologically, the reverse is true; the Indian contribution to the national gene pool continues to dominate (Porterfield, 1978).

6. This has led to a different view of race and racial mixture among Hispanics. It is symbolized by the two different names for the day that commemorates the discovery of America by Columbus. Whereas we in the United States celebrate Columbus Day, in parts of Latin America they celebrate El Dia de la Raza—the Day of the (New Mixed) Race (Fernandez, 1992). This does not mean that there is no racism in Latin America. Compared to the U.S. racism, Latin American *racismo* is a dynamic, fluid, and very contextual concept that is often associated with social class. "Regardless of color, the higher the person's social class, the whiter the person is perceived to be, and thus less subjected to racismo, therefore, people can change their color when they change their socioeconomic class" (Comas-Diaz, 1996, p. 172). This greater importance of class than race is reflected in a Brazilian saying—"A rich Negro is a White and a poor White is a Negro"—and the favored skin tone in Brazil is not white but light brown (Delger, 1971; Fernandez, 1992).

7. In his description of the Hispanic community in Chicago, Hutchison (1988) noted that although Cubans favor acculturation the most, they retain the Spanish language more than other Hispanic groups. On the other hand, Puerto Ricans are the least in favor of acculturation. They, and to a lesser extent Mexicans, view certain aspects of U.S. life with disdain and have conflicts with the U.S. lifestyle and values.

8. There are three types of definitions: biological, mystical, and administrative. Biologically, there are several genetic markers for Indians, including fingerprint patterns and organic chemical

compounds in the blood and urine. Mystical views portray them as deeply spiritual and sublimely attuned to the rhythms of nature. Administratively, the federal government has used such standards as blood quantum, tribal membership, and self-identification to delineate the Indian population. None of these is entirely satisfactory. Over the years, a hierarchy of Indian ethnic identity has emerged. There are three categories—the first includes members of federally recognized tribes, the second includes tribes that have only state recognition, and the third is made up of members of unrecognized tribes who identify themselves as American Indians (Snipp, 1997).

9. Collins (1996) studied 15 adults, each with one Japanese and one non-Japanese parent, and found that they integrated both cultures and developed an integrated identity. The overarching themes in their experiences included self-evaluation, confusion of categorization, belonging, infusion-exploration, situational use of identity, and resolution/acceptance/self-verification. Mukoyama (1998) also investigated ethnic identity, self-esteem, and adjustment among 54 Japanese-European Americans and 32 Japanese-African Americans. There was no difference between the two groups in the decision to identify monoracially versus biethnically, although monoethnic identifiers were more likely to be male. In general, all of them were well-adjusted and able to maintain a positive outlook. Chan (1993) studied the factors influencing ethnic identity of 40 biracial adults who had one Asian parent, of Chinese, Japanese, or Korean descent, and one European American parent. The majority identified more or less with both of their racial backgrounds but felt closer to groups of biracial Asian Americans than to either Asian Americans or whites. In her study of black-Japanese biracial people, Hall (1980) found that many of them saw themselves as a "new people or new race" and developed a new group to belong to. Leonard (1992) had also found that in the early 20th century, persons of mixed Punjabi-Mexican descent identified with neither of the communities in which their parents had originated but invented a community for themselves in rural northern California.

10. Allowance was made for some marriages as well. Virginia law recognized as whites those who had 1/16 Indian blood or less, so that the descendants of John Rolfe and Pocahontas could be recognized as an integral and honored part of the white race:

> The story of Rolfe and Pocahontas is a romantic one—the daughter of an Indian chief, Powhatan, she saved Captain John Smith from death at the hands of her tribe. She subsequently married him and produced a son, John Rolfe. The latter played an important part in the early history of Virginia. (Henriques, 1975, p. 32)

11. Davenport (as cited in Reuter, 1918) has provided the following designations.

- Mulatto: Negro and white

- Quadroon: mulatto and white

- Octoroon: quadroon and white

- Cascos: mulatto and mulatto

- Sambo: mulatto and Negro

- Mango: sambo and Negro

- Mustifee: octoroon and white

- Mustifino: mustifee and white

At the beginning of miscegenation between two populations presumed to be racially pure, quadroons appear in the second generation of continuing mixing with whites, and octoroons in the third. A quadroon is one-fourth African black and thus easily classified as black in the United States, yet three of this person's four grandparents are white. An octoroon has seven white great-grandparents out of eight and usually looks white or almost so. (Davis, 1991, p. 6)

12. The Upper South, composed of North Carolina and states to its north and west, had a large mulatto population.

A considerable portion of Upper South mulattoes were free, but they tended to be rural and relatively poor. Most importantly, whites in the Upper South did not usually concern themselves with the mixed-blooded nature of mulattos. They made few distinctions about color or ancestry among Negroes. Instead, they treated mulattoes very much as if they were black. (Mencke, 1979, p. 10)

On the other hand, although slavery in the Lower South was harsher, the lot of mulattoes was much better. The race relations in the Lower Southern states, particularly in South Carolina and Louisiana, evolved in a pattern borrowed from the West Indies. There was considerable miscegenation between white masters and black slave women. Planters publicly defended the practice and had a different attitude toward mulattoes (Mencke, 1979; Wood, 1974).

13. Some mulattoes had slaves of their own. During the antebellum period, many mulattoes stood aloof from the African American population. Some feared the loss of their slave property and the ire of the black masses.
14. According to Haller (1971),

For many educated Americans who shunned the stigma of racial prejudice, science became an instrument which "verified" the presumptive inferiority of the Negro and rationalized the politics of disfranchisement and segregation into a social-scientific terminology that satisfied the troubled conscience of the middle class. (p. x)

These theories also held that mulattoes were physically weak, intellectually inferior to the white man, and morally inferior to both whites and blacks.

15. The attitudes of mulattoes changed during the Civil War and Reconstruction:

This shift in attitudes can be explained in part by the altered patterns of white thought and behavior in the 1850s. During that decade mulattoes had lost most of what preferred status they did have in the eyes of whites. Mulattoes were being pushed inexorably towards an alliance with blacks, and the pressures of war, emancipation, and Reconstruction only solidified this trend. (Mencke, 1979, p. 22)

16. There were mulattoes who denied or rejected their black roots and tried to belong to the white community by "passing for white." There were others who tried to create an existence independent of both white and black communities. There were still others who did not feel accepted in the black community and painfully lived with their marginality. There were many degrees of "passing." Sometimes it involved a brief trip across the color line in order to enjoy an evening in a white restaurant or theater or a more comfortable seat on a train. At other times, it involved holding day jobs as white and returning to the African American community at night. Some passed as whites in other parts of the country away from home and periodically returned to visit family and friends. Whatever the form of passing, it was at the cost of the anxiety of operating in two antagonistic worlds while struggling to keep each world and its respective intimacies clearly separate, lest an acquaintance wittingly or unwittingly unravel the disguise (Spickard, 1989). Another variation on this theme was a collective effort resulting in the formation of elitist black bourgeois communities variously known as "blue vein," "Four Hundred," and "Talented Tenth" societies in large cities (Daniel, 1992b). By emphasizing light skin, straight hair, and sharp features as well as European

culture and thought, the multiracial members of these communities distanced themselves from the image typically held of blacks and tried to achieve parity with whites (Berzon, 1978). Whereas blue-vein societies were the urban elites within the African American community, there were some 200 or more communities called "triracial isolates." They lived apart from both blacks and whites on the fringes of villages and towns or in isolated rural enclaves and refused to accept a binary system of racial classification. "In all probability, the communities evolved from frontier settlements that became magnets for runaways slaves, trappers, homesteaders, adventurers, deserters, outlaws, and nonconformists of all racial backgrounds" (Daniel, 1992b, p. 99).

References

Abalos, D. T. (1986). *Latinos in the United States: The sacred and the political.* Notre Dame, IN: University of Notre Dame Press.

Abbott, A. (1995). Boundaries of social work or social work of boundaries? *Social Service Review, 69,* 545-562.

Abdullah, A. S. (1998). Mammy-ism: A diagnosis of psychological misorientation for women of African descent. *Journal of Black Psychology, 24*(2), 196-206.

Abramovitz, M. (1991). Putting an end to doublespeak about race, gender, and poverty: An annotated glossary for social workers. *Social Work, 36,* 380-384.

Acosta-Belen, E. (1988). *From settlers to newcomers: The Hispanic legacy in the United States.* Newport, CT: Praeger.

Acuna, R. (1981). *Occupied America: A history of Chicanos.* New York: Harper & Row.

Aguilar, M. A., DiNitto, D. M., Franklin, C., & Lopez-Pilkinton, B. (1991). Mexican American families: A psychoeducational approach to addressing chemical dependency and codependency. *Child and Adolescent Social Work, 8,* 309-326.

Ahmed, A. S. (1992). *Postmodernism and Islam.* New York: Routledge.

Allen, J. A. (1995). African Americans: Caribbean. In R. L. Edwards (Ed.), *Encyclopedia of social work* (19th ed., pp. 121-129). Washington, DC: NASW Press.

Allen, P. G. (1986). *The sacred hoop: Recovering the feminine in American Indian traditions.* Boston: Beacon.

Allman, K. M. (1996). (Un)natural boundaries: Mixed race, gender, and sexuality. In M. P. P. Root (Ed.), *The multiracial experience: Racial borders as the new frontier* (pp. 277-290). Thousand Oaks, CA: Sage.

Almeida, D. A. (1996). *Countering prejudice against American Indians and Alaska Natives through antibias curriculum and instruction.* (Report No. EDO-RC-96-4). Charleston, WV: Clearinghouse on Rural Education and Small Schools. (ERIC Document Reproduction Service No. ED 400 146)

Ambler, M. (1996). Cultural property rights: What's next after NAGPRA? Tribal College. *Journal of American Indian Higher Education, 8*(2), 8-10.

American Psychiatric Association. (1994). *Diagnostic and statistical manual of mental disorders* (4th ed.). Washington, DC: Author.

Amott, T., & Matthaei, J. (1991). *Race, gender and work.* Boston: South End.

Anderson, D. L., Barrett, R. E., & Bogue, D. J. (1997). *The populations of the United States* (3rd ed.). New York: Free Press.

Anderson, J. D. (1992). Family-centered practice in the 1990s: A multicultural perspective. *Journal of Multicultural Social Work, 1*(4), 17-29.

Andrews, J. (1989). *Poverty and poor health among elderly Hispanic Americans*. Baltimore: The Commonwealth Fund Commission on Elderly People Living Alone.

Asante, M. K. (1995). *African American history: A journey of liberation*. Maywood, NJ: The Peoples Publishing Group.

Aschenbrenner, J. (1973). *Lifelines: Black families in Chicago*. Prospect Heights, IL: Waveland Press.

Atherton, C. R., & Bolland, K. A. (1997). The multiculturalism debate and social work education: A response to Dorothy Van Soest. *Journal of Social Work Education, 33*, 143-150.

Austin, D. M. (1986). *A history of social work education*. Austin: School of Social Work, University of Texas.

Baird, B. N. (1996). *The internship, practicum, and field placement handbook: A guide for the helping professions*. Upper Saddle River, NJ: Prentice Hall.

Baker, F. M. (1988). Afro-Americans. In L. Comas-Diaz & E. E. H. Griffith (Eds.), *Clinical guidelines in cross-cultural mental health* (pp. 151-181). New York: John Wiley.

Balgopal, P. R. (1995a). Asian Americans overview. In R. L. Edwards (Ed.), *Encyclopedia of social work* (19th ed., pp. 231-237). Washington, DC: NASW Press.

Balgopal, P. R. (1995b). Asian Indians. In R. L. Edwards (Ed.), *Encyclopedia of social work* (19th ed., pp. 256-260). Washington, DC: NASW Press.

Banks, J. A. (1987). *Teaching strategies for ethnic studies*. Boston: Allyn & Bacon.

Barker, J. C., Morrow, J., & Mitteness, L. S. (1998). Gender, informal social support networks, and elderly urban African Americans. *Journal of Aging Studies, 12*, 199-223.

Barker, R. L. (Ed.). (1991). *Social work dictionary* (2nd ed.). Silver Spring, MD: NASW Press.

Barker, R. L. (Ed.). (1999). *Social work dictionary* (4th ed.). Washington, DC: NASW Press.

Barn, R. (1999). White mothers, mixed parentage children and child welfare. *British Journal of Social Work, 29*, 269-284.

Bassett, J. S. (1901). *The writings of Colonel William Byrd*. New York: Doubleday.

Bataille, G. M., & Sands, K. M. (1984). *American Indian women: Telling their lives*. Lincoln: University of Nebraska Press.

Bean, F. D., & Tienda, M. (1987). *The Hispanic population in the United States*. New York: Cambridge University Press.

Beckett, J. O., & Dungee-Anderson, D. (1992). Older minorities: Asian, Black, Hispanic, and Native Americans. In R. L. Achneider & N. P. Kroft (Eds.), *Gerontological social work: Knowledge, service settings, and special populations*. Chicago: Nelson-Hall.

Begun, A. M., Jacobs, N. R., & Quiram, J. F. (1998). *Minorities—A changing role in American society*. Wylie, TX: Information Plus.

Bejar, H. (1998). Community development and the Latin American reality: A personal view. *Community Development Journal, 30*(4), 285-291.

Belitz, J., & Valdez, D. (1994). Clinical issues in the treatment of Chicano male gang youth. *Hispanic Journal of Behavioral Sciences, 16*, 57-74.

Benjamin, R. (1995). The man from South: Reconstructing Navajo students' stories. *Youth & Society, 27*, 194-229.

Berg, I. K., & Miller, S. D. (1992). Working with Asian American clients. *Families in Society, 73*, 356-363.

Berger, R. M. (1982). The unseen minority: Older gays and lesbians. *Social Work, 27*, 236-242.

Bernal, G., & Gutierrez, M. (1988). Cubans. In L. Comas-Diaz & E. E. H. Griffith (Eds.), *Clinical guidelines in cross-cultural mental health* (pp. 233-261). New York: John Wiley.

Bernal, G., Martinez, A. C., Santisteban, D., Bernal, M. E., & Olmedo, E. E. (1983). Hispanic mental health curriculum for psychology. In J. C. Chunn, P. J. Dunston, & R. Ross-Sheriff (Eds.), *Mental health and people of color* (pp. 65-96). Washington, DC: Howard University Press.

Bernal, M. E., & Knight, G. P. (1993). *Ethnic identity: Formation and transmission among Hispanics and other minorities*. Albany: State University of New York Series, United States Hispanic Studies.

Berry, G., & Blassingame, J. W. (1982). *Long memory: The black experience in America.* New York: Oxford University Press.

Berzon, J. R. (1978). *Neither white nor black: The mulatto character in American fiction.* New York: New York University Press.

Billingsley, A. (1992). *Climbing Jacob's ladder: The enduring legacy of African American families.* New York: Simon & Schuster.

Birchett, C. (Ed.). (1992). *Biblical strategies for a community in crisis: What African Americans can do.* Chicago: Urban Ministries.

Birchfield, D. L. (1997a). Apaches. In R. J. Vecoli (Ed.), *Gale encyclopedia of multicultural America* (Vol. 1, pp. 71-80). Boston: Thomson.

Birchfield, D. L. (1997b). Choctaws. In R. J. Vecoli (Ed.), *Gale encyclopedia of multicultural America* (Vol. 1, pp. 313-324). Boston: Thomson.

Birchfield, D. L. (1997c). Navajos. In R. J. Vecoli (Ed.), *Gale encyclopedia of multicultural America* (Vol. 2, pp. 954-965). Boston: Thomson.

Birchfield, D. L. (1997d). Sioux. In R. J. Vecoli (Ed.), *Gale encyclopedia of multicultural America* (Vol. 2, pp. 1230-1239). Boston: Thomson.

Bisno, H., & Cox, F. (1997). Social work education: Catching up with the present and the future. *Journal of Social Work Education, 33*, 373-387.

Blank, R., & Slipp, S. (1994). *Voices of diversity.* New York: AMACOM.

Blumstein, P., & Schwartz, P. (1983). *American couples: Money, work, sex.* New York: Morrow.

Bonilla-Santiago, G. (1989). Legislating progress for Hispanic women in New Jersey. *Social Work, 34*, 270-272.

Boushel, M. (1996). Vulnerable multiracial families and early years services: Concerns, challenges and opportunities. *Children & Society, 10*, 305-316.

Bowser, B. P. (1991). *Black male adolescents: Parenting and education in community context.* Lanham, MD: University Press of America.

Boyer, W. H. (1989). *America's future, transition to the 21st century.* Sisters, OR: Praeger.

Bradshaw, C. K. (1992). Beauty and the beast: On racial ambiguity. In M. P. P. Root (Ed.), *Racially mixed people in America* (pp. 77-90). Newbury Park, CA: Sage.

Brandon, G. (1997). Yoruba. In D. Levinson & M. Ember (Eds.), *American immigrant cultures* (Vol. 2, pp. 946-952). New York: Macmillan.

Brille, N. I. (1998). *Working with people: The helping process* (6th ed.). New York: Longman.

Brislin, R., Cushner, K., Cherrie, C., & Yong, M. (1986). *Intercultural interactions: A practical guide.* Beverly Hills, CA: Sage.

Brislin, R. W. (1981). *Cross-cultural encounters: Face-to-face interaction.* New York: Pergamon.

Brown, N. G., & Douglass, R. E. (1996). Making the invisible visible: The growth of community network organizations. In M. P. P. Root (Ed.), *The multiracial experience: Racial borders as the new frontier* (pp. 323-340). Thousand Oaks, CA: Sage.

Browne, C., & Broderick, A. (1994). Asian and Pacific Island elders: Issues for social work practice and education. *Social Work, 39*, 252-259.

Brueggemann, W. G. (1996). *The practice of macro social work.* Chicago: Nelson-Hall.

Bryce-Laporte, R. S. (1972). Black immigrants: The experience of invisibility and inequality. *Journal of Black Studies, 3*(1), 29-56.

Burden, D., & Gottlieb, N. (1987). *The woman client.* New York: Methuen.

Buriel, R., & Vasquez, R. (1982). Stereotypes of Mexican descent persons: Attitudes of three generations of Mexican American and Anglo American adolescents. *Journal of Cross-Cultural Psychology, 13*, 59-70.

Burnam, M. A., Hough, R. L., Karno, M., Escobar, J. I., & Telles, C. A. (1987). Acculturation and lifetime prevalence of psychiatric disorders among Mexican Americans in Los Angeles. *Journal of Health and Social Behavior, 28*, 89-102.

Burston, B. W., Jones, D., & Saunders, P. R. (1995). Drug use and African Americans: Myth versus reality. *Journal of Alcohol and Drug Education, 40*(2), 19-39.

Burtt, E. A. (1959). Buddhism. In J. E. Fairchild (Ed.), *Basic beliefs* (pp. 73-90). New York: Sheridan House.

Caetano, R. (1998). Cultural and subgroup issues in measuring consumption. *Alcoholism: Clinical and Experimental Research, 22*(2), 21S.

Cafferty, S. J. P., & Chestang, L. (1976). *The diverse society: Implications for social policy.* Washington, DC: NASW Press.

Campos, A. P. (1995). Hispanics: Puerto Ricans. In R. L. Edwards (Ed.), *Encyclopedia of social work* (19th ed., pp. 1234-1252). Washington, DC: NASW Press.

Carnegie Foundation. (1990). Native Americans and higher education: New mood of optimism. *Change, 22*(1), 27-31.

Carrillo, D. F., Holzhalb, C. M., & Thyer, B. A. (1993). Assessing social work students' attitudes related to cultural diversity: A review of selected measures. *Journal of Social Work Education, 29*, 263-268.

Carr-Ruffino, N. (1996). *Managing diversity: People skills for a multicultural workplace.* Cincinnati, OH: Thomson Executive Press.

Carter, C., Coudrouglou, A., Figueria-McDonough, J., Lie, G. Y., MacEachron, A. E., Netting, F. E., Nichols-Casebolt, A., Nichols, A. W., & Risley-Curtiss, C. (1994). Integrating women's issues in the social work curriculum: A proposal. *Journal of Social Work Education, 30*, 200-216.

Casal, L., & Hernandes, A. (1975). Cubans in the U.S.: A survey of the literature. *Cuban Studies, 5*(2), 25-51.

Casas, S., & Keefe, S. (1980). *Family and mental health in Mexican American community.* Los Angeles: Spanish Speaking Mental Health Research Center.

Castex, G. M. (1994). Providing services to Hispanic? Latino populations: Profiles in diversity. *Social Work, 39*, 288-296.

Castro, F. G., Cota, M. K., & Vega, S. C. (1999). Health promotion in Latino populations: A socio-cultural model for program planning, development, and evaluation. In R. M. Huff & M. V. Klein (Eds.), *Promoting health in multicultural populations: A handbook for practitioners* (pp. 137-168). Thousand Oaks, CA: Sage.

Census will let Americans pick more than one race. (1997, October 30). *Lexington Herald-Leader,* p. A3.

Cervantes, R. C., Salgado de Snyder, V. N., & Padilla, A. M. (1989). Posttraumatic stress in immigrants from Central America and Mexico. *Hospital and Community Psychiatry, 40*, 615-619.

Champagne, D. (1993). Kinship and political change in Native American tribes. In H. P. McAdoo (Ed.), *Family ethnicity: Strength in diversity* (pp. 208-216). Newbury Park, CA: Sage.

Chan, S. (1991). *Asian Americans: An interpretive history.* New York: Twayne.

Chan, S. Q. (1993). *Ethnic identity in biracial Asian American.* Unpublished doctoral dissertation, University of California, Los Angeles.

Chandrasekhar, S. (1982). A history of United States legislation with respect to immigration from India. In S. Chandrasekhar (Ed.), *From India to America: A brief history of immigration: Problems of discrimination, admission and assimilation* (pp. 11-28). La Jolla, CA: Population Review Publications.

Chau, K. L. (1989). Sociocultural dissonance among ethnic minority populations. *Social Casework, 70*, 224-230.

Chau, K. L. (1990). A model for teaching cross-cultural practice in social work. *Journal of Social Work Education, 26*, 124-133.

Chau, K. L. (1991). Social work with ethnic minorities: Practice issues and potentials. *Journal of Multicultural Social Work, 1*(1), 23-39.

Chauce, A., Hiraga, Y., Mason, C., Aguilar, T., Ordonez, N., & Gonzales, N. (1992). Between a hard rock and a hard place: Social adjustment of biracial youth. In M. P. P. Root (Ed.), *Racially mixed people in America* (pp. 207-222). Newbury Park, CA: Sage.

Chavez, R., & Roney, C. E. (1990). Psychocultural factors affecting the mental health status of Mexican American adolescents. In A. R. Stiffman & L. E. Davis (Eds.), *Ethnic issues in adolescent mental health* (pp. 73-91). Newbury Park, CA: Sage.

Chen, M. S. (1993). Cardiovascular health among Asian Americans/Pacific Islanders: An examination of health status and intervention approaches. *International Journal of Health Promotion, 7*, 199-207.

Chew, K., Eggebeen, D., & Uhlenberg, P. (1989). American children in multiracial households. *Sociological Perspectives, 32*, 65-85.

Cho, P. J. (1997). Asian American experiences: A view from the other side. *Journal of Sociology and Social Welfare, 24*(1), 129-154.

Chow, E. N. L. (1982). *Acculturation of Asian American professional women*. Washington, DC: National Institute of Mental Health, Department of Health and Human Services.

Chow, J. (1999). Multiservice centers in Chinese immigrant communities: Practice principles and challenges. *Social Work, 44*, 70-81.

Chung, R. C., & Kagawa-Singer, M. (1993). Predictors of psychological distress among Southeast Asian refugees. *Social Science and Medicine, 36*, 631-639.

Clark, J. M., Lasaga, L. I., & Reque, R. R. (1981). *The 1980 Mariel exodus: An assessment and prospect*. Washington, DC: Council on Inter-American Security.

Clarke, C. (1983). The failure to transform: Homophobia in the black community. In B. Smith (Ed.), *Home girls: A black feminist anthology* (pp. 197-208). New York: Kitchen Table, Women of Color Press.

Clifton, J. A. (1989). *Being and becoming Indian: Biographical studies of North American frontier*. Homewood, IL: Dorsey.

Cnann, R. (1997). *Social and community involvement of religious congregations housed in historic religious properties: Finding from a six-city study*. Philadelphia: University of Pennsylvania School of Social Work.

Coile, R. C., Jr. (1990). *The new medicine: Reshaping medical practice and health care management*. Gaithersburg, MD: Aspen.

Coll, B. D. (1984). Social welfare: History. In J. B. Turner (Ed.), *Encyclopedia of social work* (17th ed., pp. 1503-1512). New York: NASW Press.

Collins, J. F. (1996). *Biracial Japanese-American identity: Hapa, double, or somewhere in between (Ethnicity)*. Unpublished doctoral dissertation, The Fielding Institute, Santa Barbara, CA.

Coltrane, S., & Valdez, E. O. (1997). Work-family role allocation in dual-earner Chicano families. In M. Romero, P. Hondagneu-Sotelo, & V. Ortiz (Eds.), *Challenging fronteras: Structuring Latina and Latino lives in the U.S.* (pp. 229-246). New York: Routledge.

Comas-Diaz, L. (1988). Cross-cultural mental health treatment. In L. Comas-Diaz & E. E. H. Griffith (Eds.), *Clinical guidelines in cross-cultural mental health* (pp. 337-361). New York: John Wiley.

Comas-Diaz, L. (1996). LatiNegra: Mental health issues of African Latinas. In M. P. P. Root (Ed.), *The multiracial experience: Racial borders as the new frontier* (pp. 167-190). Thousand Oaks, CA: Sage.

Comas-Diaz, L., & Duncan, J. W. (1985). The cultural context: A factor in assertiveness training with mainland Puerto Rican women. *Psychology of Women Quarterly, 9*, 463-476.

Comas-Diaz, L., & Greene, B. (1994). Women of color with professional status. In L. Comas-Diaz & B. Greene (Eds.), *Women of color: Integrating ethnic and gender identities in psychotherapy* (pp. 347-388). New York: Guilford.

Congress, E. P. (1994). The use of culturagrams to assess and empower culturally diverse families. *Families in Society, 75*, 531-540.

Conley, R. J. (1997). Cherokees. In R. J. Vecoli (Ed.), *Gale encyclopedia of multicultural America* (Vol. 1, pp. 271-279). Boston: Thomson.

Connor, J. W. (1974). Acculturation and family continuities in three generations of Japanese-Americans. *Journal of Marriage and the Family, 36*, 159-165.

Cooper-Lewter, N., & Mitchell, H. (1992). Soul theology: The heart of American black culture. Nashville, TN: Abingdon.

Cordova, C. B. (1998). Living in the U.S.A.: Central American immigrant communities in the United States. In F. G. Rivera & J. L. Erlich (Eds.), *Community organizing in a diverse society* (3rd ed., pp. 180-200). Needham Heights, MA: Allyn & Bacon.

Cose, E. (1997). Census at the complex issue of race. *Society, 34*, 9-13.

Council on Social Work Education. (1952). *Curriculum policy.* New York: Author.

Council on Social Work Education. (1962). *Official statement of curriculum policy for the master's degree program in graduate professional schools of social work.* New York: Author.

Council on Social Work Education. (1983). *Curriculum policy for the master's degree and baccalaureate degree programs in social work education.* New York: Author.

Council on Social Work Education. (1994). *Commission on accreditation handbook of accreditation standards and procedures.* Alexandria, VA: Author.

Cowger, C. D. (1994). Assessing client strengths: Clinical assessment for client empowerment. *Social Work, 39*, 262-268.

Cress-Welsing, F. (1991). *The ISIS papers: The keys to the colors.* Chicago: Third World.

Cruz, A. R. (1997). The Mexican-American community in the United States. In L. L. Naylor (Ed.), *Cultural diversity in the United States* (pp. 159-175). Westport, CT: Bergin & Garvey.

Cuellar, I., Arnold, B., & Maldonado, R. (1995). Acculturation rating scale for Mexican Americans-II: A revision of the original ARSMA scale. *Hispanic Journal of Behavioral Sciences, 17*, 275-304.

Cunningham, J. L. (1997). Color existence: Racial identity formation in light-skin Blacks. *Smith College Studies in Social Work, 67*, 375-400.

Curiel, H. (1995). Hispanics: Mexican Americans. In R. L. Edwards (Ed.), *Encyclopedia of social work* (19th ed., pp. 1233-1244). Washington, DC: NASW Press.

Dana, R. H. (1998). *Understanding cultural identity in intervention and assessment.* Thousand Oaks, CA: Sage.

Daniel, G. R. (1992a). Beyond black and white: The new multiracial consciousness. In M. P. P. Root (Ed.), *Racially mixed people in America* (pp. 333-341). Newbury Park, CA: Sage.

Daniel, G. R. (1992b). Passers and pluralists: Subverting the racial divide. In M. P. P. Root (Ed.), *Racially mixed people in America* (pp. 91-107). Newbury Park, CA: Sage.

Daniel, G. R. (1996). Black and white identity in the new millennium: Unsevering the ties that bind. In M. P. P. Root (Ed.), *The multiracial experience: Racial borders as the new frontier* (pp. 121-139). Thousand Oaks, CA: Sage.

Daniels, L. A. (1998). *The state of Black America 1998.* Washington, DC: National Urban League.

David, G., & Lin, J. (1997). Civil rights and Asian Americans. *Journal of Sociology and Social Welfare, 24*(1), 3-24.

Davis, F. J. (1991). *Who is black? One nation's definition.* University Park, PA: The Pennsylvania State University Press.

Davis, L. E. (1995). The crisis of diversity. In M. D. Feit, J. H. Ramey, J. S. Wodarski, & A. A. Mann (Eds.), *Capturing the power of diversity* (pp. 47-57). New York: Haworth.

Davis, R. (1980). Black suicide and the relational system: Theoretical and empirical implications of communal and family ties. *Research in Race and Ethnic Relations, 2*, 43-71.

Davis, R. E. (1997). Trauma and addiction experiences of African American women. *Western Journal of Nursing Research, 19*, 442-460.

Day, J. C. (1993). *Population projections of the United States by age, sex, race, and Hispanic origin: 1993-2050.* Washington, DC: U.S. Government Printing Office.

deBary, W. T. (1959). Confucianism. In J. E. Fairchild (Ed.), *Basic beliefs* (pp. 92-113). New York: Sheridan House.

de Haymes, M. V. (1997). The golden exile: The social construction of the Cuban-American success story. *Journal of Poverty, 1*(1), 65-79.

De Hoyos, G., De Hoyos, A., & Anderson, C. B. (1986). Sociocultural dislocation: Beyond the dual perspective. *Social Work, 31*, 61-67.

Delgado, M. (1997a). Interpretation of Puerto Rican elder research findings: A community forum of research respondents. *Journal of Applied Gerontology, 16*, 317-332.

Delgado, M. (1997b). Role of Latina-owned beauty parlors in a Latino community. *Social Work, 42*, 445-453.

Delgado, M. (2000). *Community social work practice in an urban context.* New York: Oxford University Press.

Delgado, M., & Santiago, J. (1998). HIV/AIDS in Puerto Rican/Dominican community: A collaborative project with a botanical shop. *Social Work, 43*, 183-186.

Delger, C. N. (1971). *Neither black nor white: Slavery and race relations in Brazil and the United State.* New York: Macmillan.

Deters, K. A. (1997). Belonging nowhere and everywhere: Multiracial identity development. *Bulletin of the Menninger Clinic, 61*, 368-384.

Devore, W., & Schlesinger, E. G. (1981). *Ethnic-sensitive social work practice.* St. Louis, MO: C. V. Mosby.

Dhooper, S. S. (1990). Identifying and mobilizing supports for the cardiac patient's family. *Journal of Cardiovascular Nursing, 5*(1), 65-73.

Dhooper, S. S. (1991). Toward an effective response to the needs of Asian-Americans. *Journal of Multicultural Social Work, 1*(2), 65-81.

Dhooper, S. S. (1994). *Social work and transplantation of human organs.* Westport, CT: Praeger.

Dhooper, S. S. (1997a). Poverty among Asian Americans: Theories and approaches. *Journal of Sociology and Social Welfare, 24*(1), 25-40.

Dhooper, S. S. (1997b). *Social work in health care in the 21st century.* Thousand Oaks, CA: Sage.

Dhooper, S. S., & Tran, T. V. (1987). Social work with Asian Americans. *Journal of Independent Social Work, 1*(4), 51-62.

Dhooper, S. S., & Tran, V. T. (1998). Understanding and responding to the health and mental health needs of Asian American refugees. *Social Work in Health Care, 27*(4), 65-82.

Dieppa, I. (1984). Trends in social work education for minorities. In B. W. White (Ed.), *Color in a white society* (pp. 10-21). Silver Spring, MD: NASW Press.

DiNitto, D. M., & McNeece, C. A. (1990). *Social work: Issues and opportunities in a challenging profession.* Englewood Cliffs, NJ: Prentice Hall.

Dodoo, F. N. -A. (1997). Assimilation differences among Africans in America. *Social Forces, 76*, 527-547.

Dominguez, V. R. (1975). *From neighbor to stranger: The dilemma of Caribbean peoples in the United States.* New Haven, CT: Antilles Research Program, Yale University.

Douglass, B. C. (1993). Psychotherapy with troubled African American adolescent males: Stereotypes, treatment amenability, and critical issues. *Annual Meeting of the American Psychological Association*, 2-16.

DuBrin, A. J. (1988). *Human relations for career and personal success* (2nd ed.). Englewood Cliffs, NJ: Prentice Hall.

Dunn, L. P. (1975). *Asian Americans: A study guide and sourcebook.* San Francisco: R. & E. Research Associates.

Dykeman, C., Nelson, J. R., & Appleton, V. (1996). Building strong working alliances with American Indian families. In P. L. Ewalt, E. R. Freeman, S. A. Kirk, & D. L. Poole (Eds.), *Multicultural issues in social work* (pp. 336-350). Washington, DC: NASW Press.

East-West Population Institute. (1990). *Recent Filipino immigration to the United States: A profile.* Honolulu, HI: Author.

Eitzen, D. S., & Zinn, M. B. (1997). *Social problems* (7th ed.). Needham Heights, MA: Allyn & Bacon.

Eldridge, N. S., & Gilbert, L. A. (1990). Correlates of relationship satisfaction in lesbian couples. *Psychology of Women Quarterly, 14*, 43-62.

Eliason, M., & Skinstad, A. (1995). Drug/alcohol addictions and mothering. *Alcoholism Treatment Quarterly, 12*(1), 83-96.

Enos, R. (1997). Social work practice with ethnic minority persons. In L. L. Naylor (Ed.), *Cultural diversity in the United States* (pp. 305-316). Westport, CT: Bergin & Garvey.

Epstein, M., & Moreno, R. (1997). The underreporting of deaths of American Indian children in California, 1979 through 1993. *American Journal of Public Health, 87,* 1363-1367.

Espiritu, Y. L. (1996). *Asian American women and men: Labor, laws, and love.* Thousand Oaks, CA: Sage.

Estrada, L. E., Garcia, C. E., Macias, R. F., & Maldonado, L. (1981). Chicanos in the United States: A history of exploitation and resistance. *Daedalus: Journal of the American Academy of Arts and Sciences, 110*(2), 103-131.

Evans, D. L. (1998, September 7). Lost behind prison bars. *Newsweek, 132,* 20-22.

Evans, S. E. (1996). Women. In F. E. Hoxie (Ed.), *The encyclopedia of North American Indians* (pp. 665-689). New York: Houghton Mifflin.

Face of America [Special issue]. (1993). *Time, 142*(21).

Falicov, C. (1982). Mexican families. In M. McGoldrick, J. K. Pearce, & J. Giordano (Eds.), *Ethnicity and family therapy* (pp. 134-163). New York: Guilford.

Farley, R. (1991). The new census question about ancestry: What did it tell us? *Demography, 28,* 411-429.

Fassinger, R. E., & Richie, B. S. (1997). Sex matters: Gender and sexual orientation in training for multicultural counseling competency. In D. B. Pope-Davis & H. L. K. Coleman (Eds.), *Multicultural counseling competencies: Assessment, education and training, and supervision* (pp. 83-110). Thousand Oaks, CA: Sage.

Fenster, A. (1996). Group therapy as an effective treatment modality for people of color. *International Journal of Group Psychotherapy, 46,* 399-416.

Fernandez, C. A. (1992). La raza and the melting pot: A comparative look at multiethnicity. In M. P. P. Root (Ed.), *Racially mixed people in America* (pp. 126-143). Newbury Park, CA: Sage.

Fernandez, C. A. (1996). Government classification of multiracial/multiethnic people. In M. P. P. Root (Ed.), *The multiracial experience: Racial borders as the new frontier* (pp. 15-36). Thousand Oaks, CA: Sage.

Fernandez-Kelly, M. P., & Garcia, A. M. (1997). Power surrendered, power restored: The politics of work and family among Hispanic garment workers in California and Florida. In M. Romero, P. Hondagneu-Sotelo, & V. Ortiz (Eds.), *Challenging fronteras: Structuring Latina and Latino lives in the U.S.* (pp. 215-227). New York: Routledge.

Field, L. D. (1996). Piecing together the puzzle: Self-concept and group identity in biracial black/white youth. In M. P. P. Root (Ed.), *The multiracial experience: Racial borders as the new frontier* (pp. 211-226). Thousand Oaks, CA: Sage.

Fischer, D. (1995). Young, gay and ignored? *Orana, 31*(4), 220-232.

Fitzpatrick, J. P. (1987). *Puerto Rican Americans: The meaning of migration.* Englewood Cliffs, NJ: Prentice Hall.

Fong, L. Y. S. (1997). Asian-American women: An understudied minority. *Journal of Sociology and Social Welfare, 24*(1), 91-111.

Forbes, J. D. (1988). *Black Africans and Native Americans: Color, race and caste in the evolution of Red-Black people.* New York: Basil Blackwell.

Fowers, B. J., & Richardson, F. C. (1994). Why is multiculturism good? *American Psychologist, 51,* 609-621.

Fox, P. G. (1991). Stress related to family change among Vietnamese refugees. *Journal of Community Health Nursing, 8,* 45-56.

Franklin, A. J. (1992). Therapy with African American men. *Families in Society, 73,* 350-355.

Franklin, C., Waukechon, J., & Larney, P. S. (1995). Culturally relevant school programs for American Indian children and families. *Social Work in Education, 17,* 183-194.

Frazier, F. (1966). *The Negro family in the United States.* Chicago: University of Chicago Press.

Frye, B. A. (1995). Use of cultural themes in promoting health among Southeast Asian refugees. *American Journal of Health Promotion, 9,* 269-280.

Frye, B. A., & D'Avanzo, C. (1994). Themes in managing culturally defined illness in the Cambodian refugee family. *Journal of Community Health Nursing, 11*, 89-98.

Fuchs, L. H. (1997). What we should count and why. *Society, 34*(6), 24-27.

Fullilove, M., Fullilove, R., Smith, M., Winkler, K., Micheal, C., Panzer, P., & Wallace, R. (1993). Violence, trauma, and post-traumatic stress disorder among women drug users. *Journal of Traumatic Stress, 6*, 533-543.

Funderberg, L. (1994). *Black, white, other: Biracial Americans talk about race and identity*. New York: William Morrow.

Gallegos, J. S. (1984). The ethnic competence model for social work education. In B. W. White (Ed.), *Color in a white society* (pp. 1-9). Silver Spring, MD: NASW Press.

Gann, L. H., & Duignan, P. J. (1986). *Hispanics in the United States: A history*. Boulder, CO: Westview.

Garcia, M., & Lega, L. I. (1979). Development of a Cuban ethnic identity questionnaire. *Hispanic Journal of Behavioral Sciences, 1*, 247-261.

Garrett, M. T. (1999). Understanding the "medicine" of Native American traditional values: An integrative review. *Counseling & Values, 43*(2), 84-99.

Garrison, L. (1993). Professionals of the future: Will they be female? Will they be ethnically diverse? *Roeper Review, 15*(3), 161-165.

Garvin, C. D., & Seabury, B. A. (1997). *Interpersonal practice in social work*. Needham Heights, MA: Allyn & Bacon.

Gavagan, T., & Brodyaga, L. (1998). Medical care for immigrants and refugees. *American Family Physician, 57*, 1061-1066.

Gellar, S. (1986). The colonial era. In Martin, P. M. & O'Mera, P. (Eds.), *Africa* (2nd ed.) (pp. 122-140). Bloomington: Indiana University Press.

Germain, C. B., & Gitterman, A. (1995). Ecological perspective. In R. L. Edwards (Ed.), *Encyclopedia of social work* (19th ed., pp. 816-824). Washington, DC: NASW Press.

Gibbs, J. T. (1988). Young, black, male in America: Endangered, embittered and embattled. In J. T. Gibbs, A. F. Brunswick, M. E. Connor, R. Dembo, T. E. Larson, R. J. Reed, & B. Solomon (Eds.), *Young, Black and male in America* (pp. 1-36). Dover, MA: Auburn House.

Gibbs, J. T. (1989). Biracial adolescents. In J. T. Gibbs & L. N. Huang (Eds.), *Children of color: Psychological interventions with minority youth* (pp. 322-350). San Francisco: Jossey-Bass.

Gibbs, J. T., & Hines, A. (1992). Negotiating ethnic identity: Issues for black-white biracial adolescents. In M. P. P. Root (Ed.), *Racially mixed people in America* (pp. 223-238). Newbury Park, CA: Sage.

Gibson, M. A., & Ogbu, J. U. (1991). *Minority status and schooling: A comparative study of immigrant and involuntary minorities*. New York: Garland.

Gilbertson, G. A., Fitzpatrick, J. P., & Yang, L. (1996). Hispanic intermarriage in New York City: New evidence from 1991. *International Migration Review, 30*, 445-459.

Gilkes, C. T. (1980). The black church as a therapeutic community: Suggested areas for research into the Black religious experience. *Journal of Interdenominational Theological Center, 8*, 29-44.

Gilliland, H. (1992). *Teaching the Native American*. Dubuque, IA: Kendall/Hunt.

Glass, R. D., & Wallace, K. R. (1996). Challenging race and racism: A framework for educators. In M. P. P. Root (Ed.), *The multiracial experience: Racial borders as the new frontier* (pp. 341-358). Thousand Oaks, CA: Sage.

Glazer, N. (1976). Foreword. In P. Saran & E. Eames (Eds.), *The new ethnics: Asian Indians in the United States* (pp. vi-viii). New York: Praeger.

Gonsalves, C. J. (1992). Psychological stages of the refugee process: A model for therapeutic interventions. *Professional Psychology: Research and Practice, 23*, 382-389.

Goodluck, C. T. (1993). Social services with Native Americans: Current status of the Indian Child Welfare Act. In H. P. McAdoo (Ed.), *Family ethnicity: Strength in diversity* (pp. 217-228). Newbury Park, CA: Sage.

Goodman, H., Getzel, G. S., & Ford, W. (1996). Group work with high-risk urban youths on probation. *Social Work, 41*, 375-381.

Gottlieb, B. H. (1985). Assessing and strengthening the impact of social support on mental health. *Social Work, 30*, 293-300.

Gould, J. (1994). Disobedience (in language) in texts by lesbian Native Americans. *ARIEL, 25*(1), 32-44.

Gould, M. (1997). Statutory oppressions: An overview of legalized homophobia. In M. P. Levine (Ed.), *Gay men: The sociology of male homosexuality* (pp. 51-67). New York: Harper & Row.

Graham, L. O. (1999). Our kind of people: Inside America's Black upper class. New York: HarperCollins.

Graham, S. R. (1996). The real world. In M. P. P. Root (Ed.), *The multiracial experience: Racial borders as the new frontier* (pp. 37-48). Thousand Oaks, CA: Sage.

Grant, L. M., & Gutierrez, L. M. (1996). Effects of culturally sophisticated agencies on Latino social workers. *Social Work, 41*, 624-631.

Green, H. (1994). Refugees in transition—Educational opportunity to promote the advancement of women. *Convergence, 27*(2/3), 175-184.

Green, J. W. (1982). *Cultural awareness in the human services*. Englewood Cliffs, NJ: Prentice Hall.

Green, R. (1987). *The "sissy boy syndrome" and the development of homosexuality*. New Haven, CT: Yale University Press.

Greenberg, D. F. (1988). *The construction of homosexuality*. Chicago: University of Chicago Press.

Greene, B. (1994). Ethnic-minority lesbians and gay men: Mental health and treatment issues. *Journal of Consulting and Clinical Psychology, 62*, 243-252.

Greif, G. L. (1986). The ecosystems perspective "meets the press." *Social Work, 31*, 225-226.

Grosfoguel, R. (1997). Migration and geopolitics in the Greater Antilles: From the Cold War to the Post-Cold War. *Review, 20*(1), 115-145.

Grossman, R. G. (1990). *A study of immigrant Hispanic alcoholics in a treatment program*. Unpublished doctoral dissertation, Yeshiva University, New York.

Guarnizo, L. E. (1997). Los Dominicanyorks: The making of a binational society. In M. Romero, P. Hondagneu-Sotelo, & V. Ortiz (Eds.), *Challenging fronteras: Structuring Latina and Latino lives in the U.S.* (pp. 161-174). New York: Routledge.

Gurak, D. T., & Kritz, M. M. (1985). Hispanic immigration to the Northeast in the 1970s. *Migration Today, 13*(2), 6-12.

Gutierrez, L., Alvarez, A. R., Nemon, H., & Lewis, E. A. (1996). Multicultural community organizing: A strategy for change. *Social Work, 41*, 501-508.

Gutierrez, L., & Nagda, B. A. (1996). The multicultural imperative in human services organizations: Issues for the twenty-first century. In P. R. Raffoul & C. A. McNeece (Eds.), *Future issues for social work practice* (pp. 203-213). Needham Heights, MA: Allyn & Bacon.

Gutierrez, L. M. (1990). Working with women of color: An empowerment perspective. *Social Work, 35*, 149-153.

Gutierrez, L. M., & Lewis, E. A. (1998). A feminist perspective on organizing with women. In F. G. Rivera & J. L. Erlich (Eds.), *Community organizing in a diverse society* (3rd ed., pp. 97-116). Needham Heights, MA: Allyn & Bacon.

Guzzetta, C. (1995). White ethnic groups. In R. L. Edwards (Ed.), *Encyclopedia of social work* (19th ed., pp. 2508-2517). Washington, DC: NASW Press.

Hacker, A. (1992). Two nations: Black and white, separate, hostile, unequal. New York: Scribner.

Hagan, J. W., House, T., & Skenadore, A. H. (1995). Kanuhkwene: An empowering concept by and for Oneida women. *Journal of Humanistic Education & Development, 33*(3), 123-131.

Haizlip, S. T. (1994). *The sweeter the juice: A family memoir in black and white*. New York: Simon & Schuster.

Haizlip, S. T. (1995, February/March). Passing. *American Heritage, 46*(1), 46-53.

Hall, C. C. I. (1980). *The ethnic identity of racially mixed people: A study of Black-Japanese*. Unpublished doctoral dissertation, University of California, Los Angeles.

Hall, C. C. I. (1992). Coloring outside the lines. In M. P. P. Root (Ed.), *Racially mixed people in America* (pp. 326-329). Newbury Park, CA: Sage.

Hall, C. C. I. (1996). A race odyssey. In M. P. P. Root (Ed.), *The multiracial experience: Racial borders as the new frontier* (pp. 395-410). Thousand Oaks, CA: Sage.

Hall, C. C. I. (1997). Best of both worlds: Body image and satisfaction of a sample of black-Japanese biracial individuals. *Amerasia Journal, 23*, 87-97.

Hall, L. (1997a). Creeks. In R. J. Vecoli (Ed.), *Gale encyclopedia of multicultural America* (Vol. 1, pp. 347-358). Boston: Thomson.

Hall, L. (1997b). Iroquois Confederacy. In R. J. Vecoli (Ed.), *Gale encyclopedia of multicultural America* (Vol. 2, pp. 750-763). Boston: Thomson.

Haller, J. S., Jr. (1971). *Outcastes from evolution: Scientific attitudes of racial inferiority, 1859-1900.* Urbana: University of Illinois Press.

Hamilton, N., & Chinchilla, N. S. (1997). Central American migration: A framework for analysis. In M. Romero, P. Hondagneu-Sotelo, & V. Ortiz (Eds.), *Challenging fronteras: Structuring Latina and Latino lives in the U.S.* (pp. 81-100). New York: Routledge.

Hann, R. S. (1994). Tuberculosis. In N. W. S. Zane, D. T. Takeuchi, & K. N. J. Young (Eds.), *Confronting critical health issues of Asian and Pacific Islander Americans* (pp. 289-301). Thousand Oaks, CA: Sage.

Hardy-Fanta, C. (1991). *Latina women, Latino men, and political participation in Boston: La Chispa que Prende.* Unpublished doctoral dissertation, Brandeis University, Waltham, MA.

Hare, B. (1988). Black youth at risk. In J. Dewart (Ed.), *The state of Black America, 1988* (pp. 81-93). New York: National Urban League.

Harel, Z., McKinney, E. A., & Williams, M. (1990). *Black aged: Understanding diversity and service needs.* Newbury Park, CA: Sage.

Harjo, S. S. (1993). The American Indian experience. In H. P. McAdoo (Ed.), *Family ethnicity: Strength in diversity* (pp. 199-207). Newbury Park, CA: Sage.

Harmon, A. (1990). When is an Indian not an Indian? The friends of the Indian and the problems of Indian identity. *Journal of Ethnic Studies, 18*, 95-123.

Hartman, A., & Laird, J. (1983). *Family-centered social work practice.* New York: Free Press.

Harvey, A. R. (1985). Traditional African culture as the basis for the Afro-American church in America. In A. R. Harvey (Ed.), *The black family: An afrocentric perspective* (pp. 1-22). New York: United Church of Christ Commission on Racial Justice.

Hatchett, S. (1991). Family life. In J. Jackson (Ed.), *Life in black America* (pp. 46-83). Newbury Park, CA: Sage.

The hate debate. (1998, November 23). *The New Republic, 219*(18), 7-9.

Hayes-Bautista, D. E., & Chapa, J. (1987). Latino terminology: Conceptual bases for standardized terminology. *American Journal of Public Health, 77*, 61-68.

Haynes, A. W., & Singh, R. N. (1992). Ethnic-sensitive social work practice: An integrated, ecological, and psychodynamic approach. *Journal of Multicultural Social Work, 2*(2), 43-52.

Haynes, K. S., & Holmes, K. A. (1994). *Invitation to social work.* New York: Longman.

Heaton, T. B., & Albrecht, S. L. (1996). The changing pattern of interracial marriage. *Social Biology, 43*, 203-217.

Helms, J. E. (1990). *Black and white racial identity: Theory, research and practice.* New York: Greenwood.

Hendricks, L. E. (1988). Outreach with teenage fathers: A preliminary report on three ethnic groups. *Adolescence, 23*, 711-720.

Henriques, F. (1975). *Children of conflict: A study of interracial sex and marriage.* New York: E. P. Dutton.

Hepworth, D. H., & Larsen, J. A. (1993). *Direct social work practice: Theory and skills.* Pacific Grove, CA: Brooks/Cole.

Hernandez, L., & Carlquist-Hernandez, K. (1997). Humanization of the counseling-teaching process for Latinos: Learning principles. *Journal of Non-White Concerns, 7*, 150-158.

Herring, R. D. (1990). Understanding Native-American values: Process and content concerns for Counselors. *Counseling & Values, 34*(2), 134-138.

Herring, R. D., & Meggert, S. S. (1994). The use of humor as a counselor strategy with Native American Indian children. *Elementary School Guidance & Counseling, 29*(1), 67-77.

Hill, R. B. (1997). *The strengths of African American families: Twenty-five years later*. Washington, DC: R & B Publishers.

Hilton, R. (1973). *The Latin Americans: Their heritage and their destiny*. Philadelphia: J. B. Lippincott.

Hirschfelder, A., & Kreipe de Montano, M. (1993). *The Native American almanac: A portrait of Native America today*. New York: Prentice Hall.

Ho, M. K. (1987). *Family therapy with ethnic minorities*. Newbury Park, CA: Sage.

Ho, M. K. (1991). Use of Ethnic-Sensitive Inventory (ESI) to enhance practitioner skills with minorities. *Journal of Multicultural Social Work, 1*(1), 57-67.

Ho, M. K. (1992). *Minority children and adolescents in therapy*. Newbury Park, CA: Sage.

Hodes, M. (1998). Refugee children. *British Medical Journal, 316*(7134), 793-795.

Hodge, W. H. (1981). *The first Americans*. New York: Holt, Rinehart & Winston.

Hodgkinson, H. (1992). *The current condition of Native Americans*. (Report No. EDO-RC-92-7). Charleston, WV: Clearinghouse on Rural Education and Small Schools. (ERIC Document Reproduction Service No. RC 081 910)

Hoffman, K. S., & Sallee, A. L. (1994). *Social work practice: Bridges to change*. Needham Heights, MA: Allyn and Bacon.

Hogan-Garcia, M. (1999). *The four skills of cultural diversity competence: A process for understanding and practice*. New York: Brooks/Cole, Wadsworth, International Thompson Publishing.

Hoopes, D., & Ventura, P. (1979). *Intercultural sourcebook cross-cultural training methodologies*. Washington, DC: Sietar International.

Hoopes, D. S. (1981). Intercultural communication concepts and the psychology of intercultural experience. In M. D. Pusch (Ed.), *Multicultural education: A cross cultural training approach* (pp. 17-22). Yarmouth, ME: Intercultural Press.

Hornby, R. (1992). *Training culturally appropriate interventions for Native Americans*. Washington, DC: Comprehensive Program Fund for the Improvement of Secondary Education.

Horton, H. D., Thomas, M. E., & Herring, C. (1995). Rural-urban differences in black family structure. *Journal of Family Issues, 16*, 298-313.

Huggins, S. E. (1997). Pooling community dollars. *Black Enterprise, 27*(10), 32.

Hughes, M. J. (1995). *Breaking the cycle of destructive behaviors: Facilitating positive developmental change in African and Latino-American males, 18-28*. Unpublished doctoral dissertation, Brandeis University, Waltham, MA.

Hurtado, A. L. (1996). When strangers meet: Sex and gender on three frontiers. *Frontiers: A Journal of Women Studies, 17*(3), 52-74.

Hutchinson, E. O. (1996). *The assassination of the black male image*. New York: Simon & Schuster.

Hutchison, R. (1988). The Hispanic community in Chicago: A study of population growth and acculturation. *Research in Race and Ethnic Relations, 5*, 193-229.

Icard, L. D., Longres, J. F., & Spencer, M. (1999). Racial minority status and distress among children and adolescents. *Journal of Social Service Research, 25*(1/2), 19-40.

Ifill, D. (1989). Teaching minority practice for professional application. *Journal of Social Work Education, 25*, 29-35.

Inclan, J., & Hernandez, M. (1992). Cross-cultural perspectives and codependence: The case of poor Hispanics. *American Journal of Orthopsychiatry, 62*, 245-255.

Isaacs, H. R. (1972). *Images of Asia: American views of China and India*. New York: Harper & Row.

Ishisaka, H. A., Nguyen, Q. T., & Okimoto, J. T. (1985). The role of culture in the mental health treatment of Indochinese refugees. In T. C. Owen (Ed.), *Southeast Asian mental health: Treatment, prevention, services, training, and research* (pp. 41-63). Washington, DC: National Institute of Mental Health.

Ishisaka, H. A., & Takagi, C. Y. (1982). Social work with Asian- and Pacific-Americans. In J. W. Green (Ed.), *Cultural awareness in the human services* (pp. 122-156). Englewood Cliffs, NJ: Prentice Hall.

Ito, M. (1998). The status of the individual in Japanese religions: Implications for Japan's collectivistic social values. *Social Compass, 45*, 619-633.

Jacobs, N. R., Siegal, M. A., & Quiram, J. (1996). *Profile of the nation: An American portrait.* Wylie, TX: Information Plus.

Jimenez, M. A., & Jimenez, D. R. (1992). Latinos and HIV disease: Issues, practice and policy implications. *Social Work in Health Care, 17*(2), 41-51.

Jimenez-Vazquez, R. (1990). Social work research on mental health in the Cuban community in the United States: The state of the art. In I. Dieppa & D. F. Arguello (Eds.), *Proceedings of the conference "Social Work Research in Mental Health and the Hispanic Community"* (pp. 17-37). Rockville, MD: National Institute of Mental Health.

Jimenez-Vazquez, R. (1995). Hispanics: Cubans. In R. L. Edwards (Ed.), *Encyclopedia of social work* (19th ed., pp. 1223-1232). Washington, DC: NASW Press.

Jones, L., Agbayani-Siewert, P., & Friaz, G. (1998). Effects of economic stress on high school students' views of work and future. *Social Work in Education, 20*, 11-24.

Jordan, W. D. (1968). *White over black.* Chapel Hill: University of North Carolina Press.

Jung, M. (1984). Structural family therapy: Its applications to Chinese families. *Family Process, 23*, 365-374.

Kamya, H. A. (1997). African immigrants in the United States: The challenge for research and practice. *Social Work, 42*, 154-166.

Kang, D. S., Kahler, L. R., & Tesar, C. M. (1998). Cultural aspects of caring for refugees. *American Family Physician, 57*, 1245-1252.

Kanuha, V. (1990). Compounding the triple jeopardy: Battering in lesbian of color relationships. *Women and Therapy, 9*, 169-184.

Kasee, C. R. (1995). Identity, recovery and religious imperialism: Native American women and the New Age. In J. Ochshorn & E. Cole (Eds.), *Women's spirituality, women's lives* (pp. 83-93). Binghamton, NY: Haworth.

Kawagley, O. (1997). Yupait. In R. J. Vecoli (Ed.), *Gale encyclopedia of multicultural America* (Vol. 2, pp. 1420-1426). Boston: Thomson.

Kemp, C. (1993). Health services for refugees in countries of second asylum. *International Nursing Review, 40*, 21-24.

Kim, D. S. (1977). How they fared in American homes: A follow-up study of adopted Korean children. *Children Today, 6*, 2-6, 31.

Kim, S. C. (1985). Family therapy for Asian Americans: A strategic-structural framework. *Psychotherapy, 22*, 342-348.

King, A. E. O. (1997). Understanding violence among young African American males: An Afrocentric perspective. *Journal of Black Studies, 28*(1), 79-96.

King, R. C., & DaCosta, K. M. (1996). Changing face, changing race: The remaking of race in the Japanese American and African American communities. In M. P. P. Root (Ed.), *The multiracial experience: Racial borders as the new frontier* (pp. 227-244). Thousand Oaks, CA: Sage.

Kirst-Ashman, K. K., & Hull, G. H., Jr. (1993). *Understanding generalist practice.* Chicago: Nelson-Hall.

Kitano, H. H. L. (1990). Asian Americans. In A. Minahan (Ed.), *Encyclopedia of social work* (18th ed., pp. 156-169). Silver Spring, MD: NASW Press.

Kitano, H. L., & Daniels, R. (1988). *Asian Americans: Emerging minorities.* Englewood Cliffs, NJ: Prentice Hall.

Klein, P. (1968). *From philanthropy to social welfare: An American cultural perspective.* San Francisco: Jossey-Bass.

Klor de Alva, J. J. (1988). Telling Hispanics apart: Latino sociocultural diversity. In E. Acosta-Belen & B. R. Sjostrom (Eds.), *The Hispanic experience in the United States: Contemporary issues and perspectives* (pp. 107-136). Westport, CT: Praeger.

Kluckhohn, F. (1961). *Variations in value orientations.* Evanston, IL: Row, Peterson.

Kook, R. (1998). The shifting status of African Americans in the American collective identity. *Journal of Black Studies, 29*(2), 154-179.

Kropf, N. P., & Isaac, A. R. (1992). Cultural diversity and social work practice: An overview. In D. F. Harrison, J. S. Wodarski, & B. A. Thyer (Eds.), *Cultural diversity and social work practice* (pp. 3-12). Springfield, IL: Charles C Thomas.

Kulig, J. C. (1994). "Those with unheard voices": The plight of a Cambodian refugee woman. *Journal of Community Health Nursing, 11*, 99-107.

Kumagai, F. (1995). Families in Japan: Beliefs and realities. *Journal of Comparative Family Studies, 26*, 135-163.

Ladner, J. (1984). Providing a healthy environment for interracial children. *Interracial Books for Children Bulletin, 15*, 7-8.

Land, H., & Hudson, S. (1997). Methodological considerations in surveying Latina AIDS caregivers: Issues in sampling and measurement. *Social Work Research, 21*, 233-246.

Landon, J. W. (1986). *The development of social welfare*. New York: Human Sciences Press.

Larson, T. E. (1988). Employment and unemployment of young black males. In J. T. Gibbs, A. F. Brunswick, M. E. Connor, R. Dembo, T. E. Larson, R. J. Reed, & B. Solomon (Eds.), *Young, black and male in America*. Dover, MA: Auburn House.

Leashore, B. R. (1995). African Americans overview. In R. L. Edwards (Ed.), *Encyclopedia of social work* (19th ed., pp. 101-114). Washington, DC: NASW Press.

Lee, I. C. (1992). The Chinese-American's community organizing strategies and tactics. In F. G. Rivera & J. L. Erlich (Eds.), *Community organizing in a diverse society* (pp. 133-158). Boston: Allyn & Bacon.

Leiby, J. (1971). Social welfare: History of basic ideas. In R. Morris (Ed.), *Encyclopedia of social work* (16th ed., pp. 1461-1476). New York: NASW Press.

Leiby, J. (1984). Social welfare: History of basic ideas. In J. B. Turner (Ed.), *Encyclopedia of social work* (17th ed., pp. 1512-1529). New York: NASW Press.

Leonard, K. I. (1992). *Making ethnic choices: California's Punjabi Mexican Americans*. Philadelphia: Temple University Press.

Lewis, R. G. (1995). American Indians. In R. L. Edwards (Ed.), *Encyclopedia of social work* (19th ed., pp. 216-225). Washington, DC: NASW Press.

Lex, B. W. (1987). Review of alcohol programs in ethnic community groups. *Journal of Consulting and Clinical Psychology, 55*, 293-300.

Lightfoot-Klein, H., & Shaw, E. (1990). Special needs of ritually circumcised women patients. *JOGNN, 20*(2), 102-107.

Lincoln, C. E., & Mamiya, L. H. (1990). *The black church in the African American experience*. Durham, NC: Duke University Press.

Lindsey, L. L. (1990). *Gender roles: A sociological perspective*. Englewood Cliffs, NJ: Prentice Hall.

Lipson, J. G., Omidian, P. A., & Paul, S. M. (1995). Afgan health education project: A community survey. *Public Health Nursing, 12*(3), 143-150.

Lister, L. (1987). Curriculum building in social work education: The example of ethnocultural content. *Journal of Social Work Education, 23*, 31-39.

Littlefield, D. F., Jr. (1979). *Africans and Creeks: From the colonial period to the civil war*. Westport, CT: Greenwood.

Locke, D. C. (1998). *Increasing multicultural understanding: A comprehensive model* (2nd ed.). Thousand Oaks, CA: Sage.

Logan, S. M., Freeman, E. M., & McRoy, R. G. (1990). *Social work with black families: A cultural specific perspective*. White Plains, NY: Longman.

Longres, J. F. (1982). Minority groups: An inter-group perspective. *Social Work, 26*, 7-14.

Longres, J. F. (1995a). Hispanic overview. In R. L. Edwards (Ed.), *Encyclopedia of social work* (19th ed., pp. 1214-1222). Washington, DC: NASW Press.

Longres, J. F. (1995b). Richmond, Mary Ellen (1861-1928). In R. L. Edwards (Ed.), *Encyclopedia of social work* (19th ed., p. 2605). Washington, DC: NASW Press.

Longres, J. F., & Seltzer, G. B. (1994). *Racism: Its implications for the education of minority social work students*. Binghamton, NY: Haworth.

Lord, N. (1996). Native tongues. *Sierra, 81*(6), 46-52.

Lord, S., & Kennedy, E. (1992). Intervening in urban poverty at the grassroots level: A school-community partnership in the United States. *International Social Work, 35*, 255-266.

Lott, J. T. (1997). Demographic changes transforming the Filipino American community. In M. P. P. Root (Ed.), *Filipino Americans: Transformation and identity* (pp. 11-20). Thousand Oaks, CA: Sage.

Loving v. Virginia, 388 U.S. (1968).

Lum, D. (1986). *Social work practice and people of color: A process-stage approach*. Monterey, CA: Brooks/Cole.

Lum, D. (1992). *Social work practice and people of color: A process-stage approach* (2nd ed.). Belmont, CA: Brooks/Cole.

Lum, D. (1996). *Social work practice and people of color: A process-stage approach* (3rd ed.). Pacific Grove, CA: Brooks/Cole.

Lum, D. (1999). *Culturally competent practice: A framework for growth and action*. Pacific Grove, CA: Brooks/Cole.

Luu, V. (1989). The hardship of escape for Vietnamese women. In Asian Woman United of California (Ed.), *Making waves: An anthology by and about Asian American women* (pp. 60-72). Boston: Beacon.

Lyman, S. M. (1977). *The Asians in North America*. Santa Barbara, CA: ABC-CLIO.

Mahmoud, V. (1996). African American Muslim families. In M. McGoldric, J. Giordano, & J. K. Pearce (Eds.), *Ethnicity and family therapy* (2nd ed., pp. 112-128). New York: Guilford.

Mangiafico, L. (1988). *Contemporary American immigrants: Patterns of Filipino, Korean, and Chinese settlement in the United States*. Westport, CT: Praeger.

Marcos, L. R. (1994). The psychiatric examination of Hispanics: Across the language barrier. In R. G. Malgady & O. Rodriquez (Eds.), *The theoretical and conceptual issues in Hispanic mental health* (pp. 144-153). Malabar, FL: Krieger.

Marin, G., & Marin, B. V. (1991). *Research with Hispanic populations*. Newbury Park, CA: Sage.

Martinez, C. (1988). Mexican-Americans. In L. Comas-Diaz & E. E. H. Griffith (Eds.), *Clinical guidelines in cross-cultural mental health* (pp. 182-203). New York: John Wiley.

Martinez, D. (1996). First people, firsthand knowledge. *Sierra, 81*(6), 50-54.

Mary, N. L., & Morris, T. (1994). The future and social work: A global perspective. *Journal of Multicultural Social Work, 3*(4), 89-101.

Mass, A. I. (1992). Interracial Japanese Americans: The best of both worlds or the end of the Japanese American community? In M. P. P. Root (Ed.), *Racially mixed people in America* (pp. 265-279). Newbury Park, CA: Sage.

Matsuoka, J. K., Breaux, C., & Ryujin, D. H. (1997). National utilization of mental health services by Asian Americans/Pacific Islanders. *Journal of Community Psychology, 25*, 141-145.

Mattson, S. (1993). Mental health of Southeast Asian refugee women: An overview. *Health Care for Women International, 14*, 155-165.

Matute-Bianchi, M. E. (1986). Ethnic identities and patterns of school success and future among Mexican-descent and Japanese American students in a California high school: An ethnographic analysis. *American Journal of Education, 95*, 233-255.

Mayadas, N., & Elliot, D. (1989). Traditions and innovation in the ethics of social group work. *Proceedings of the 11th Annual Symposium of the Association for the Advancement of Social Work With Groups, 2*, 1274-1289.

Mayeno, L., & Hirota, S. M. (1994). Access to health care. In N. W. S. Zane, D. T. Takeuchi, & K. N. J. Young (Eds.), *Confronting critical health issues of Asian and Pacific Islander Americans* (pp. 347-376). Thousand Oaks, CA: Sage.

Mazumdar, S. (1984). Punjabi agricultural workers in California, 1905-1945. In L. Cheng & E. Bonacich (Eds.), *Labor immigration under capitalism: Asian workers in the United States before World War II* (pp. 549-578). Berkeley: University of California Press.

McAdoo, H. P. (1987). Blacks. In A. Minahan (Ed.), *Encyclopedia of social work* (18th ed., Vol. 1, pp. 194-204). Silver Spring, MD: NASW Press.

McCarthy, C. (1993). After the canon: Knowledge and ideological representation in the multicultural discourse on curriculum reform. In C. McCarthy & W. Crichlow (Eds.), *Race, identity, and representation in education* (pp. 289-305). New York: Routledge.

McCollum, E., & Trepper, T. (1995). "Little by little, pulling me through"—Women's perceptions of successful drug treatment: A qualitative inquiry. *Journal of Family Psychotherapy, 6*(1), 63-82.

McGill, D. W. (1992). The cultural story in multicultural family therapy. *Families in Society, 73*, 339-349.

McInnis, K. (1991). Ethnic-sensitive work with Hmong refugee children. *Child Welfare, 70*, 571-580.

McIntosh, P. (1998). White privilege: Unpacking the invisible knapsack. In P. S. Rothenberg (Ed.), *Race, class, and gender in the United States* (pp. 165-169). New York: St. Martin's.

McMahon, M. O. (1994). *Advanced generalist practice with an international perspective.* Englewood Cliffs, NJ: Prentice Hall.

McPhatter, A. R. (1991). Assessment revisited: A comprehensive approach to understanding family dynamics. *Families in Society, 8*(1), 11-22.

McRae, M. B., Carey, P. M., & Anderson-Scott, R. (1998). Black churches as therapeutic systems: A group process perspective. *Health Education & Behavior, 25*, 778-790.

McRoy, R. G., & Freeman, E. (1986). Racial identity issues among mixed-race children. *Social Work in Education, 8*, 164-174.

McWilliams, C. (Ed.). (1990). *North from Mexico.* Westport, CT: Greenwood.

Meier, M. S. (1990). Politics, education and culture. In C. McWilliams (Ed.), *North from Mexico* (pp. 285-308). Westport, CT: Greenwood.

Meier, M. S., & Rivera, F. (1972). *The Chicanos: A history of Mexican Americans.* New York: Hill & Wang.

Melendy, H. B. (1977). *Asians in America: Filipinos, Koreans, and East Indians.* Boston: Twayne.

Melwani, L. (1994, January 31). Dark side of the moon. *India Today,* pp. 60C-60F.

Mencke, J. G. (1979). *Mulattoes and race mixture: American attitudes and images, 1865-1918.* Ann Arbor, MI: UMI Research Press.

Mendoza, R. H. (1989). An empirical scale to measure type and degree of acculturation in Mexican-American adolescents and adults. *Journal of Cross-Cultural Psychology, 20*, 372-385.

Merida, K. (1999, December/January). Decriminalizing "Driving While Black." *Emerge, 10*(3), 26.

Miah, M. R., & Kahler, D. R. (1997). Asian-American elderly: A review of the quality of life and social service needs. *Journal of Sociology and Social Welfare, 24*(1), 79-89.

Mihesuah, D. A. (1996). Commonality of differences: American Indian women and history. *American Indian Quarterly, 20*(1), 15-28.

Mirande, A. (1988). Que gacho es ser macho: It's a drag to be a macho man. *Aztlan, 17*, 63-89.

Mohan, B. (1997). Notes toward a theory of secondary integration: Aporias of a lost paradigm. *Journal of Sociology and Social Welfare, 24*(1), 113-127.

Mohr, R. D. (1998). Anti-gay stereotypes. In P. S. Rothenberg (Ed.), *Race, class and gender in the United States* (pp. 452-457). New York: St. Martin's.

Montiel, M., & Ortego y Gasca, F. (1998). Chicanos, communities and change. In F. G. Rivera & J. L. Erlich (Eds.), *Community organizing in a diverse society* (3rd ed., pp. 43-61). Needham Heights, MA: Allyn & Bacon.

Montserrat, J. (1994). The year 2000. In K. Wagenheim & O. J. de Wagenheim (Eds.), *The Puerto Ricans: A documentary history* (pp. 315-322). Princeton, NJ: Markus Wiener.

Moore, S. E. (1998). [Review of E. O. Hutchinson's book *The assassination of the Black male image*]. *Black Issues in Higher Education, 15*(1), 41.

Morales, J., & Reyes, M. (1998). Cultural and political realities for community social work practice with Puerto Ricans in the United States. In F. G. Rivera & J. L. Erlich (Eds.), *Community organizing in a diverse society* (pp. 75-96). Boston: Allyn & Bacon.

Morokvasic, M. (1984). Birds of passage are also women. *International Migration Review, 18*, 886-907.

Motoyoshi, M. M. (1990). The experience of mixed-race people: Some thoughts and theories. *Journal of Ethnic Studies, 18*, 77-94.

Mukoyama, T. H. J. (1998). *Effects of heritage combination on ethnic identity, self-esteem, and adjustment among American biethnic adults.* Unpublished doctoral dissertation, California School of Professional Psychology, Los Angeles.

Munoz, A. N. (1971). *The Filipinos in America.* Los Angeles: Mountainview.

Murase, K. (1995). Asian American: Japanese. In R. L. Edwards (Ed.), *Encyclopedia of social work* (19th ed., pp. 241-248). Washington, DC: NASW Press.

Murrell, A. J., & Jones, R. (1996). Assessing affirmative action: Past, present, and future. *Journal of Social Issues, 52*(4), 77-92.

Nah, K. H. (1993). Perceived problems and service delivery for Korean immigrants. *Social Work, 38*, 289-296.

Nakanishi, M., & Rittner, B. (1992). The inclusionary cultural model. *Journal of Social Work Education, 28*, 27-35.

Nakashima, C. L. (1992). An invisible monster: The creation and denial of mixed-race people in America. In M. P. P. Root (Ed.), *Racially mixed people in America* (pp. 162-178). Newbury Park: Sage.

Nakashima, C. L. (1996). Voices from the movement: Approaches to multiraciality. In M. P. P. Root (Ed.), *The multiracial experience: Racial borders as the new frontier* (pp. 79-97). Thousand Oaks, CA: Sage.

Nash, G. B. (1974). *Red, white and black: The peoples of early America.* Englewood Cliffs, NJ: Prentice Hall.

Nash, P. T. (1992). Multicultural identity. In M. P. P. Root (Ed.), *Racially mixed people in America* (pp. 24-36). Newbury Park, CA: Sage.

National Association of Social Workers. (1996). *Code of ethics.* Washington, DC: Author.

Neff, J. A., & Hoppe, S. K. (1993). Race/ethnicity, acculturation, and psychological distress: Fatalism and religiosity as cultural resources. *Journal of Community Psychology, 21*, 3-20.

Neighbors, H. W., Musick, M. A., & Wiliams, D. R. (1998). The African American minister as a source of help for serious personal crisis: Bridge or barrier to mental health care? *Health Education & Behavior, 25*, 759-778.

Nelson, C., & Tienda, M. (1997). The structuring of Hispanic ethnicity: Historical and contemporary perspectives. In M. Romero, P. Hondagneu-Sotelo, & V. Ortiz (Eds.), *Challenging fronteras: Structuring Latina and Latino lives in the U.S.* (pp. 7-29). New York: Routledge.

Newman, B. S. (1989). Including curriculum content on lesbian and gay issues. *Journal of Social Work Education, 25*, 202-211.

Ngwainmbi, E. K. (1999). Exporting communication technology to developing countries: Sociocultural, economic and educational factors. Lanham, MD: University Press of America.

Nichols-Casebolt, A., Krysik, J., & Hamilton, B. (1994). Coverage of women's issues in social work journals: Are we building an adequate knowledge base? *Journal of Social Work Education, 30*, 348-362.

Nolte, W. W., & Wilcox, D. L. (1984). *Effective publicity: How to reach people.* New York: John Wiley.

Norman, J., & Wheeler, B. (1996). Gender-sensitive social work practice: A model for education. *Journal of Social Work Education, 32*, 203-213.

Norris, A. E., Ford, K., & Bova, C. A. (1996). Psychometrics of a brief acculturation scale for Hispanics in a probability sample of urban Hispanic adolescents and young adults. *Hispanic Journal of Behavioral Sciences, 18*, 29-38.

Norton, D. (1978). *The dual perspective: Inclusion of ethnic minority content in social work curriculum.* New York: Council on Social Work Education.

Nwadiora, E., & McAdoo, H. (1996). Acculturative stress among Amerasian refugees: Gender and racial differences. *Adolescence, 31*, 477-487.

O'Hare, W., & Felt, J. C. (1991). *Asian Americans: America's fastest-growing minority group*. Washington, DC: Population Reference Bureau.

O'Hare, W. P. (1992). America's minorities—The demographics of diversity. *Population Bulletin, 47*(4), S2(44).

Okamura, J. Y., & Agbayani, A. R. (1997). Parmantsan: Filipino American higher education. In M. P. P. Root (Ed.), *Filipino Americans: Transformation and identity* (pp. 183-197). Thousand Oaks, CA: Sage.

Olson, D. H. (1986). Circumplex model VII: Validation studies and FACES. *Family Process, 25*, 337-351.

Olson, D. H., Portner, J., & Lavee, Y. (1985). *FACES III*. St. Paul: Family Social Science, University of Minnesota.

Ong, P. (1984). Chinatown unemployment and the ethnic labor market. *Amerasia Journal, 11*, 35-54.

Ong, P., & Hee, S. (1994). Economic diversity. In P. Ong (Ed.), *The state of Asian Pacific America: Economic diversity, issues, and policies* (pp. 31-56). Los Angeles: LEAP Asian Pacific American Public Policy Institute and University of California at Los Angeles Asian American Studies Center.

Ortiz, V. (1997). Demographic overview of Latinos. In M. Romero, P. Hondagneu-Sotelo, & V. Ortiz (Eds.), *Challenging fronteras: Structuring Latina and Latino lives in the U.S.* (pp. xvi-xix). New York: Routledge.

Padilla, A. M., Alvarez, M., & Lindholm, K. J. (1986). Generational status and personality factors as predictors of stress in students. *Hispanic Journal of Behavioral Sciences, 8*, 257-288.

Padilla, A. M., Carlos, M., & Keefe, S. (1976). Mental health service utilization by Mexican Americans. In M. R. Miranda (Ed.), *Psychotherapy with the Spanish-speaking: Issues in research and service delivery*. Los Angeles: Spanish Speaking Mental Health Research Center, University of California.

Padilla, A. M., Lindholm, K. J., Chen, A., Duran, R., Hakuta, K., Lambert, W., & Tucker, G. R. (1991). The English-only movement: Myths, reality, and implications for psychology. *American Psychologist, 46*, 120-130.

Padilla, A. M., & Ruiz, R. A. (1976). *Latino mental health: A review of literature*. Rockville, MD: U.S. Department of Health, Education and Welfare.

Palacios, M., & Franco, J. N. (1986). Counseling Mexican American women. *Journal of Multicultural Counseling and Development, 14*, 124-131.

Paniagua, F. A. (1994). *Assessing and treating culturally diverse clients: A practical guide*. Thousand Oaks, CA: Sage.

Pantoja, A., & Perry, W. (1998). Community development and restoration: A perspective and case study. In F. G. Rivera & J. L. Erlich (Eds.), *Community organizing in a diverse society* (3rd ed., pp. 220-243). Needham Heights, MA: Allyn & Bacon.

Parsons, R. D. (1995). *The skills of helping*. Needham Heights, MA: Allyn and Bacon.

Parsons, S., Simmons, W., Shinhoster, F., & Kilburn, J. (1999). A test of the grapevine: An empirical examination of conspiracy theories among African Americans. *Sociological Spectrum, 19*(2), 201-223.

Payne, R. J. (1998). *Getting beyond race: The changing American culture*. Boulder, CO: Westview.

Pederson, P. B. (1988). *A handbook for developing multicultural awareness*. Alexandria, VA: American Counseling Association.

Peplau, L. A., Cochran, S. D., & Mays, V. M. (1997). A national survey of the intimate relationships of African American lesbians and gay men: A look at commitment, satisfaction, sexual behavior, and HIV disease. In B. Greene (Ed.), *Ethnic and cultural diversity among lesbians and gay men* (pp. 11-38). Thousand Oaks, CA: Sage.

Perdue, T. (1979). *Slavery and the evolution of Cherokee society, 1540-1866*. Knoxville: University of Tennessee Press.

Pido, A. J. A. (1997). Macro/micro dimension of immigration to the United States. In M. P. P. Root (Ed.), *Filipino Americans: Transformation and identity* (pp. 21-38). Thousand Oaks, CA: Sage.

Pinderhughes, E. (1979). Teaching empathy in cross-cultural social work. *Social Work, 24*, 312-316.

Plous, S. (1996). Ten myths about affirmative action. *Journal of Social Issues, 52*(4), 25-31.

Ponchillia, S. V. (1993). The effect of cultural beliefs on the treatment of Native peoples with diabetes and visual impairment. *Journal of Visual Impairment & Blindness, 87*, 333-336.

Popple, P. R. (1983). Contexts of practice. In A. Rosenblatt & D. Waldfogel (Eds.), *Handbook of clinical social work* (pp. 70-96). San Francisco: Jossey-Bass.

Popple, P. R. (1995). Social work profession: History. In R. L. Edwards (Ed.), *Encyclopedia of social work* (19th ed., pp. 2282-2292). Washington, DC: NASW Press.

Porterfield, E. (1978). *Black and white mixed marriages*. Chicago: Nelson-Hall.

Portes, A. (1982). Illegal immigration and the international systems: Lessons from recent legal immigrants to the United States. In N. R. Yetman (Ed.), *Majority and minority* (pp. 509-520). Boston: Allyn & Bacon.

Portes, A., & Truelove, C. (1987). Making sense of diversity: Recent research on Hispanic minorities in the United States. *Annual Review of Sociology, 13*, 359-385.

Potocky, M. (1996). Refugee children: How are they faring economically as adults? *Social Work, 41*, 364-373.

Poussaint, A. F. (1984). Study of interracial children presents positive picture. *Interracial Books for Children Bulletin, 15*, 9-10.

Poyo, G. E. (1984). Cuban communities in the United States: Toward an overview of the 19th century experience. In M. Uriarte-Gaston & J. C. Martinez (Eds.), *Cubans in the United States* (pp. 44-64). Boston: Center for the Study of the Cuban Community.

Publisher's note. (1994). In S. Auerbach (Ed.), *Encyclopedia of multiculturalism* (pp. v-vi). New York: Marshall Cavendish.

Purdy, J. K., & Arguello, D. (1992). Hispanic familism in caretaking of older adults: Is it functional? *Journal of Gerontological Social Work, 19*(2), 29-43.

Queralt, M. (1984). Understanding Cuban immigrants: A cultural perspective. *Social Work, 29*, 115-121.

Ramirez, D. A. (1996). Multiracial identity in a color-conscious world. In M. P. P. Root (Ed.), *The multiracial experience: Racial borders as the new frontier* (pp. 49-62). Thousand Oaks, CA: Sage.

Ramirez, M. (1984). Assessing and understanding biculturalism-multiculturalism in Mexican-American adults. In J. L. Martinez & R. H. Mendoza (Eds.), *Chicano psychology* (pp. 77-94). Orlando, FL: Academic Press.

Ramirez, M. (1999). *Multicultural psychotherapy: An approach to individual and cultural differences*. Boston: Allyn and Bacon.

Ramirez, R. (1985). Hispanic spirituality. *Social Thought, 11*(3), 6-13.

Randall, D. (1971). *The black poets*. New York: Bantam.

Rarick, C. A. (1994). The philosophical impact of Shintoism, Buddhism, and Confucianism on Japanese management practices. *International Journal of Value-Based Management, 7*, 219-226.

Raveis, V. H., & Siegel, K. (1998). Factors associated with HIV-infected women's delay in seeking medical care. *AIDS Care, 10*, 549-562.

Rees, S. (1991). *Achieving power: Practice and policy in social welfare*. North Sydney, Australia: Allyn & Bacon.

Reese, D. J., & Ahern, R. E. (1999). Hospice access and use by African Americans: Addressing cultural and institutional barriers through participatory action research. *Social Work, 44*, 549-560.

Reid, M. (1993). *Native Americans: Leaders in the 21st century: A comprehensive statewide plan for Indian Education*. Tulsa, OK: State Department of Education Printing Services.

Reid, W. C. (1978). *The task-centered system*. New York: Columbia University Press.

Reid, W. C. (1985). *Family problem solving*. New York: Columbia University Press.

Repack, T. A. (1997). New roles in a new landscape. In M. Romero, P. Hondagneu-Sotelo, & V. Ortiz (Eds.), *Challenging fronteras: Structuring Latina and Latino lives in the U.S.* (pp. 247-263). New York: Routledge.

Reuter, E. B. (1918). *The mulatto in the United States*. Boston: Richard G. Badger, The Gorham Press.

Rhee, S. (1997). Domestic violence in the Korean immigrant family. *Journal of Sociology and Social Welfare, 24*(1), 63-77.

Richmond, M. E. (1897). The need of a training school in applied philanthropy. In *Proceedings of the National Conference of Charities and Correction* (pp. 181-189). Boston: George H. Ellis.

Richmond, M. E. (1917). *Social diagnosis.* New York: Russell Sage Foundation.

Rivera, F. G., & Erlich, J. L. (1992). Prospectives and challenges. In F. G. Rivera & J. L. Erlich (Eds.), *Community organizing in a diverse society* (pp. 1-26). Boston: Allyn & Bacon.

Rivera, F. G., & Erlich, J. L. (Eds.). (1995). *Community organizing in a diverse society* (2nd ed.). Boston: Allyn & Bacon.

Rivera, F. G., & Erlich, J. L. (1998). A time of fear, a time of hope. In F. G. Rivera & J. L. Erlich (Eds.), *Community organizing in a diverse society* (3rd ed., pp. 1-24). Needham Heights, MA: Allyn & Bacon.

Rodriquez, C. E. (1989). *Puerto Ricans born in the U.S.A.* Boston: Unwin Hyman.

Rodriguez, C. E. (1996). Puerto Ricans: Between black and white. In C. E. Rodriguez & V. S. Korrol (Eds.), *Historical perspectives on Puerto Rican survival in the United States* (pp. 25-35). Princeton, NJ: Markus Wiener.

Romero, J. T. (1983). The therapist as a social change agent. In G. Gibson (Ed.), *Our kingdom stands on brittle glass* (pp. 86-95). Silver Spring, MD: NASW Press.

Romero, M. (1997). Introduction. In M. Romero, P. Hondagneu-Sotelo, & V. Ortiz (Eds.), *Challenging fronteras: Structuring Latina and Latino lives in the U.S.* (pp. xiii-xix). New York: Routledge.

Root, M. P. P. (1985). Guidelines for facilitating therapy with Asian-American clients. *Psychotherapy, 22*, 349-356.

Root, M. P. P. (1990). Resolving "other" status: Identity development of biracial individuals. In L. Brown & M. P. P. Root (Eds.), *Complexity and diversity in feminist theory and therapy* (pp. 185-205). New York: Haworth.

Root, M. P. P. (Ed.). (1992). *Racially mixed people in America.* Newbury Park, CA: Sage.

Root, M. P. P. (1994). Mixed-race women. In L. Comas-Diaz & B. Greene (Eds.), *Women of color: Integrating ethnic and gender identities in psychotherapy* (pp. 455-478). New York: Guilford.

Root, M. P. P. (1996). Introduction. In M. P. P. Root (Ed.), *The multiracial experience: Racial borders as the new frontier* (pp. xiii-xxviii). Thousand Oaks, CA: Sage.

Root, M. P. P. (1997). Mixed-race women. In N. Zack (Ed.), *Race/sex: Their sameness, difference, and interplay* (pp. 157-172). New York: Routledge.

Rosaldo, R., & Flores, W. V. (1997). Identity, conflict, and evolving Latino communities: Cultural citizenship in San Jose, California. In W. V. Flores & R. Benmayor (Eds.), *Latino cultural citizenship: Claiming identity, space, and rights* (pp. 57-96). Boston: Beacon.

Rose, I. G. (1984). An Hispanic perspective on biracial, bicultural families. *Interracial Books for Children Bulletin, 15*, 12.

Ross-Sheriff, F. (1995). African Americans: Immigrants. In R. L. Edwards (Ed.), *Encyclopedia of social work* (19th ed., pp. 130-136). Washington, DC: NASW Press.

Rothman, J. (1995). Approaches to community interventions. In J. Rothman, J. L. Erlich, & J. E. Tropman (Eds.), *Strategies of community intervention: Macro practice* (5th ed., pp. 26-64). Itasca, IL: F. E. Peacock.

Rounds, K. A., Weil, M., & Bishop, K. K. (1994). Practice with culturally diverse families of young children with disabilities. *Families in Society, 75*, 3-15.

Ruffins, P. (1998). The Tuskegee experiment's long shadow. *Black Issues in Higher Education, 15*(18), 26-32.

Rumbaut, R. G., Chavez, L. R., Moser, R. J., Pickwell, S. M., & Wishnik, S. M. (1988). The politics of migrant health care: A comparative study of Mexican immigrants and Indochinese refugees. *Research in the Sociology of Health Care, 7*, 143-202.

Ryan, A. S. (1985). Cultural factors in casework with Chinese-Americans. *Social Casework, 66*, 333-340.

Safa, H. I. (1988). Migration identity: A comparison of Puerto Rican and Cuban migrants in the United States. In E. Acosta-Belen & B. R. Sjostrom (Eds.), *The Hispanic experience in the United States: Contemporary issues and perspectives* (pp. 137-150). Westport, CT: Praeger.

Saleebey, D. (1992). Introduction: Power in the people. In D. Saleebey (Ed.), *The strength perspective in social work practice* (pp. 3-17). New York: Longman.

Sanchez, G. I. (1977). Pachucos in the making. In R. Rosaldo, R. Calvert, & G. Seligman (Eds.), *Chicano: The evolution of a people* (p. 210). Huntington, NY: Robert E. Krieger.

Sanchez Korrol, V. E. (1993). *From colonia to community: The history of Puerto Ricans in New York City, 1917-1948.* Westport, CT: Greenwood.

Sandoval, C. (1990). Feminism and racism: A report on the 1981 National Women's Studies Association Conference. In G. Anzáldua (Ed.), *Making face, making soul (haciendo caras): Creative and critical perspectives by women of color* (pp. 55-71). San Francisco: Aunt Lute Foundation.

Sarkodie-Mensah, K. (1995). Nigerian Americans. In R. J. Vecoli, J. Galens, A. Sheets, & R. V. Young (Eds.), *Gale encyclopedia of multicultural America* (Vol. 2, pp. 987-1003). (Irish Americans-Yupiat Index). Detroit: International Thomas.

Schafer, J. R., & McIlwaine, B. D. (1992). Investigating child sexual abuse in the American Indian Community. *American Indian Quarterly, 16*(2), 157-168.

Schinke, S. (1996). Behavior approaches to illness prevention for Native Americans. In P. M. Kato & T. Mann (Eds.), *Handbook of diversity issues in health psychology* (pp. 367-388). New York: Plenum.

Sears, J. (1991). *Growing up gay in the south: Race, gender, and journeys of the spirit.* London: Hawthorn Press.

Shackford, K. (1984). Interracial children: Growing up healthy in an unhealthy society. *Interracial Books for Children Bulletin, 15,* 4-6.

Shimon, L. C. (1976). I know something good about you. In H. Felleman (Ed.), *The best loved poems of the American people* (p. 116). New York: Doubleday.

Shon, S., & Ja, D. (1982). Asian families. In M. McGoldrick, J. K. Pearce, & J. Giordano (Eds.), *Ethnicity and family therapy* (pp. 208-228). New York: Guilford.

Shulman, L. (1999). *The skills of helping individuals, families, groups, and communities* (4th ed.). Itasca, IL: F. E. Peacock.

Siefert, K. (1983). An exemplar of primary prevention in social work: The Sheppard-Towner Act of 1921. *Social Work in Health Care, 9*(1), 87-103.

Simon, B. L. (1994). *The empowerment tradition in American social work: A history.* New York: Columbia University Press.

Simon, H. (1976). *Administrative behavior* (3rd ed.). New York: Free Press.

Singleton-Bowie, S. M. (1995). The effects of mental health practitioners' racial sensitivity on African Americans' perceptions of service. *Social Work Research, 19,* 238-244.

Sinha, L. (1996). A patchwork of ethnicity. *Latino Studies Journal, 7,* 80-89.

Siporin, M. (1975). *Introduction to social work practice.* New York: Macmillan.

Siporin, M. (1989). The social work ethic. *Social Thought, 15*(3/4), 42-52.

Skabelund, G. P. (1995). *Culturgrams: The nations around us: Vol. 1. The Americas and Europe.* Garrett Park, MD: Garrett Park Press.

Slucher, M. P., Mayer, C. J., & Dunkle, R. (1996). Gays and lesbians older and wiser (GLOW): A support group for older gay people. *Gerontologist, 36*(1), 118-123.

Smart, J. F., & Smart, D. W. (1995). Acculturation stress: The experience of the Hispanic immigrant. *Counseling Psychology, 23,* 25-42.

Smith, E. J. (1981). Cultural and historical perspectives in counseling blacks. In D. W. Sue (Ed.), *Counseling the culturally different: Theory and practice* (pp. 141-185). New York: John Wiley.

Smith, J. C., & Johns, R. L. (1995). *Statistical record of Black America* (3rd ed.). Detroit: Gale Research.

Smith, R. F. (1995). Settlements and neighborhood centers. In R. L. Edwards (Ed.), *Encyclopedia of social work* (19th ed., pp. 2129-2135). Washington, DC: NASW Press.

Smith, W. C. (1985). *The church in the life of the Black family.* Valley Forge, PA: Judson Press.

Smither, R., & Rodriguez-Geigling, M. (1982). Personality, demographics, and acculturation of Vietnamese and Nicaraguan refugees to the United States. *International Journal of Psychology, 17,* 19-25.

Snipp, C. M. (1997). Some observations about racial boundaries and the experiences of American Indians. *Ethnic and Racial Studies, 20,* 667-689.

Sodowsky, G. R., Kuo-Jackson, P. Y., & Loya, G. J. (1997). Outcome of training in the philosophy of assessment: Multicultural counseling competencies. In D. B. Pope-Davis & H. L. K. Coleman (Eds.), *Multicultural counseling competencies: Assessment, education and training, and supervision* (pp. 3-42). Thousand Oaks, CA: Sage.

Solomon, B. (1976). *Black empowerment: Social work in oppressed communities.* New York: Columbia University Press.

Specht, H., & Courtney, M. E. (1994). *Unfaithful angels: How social work has abandoned its mission.* New York: Free Press.

Spencer, J. M. (1997). *The new colored people: The mixed-raced movement in America.* New York: New York University Press.

Spickard, P. R. (1989). *Mixed blood: Intermarriage and ethnic identity in twentieth-century America.* Madison: University of Wisconsin Press.

Spickard, P. R. (1997). What must I be? Asian Americans and the question of multiethnic identity. *Amerasia Journal, 23,* 43-60.

Spickard, P. R., Fong, R., & Ewalt, P. L. (1995). Undermining the very basis of racism—Its categories. *Social Work, 40,* 581-584.

Spring, J. (1997). *Deculturalization and the struggle for equality* (2nd ed.). San Francisco: McGraw-Hill.

Stack, S., & Wasserman, I. (1995). The effects of marriage, family, and religious ties on African American suicide ideology. *Journal of Marriage and the Family, 57,* 215-223.

Standen, B. C. S. (1996). Without a template: The biracial Korean/white experience. In M. P. P. Root (Ed.), *The multiracial experience: Racial borders as the new frontier* (pp. 245-259). Thousand Oaks, CA: Sage.

Staples, L. (1984). Roots to power: A manual for grassroots organizing. New York: Praeger.

Steiner, S. (1971). The new Indians. In J. David (Ed.), *The American Indian: The first victim* (pp. 175-192). New York: William Morrow.

Suarez, L., & Ramirez, A. G. (1999). Hispanic/Latino health and disease: An overview. In R. M. Huff & M. V. Klein (Eds.), *Promoting health in multicultural populations: A handbook for practitioners* (pp. 115-136). Thousand Oaks, CA: Sage.

Sue, D. W. (1997). Foreword. In D. B. Pope-Davis & H. L. K. Coleman (Eds.), *Multicultural counseling competencies: Assessment, education and training, and supervision* (pp. ix-xi). Thousand Oaks, CA: Sage.

Sue, D. W., & Morishima, J. K. (1982). *The mental health of Asian Americans.* San Francisco: Jossey-Bass.

Suinn, R., Rikard-Figueroa, K., Lew, S., & Vigil, P. (1987). The Suinn-Lew Asian Self-Identity Acculturation Scale: An initial report. *Educational and Psychological Measurement, 47,* 401-407.

Sullivan, P. (1998). "What are you?" Multiracial families in America. *Our Children, 23*(5), 34-35.

Swanson, W., & Breed, W. (1976). Black suicide in New Orleans. In E. Shneidan (Ed.), *Sociology: Contemporary developments* (pp. 103-128), New York: Grune & Stratton.

Swerdlow, M. (1992). "Chronicity," "nervios," and community care: A case of Puerto Rican psychiatric patients in New York City. *Culture, Medicine, and Psychiatry, 16,* 217-235.

Szapocznik, J., & Hernandez, R. (1990). The Cuban family. In C. Mindel, R. W. Haberstein, & R. Wright, Jr. (Eds.), *Ethnic families in America: Patterns and variations* (pp. 160-172). New York: Elsevier.

Takaki, R. (1989). *Strangers from a different shore: A history of Asian Americans.* New York: Little, Brown.

Takaki, R. (1990). *Iron cages: Race and culture in 19th century America*. New York: Oxford University Press.

Taylor, R. L. (1994). *Minority families in America: A multicultural perspective*. Englewood Cliffs, NJ: Prentice Hall.

Thangavelu, V. (1980). *The Samsar model of social work practice*. Mangalore, India: Preeti.

Thom, L. (1992). *Becoming brave: The path to Native American manhood*. San Francisco: Chronicle.

Thornton, M. C. (1983). *A social history of a multiethnic identity: The case of black Japanese Americans*. Unpublished doctoral dissertation, University of Michigan, Ann Arbor.

Thornton, M. C. (1992). The quiet immigration: Foreign spouses of U.S. citizens, 1945-1985. In M. P. P. Root (Ed.), *Racially mixed people in America* (pp. 64-76). Newbury Park, CA: Sage.

Tienda, M. (1989). Puerto Ricans and the underclass debate. *Annals of the American Academy of Political and Social Sciences, 501*, 105-119.

Torres, A. (1995). *Between melting pot and mosaic: African Americans and Puerto Ricans in the New York political economy*. Philadelphia: Temple University Press.

Torres, J. B. (1998). Masculinity and gender roles among Puerto Rican men: Machismo on the U.S. mainland. *American Journal of Orthopsychiatry, 68*, 16-26.

Tran, T. V., & Dhooper, S. S. (1996). Ethnic and gender differences in perceived needs for social services among elderly Hispanic groups. *Journal of Gerontological Social Work, 25*(3/4), 121-147.

Tran, T. V., & Dhooper, S. S. (1997). Poverty, chronic stress, ethnicity and psychological distress among elderly Hispanics. *Journal of Gerontological Social Work, 27*(4), 3-19.

Trattner, W. (1989). *From poor law to welfare state: A history of social welfare*. New York: Free Press.

Trattner, W. I. (1994). *From poor law to welfare state: A history of social welfare in America* (5th ed.). New York: Free Press.

Trimble, J. E., Fleming, C. M., Beauvais, F., & Jumper-Thurman, P. (1996). Essential cultural and social strategies for counseling Native American Indians. In P. B. Pedersen, J. G. Draguns, W. J. Lonner, & J. Trimble (Eds.), *Counseling across cultures* (pp. 177-209). Thousand Oaks, CA: Sage.

Trolander, J. A. (1975). *Settlement houses and the great depression*. Detroit: Wayne State University Press.

Tucker, M. (1990). Director's foreword. In R. Ferguson, M. Gever, M. H. Trinh, & C. West (Eds.), *Marginalization and contemporary cultures* (pp. 7-9). New York: MIT Press.

Tucker, M. B., & Mitchell-Kernan, C. (1995). *The decline in marriage among African Americans: Causes, consequences, and policy implications*. New York: Russell Sage Foundation.

Turner, J. B. (1971). Racial and other minority groups. In R. Morris (Ed.), *Encyclopedia of social work* (16th ed., pp. 1068-1077). New York: NASW Press.

Turner, J. B. (1995). Group work and ethnic diversity. In M. D. Feit, J. H. Ramey, J. S. Wodarski, & A. A. Mann (Eds.), *Capturing the power of diversity* (pp. 7-17). New York: Haworth.

Turner, R. J. (1991). Affirming consciousness: The Africentric perspective. In J. R. Everett, S. Chipungu, & B. R. Leashore (Eds.), *Child welfare: An Africentric perspective* (pp. 36-57). New Brunswick, NJ: Rutgers University Press.

Twine, F. W. (1996). Heterosexual alliances: The romantic management of racial identity. In M. P. P. Root (Ed.), *The multiracial experience: Racial borders as the new frontier* (pp. 291-304). Thousand Oaks, CA: Sage.

Uchida, Y. (1982). *Desert exile: The uprooting of a Japanese American family*. Seattle: University of Washington Press.

Uehara, E. D., Sohng, S. L. S., Bending, R. L., Seyfried, S., Richey, C. A., Morelli, P., Spencer, M., Ortega, D., Keenan, L., & Kanuha, V. (1996). Toward a value-based approach to multicultural social work research. *Social Work, 41*, 613-621.

Ulincy, L. D., Hu, F., Lock, A., Liu, R., Lin-Fu, J. S., & Alexander, G. A. (1995). *Asian/Pacific Islander American health: Current bibliographies in medicine*. Bethesda, MD: U.S. Department of Health and Human Services, National Institute of Health.

U.S. Bureau of the Census. (1990). *The Hispanic population in the United States*. Washington, DC: U.S. Government Printing Office.

U.S. Bureau of the Census. (1991). Race and Hispanic origin. In U.S. Bureau of the Census (Ed.), *1990 census profile, No. 2*. Washington, DC: U.S. Government Printing Office.

U.S. Bureau of the Census. (1992a). *Current population reports, population characteristics. P. 20-459. The Asian and Pacific Islander Population in the United States, March 1991 and 1990*. Washington, DC: U.S. Government Printing Office.

U.S. Bureau of the Census. (1992b). *Marital status and living arrangements: March 1992* (Current Population Reports, Population Characteristics, Series P20-468). Washington, DC: U.S. Government Printing Office.

U.S. Bureau of the Census. (1992c). *Populations projections of the United States by age, sex, race, and Hispanic origin: 1992 to 2050*. Washington, DC: U.S. Government Printing Office.

U.S. Bureau of the Census. (1993a). *Census of the population: Socioeconomic characteristics* (Series CP-2-1-M). Washington, DC: U.S. Government Printing Office.

U.S. Bureau of the Census. (1993b). *Hispanic Americans today* (Current Population Reports, Population Characteristics, Series P-23, No. 183). Washington, DC: U.S. Government Printing Office.

U.S. Bureau of the Census. (1994). *Current population reports: Marital status and living arrangements*. Washington, DC: U.S. Government Printing Office.

U.S. Commission on Civil Rights. (1986). *Recent activities against citizens and residents of Asian descent*. Washington, DC: Author.

U.S. Commission on Civil Rights. (1992). *Civil rights issues facing Asian Americans in the 1990s*. Washington, DC: Author.

U.S. Department of Commerce. (1993a). *We the American . . . foreign born*. Washington, DC: Bureau of the Census.

U.S. Department of Commerce. (1993b). *We the American . . . Hispanics*. Washington, DC: Bureau of the Census.

U.S. Department of Commerce. (1997). *Statistical abstract of the United States* (117th ed.). Washington, DC: U.S. Government Printing Office.

Valle, R. (1980). Social mapping techniques: A preliminary guide for locating and linking to natural networks. In R. Valle & W. Vega (Eds.), *Hispanic natural support systems* (pp. 113-121). Sacramento: State of California Department of Mental Health.

Valverde, K. C. (1992). From dust to gold: The Vietnamese Amerasian experience. In M. P. P. Root (Ed.), *Racially mixed people in America* (pp. 144-161). Newbury Park, CA: Sage.

Van Soest, D. (1995). Multiculturalism and social work education: The non-debate about competing perspectives. *Journal of Social Work Education, 31*, 55-66.

Van Soest, D. (1996). The influence of competing ideologies about homosexuality on nondiscrimination policy: Implications for social work education. *Journal of Social Work Education, 32*, 53-64.

Vargas, L. A. (1992). Diversity of aging experience in Latin America and the Caribbean. *Clinical Gerontologist, 11*(3/4), 5-19.

Vasquez, M. J. T. (1994). Latinas. In L. Comas-Diaz & B. Greene (Eds.), *Women of color: Integrating ethnic and gender identities in psychotherapy* (pp. 114-138). New York: Guilford.

Vecoli, R. J. (1995). Ghanians. In R. J. Vecoli, J. Galens, A. Sheets, & R. V. Young (Eds.), *Gale encyclopedia of multicultural America* (Vol. 2, pp. 331-335). (Irish Americans-Yupiat Index). Detroit: International Thomas.

Vega, W. A. (1990). Hispanic families in the 1980s: A decade of research. *Journal of Marriage and the Family, 52*, 1015-1024.

Walker, L., & Wilson, B. C. (1997). African Americans. In D. Levison & M. Ember (Eds.), *American immigrant cultures* (Vol. 1, pp. 10-20). New York: Macmillan.

Wardle, F. (1992). *Biracial identity: An ecological and developmental model*. Denver, CO: Center for the Study of Biracial Children.

Wardle, F. (1993). Interracial families and biracial children. *Child Care Information Exchange, 90*, 45-48.

Warheit, G. J., Vega, W. A., Khourey, E. L., Gil, A. A., & Elfenbein, P. H. (1996). A comparative analysis of cigarette, alcohol, and illicit drug use among an ethnically diverse sample of Hispanic, African American, and non-Hispanic white adolescents. *Journal of Drug Issues, 26*, 901-922.

Warren, R. C. (1993). The morbidity/mortality gap: What is the problem? *Annals of Epidemiology, 3*, 127-129.

Washington, H. A. (1994, October). Human guinea pigs. *Emerge, 6*(1), 24-35.

Wax, M. L. (1971). *Indian Americans*. Englewood Cliffs, NJ: Prentice Hall.

Weaver, H. N. (1999a). Indigenous people and the social work profession: Defining culturally competent services. *Social Work, 44*, 217-226.

Weaver, H. N. (1999b). Through indigenous eyes: Native Americans and the HIV epidemic. *Health & Social Work, 24*(1), 27-35.

Wehrly, B. (1996). *Counseling interracial individuals and families*. Alexandria, VA: American Counseling Association.

Weil, M. O., & Gamble, D. N. (1995). Community practice models. In R. L. Edwards (Ed.), *Encyclopedia of social work* (19th ed., pp. 577-593). Washington, DC: NASW Press.

Weisman, J. R. (1996). An "other" way of life: The empowerment of alterity in the interracial individual. In M. P. P. Root (Ed.), *The multiracial experience: Racial borders as the new frontier* (pp. 152-166). Thousand Oaks, CA: Sage.

Weyr, T. (1988). *Hispanic U.S.A.: Breaking the melting pot*. New York: Harper & Row.

White, E. (Ed.). (1990). *The black women's health book*. Seattle, WA: Seal Press.

Whitler, T. E., & Calantone, R. J. (1991). Strength of ethnic affiliation: Examining Black identification with Black culture. *Journal of Social Psychology, 131*, 461-468.

Williams, E., & Ellison, F. (1996). Culturally informed social work practice with American Indian clients: Guidelines for non-Indian social workers. *Social Work, 41*, 147-151.

Williams, T. K. (1992). Prism lives: Identity of binational Americans. In M. P. P. Root (Ed.), *Racially mixed people in America* (pp. 280-303). Newbury Park, CA: Sage.

Williams, T. K. (1996). Race as a process: Reassessing the "What are you?" encounters of biracial individuals. In M. P. P. Root (Ed.), *The multiracial experience: Racial borders as the new frontier* (pp. 191-210). Thousand Oaks, CA: Sage.

Williamson, J. (1984). *New people: Miscegenation and mulattoes in the United States*. New York: New York University Press.

Wilson, A. (1987). *Mixed race children: A study of identity*. Boston: Allen and Unwin.

Wilson, T. P. (1992). Blood quantum: Native American mixed bloods. In M. P. P. Root (Ed.), *Mixed race people in America* (pp. 108-125). Newbury Park, CA: Sage.

Wingfield, H. L. (1988). The church and Blacks in America. *Western Journal of Black Studies, 12*(3), 127-133.

Winkelman, M. (1999). *Ethnic sensitivity in social work*. Dubuque, IA: Eddie Bowens.

Winn, N. N., & Priest, R. (1993). Counseling biracial children: A forgotten component of multicultural counseling. *Family Therapy, 20*, 29-36.

Winter, G. (1966). *Elements of a social issue: The role of social science in public policy*. New York: Macmillan.

Wodarski, J. S. (1992a). Social work practice with Asian-Americans. In D. F. Harrison, J. S. Wodarski, & B. A. Thyer (Eds.), *Cultural diversity and social work practice* (pp. 45-69). Springfield, IL: Charles C Thomas.

Wodarski, J. S. (1992b). Social work practice with Hispanic Americans. In D. F. Harrison, J. S. Wodarski, & B. A. Thyer (Eds.), *Cultural diversity and social work practice* (pp. 71-105). Springfield, IL: Charles C Thomas.

Wohl, B. J. (1995). Group work for what? Group work linkage of micro- and macro-social policy issues. In M. D. Feit, J. H. Ramey, J. S. Wodarski, & A. A. Mann (Eds.), *Capturing the power of diversity* (pp. 77-88). New York: Haworth.

Wong-Rieger, D., & Quintana, D. (1987). Compartive acculturation of Southeast Asians and Hispanic immigrants and sojourners. *Journal of Cross-Cultural Psychology, 18*, 145-162.

Wood, P. H. (1974). *Black majority: Negroes in colonial South Carolina from 1670 through the Stono rebellion*. New York: Knopf.

Wright, L. (1994, July 25). One drop of blood. *The New Yorker, 70*(22), 46-49.

Wright, M. A. (1998). *I'm chocolate, you're vanilla: Raising healthy black biracial children in a race-conscious world*. San Francisco: Jossey-Bass.

Yamashiro, G., & Matsuoka, J. K. (1997). Help-seeking among Asian and Pacific Americans: A multiperspective analysis. *Social Work, 42*, 176-186.

Zastrow, C. (1985). *The practice of social work*. Homewood, IL: Dorsey.

Author Index

Subject Index

About the Authors

Surjit Singh Dhooper is Professor of Social Work at the University of Kentucky, Lexington. His professional experience, spread over 36 years, includes both practice and teaching. He has done direct practice as well as administrative and community organizational work in health care settings for 18 years and has taught at both graduate and undergraduate levels for over 18 years. He is Codirector of the Joint University of Kentucky-University of Louisville Ph.D. in Social Work Program. He has authored or coauthored five books, more than 40 journal articles, and over 20 book reviews, and he has presented papers at many national and international conferences. His books include *Social Work and Transplantation of Human Organs* (1994) and *Social Work in Health Care in the 21st Century* (1997). He was included among the 250 nationally prominent and most published social work scholars in the 1980s in a study by the Virginia Commonwealth University School of Social Work. He is the consulting editor or book reviewer for many professional journals, including *Journal of Social Work Education, Social Work, Health and Social Work*, and *Journal of Gerontological Social Work*. He has been a member of several university-, community-, and national-level committees and boards, such as the National Committee on Racial and Ethnic Diversity and the Legal Defense Service of the National Association of Social Workers.

Sharon E. Moore is Associate Professor at the Raymond A. Kent School of Social Work at the University of Louisville in Louisville, Kentucky. She has several years of direct practice experience in the fields of medical social work and substance abuse counseling. She is the author of journal articles on substance abuse treatment for adolescent African American males, on the role of the African American church in community empowerment, and on tenure and publication issues for African American faculty. Her articles include *The ABCs of Tenure: What All African American Faculty Should Know* (1998), *Adolescent Black Males, Drug Trafficking, and Addiction: Three Theoretical Perspectives* (1995) *and The Role of the Black Church in Changing Times: Empowering the Community for Survival* (1995). She has also worked extensively with African American youth outreach initiatives and received an Outstanding Citizens Award from the Pittsburgh Federal Executive Board.